BOSTON'S
"CHANGEFUL TIMES"

CREATING THE
NORTH AMERICAN LANDSCAPE

Gregory Conniff
Bonnie Loyd
Edward K. Muller
David Schuyler
Consulting Editors

George F. Thompson
Series Founder and Director

*Published in
cooperation with the
Center for American Places,
Harrisonburg, Virginia*

BOSTON'S "CHANGEFUL TIMES"

Origins of
Preservation & Planning
in America

MICHAEL HOLLERAN

The Johns Hopkins University Press
BALTIMORE AND LONDON

© 1998 The Johns Hopkins University Press
All rights reserved. Published 1998
Printed in the United States of America on acid-free paper

Johns Hopkins Paperbacks edition, 2001
2 4 6 8 9 7 5 3 1

The Johns Hopkins University Press
2715 North Charles Street
Baltimore, Maryland 21218-4363
www.press.jhu.edu

Library of Congress Cataloging-in-Publication Data will be found
at the end of this book.
A catalog record for this book is available from the British Library.

ISBN 0-8018-6644-8 (pbk.)

For Aimée

We have passed together through changeful times.
—REV. CHANDLER ROBBINS

Contents

Contents

Acknowledgments

Good history relies on good archivists, and I have relied above all on Lorna Condon of the Society for the Preservation of New England Antiquities. Thanks to Lorna, and to Ellie Reichlin; thanks to the staff of the Boston Public Library, especially John Dorsey, Aaron Schmidt, Sinclair Hitchings, and Katherine Dibble. Thanks to Philip Bergen and Douglas Southard at the Bostonian Society Library; to Jane S. Knowles, Trevor Johnson, and Catharina Slautterback at the Boston Athenaeum; to Elizabeth Bouvier of the Massachusetts Supreme Judicial Court Archives, Linda McCorkle and the Harvard Business School Baker Library, Laurie Whitchill and Marilyn Simpson at the Rhode Island School of Design Library, Nina Zannieri at the Paul Revere Memorial Association, Paul R. Tierney at the Suffolk County Registry of Deeds, Joyce Connolly at the Frederick Law Olmsted National Historic Site, Herbert Finch at the Cornell Collection of Regional History and Archives, and Janice Madhu at the George Eastman House/International Museum of Photography. Thanks to Harvard's Loeb Library, M.I.T.'s Rotch Library, Boston University's Beebe Communications Center, the Massachusetts Historical Society, and the Massachusetts State Archives and State Library, especially its Special Collections. Thanks to David Bohl for his magic touch in the darkroom.

Thanks to Antoinette Downing, Marc Weiss, Gary Hack, Christine Cousineau, David Schuyler, Seymour Mandelbaum, Stephen Mrozowski, Patricia Burgess, Garrett Power, James M. Lindgren, Yuk Lee, and the late William Jordy for comments on early versions of some of this work and for generously making available unpublished materials. Thanks to my graduate research assistants, John Baloga and Debbie Fuller Penn. The National Endowment for the Humanities helped fund my research, and the University of Colorado at Denver provided both funding and precious release time.

I am grateful to George F. Thompson, president of the Center for Ameri-

Acknowledgments

can Places, David Schuyler, Mary V. Yates, and Julie Burris for their able help in making this a book.

Finally, thanks to Robert M. Fogelson for his guidance and generous support at every phase of this project. And to Aimée, Max, and Sam, thanks for your patience when my mind has seemed two thousand miles away.

BOSTON'S "CHANGEFUL TIMES"

Introduction

Change is the order of Divine Providence; nothing is permanent
or enduring upon earth.
— REV. SAMUEL KIRKLAND LOTHROP

Today Americans take for granted the shared value of continuity in the built environment. Though our urban areas may change rapidly, neighborhood stability and historic preservation are universally approved as principles. We agree that they are good, and argue only about what price we are willing to pay for them in practice.

In the middle of the nineteenth century, expectations and experience both were profoundly different. The whole American culture of city building relied on continual change. After the Civil War, Bostonians watched approvingly as row after row of old houses were pulled down to make way for mercantile "palaces," which they cheerfully expected to see replaced in their time by still more wonderful buildings. By the turn of the century, Boston was almost completely remade. In whole districts, not a single original building stood; indeed, much of the ground beneath the city had not existed. Old buildings were regarded with distaste. They were "firetraps," "eyesores," often converted to unintended uses with unsightly results. Historically significant buildings were not exempt from this perception; while many Bostonians took great pride in them, their appreciation was not aesthetic, and in any case antiquarianism was an attitude of connoisseurship, not a prescription for action.

Real estate investors anticipated ever more intensive use. They valued and developed residential property with an eye to its eventual conversion for commercial purposes. Subdivisions were sometimes replatted during the development process to allow denser building. Neighborhood deterioration, if unwelcome, was accepted as inevitable. When residents felt forced to move, they tried to cash in on the changing land uses as profitably as they could, in order once again to secure a suitable home. The cycle from fashionable new residential area to commercial use or slum could take as little as ten or fifteen years.[1] Trying to defend one's neighborhood from the changing city seemed as futile as defending a sandcastle from the rising tide.

During the last third of the nineteenth century, Americans grew uncomfortably aware of the pace of change in the urban environment, and in various ways they began to seek instead environmental permanence. They sought homes protected from change, and developers responded with long-term deed restrictions. They defended features of the city they had come to value: not only historic buildings but also neighborhoods, landscapes, burial grounds, views, trees. They sought to create new pieces of the city that would both deserve and achieve permanence: parks, public buildings, and public spaces. Eventually they used public powers to restrain disruptive changes throughout the city.

As the city became a more elaborate artifact, it gained physical momentum; continual change became more expensive and inconvenient. At the beginning of the nineteenth century, Boston was mainly a collection of buildings, but by the end of the century, it was knitted together by pipes, wires, and conduits as well as more complex infrastructure such as America's first subway. More elaborate and expensive building types, and the considerable social and economic costs of continual reconstruction and relocation, lent increasing attractiveness to what planner Charles H. Cheney later called "building for permanency."[2] If the city could begin to take a permanent shape, then durable infrastructure such as streets, lots, utilities, and transit lines could be configured for particular land uses rather than for generalized speculative potential. Building for permanency produced romantic suburbs notable for their quality as residential environments, and also for the very idea that a subdivision could be designed to remain residential, actively shaped to resist conversion to other uses. The City Beautiful movement created civic and institutional centers meant to express and retain their centrality, and at its most ambitious aimed to make a whole urban environment worthy of permanence.

Real estate thinking, the main normative theory of urban form during this period, underwent a subtle but fundamental shift from a speculative outlook to one focused on stability of investment and permanence of value. Deed restrictions established a permanent form and use for the urban fabric, imposing legally what subdivisions and civic centers attempted spatially. While real estate wisdom had once held that restrictions on the use of land diminished its value, turn-of-the-century homeowners were more likely to consider them essential. Affluent Americans had their pick of neighborhoods where they might remain for the rest of their days without worrying about encroachments from businesses or tenements.

4

Introduction

Historic preservation addressed the stability of existing pieces of the environment. In two generations it emerged from an extreme form of antiquarianism, seemingly out of place in the New World, to an accepted approach for extraordinary features of the city and, by the end of the period, an institutionalized public policy and even a way of thinking about whole urban districts. Conflict between change and permanence often appeared as historically informed opposition to redevelopment of public spaces and landscapes—such as Boston's Common and its old burial grounds—although these are not traditionally defined as the mainstream of historic preservation. Early parks advocates created landscapes intended to be permanent, and their successors fought to preserve them.

Beginning in the late nineteenth century, American cities adopted a great array of new public measures to shape their growth. While the origins of public control lie in sanitation, safety, and the need to regulate private use of public space, by the early twentieth century some public powers had evolved specifically for controlling visible change in the environment. For the first time, American cities explicitly sought to avert change in their patterns of land use and built form, viewing government no longer as a means of promoting environmental change but rather as the only agency able to secure environmental stability. Building-height restrictions, front-yard setbacks, and land-use districts were all brought together finally as comprehensive zoning, a degree of public control once unthinkable, and for the equally unthinkable end of limiting rather than encouraging change in the city.

Other examples of the search for permanence can be found in a variety of fields. Architects began adopting the Colonial Revival style in the late nineteenth century, reinforcing preservationism and creating the potential for a permanently established community architectural identity. New "perpetual care" cemeteries aimed to secure an earthly setting corresponding to spiritual eternity. The same period saw the first movement to forever set aside wilderness areas as national and state parks and the beginning of efforts to preserve archaeological remains of pre-Columbian settlement.

The pursuit of permanence was not a single coordinated "movement," because its participants did not identify it as one. Nonetheless, people in diverse fields were saying similar things as they pursued similar goals. Often the same people were active in a number of causes, responding to threats they perceived as somehow connected.

The changes that form the subject of this book are, first of all, deliberate physical alterations in places. These actions individually were intentional on someone's part, even if their aggregate effects were often unanticipated or even incomprehensible. Inadvertent changes—fires, erosion, and other natural phenomena—are outside our scope. Intangible changes—in community ethnicity, in economic control—are not directly our subject either, though they often worked upon the physical environment, and it in turn became their symbol. When one Bostonian in 1844 observed that he lived in "changeful times," his comment was prompted by an impending physical change, the demolition of a church. But the phrase resonated on many levels: change in the building, change in the neighborhood and the life of the congregation, change in the city and the society. Change in the urban environment was a significant physical phenomenon, and it was a cultural phenomenon as well.

Nineteenth-century Americans not only acted to change their environment; they frequently exchanged one environment for another. Alexis de Tocqueville described American restlessness in the first half of the century: "In the United States a man builds a house in which to spend his old age, and he sells it before the roof is on; he plants a garden and lets it just as the trees are coming into bearing; he brings a field into tillage and leaves other men to gather the crops; he embraces a profession and gives it up; he settles in a place, which he soon afterwards leaves to carry his changeable lodgings elsewhere." [3] A population forever moving on was the flywheel of the culture of change. If dwellers changed faster than dwelling, physical change did not matter in anyone's experience. Only the people who stayed put found environmental change disturbing.

Increasing numbers of Americans did conclude that their cities changed too much, too fast, and adopted the opposite ideal of environmental "permanence." They did not define this term; permanence was more of a visceral reaction against change than a well-articulated alternative to it. Nor could permanence ever be accomplished in fact the way change was a fact. Permanence was a goal, and sometimes a practical intention. Americans set out to make buildings and landscapes and neighborhoods that could last a very long time, and set out to create the conditions under which they would last.

Environmental permanence cannot be absolute. Even Niagara and the pyramids erode (and their meanings and their surroundings change faster still). Within the mid-nineteenth-century city, the word *permanent* was commonly applied in a narrow sense, to all durable construction that was not intended as temporary, but this usage began to seem unsatisfactory. Did *permanent* mean potentially durable, without any commitment to actual duration? Or was it to be taken more literally, as unlimited duration, real perpetuity? More and more Americans thought that it should, that some buildings and landscapes should indeed embody a permanence of centuries, of as long as human intentions could reach. John Ruskin, the nineteenth-century architectural theorist, sought structures that, like the pyramids, would decay only at a geological pace. This required human maintenance to be consistent

6

over generations and centuries; it was perhaps the idea of such steadiness of human purpose that felt so reassuring. And to the extent that environment conditions culture, physically durable cities could help reinforce steadiness of human purpose. The scope of intentions was lengthening as complex construction lengthened the economic life of buildings, but permanence was also becoming a cultural goal beyond any utilitarian motivations.

Permanence had not only an implicit length but also two directions, toward the past and the future. Ancient buildings and settled landscapes from the past appeared already to have achieved some kind of permanence. Places built for permanence projected durability into the future. When architects designed new places to look old, they were combining both directions, invoking an ersatz past to promise a real future. Prospective and retrospective permanence also ran together when neighborhoods designed for permanence—the Back Bay in Boston, elite subdivisions in Brookline and Cambridge—began to mature, and their residents defended them from change. The pursuit of permanence, whether looking forward or backward, is the story of Americans coming to think of their cities as having a time dimension, and beginning to think as ambitiously in that dimension as in the other three.

Is permanence inherently good? Planning theorist Kevin Lynch considered and rejected durability as one performance criterion for cities. Other scholars have noted the benefits of change and the drawbacks of increasing durability in urban form. Josef W. Konvitz describes the permanence of infrastructure in the late nineteenth century as a problem rather than a goal, making cities less adaptable and their fabric more liable to obsolescence. Christine Meisner Rosen, similarly, describes the durability of imperfect urban form in the face of opportunities for improvement, such as reconstruction after great fires. Anne Vernez Moudon examines San Francisco's Alamo Square district, suggesting in her book's title that it was "built for change," or at least (as she explains inside) that its spatial pattern proved adaptable to continual changes in physical fabric, and that whether intentional or not this adaptability was generally found satisfactory. Stewart Brand adopts Moudon's phrase to describe deliberate adaptability by design. When Brand or Moudon write "built for change," they are talking, paradoxically, about a kind of permanence through flexibility. Lynch, Konvitz, Rosen, Moudon, and Brand all seek a city whose fabric evolves to maintain good fit with its inhabitants—healthy change.[4] But Bostonians at the end of the nineteenth century found change so disorienting that for increasing numbers of them, no change seemed healthy.

John J. Costonis focuses on environmental change in his discussion of the proper place for aesthetics in the law. People understand change, he says, in terms of "icons" and "aliens." Icons are "features invested with values that confirm our sense of order and identity." Aliens are features, or proposals, that threaten icons. "We bond to our icons for reassurance," writes Costonis, "and they, in turn, reinforce our sense of order in the world no less than religion or popular culture. An icon's loss or contamination is accompanied by reactions quite similar to those that, for many, accompanied the elimination of Latin from the Roman Catholic Mass, the death of Bing Crosby, Judy Garland or John Lennon, or even Coca-Cola's decision to change its 'classic' formula."[5] In Costonis's terms, this book is an historical examination of the ways people defined and defended icons in one American city.

Icons are often called "landmarks" or, especially in the nineteenth century, "monuments." Both words refer to the boundary markers that let us know our territory, the "landmarks" the Old Testament enjoins us not to disturb.[6] The terms have been adapted metaphorically to express a deeper cognitive reality: historic monuments, and the familiar landmarks of our past, organize our knowledge of our own territories and therefore of our selves. People orient themselves through mental maps incorporating stable features of the environment. Recognizing our place in the world helps define our identities, as Henry James discovered upon watching the demolition of a Boston house where he had lived as a youth. "It was as if the bottom had fallen out of one's own autobiography," he wrote, "and one plunged backward into space without meeting anything."[7]

Change and its antithesis, permanence, might be balanced against one another to arrive at some ideal synthesis—Costonis seeks "stability"; Lynch proposed "continuity." The pursuit of permanence described here did not arrive at any such coherent resolution. Instead, Americans discovered that the tools they had fashioned for preventing change could also be used to control it, and many people for various reasons found controlled change even more appealing than no change at all. Once environmental change came under control, Americans faced new questions in how to use that control, which could work for many ends besides permanence or stability. These questions have occupied American planners since the 1920s.

This book examines the culture of city building, the working suppositions of the many people who were involved in making cities: real estate speculators; legislators and municipal officials; lawyers, surveyors, engineers, architects, and their emerging professional kin, landscape architects and city planners; and, in general, the well-to-do third of the population who made up these other groups' customers, clients, and activist constituencies. The inquiry inevitably focuses on the upper and substantial middle classes. Its subjects are perceptions and decision-making about urban change; these were the classes who left written records of their perceptions, and since they made the decisions, they left the built record, too. They exercised the control.

Historians who focus on class structure look at efforts to control urban development and to preserve monuments of national and ancestral origins, and they see attempts to consolidate elite status and identity. There is ample evidence to support this reading. In some of the issues I explore, upper- or middle-class Americans clearly acted against perceived threats from lower classes. Much of the preservation movement, as historians have traditionally defined it, can be explained as elite assertiveness of a class- and ethnicity-based traditionalism.[8] But if we look at a broader set of preservation issues— not just overt public efforts at saving historic buildings but also attempts to prevent alien intrusions into neighborhoods, to maintain historic spaces such as graveyards, and to continue institutions in their historic structures —we find that many episodes pitted different elites against one another. Wealthy householders fought wealthy developers; factions faced off within the congregations of upper-class churches and within the membership of the Boston Athenaeum. Many land-use and preservation controversies were intraclass disagreements about which parts of the environment were meant as symbolic and which utilitarian, and how to weigh these disparate values. Typically both sides acknowledged patriotic and historical significance, but they disagreed whether it should have any operational weight against the practical forces that drove change in the environment.

Were these issues mainly about class or were elites simply the only people with the luxury of addressing them? Only the well-to-do were likely to stay in one place long enough even to know about the pace of environmental change. Working-class Bostonians presumably had worries more immediate than change in their surroundings, though they also bore more of its disruption and profited less by it than their upper-class contemporaries. We can surmise that the agreeable surroundings of elite restricted subdivisions were attractive to other classes, by the determination with which ordinary Americans pursued similar environments within the limits of their means. Even lowbrow suburbs eventually used deed restrictions to protect their modest houses from incompatible land uses and encroachments by lower-status residents.[9] But if the working classes were equally interested in neighborhood stability, their disputes were less likely to end up in the courts or before the legislature. Disputes of the well-to-do, on the other hand, forged attitudes and legal tools later used by the rest of society.

Boston was in the forefront of American reactions against environmental change. It was one of the earliest centers of urban preservationism. It was the source of critical case law establishing deed restrictions as a tool for private planning. It made the first public efforts at preserving landscapes threatened by metropolitan growth. Its regulation of building heights, the first such restriction in the country, served as a national precedent for zoning. Responses to change were earlier, stronger, and more successful in Boston than elsewhere.

Why did these issues arise first in Boston? Why did Bostonians resolve them in such distinctive ways? Boston's history was long and distinguished, and Bostonians savored their history as New Yorkers and even Philadelphians did not. Boston's townscape too was distinguished, an architectural legacy from Charles Bulfinch and his successors. Boston's peculiar geography, originally a hilly little peninsula surrounded by mostly shallow bays, eased some of the pressure to rebuild this existing fabric, because the city could grow by making new land throughout the nineteenth century. Boston was a wealthy city. Eighteenth-century trading fortunes spawned nineteenth-century industrial fortunes, which in turn made Boston a nationwide source of investment capital. The heirs to these fortunes emerged during the nineteenth century as Boston's "Brahmin" aristocracy, defined not only by wealth and privilege but also by an ethic of community responsibility and intellectual and artistic excellence. They turned local institutions such as Harvard College into national institutions and made Boston the center of American high culture. Wealth held by a stable elite, closely identified with and involved in civic affairs, made for less resistance in Boston than elsewhere to public regulation of property. This identification of individual interests with the community broke down in the twentieth century, as a new politics of polarization turned the environment into a battleground of class and ethnic conflict, but during the nineteenth century, Boston's politics remained sufficiently deferential that Brahmins were confident that they articulated broadly shared values.

This story is important not because of Boston's uniqueness, but just the opposite, because other cities followed Boston's example. A predilection for permanence soon appeared elsewhere across the country. Citizens and architects defended landmarks, even in such comparatively young places as Chicago and California. By the early 1880s, westerners were already working to save some of the region's heritage of Spanish colonial settlement, and by the end of the decade their interest had expanded to include the remnants of Anglo-American arrival only forty years before.[10] Developers wrote deed restrictions all around the country, even though other states' courts were less likely to enforce them. Other cities imposed public controls on development. Chicago enacted building-height restrictions only a year after Boston, and they were later adopted or urged with preservationist rationales in Baltimore and on Fifth Avenue in New York.[11]

Introduction

Boston could serve as a model because, despite its distinctive local conditions and culture, it was a big commercial and industrial city in many respects similar to others. It was growing fast, through Yankee migration from elsewhere in New England and through greater immigration than ever before, starting in the 1840s from Ireland and later in the century from Italy and eastern Europe. Old residents, new immigrants, and the expansion of business and industry set up a keen competition for space that forced change at the center of the city. Many of the middle classes opted out of this competition to some of America's earliest commuter suburbs, where they worked transformations of surrounding towns and then watched as their neighborhoods in turn were altered out of all recognition. All of this looked familiar from other American cities; Boston was fully a part of the nineteenth century's prevailing culture of change.

PART I

CHANGE

CHAPTER 1

❧❧❧

The Culture of Change

Let us welcome whatever change may come.
— NATHANIEL HAWTHORNE

At 7:24 P.M., on Saturday, November 9, 1872, the Boston fire department logged a report from alarm box 52 at Summer and Kingston Streets in downtown Boston. An epidemic had idled most horses in the city, so a team of men pulled a single pumping engine to the scene. When they got there the fire had already spread up an elevator shaft and completely consumed the four-story building. They discovered to their horror that water mains laid when this was a residential area carried only enough water to reach two or three stories, and as more engines arrived and connected their hoses, the pressure dropped even lower. The fire easily jumped the narrow streets, aided by fashionable new mansard roofs that jutted their wooden cornices toward one another out of reach of the firefighters' streams. London and Liverpool insurance underwriters had recently looked at the combination of dangerous buildings and inadequate protection and concluded that downtown Boston was a disaster waiting to happen.[1] It was happening.

During the night Chief Engineer John S. Damrell ordered his men to begin dynamiting buildings to clear firebreaks, but their untrained efforts simply spread the flames. The fire stopped at the walls of the Old South Church only through some combination of divine intervention and the heroic efforts of firefighters. When the Great Fire was brought under control after two days, fourteen people had died and sixty-five acres of the heart of the city were smoking rubble and surreal heat-sculpted granite.[2]

"Changeful Times"

In spite of the fire's immense destruction and the magnificence of the buildings it consumed, the city was strangely free of mourning for them. Bostonians hardly knew the place. The "burnt district" had already changed out of

FIGURE 1.1   *The Great Fire: heroic efforts to save the Old South Church. Courtesy Boston Public Library, Print Department*

all recognition when it became a downtown business area. If the public felt any sentimental attachments here, they were to the residences and gardens that only recently had been displaced. The fire spared Old South Church, "almost the only building of historic significance within the burnt district," said the *Boston Globe*.[3] Yet the Old South, like burned-out Trinity Church, had already decided to move elsewhere; they were lost in plans if not yet in fact. Perhaps the fire was not traumatic because the city had sustained its trauma here piecemeal as the area was transformed. The burnt district was already scar tissue. The fire was only a more dramatic instance of what Bostonians were doing for themselves.

For most Bostonians the area's recent reconstruction operated in another way to forestall nostalgia. Memories of building it were so fresh, and the result considered so successful, that it seemed no real problem to do it again. In this widely held view, rebuilding Boston was an opportunity. Crooked and narrow old streets could be made wide and straight, and buildings more fire-resistant; in the end the Great Fire would leave Boston bigger and better. To support this view Boston had only to look to Chicago, which had suffered a vastly more damaging fire just a year earlier. Despite fears—or, in some quarters, hopes—that the disaster would set Chicago back permanently, Chicago's ambitious reconstruction, said the *Globe,* had already made it "beautified, stronger, more successful than ever."[4] The fire only enhanced Chicago's legend.

Chicago was the prodigy of nineteenth-century urbanization, but cities throughout the western world were growing at prodigious rates, especially in North America. Many founded during the century would grow to hundreds of thousands. As Homer Hoyt wrote in 1933, with a mixture of awe and pride: *Chicago*

The growth of Chicago in the nineteenth century has been paralleled by that of no other great city of a million population or over in either ancient or modern times. . . . It compressed within a single century the population growth of Paris for twenty centuries. From 1840 to 1890, the rapidity of its development outstripped that of every other city in the world. An insignificant town in 1840, . . . by 1890 it was the second city in point of numbers in the United States. In 1930 only London, New York and Berlin—all much older—contained more people.[5]

The growth of established seaport cities like Boston and Philadelphia was less impressive only by comparison. Before Chicago took its place as the emblem of American urban growth, its symbol was Boston's own industrial satellite of Lowell, "the American Manchester," the nation's fourteenth largest city in 1840, where nineteen years earlier stood only a few farms.[6]

Bostonians were no less aggressive in developing their own city and its suburbs. By any objective standard—population, wealth, building—the city grew fast. When the Town of Boston became a municipality in 1822, its real estate was assessed at $23 million. By the decade after the Civil War, the city added that much to its valuation each year.[7] Up to 1880, Boston's population grew by a third to a half each decade. *?°?.*

These new residents had to live somewhere. Boston in 1840 was a city of ninety-three thousand crammed into substantially the same square-mile peninsula as the colonial town of two hundred years earlier. This circumstance had already resulted in complete abandonment of detached houses,

FIGURE 1.2 (TOP) *The "burnt district." In the background is the unburned Old South. Courtesy Boston Public Library, Print Department*

FIGURE 1.3 (BOTTOM) *Basement crypts in the ruins of old Trinity Church after the fire, photographed by John P. Soule, 1872. Society for the Preservation of New England Antiquities*

even for the rich, and extreme overcrowding for the poor. Those who were in between increasingly left for the suburbs—the working classes walking across bridges to Charlestown, Cambridgeport, or South Boston, the middle classes settling the nation's first commuter suburbs along railroads leading out of the city.[8] Boston had no room for more people, yet it continued to grow. Even though its suburbs consistently grew faster than the city, Boston added, on average, its entire 1840 population each decade from 1860 to 1920.

In order to accomplish this growth, Bostonians completely remade their whole environment, over and over, working "such a transformation as no other great city of the world has ever undergone at the hands of man," as a contemporary historian described it.[9] They shoveled hills into bays, more than doubling the peninsula's area. They turned to new forms of housing, such as buildings intentionally designed as tenements, and the American premiere of "French flats," or apartments. Boston also annexed adjacent suburbs, though with less success than other American big cities. Whether annexed or not, the once rural landscapes near the city soon sprouted densely built houses and streets as far as the eye could see.

While these new areas spread, Boston was also reworking the old city plan at its center. Mayor Alexander H. Rice, in his 1856 annual review of the city's finances, reminded citizens that "Boston is subjected to one item of expense which is almost unknown in cities of modern origin . . . the numerous narrow and crooked streets which well enough answered the convenience of a provincial town, are found to be totally inadequate to the wants of a great city, daily becoming more and more crowded with business and population."[10] So Boston widened and cut through new arteries. The pace increased when the legislature in 1868 finally granted the city the right to recover some of the costs from property owners who benefited.[11] "It seems inevitable," said Mayor Rice, "that these improvements must continue, until a considerable portion of our original territory has been rebuilt."[12]

Government involvement in shaping new urban form was conceived as public preparation for essentially private processes. Municipalities graded and paved roadways, provided or encouraged private corporations to provide other infrastructure systems, located parks, markets, and a host of other public facilities, and often subsidized private enterprises such as railroads that they hoped would attract still further growth. While these powers if coordinated had tremendous potential for consciously shaping the city, Americans not only failed to realize this potential but saw little point in it. "All urban growth was good," says historian Sam Bass Warner, "and therefore needed no special attention." The fabric of the city emerged instead from what Warner calls a tradition of "privatism." As historian Hendrik Hartog explains of New York's grid, "The formal design of the city was public;

but that design remained only a context for private decision making." In previous centuries, says Hartog, governments confined themselves to conservatively protecting property rights. But government in America existed not for conserving static accumulations of wealth but for increasing aggregate wealth by promoting growth.[13]

What was life like in such a changing environment? City dwellers' lives in the mid-nineteenth century were so unsettled as to make this question unimportant for many of them. Peter R. Knights's research on residential persistence and mobility in Boston before the Civil War reaches the startling conclusion that "one-half of Boston's population would disappear and be replaced every one or two years."[14] Those who remained moved around within the city, and the rate at which they moved was increasing. If Knights's samples are representative, then Boston's 1860 population of 178,000 included fewer than 4,000 household heads who had lived in the city in 1830.[15] Since this stable minority consisted disproportionately of the well-to-do, it was mainly these classes who had the chance to see environmental change affecting their own lives. We can begin to understand those effects by looking at changes in elite neighborhoods.

Before the end of the eighteenth century, the city had no exclusively elite sections. Merchants and the wealthy lived in many parts of colonial Boston, especially the center of town, the pleasant high grounds overlooking it, and the North End, which was if anyplace the preferred neighborhood. When the North End's royalists left with evacuating British troops, the area began a slow decline in fortunes, eventually to become an immigrant tenement district. The center of the city, around State Street, also lost its residential attractiveness with the growth of business after the war. Movement from these two areas, together with growth of the city's upper classes, made fashionable neighborhoods expand in other directions. In 1795 the Mount Vernon Proprietors began developing Beacon Hill, changing it from a ragged wasteland into a homogeneous upper-class district. South of State Street, pleasant houses and gardens grew up in the old "South End" of Summer, Franklin, and Pearl Streets and Fort Hill, and after 1810 this district spread westward to Tremont Street and Park Street, facing Beacon Hill across the Common. Increasing land-use segregation yielded a growing turf for the well-to-do, but even in the North End where it was shrinking, the process was reassuringly gradual. As the peninsula filled in to urban densities, elite residential areas maintained stable locations but changed in form, as when Patrick T. Jackson in the early 1830s leveled almost-rural Pemberton Hill and its mansions to create Pemberton Square and its fine row houses.[16]

By the next decade, however, intensifying competition for space was having less benign effects on these neighborhoods. "The alterations here sur-

FIGURE 1.4   *Colton map of Boston, 1855. Boston Athenaeum*

pass all you can conceive," wrote Charles Bulfinch to his son in 1843.[17] The business district expanded south into Franklin and Pearl Streets; from the other direction waterfront warehouses encroached on Fort Hill. Residents sold out to speculators, and this time neighborhood change was not gradual. While Fort Hill's new owners waited to build business blocks, they carried their investments by packing houses from cellar to attic with the Irish who were arriving at and working on the docks below. The Irish were the first great wave of European immigrants whom Bostonians did not consider assimilable. Their arrival recast economic competition as ethnic conflict.

The Fort Hill and Pearl Street aristocracy moved to Tremont Street, Temple Place, and Bedford Street, expanding the old South End below Summer Street. They found themselves almost immediately in the path of the newly emerging retail district, which by 1847 had an outpost on Washington Street as far south as Summer Street.[18] A horsecar line on Washington Street in 1856 gave additional impetus to this retail invasion, but it also provided a residential alternative.

The streetcars ran to the new South End, a comparatively vast area of land being filled along the neck that connected Boston to the mainland. The city had been trying for decades to lure suburban-minded middle-class residents here, and starting in 1856 it succeeded. The South End, according to historian Walter Firey, was "the distinctly preferred residential district of the city" during the 1860s, while the sale of Summer and Tremont Street homes for business blocks financed new mansions. Upper-class preferences soon switched to the Back Bay, and the South End quickly declined into a roominghouse district. In his 1885 novel *The Rise of Silas Lapham*, William Dean Howells describes nouveau-riche Lapham's move to the South End in 1872, his house "bought very cheap of a terrified gentleman of good extraction who discovered too late that the South End was not the thing, and who in the eagerness of his flight to the Back Bay threw in his carpets and shades for almost nothing."[19] Of all the changing neighborhoods, the South End's fall was the most traumatic. Not only was its fashionable life span the shortest yet, but unlike Fort Hill and the Summer Street district, its departing residents generally sold not at a handsome gain but at a loss.

So long as fashionable neighborhoods moved around within the limits of Boston's original peninsula, they were within easy walking distance of the shared environment of public spaces and buildings, particularly churches, which anchored the changes in people's individual environments. By the 1840s neighborhood changes were tearing these anchors loose. Churches began moving, pulled by wholesale migration of their congregations and pushed by the altered character of their old locations. Deacon Frederick D. Allen of the Old South Church reported in 1872 that of the thirteen churches

22

FIGURE 1.5   *The old Second Church, built 1721. Society for the Preservation of New England Antiquities*

that in 1845 served the old Summer Street district east of Washington Street, one had closed its doors and eleven had moved elsewhere. Only the Old South remained, and its leaders, said Allen, "have long regarded the ultimate removal of our place of worship as inevitable."[20]

One of the departures on Allens's list was the Second Church. When Chandler Robbins succeeded Ralph Waldo Emerson to its pulpit in 1833, the congregation occupied the oldest church structure in the city, on Hanover Street in the North End.[21] Before Robbins retired in 1874, the church would make its home in five different buildings, not counting temporary accommodations.

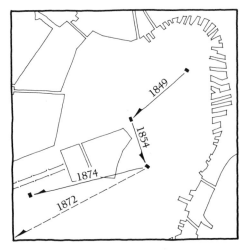

MAP 1   *Second Church moves. Maps by author.*

Even before Robbins's ministry, Second Church members had begun agi-
tating to move from the hundred-year-old building, its maintenance burdensome and its location increasingly unattractive to the congregation. During
Emerson's tenure their dissatisfaction was sufficiently public that the Roman Catholic Diocese in 1832 inquired about buying the building, an offer
that was itself an indicator of ethnic change in the neighborhood. By 1840
most of the congregation, including its wealthiest members, had moved
away from the neighborhood; they bought a site on Beacon Hill for a new
church, but the North End minority resisted. Robbins thought he had found
a compromise to keep the congregation intact, through the symbolic renewal of demolishing and rebuilding on the same site.[22] "We have passed
together through changeful times," Robbins told his congregation, but the
changeful times were just beginning.[23] The new building saddled the church
with debt while members continued drifting away, and in 1849, by necessity
rather than by choice, the congregation sold it and left the church's historic
neighborhood. Wealthy parishioners had offered to save the building, Robbins afterward claimed, but he felt that the church would fail if it remained
in the changing North End. Instead it was set adrift. For a while Robbins preached in the Masonic Temple, until the parishioners bought a small
chapel at almost the same spot on Beacon Hill to which they had refused
to move ten years earlier. In 1854 they absorbed another congregation in
order to take over its church south of Summer Street on pleasant, tree-lined
Bedford Street, just the sort of home they had been looking for. But even as
Robbins moved his flock into their new quarters, businesses were moving in

24

around them. In only eighteen years, church members dispersed even more thoroughly than they had done from the North End, and once more they decided to move on. This time they packed up to bring with them the pulpit, pews, stained glass, and the very stones of their building. When they did so, early in 1872, they were not yet sure where they would go. They bought a lot in the South End, but this time sensed impending neighborhood change before they moved. They rebuilt instead at Copley Square, in the Back Bay.[24]

The Second Church's move was part of an institutional stampede to the Back Bay. Federal Street (thereafter Arlington Street) Church in 1859 bought one of the first lots filled, helping to establish the area's aristocratic character, and three more churches followed in the 1860s. In 1871 and 1872, Brattle Square and Old South Churches laid cornerstones in the Back Bay, and Trinity Church, which had hesitated momentarily about venturing out "upon the new land," acquired a site there.[25] These were three of Boston's most prestigious congregations, and their decisions to move to the Back Bay, coming in quick succession, must have deflated in the South End any lingering hopes of social preeminence. The Old South's building committee displayed the spirit of the move in requesting contractors' estimates for a new building "in every respect equal in finish" to the First Church, the most recently completed arrival.[26] The Back Bay filled up in a tide of ostentatious fashion.

The very idea of "fashion" in objects as durable as buildings and urban districts underscores the era's increasing assumptions of mutability. During the eighteenth century the simple Georgian style served as enough of an architectural constant that when Faneuil Hall was enlarged in 1805, its 1747 exterior details could be copied without any sense of anachronism.[27] Most structures were designed in an architectural vernacular that evolved slowly enough that new buildings looked not too different from the old buildings they replaced, so the city remained familiar even as its components changed. This continuity broke down by the middle of the nineteenth century with the advent of widespread self-conscious architecture. A bewildering succession of styles clothed buildings that previously would not have pretended to any style at all, and even humble cottages became subjects for pattern books promoting the latest architectural fashions. As each new building sought to differentiate itself from its surroundings, environmental change, no matter what its objective rate, became subjectively more noticeable.

Change Is Good

A month before the 1872 fire, the *Globe* cheerfully described just how noticeable change had become:

Bostonians who have been absent from their native city for a few years, return to express astonishment as they regard the rapid growth of the city. . . . Extended avenues, squares, and elegant blocks of buildings are springing up every twelvemonth, and the town is increasing in its number of inhabitants with unprecedented rapidity. . . . Old landmarks and localities have almost completely disappeared, and about one-half of Boston to-day is built upon made ground, reclaimed from the tide waters. The Back Bay—scene of past skatings, and boatings, and smeltings, and snipe shootings, has vanished, giving place to palatial residences, elegant parks, superb avenues, and scores of stone churches whose architectural beauty cannot be excelled.[28]

Like the *Globe*'s editor, most nineteenth-century Americans sensed the acceleration of change, and by and large they approved. David Lowenthal describes two distinct strains of thought according to which change was good.[29] The *Globe*'s comments belonged to the newer one, optimistic and imbued with rationality, viewing change as improvement and emphasizing material progress, gradual and continual. The older strain thought of change as renewal, emphasizing less the good to come than the corruption of what was old, and thus the necessity of starting anew. These two views reinforced one another, as Nathaniel Hawthorne showed a few years earlier in recounting an American's reflections on a perfectly preserved English village:

His delight at finding something permanent begins to yield to his Western love of change. . . . Better than this is the lot of our restless countrymen, whose modern instinct bids them tend always towards "fresh woods and pastures new." Rather than the monotony of sluggish ages, loitering on a village-green, toiling in hereditary fields, listening to the parson's drone lengthening through centuries in the gray Norman church, let us welcome whatever change may come—change of place, social customs, political institutions, modes of worship—trusting that, if all present things shall vanish, they will but make room for better systems, and for a higher type of man to clothe his life in them, and fling them off in turn.[30]

The older strain of thought, viewing change as renewal, was a remnant of American revolutionary ideology. Bostonians evoked even earlier roots in the Puritan founders' search for a new beginning. The view is akin to the millennial tradition, which anticipated the ultimate end of a corrupt world and the beginning of a good one. Americans in each generation saw their

FIGURE 1.6 *The Back Bay, c. 1870, photographed over the Common and the Public Garden. At left is the 1861 Arlington Street (formerly Federal Street) Church; at right, the beginning of Commonwealth Avenue. The vast expanse of the as-yet unfilled Back Bay extends behind them. Society for the Preservation of New England Antiquities*

own time marking this divide. In the Enlightenment's secularized version, renewal was cyclical: each generation had a right and a responsibility to make its world anew. Legal theorists of the early Republic argued that the law, instead of following ancient precedent, should expire to be rewritten every nineteen years. Thomas Jefferson stated the principle most starkly: "The dead have no rights."[31]

While Puritan and Republican thought dealt mainly with society and institutions, they easily translated into principles for the environment. Puritans rejected the notion of hallowed ground and thus, in theory, the stabilizing influence of consecrated houses of worship. As for Americans of the early nineteenth century, while their architecture sought to validate the Republic through timeless Greek Revival buildings in durable granite, Hawthorne suggested in *The House of the Seven Gables* that statehouses ought to crumble every twenty years as a hint to reexamine the institutions within them.[32]

law

American land law during the first two-thirds of the nineteenth century evolved along similar lines. Legislatures and courts consistently ignored expectations of continuity, favoring instead productive use and change. Past generations' legal edifices, like their physical ones, could be torn down and built over to suit the living. For example, American states abandoned the English common-law doctrine of "ancient lights," the right to prevent a new structure from blocking an existing window. It was incompatible with "the rapidly growing cities in this country," explained a legal commentator in 1832.[33] Similarly, nuisance doctrine was progressively relaxed to avoid fettering the growth of industries and railroads. Even ownership itself became subject to changing circumstances, through the doctrine of adverse possession, under which a person openly using another's land as if it were his own would, after a period of years, gain title to it. While this doctrine originated in English common law, nineteenth-century Americans made it easier to invoke. Adverse possession made sense to them because it rewarded action and reflected their impatience with absentee paper ownership.[34]

The most direct interference by past generations brought the most severe reactions: while bequests often expressed their donors' explicit wishes, courts were reluctant to let the dead bind the living. The legal version of this Jeffersonian principle was the "rule against perpetuities," which according to Bouvier's 1858 *Law Dictionary* prohibited "any limitation tending to take the subject of it out of commerce" for an unacceptably long period.[35] "A perpetual entail of real estate for special uses, in a town destined to grow and expand, was likely in the end to become a public nuisance," complained one clergyman who, through such an entail, had to live in his predecessors' eighteenth-century parsonage on what by 1851 had become a noisy downtown street. The Massachusetts Supreme Judicial Court agreed with him and overturned the restriction four years later.[36] Courts routinely read such stipulations not as strict requirements but as general intentions subject to reinterpretation in light of changing circumstances.

Unlike the older thinking, which looked for renewal mainly in society, the improvement strain concerned itself with progress in the material world. Even people who were more interested in spiritual progress could not help but be impressed at the nineteenth century's tangible accomplishments. Rev. Chandler Robbins of the Second Church, for example, turned his eyes from heaven to earth as the congregation in 1844 prepared to leave its 123-year-old building: "What progress has society made since the corner-stone of this edifice was laid! . . . And we and our children, if we are but faithful to the mighty trust of the most glorious present which the world has yet seen, may turn our faces forward with a still more hopeful gaze, and expect, that ere the new temple which we are about to rear shall crumble with age, or be exchanged for a more spacious and beautiful house, . . . its worshipers [shall] rejoice in a yet more perfect manifestation of the kingdom of Heaven on earth."[37]

Faith in material progress was easy in the nineteenth century. The radical but continual improvement familiar today in computers was then the norm in every department of domestic and urban technology. Candles gave way to oil lamps and gaslight and then to the miraculous electric light. Omnibuses appeared and then gave way to horsecars and electric streetcars and, in few places, rapid transit. Water systems, and the sewage and drainage systems they enabled and required, rearranged both houses and streets. In the process many technological dead ends—pneumatic transit, for example, or the many waste disposal methods that competed with flush toilets—were explored and then abandoned, making the march of improvement all the more bewildering. "They invent everything all over again about every five years," explained Arthur Townsend in Henry James's 1881 *Washington Square*, "and it's a great thing to keep up with the new things."[38]

A nation that was then building the Brooklyn Bridge and entertaining projects to harness Niagara thought its own powers as sublime as Nature's, and its material progress potentially limitless. Indeed, the most insidious check on progress was inability to imagine the future's still greater improvements. As Rev. Dr. Jacob H. Manning prayed at the dedication of the new Old South in 1875, "Spare it only so long as it shall serve Thy loving purpose. . . . When its noble walls must crumble, teach thy people to bow in the faith of something better to come."[39]

Even apart from technological change, the country's increasing wealth brought evident improvements in its standard of living, at least for the classes then visible to polite society. "In ten years," predicted one Gothamite in 1855, "the finest buildings now in New York will be far surpassed by the growing taste and wealth of builders."[40] Prosperity in turn spurred technological innovation, and mass marketing brought these innovations to more people faster than ever before.

A special intersection of technology, prosperity, and marketing gave rise to the suburbanization that contemporaries found perhaps the most striking evidence of material progress. Railroads and then streetcars made vast new tracts available for urban housing, while growing middle classes commanded the resources to take advantage of them. Detached houses with sunlight on four sides and their own gardens, however tiny, validated material progress through the moral and spiritual accomplishment of better homes for families. Businesses' invasion of downtown residential areas was by this thinking a positive force, since it pushed even the timid or nostalgic out to suburban Arcadia. Nor was the migration solely to the benefit of these former urbanites. Their arrival improved the suburbs themselves, as at the Roxbury Highlands outside Boston, once "a rough, ragged tract of wilderness," according to an observer in 1872, "but now covered with elegant dwellings, embowered in trees and flowers, presenting, at every turn, density of population and charming residences."[41]

"Whatever is old," said Emerson, "is corrupt"; whatever was new was good. Henry James's Arthur Townsend expressed this faith in reflecting on his new home: "It doesn't matter, . . . it's only for three or four years. At the end of three or four years, we'll move. That's the way to live in New York— to move every three or four years. Then you always get the last thing. It's because the city's growing so quick—you've got to keep up with it. . . . [W]hen we get tired of one street we'll go higher." Sam Bass Warner explains the implications of streetcar suburbs' "omnipresent newness": "Whether a man lived in a lower middle class quarter of cheap triple-deckers, or on a fashionable street of expensive singles, the latest styles, the freshly painted houses, the neat streets, the well-kept lawns, and the new schools and parks gave him a sense of confidence in the success of his society and a satisfaction at his participation in it."[42] The new suburban environment, with its emphasis on landscape and nature, was partly a rejection of the old neighborhoods of the city, built up to the street with houses in past generations' styles.

If historic buildings were important or worthwhile, it was in spite of their age, not because of it. Historical significance resided in sites rather than structures; tearing down the oldest church in Boston made sense to members of the Second Church in 1844 because it allowed them to build anew at their traditional location. Some of Boston's historically minded citizens in 1826 proposed demolishing the Old State House because its site would be an appropriate location for a statue honoring George Washington. Without any reluctance they recommended "the removal of such an encumbrance": "If no statue of Washington had been procured, the committee thought that the City could do no act more worthy of its reputation . . . than to raze the present edifice, and to erect a column, or obelisk, as a memorial of the important use, to which that spot had been devoted, and by which it had been consacrated [sic]."[43]

Over the next half-century this philosophy retained its force. Franklin Haven, president of the Merchants' Bank, in 1881 led another attempt to get rid of the Old State House, where "a shaft or other monument" could "best commemorate the spot and cherish its patriotic associations."[44] The same argument was applied to other historic structures as well. The Old South was "a hideous structure, offensive to taste," testified a Glocester resident in 1878, and "a handsome building could be erected there, upon the front of which might be placed an attractive model of the old church, which would answer every purpose of the present structure as a monument."[45]

Old buildings without such historic associations were even more subject to negative feelings. They were eyesores and firetraps, and any project that eliminated them was to be encouraged. The anonymously ancient structures of Italian hill towns inspired revulsion in Americans, according to Hawthorne, and "gazing at them, we recognize how undesirable it is to build the tabernacle of our brief lifetime out of permanent materials." A decade before Boston's conflagration, he reflected that "all towns should be made capable of purification by fire, or of decay within each half-century. Otherwise, they become the hereditary haunts of vermin and noisomeness, besides standing apart from the possibility of such improvements as are constantly introduced into the rest of man's contrivances and accommodations."[46] Americans had an interest in deciding that a continually changing environment was good, because they believed that it was their natural condition.

Change Is Inevitable

Pervasive faith in progress led to a certain resignation on the part of anyone who doubted its benefits (and such people did exist, as we will see in the next chapter). Change was inevitable, most Americans thought, so even if change was not good, there was no point in resisting it. This was, of course, a self-fulfilling prophesy: historic structures would come down if no one acted to save them; threatened neighborhoods would deteriorate if their residents' instinctive response to undesirable change was to move rather than to resist.

Belief in the inevitability of change did not lead merely to passive resignation; nineteenth-century city people actively anticipated, planned for, and depended on change. All planning, financial and personal as well as topo-

31

graphical, incorporated the expectation of rapid and continual change. According to historian Edward K. Spann, New Yorkers before the Civil War thought "nothing was permanent and nothing more valuable than the money needed to take advantage of changing times." Financial practice, even in Boston where family trusts might hold their property for generations, emphasized liquidity of assets: short-term leases and short-term balloon mortgages.[47] For all but the most established tenants and borrowers, these practices implied an instability of tenancy that became painfully evident with each financial crisis. At other times it loomed as a possibility which would have seemed more disturbing except that so many people moved so often anyway.

Making change part of the calculus of all decisions about the urban environment helped bring about that change. In anticipation of redevelopment, New Yorkers built their city as "an irregular collection of temporary buildings," as one English visitor described it, "not meant to endure for any length of time." Naturally such buildings deteriorated quickly, and their owners replaced them frequently. "Build better, build something immortal?" asks Spann. "Why, when a new and, one hoped, better world would soon appear in some new and better uptown?"[48]

The assumption of change encouraged change also by buffering people—some people, the ones making decisions—from the effects of change, and thus forestalling their resistance to it. New Yorkers with a choice settled the central spine of Manhattan Island because they assumed that its waterfronts would eventually become tenement and warehouse districts, and so they were neither affected by nor much interested in the neighborhood succession that in fact took place there.[49] Bostonians, like residents of other American cities, increasingly buffered themselves from urban change by leaving the city altogether, for outlying towns they believed would remain more stable.

The pervasiveness of the assumption of change can be seen in its infiltration even of subjects traditionally assumed permanent. The most dramatic example was the treatment of graveyards. "It is often said by poor people," said Harriet H. Robinson, from the Boston suburb of Malden, "that the time will come when they will own six feet of earth, and occupy it until the last trump sounds."[50] Mrs. Robinson spoke in 1884 as the Boston Common Council considered selling part of the South Burying Ground, where her father lay, for a building site.

Despite popular expectations of permanence, actual usage in most urban graveyards was in every way the opposite. From the South Burying Ground alone the city had already given up sections for a piano factory, an alley to service neighboring residential development, a street, a hotel, and even a music hall. Not only did abutting landowners treat the burial ground as available space for their own continuing expansion; the city itself did not consider it a permanent use of the land. It was a place for putting bodies, not for keeping them. Tombs were built there not to mark permanent resting places but to allow removal of bodies without the inconvenience of digging them up. As for the three thousand or so bodies buried in the ordinary manner in the ground, the city had no apparent intention of maintaining their graves indefinitely. Shortly after active burials ceased, the city closed the graveyard's gates and stopped taking care of it. Nor were these attitudes directed only toward the paupers' graves of the South Burying Ground. The aristocratic Granary and King's Chapel burial grounds downtown received better landscape care, but they too held "speculative tombs" owned by undertakers who regularly removed bodies from them in order to free up space for new interments.[51] Directory publisher George Adams, carrying out a city-sponsored program of street renumbering in 1850, reserved addresses for their frontage, explaining that "buildings will, no doubt, cover these grounds within the present century."[52] Trinity Church, having sold tombs in a basement crypt, later insisted that the sales were revocable in order to reuse the property as a business block.[53]

Relatives of the dead tacitly acquiesced in this treatment of burial as a potentially temporary land use. They often moved the remains of their relatives, usually to some place like Mount Auburn Cemetery in Cambridge, located far enough outside the city that the departed seemed more likely to rest in peace. But the ancestors brought there by their nineteenth-century descendants might well have expected the same of their original resting places, and even within rural cemeteries, families moved their loved ones' remains from place to place.[54] At the hearing where Mrs. Robinson objected to disturbing the South Burying Ground, she was outnumbered by speakers who raised no objections to respectfully executed relocation of bodies and in some cases welcomed it for the potential to improve their loved ones' posthumous neighborhoods. In a revealing paradox, the city registrar testified that the graveyard was ripe for discontinuation, giving as his evidence the fact that he had ceased receiving requests for the removal of bodies from it.

Churches, like graveyards, were popularly considered permanent. While seventeenth-century Puritans rejected consecration as a worldly distraction, in practice their descendants believed that places of worship should be permanent, even in the absence of any formal ritual affirming it. Chandler Robbins expressed these popular expectations when he said of the old Second Church that "a hundred and thirty years of occupancy by a Christian church make it a consecrated spot."[55] As with graveyards, actual practice revealed these expectations to be confused and subservient to the demands of a changing city.

While Robbins's rhetoric paid homage to continuity and tradition, these often took token or intangible forms: the congregation's name, for example, or its communion vessels, which "have survived the burning of one house of worship, and the demolition of three. They have accompanied this church in all its vicissitudes and wanderings." Robbins in 1874 invoked this silverware as he prepared his followers for yet another move to yet another building: "How immediately they transfer to it the hallowed associations which our hearts have twined about them in other temples! How they impart to it at once the air of home!"[56]

Even this tenuous and contrived continuity allowed Robbins and his followers a high tolerance for environmental instability, which they did not just passively accept but actively initiated. In the 1840s both halves of the congregation sought change. The ostensibly conservative North End faction did not seek to preserve the oldest church in the city or even to construct a new building reminiscent of it; like their South End counterparts, they wanted a new building of new design. A generation later, packing and numbering like an archaeological treasure the stones of a twenty-eight-year-old church built for another congregation smacked of desperation for continuity. Yet the congregation began its move before fixing on a destination, and they did not follow through with the fetishistic process of bringing their Bedford Street building with them; they improved the building so far as to make the carefully numbered stones unrecognizable. Another minister moving his flock to the Back Bay at the same time invoked the heroic Pilgrims who "turned their backs upon the dear old churches" and articulated the principle that underlay all this motion: "As we cannot annul, we should cheerfully submit to that law of change which is a necessary condition of our being on earth."[57]

While change itself might be a law, the direction of change was by no means certain. Bostonians did not know where their city was going, as they demonstrated during a decade of arguing where to put a new courthouse that was first proposed in the early 1870s. One writer urged the city to build "such a Court House as will suffice for the next twenty years," since "twenty years from now we may require a house in another part of the city." Another suggested letting the courts take over the Beacon Hill State House, so that a new one could be built on the Back Bay.[58]

The Back Bay complicated any understanding of the city's future growth. Downtown had been expanding to the south, but the new land opened a westward direction that had not existed before. Would the business district, like residences and institutions, change its course? If it turned toward the Back Bay, would it engulf intervening Beacon Hill, as some people expected?[59] All American cities faced similar uncertainties, none more than Chicago, where the fire in 1871 suddenly turned all the contingencies of evolving urban form into a single immediate question. "Some do not [re]-build," reported the *Globe*'s Chicago correspondent, "because they do not know what to build. There is great uncertainty as to where business centres are to be, as to which streets will be plebeian and which aristocratic. The sweeping fire abolished all distinctions, . . . and men are waiting until causes over which they have little control have decided whether they are to put up shanties or palaces."[60]

Projecting the answers to such questions was the stock in trade of real estate speculators. Real estate thinking was important not merely because it produced most of the built environment but also because it provided the contemporary terms for understanding that environment. Before the advent of city planning at the turn of the century, the implicit rules of real estate were the main available body of theory for explaining urban growth and form.

Real estate development was a fragmented process in the nineteenth century, especially in Boston. No single developer produced finished pieces of the environment by taking them from raw land through occupancy; instead each step of this process was undertaken separately, mostly by small-scale operators. Land developers made a minimum of tangible improvements, simply packaging land for speculation by recording a plat and staking lots. They often marketed aggressively; larger subdividers hired trains for free weekend excursions to their sites, where clambakes and brass bands were calculated to heighten auction fever. Their product was popular. Most people could flatter themselves that they understood it, and real estate looked like a safe investment at a time when banks sometimes were not. Even the working class could afford the cheapest lots when they were offered on easy credit, and wealthier investors could gamble on land near the center, which might or might not become part of downtown. Everyone could be a speculator.[61]

The word *speculation* had in the nineteenth century, as it does now, many shades of meaning. In a matter-of-fact sense it means gaining unearned increment from change. James E. Vance, using this definition, emphasizes the importance of anticipating and understanding change in order to profit by it. Richard Sennett, on the other hand, describes nineteenth-century speculation as almost pure gambling. People anticipated change in the sense of expecting it to happen, but when and how was a matter of chance, largely beyond comprehension. Genteel opinion in general, and the Boston elite in particular, was appalled by "speculation," but their definition focused not on gain but on gamble. A latent Puritanism rebelled at truly unearned profit;

investors properly earned their gain by understanding their investments, by correctly predicting change.[62]

Investors were aided in their understanding by the pervasive anticipation of change. Our late-twentieth-century sensibilities can be disturbed when we look at a nineteenth-century city street map and realize that much of it shows paper streets that existed on the ground as nothing more than surveyors' stakes, if that. Such a map does not, in our view, correctly represent reality. But its contemporary users were less likely to be bothered by this distinction. Their view of reality was compounded of what was becoming as well as what had already come about. A view that is today found mainly among those involved in real estate development was then common among average citizens, each of whom was at least potentially a speculative lot investor.

The all-encompassing awareness of potential land-use change extended to the domestic environment. Just as homeowners today seldom entirely lose sight of their property as accumulated equity—a consideration that ordinarily leads them to value neighborhood stability—so their counterparts in the mid-nineteenth century were ever conscious of it as a speculation, always aware of its potential for conversion, perhaps at some distant date, to something other than a house. Thus even those developers marketing a suburban residential environment, an escape from the city, often felt that they had to promise an investment in what would later become a city.[63]

This attitude is explained by a sobering corollary of the axiom of inevitable change. When good neighborhoods changed, they generally changed for the worse, as places to live, and neighborhood decline was accepted as a rule of real estate. Nineteenth-century Americans viewed their homes as speculative investments in part by necessity, a defensive adaptation to the changing city. Since they would eventually be forced to vacate their homes, they wanted to do so on favorable terms.

The spatial expression of this philosophy was the city of gridded streets of standard lots. "Since the growth of cities leads normally to the ultimate conversion of residence land into business land," explained real estate writer Richard Hurd, "a uniform system of platting suitable for business purposes throughout the entire city is generally preferable." No lot, no locality, made any commitment as to its intended use; all were designed to accommodate the most intense uses they might later be called on to serve. In the ideal urban fabric, every street was wide and straight enough to become a main business thoroughfare. The grandfather of the speculative grid was the 1811 plan for Manhattan, where "some two thousand blocks were provided," as Frederick Law Olmsted later explained, "each theoretically 200 feet wide, no more, no less; and ever since, if a building site is wanted, whether with a view to a church or a blast furnace, an opera house or a toy shop, there is, of intention, no better a place in one of these blocks than in another."[64] In Boston as in many eastern cities the grid was not such a transcendent Cartesian reality imposed by public authority but a hypothetical norm interpreted by each developer within his own domain, so that the map of the city showed not one grid but a crazy quilt of little gridlets.

What developers could interpret they also could and did reinterpret, by replatting streets and lots. The practice of resubdivision grew naturally out of the uncertainties of real estate development. Of all residential land, fashionable upper-class building lots drew the highest prices, so subdividers with even the slimmest hopes of attracting such buyers laid out their plats for this market. Only a few of them could succeed. But did the others really fail? When they redrew their plats as more modest lots a fraction of their original size—often by cutting additional streets through them—the cachet of the imaginary upper-class neighborhood could help in subsequent marketing.[65] The potential for resubdivision was thus a valuable tool in the land developer's kit. Plats might be resubdivided while they were still raw land, or they might be redrawn around those lots that had already been sold and perhaps built upon.

Resubdivision was also carried out at a smaller scale by individual lot owners. In the literature of housing reform this process is familiar as the way back courts and rear tenements were created out of already small yards. But the practice was also common at the other end of the social scale, where the owners of great houses sold off their gardens as building lots, often remaining in the mansion and therefore taking an interest in the quality of the new development.[66] In at least some cases the potential for individual resubdivision was anticipated in the original design of plats, as in the suburbs of another New England city where subdividers laid out large one-hundred-by one-hundred-foot lots, "for houses or dividing to sell again": "Our object is to WHOLESALE land rather than to retail," said their advertisement, "giving the buyer the opportunity to sell a considerable portion at advanced prices, thereby securing his own home site at a practically nominal figure."[67] While resubdivision of individual lots changed neighborhoods more gradually than wholesale replatting, in the aggregate it could be more disruptive because it was less orderly and predictable.[68] For homeowners, however, it was always in the lexicon of possibilities, a last resort to pull the full speculative value out of their property.

In nineteenth-century Boston there was an intimate relationship between rapid growth that made the physical environment unstable and a culture that approved and even celebrated such change. But people naturally enough did not like feeling forced from their homes. In spite of a prevailing ideology that change was both inevitable and productive, for the greater good and for themselves as individuals, nineteenth-century Bostonians expressed much the same feelings of regret, fear, and anger we would expect under similar circumstances today. During the 1870s and 1880s, Bostonians began to decide that these were not merely self-indulgent sentiments to be set aside but valid objections to the culture of change.

CHAPTER 2

❧❧❧

Problems with Change

Progress is a terrible thing.
—WILLIAM JAMES

Change was the norm in nineteenth-century America in other realms aside from the urban environment, and much of the change was not pleasant. A modern urban industrial society was emerging from an agrarian country, and this was a disturbing process. These larger social forces helped create the preconditions for a shift in the way Americans viewed environmental change.

Unfamiliar Society

From the 1840s onward Boston's in-migration from the New England countryside began to be overwhelmed by waves of migration from across the Atlantic, first from Ireland and then from southern and eastern Europe. Bostonians who were happy to see their city grow by assimilating the sons and daughters of Maine farmers were less happy about assimilating the children of Ireland. An anti-Irish and anti-Catholic mob in 1834 burned the Ursuline convent in Charlestown, an early and virulent manifestation of antebellum xenophobia.[1] By the last third of the nineteenth century, nativism had subsided from a political movement into a pervasive and uncomfortable consciousness that much of the urban population was not "wholesome American stock" but something else, poor or transient or especially foreign, a population whose ways were at best strange, and one that was growing at an alarming rate. One by-product of this growth was ethnically based machines of political power and patronage which seemed to make a mockery of America's republican principles, and which encouraged a growing nostalgia for apparently simpler times.

At the other end of the social scale, old urban aristocracies such as Boston's Brahmins were being displaced from the apex of wealth by a numbingly rich kind of newcomer to the national scene. Brahmin wealth, mostly inherited, was tied to position within a local community and to an ethic of responsibility to that community. The new larger fortunes of industrial America were embodied in impersonal and placeless corporations or held by the flamboyant robber barons who could buy and sell businesses at this modern scale. Boston remained one of the nation's centers of capital, but its conservative bankers and trustees frowned on excess and took a dim view of their new financial more-than-peers elsewhere. Bostonians ranging from the old-money elite to the native-born working classes thus saw unwelcome social extremes emerging both above and below them. "Two enemies, unknown before, have risen like spirits of darkness on our social and political horizon," wrote Boston historian Francis Parkman in 1878, "an ignorant proletariat and a half-taught plutocracy."[2]

A growing incidence of civil unrest seemed to come hand in hand with this stark class differentiation. Mob violence grew more common in American cities in the middle years of the nineteenth century and then erupted at an unprecedented scale during the Civil War. When the Union imposed a military draft in July 1863, rioting Irish immigrants lynched blacks in New York and plunged the city into virtual anarchy; by the time the army reestablished control several days later, rioters and troops together had killed more than a hundred people. In Boston's North End a mob attacked an armory, which the militia defended by firing a cannon into the crowd, killing several people.[3] While these riots could not compare in ferocity with the battles of the Civil War itself, to many Boston residents they were more disturbing. They brought the war's chaos home to otherwise secure northern territory and undermined whatever ideas of common purpose people used for making sense of the great national self-destruction.

After the war this sense of looming conflict did not abate but arose increasingly from labor strife. In 1877, at the depth of the worst depression the nation had yet experienced, railroads cut wages, triggering a strike which turned violent when the companies tried to keep trains running with nonunion labor backed by police and the militia. Federal troops killed scores of people to take control of cities from Baltimore to Chicago. In comparatively placid Boston, Harvard president Charles W. Eliot began drilling riflemen in the college yard. The violence in 1877, wrote one historian a generation later, "seemed to threaten the chief strongholds of society and came like a thunderbolt out of a clear sky, startling us rudely. For we had hugged the delusion that such social uprisings belonged to Europe and had no reason of being in a free republic."[4]

It seemed possible that American cities could be engulfed in European-style class warfare. Commentators drew parallels between the 1877 disturbances and the Paris Commune six years earlier. The experience of pitched

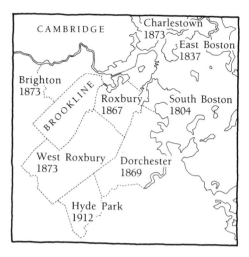

MAP 2 *Boston annexations*

battles in the streets on this side of the Atlantic energized previously sluggish efforts to build fortresslike armories for the militia in American cities;
in Boston the First Corps of Cadets began a fundraising campaign in 1878.
"The skies may be clear today," they said of the city's restless classes, "but no
man knows when the storm may burst."[5] Americans regularly invoked the
metaphor of a volcano under the city; hidden social forces of untold power
waited to erupt. The whole fabric of society threatened to fall apart; it was
no longer clear that there were any limits to the potential disruption.[6]

Concerns such as these shaped a watershed in the history of American
cities: the town of Brookline's 1873 decision to decline annexation by Boston. Annexation advocates held out promises of limitless pure water, street
lighting, and other material improvements; for Brookline residents who
identified the city's prosperity with their own they painted a vision of a
greater Boston growing to become second city of the nation. But Brookline's
comfortable suburbanites, by the resounding vote of 706 to 299, were not
impressed with these incantations of the culture of change.[7] They liked what
they had. "It is better to keep the town pure," said one Brookline resident,
"than to mix with the city affairs and attempt to purify them."[8] Brookline
became a new prototype in American metropolitan development: the independent commuter suburb, functionally a part of the city but socially and
politically separate, taking its sustenance from the urban economy but in-
sulating itself as much as possible from urban population and problems.
Other towns around Boston and other cities quickly saw Brookline's point
and backed away from the rim of the urban vortex.[9]

The metropolis grew bigger even if municipal boundaries did not, and it also grew fundamentally different. Rapid changes in the physical environment expressed far-reaching changes in social structure. The revolution in urban transportation wrought by railroads and streetcars, says historian David Schuyler, "literally turned the city inside out," reversing the structure of the walking city by "enabling the rich to move to homes in the suburbs, while the poor huddled in increasingly congested downtown areas." Spatial differentiation was carried further as increasingly fine distinctions of class and ethnicity were expressed in residential location. This increasing neighborhood segregation, Edward K. Spann notes of New York City, "was both imprecise and unstable; the expansion of commerce and the growth in the number of poor people was too rapid for either to be contained within an established zone." Because the intimately mixed social classes and land uses of the old walking city were no longer acceptable to middle-class America, almost any land-use change appeared threatening. The consequences of neighborhood change became potentially more drastic. No longer would a neighborhood merely become denser; it would change in type, and a person who once belonged there would no longer belong. People reacted to neighborhood change with a heightened sensitivity. In John P. Marquand's novel *The Late George Apley,* Apley's father sees opposite the family's South End mansion a man wearing no dress coat. "The next day," recalls Apley, "he sold his house for what he had paid for it and we moved to Beacon Street [in the Back Bay]. Father had sensed the approach of change; a man in his shirt sleeves had told him that the days of the South End were numbered."[10]

When people became uneasy about the directions and pace of social change, then the city's physical change no longer seemed reassuring. Suddenly change in general seemed perhaps negative rather than positive. This was not a reasoned conclusion but a cultural gestalt-switch, a shift in perception like the silhouette of a vase that suddenly reveals itself as the space between two human profiles. People reinterpreted what they knew of the world, seeing it in a new light. The rapidly changing face of the city could still be seen as a sign of material progress, but it could just as easily be seen as a symptom of the disturbing social changes it housed. It was the aggregate of these individual shifts in perception that was ultimately important; the particular times and catalytic events that changed individual minds varied. "The party of Memory for the first time began to outvote the party of Hope," says David Lowenthal of the 1880s and 1890s.[11] The culture of change was a matter of faith, and once questioned, that faith quickly evaporated.

As individual Americans lost their faith in change, they grew more keenly aware of its disadvantages—problems they already knew about but had dis-

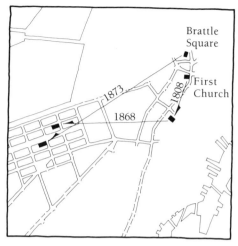

MAP 3   *First Church, Brattle Square Church*

missed either as sentimentalism unbefitting a practical nation or as regrettable but inevitable side effects of a necessary and healthy progress. As faith in change slipped away, awareness of these drawbacks remained and assumed a life of its own as a criticism of the culture of change. People began to acknowledge the disorientation that resulted from rapid change. They sought refuge from change in their own lives. Finally they began to formulate new theories of urban growth and form based not on change but on permanence.

Disappearing Landmarks and the Unfamiliar City

People regretted the loss of familiar scenes and landmarks, but their sadness often took them by surprise, because the culture of change had taught them to reject such sentimentality. The Second Church congregation felt unexpectedly bereft at the demolition of its old home in 1844. "We knew not how dear were its old walls, till they began to disappear," confessed Rev. Chandler Robbins. "We never realized how strong and tender were the associations that bound it to our hearts, till we saw it dismantled, desolate, and ruinous, whilst the work of its destruction was going on."[12]

Possibly the first recorded preservation controversy in America was the unsuccessful opposition to demolishing Boston's "Old Brick" First Church meetinghouse in 1808, as the congregation moved from State Street to then bucolic Chauncy Place.[13] Sixty years later the expanding business district had overtaken that spot, too. Rev. Rufus Ellis, in his 1868 farewell sermon at Chauncy Place, was less circumspect about his regrets than others in his position had been a decade or so earlier. "For myself," he said,

as the time for our departure has drawn nearer and nearer, I am less and less willing to go. I was sorry when I found that our stay must be shortened by only so much as a week. I am thankful that it is no part of my duty to disturb the headstone of the old building, as it was to aid in placing the corner-stone of the new. I am sorry that I ever assented when they called the church gloomy. . . . I shall try not to be near when the first axe falls upon the old timbers. . . . [T]he glory has not been lifted from this house, and our hearts are in the old places.

"I sincerely hope that more abiding things are in store for the congregation," said Ellis. "Such changes are not good for us."[14]

The lost landmark that raised the most serious questions about the culture of change was Brattle Square Church, razed in the early 1870s. Bostonians had watched in dismay as John Hancock's house was torn down ten years earlier, and this was Hancock's church. The peculiar power of its loss came from the relationship between two parts of its story. First, it was seen as perhaps the most historically significant structure to go since the Old Brick meetinghouse in 1808, and much of the community mourned it. Second, the subsequent fate of its congregation suggested new and disturbing lessons about the loss of the building, and about change in general.

Brattle Square was one of the great Brahmin churches, built in 1772–73 largely at Hancock's instigation; its proprietors included both Presidents Adams as well as governors and chief justices of the commonwealth and some of its wealthiest merchants. The building, designed by Thomas Dawes, was among the earliest of Boston's churches that later generations would find architecturally respectable. Additional historical interest accrued when British troops took over the new building for a barracks and endeared themselves to nineteenth-century antiquarians by chiseling Hancock's name off the cornerstone. A patriot cannonball said to have struck the church was installed in the exterior wall in 1825, cementing the building's revolutionary associations in the public mind.[15]

Twenty years later Brattle Square, just off State Street, was at the very center of the business district, a too worldly destination for churchgoers' Sunday tastes. The congregation considered moving in the 1840s and discussed the question again and again during the next two decades. In the 1850s church lawyers, asking the Supreme Judicial Court to modify an eighteenth-century will by which the society held its nearby parsonage, argued that the area had changed so thoroughly that it was no longer reasonable to expect the minister to live there. The court agreed. Rev. Samuel K. Lothrop's fare-

FIGURE 2.1 *Old Brattle Square Church, photographed by Josiah Johnson Hawes, 1859. Above the entry on the right is the British cannonball said to have struck the building; at the far right, down Brattle Street, Faneuil Hall is just visible. Society for the Preservation of New England Antiquities*

well sermon conveys the sense that the neighborhood finally forced them, almost physically, to leave.[16]

Lothrop and his flock looked upon their relocation with foreboding because of the beloved structure they would be leaving. Of the many migrating churches, this move was the least hopeful yet. In his farewell to the old building, Lothrop mouthed mechanically the usual formulas about the importance of the church as an institution rather than as a tangible structure: "Are our religious feelings and associations so much more local and confined than those of every other part of our nature, that we cannot meet the changes that require us to transfer them to new scenes? Is our worship . . .

so dependent upon the influence of outward and accustomed surroundings . . . ?"[17] He went on to deny this rhetorical premise, but the passion
in his sermon reinforced what many of his parishioners must have felt: that
Brattle Square Church really was a particular building in a particular place,
and not an abstract and transportable institution.

The congregation forced itself to sacrifice its church because, faced with
the altered neighborhood around it, the culture of change dictated that this
was the appropriate response. Even though they would all understandably
feel regrets about the move, said Lothrop, to give in to their "attachment
and reverence for this spot and this house" would be a self-indulgent "grati-
fication of our personal feelings." When nostalgia became an impediment to
change, it was in this view a "morbid" impulse.[18]

The prospect of losing Brattle Square Church brought the greatest public outcry yet from Boston's "citizens generally, who feel that they have, as it
were, some right of property in this old landmark of the past."[19] These protests, however, were not yet channeled into any effective avenues of opposition. Old Brattle Square Church held its last service on July 30, 1871. Elite
churches were usually empty in the summer, as their congregations fled to
the country and the shore, but this service was packed. The society sold the
building, which then stood for many months as a forlorn shell. That fall they
laid the cornerstone for their new building, designed by H. H. Richardson,
on Commonwealth Avenue in the Back Bay.

The new building's dedication on December 22, 1873, followed a few
weeks after that year's financial panic, which together with the fire reduced
the congregation's ability to subscribe the hefty pew sales needed to pay
for it, even as budget overruns made such sales all the more imperative.
The church opened under a mortgage, a common practice which ordinarily
seemed prudent enough, when at Lothrop's dedication sermon all could hear
yet another disaster: the new building's acoustics were appalling.[20]

Now Bostonians saw revealed an unhappy side to churches' Back Bay
migration. If their leaders sincerely believed them durable institutions continuing on new sites, the churchgoing public was willing to treat them in the
same spirit of change they had already shown for their neighborhoods. The
Back Bay's oversupply of churches in a small area was convenient for a sort
of religious comparison-shopping. As each new church opened, the curious thronged it for a season. The new Brattle Square Church and its tower
succeeded as an architectural presence on Commonwealth Avenue, but its
elderly minister and difficult acoustics made it fare badly once people ven-
tured inside. Within a year it was searching for a new pastor so that Lothrop
could retire; with uncertainty in both treasury and pulpit, even those parishioners who were inclined to stay hesitated to make a financial commitment.

By 1875 the new building's mortgage was overdue, and the congregation openly discussed selling it. The debt was easily within reach of the society's wealthy members, but they had already given, and before they would give more they wanted to see a more general support that was not forthcoming. When the proprietors announced a parish meeting to consider ways of avoiding a sale, almost no one came. Lothrop, his health failing, took a leave of absence, and the church closed in the summer of 1875. The congregation disbanded.

So the Brattle Square Church, after much talk about the necessity of moving to avoid a slow death in its old location, moved and instead died quickly. What killed it? Not bad acoustics or debt. Both could have been remedied, but the parishioners lacked the will and instead fled. Bostonians saw two possible interpretations. One, in keeping with the culture of change, was that they had waited too long. In this view the congregation killed itself in the 1850s and 1860s, when it clung morbidly to the past. If the congregation had dwindled slowly in its old church so that it could not be rebuilt in the new, this explanation would be compelling. But the congregation left for the Back Bay more or less intact, ample in both numbers and wealth, and fell away only after it arrived.

The other explanation is the one that Lothrop and his contemporaries were so eager to discount: that Brattle Square Church really was an irreplaceable building, that the parishioners' embarrassment was over not their architect's acoustical miscalculation but the act of desecration they had committed in selling the old church to be torn down. This explanation led to dark conclusions, for it did not follow that the congregation could have continued its life permanently in its old meetinghouse. If it could not live apart from its Brattle Square building, and if the square itself was so inhospitable as to be lethal to the congregation, then Boston's growth had strangled this church dead.

Brattle Square Church raised one further question that was at the heart of any ideas of permanence for architectural landmarks: Was it the union of institution and structure that was consecrated, or the structure itself? Had the congregation committed its act of desecration when it moved from its Brattle Square church, or when it allowed the building to be demolished? The idea of preserving landmarks independently of institutions seemed grotesque to Lothrop, who asked, "Would we leave these churches stranded and useless on their old spots, to be monuments then not simply of change, but of decay and death?"[21] His contemporaries were ill equipped to answer these questions, but in a few years they would ask them again for the Old South Church.

How were people to respond to the sadness they felt at these changes in the city around them? Those who had begun to lose their faith in change treated such emotions as more than anomalies. The destruction of culturally significant buildings and landscapes could reverberate with the same jarring notes as the increasing disharmony of society at large. The destruction of visually prominent structures could be disorienting, and this disorientation was itself yet another stimulus helping to re-form attitudes toward change.

One current conceptual framework for questioning change was the nineteenth-century romantic tradition in the arts, but only in the second half of the century did Americans connect that tradition with the process of shaping the urban environment. By the 1840s some Americans were expressing an awareness of the dark side of progress, a growing sympathy with the wilderness that was being vanquished as settlement spread across the continent and across the new suburbs. But these were literary qualms; they had no place in the practical culture of city building. Since they were framed as a conflict between civilization and nature, they made few distinctions within the city and so had little to say about any changes there other than its overall growth.

These qualms about lost nature were often expressed in the vicinity of cities, as they extended into and destroyed or transformed the countryside. The Hudson River school of landscape painting made people particularly sensitive to change in that region above New York City; painter Thomas Cole complained that "they are cutting down all the trees in the beautiful valley on which I have looked so often with a loving eye." New York native Henry P. Tappan, chancellor of the University of Michigan, returned to the city in 1855 and bemoaned its expansion over an island once "remarkable for its natural beauty." Just across the rivers, "the heights of Brooklyn, the shores of Hoboken, might have been preserved for enchanting public grounds. They, too, are lost forever."[22] After Boston annexed the town of Roxbury, one resident described its transformation:

Parker's Hill with its gray ledges, seamed by the frost of ages, but painted with the soft and parti-colored lichens, and decorated with ferns and nodding grasses, has yielded to the ravages of the drill and sledge hammer, to the pick and shovel. . . . The dog-tooth violets, the cowslips, the columbines, the anemones, the gentians have fled . . . and blank, unadorned highways have taken their places, fringed no longer with beauty of any kind, but presenting rows and blocks of very inferior houses.[23]

With the growth of cities, their residents found increasing occasion to rue disruption not only of their sylvan settings but of streetscapes within the city itself, as familiar and pleasing scenes were lost. "New York is notori-

NY

ously the largest and least loved of any of our great cities," said *Harper's Monthly* in 1856. "Why should it be loved as a city? It is never the same city for a dozen years together. A man born in New York forty years ago finds nothing, absolutely nothing, of the New York he knew."[24]

The cumulative effect of losing landmarks and whole swaths of the city was more than sadness; it was actual cognitive disorientation, the uncomfortable sensation of a reality not in accordance with internalized mental maps. When the environment changed so thoroughly that people could no longer tell where they were—literally, in the case of returning residents, but figuratively true for many others—then change in the environment alone could bring into question the idea of change as improvement.

The shift from vernacular to self-conscious architecture reinforced the disorienting effects of environmental change. Vernacular replacement of ordinary buildings by similar structures had hidden the pace of change, but the rapid succession of exotic styles and frenzied eclecticism exaggerated it. So long as change seemed good, this was encouraging. But as soon as change was potentially disturbing, then the urban environment was among the most disturbing phenomena around. Surviving old buildings, even ordinary ones, took on a reassuring aspect, not merely for the sentimental associations particular to each of them but also for their general suggestion of continuity.

But as Americans looked around themselves they found little such reassurance. An awareness of the pervasive newness of their environment, its complete lack of remnants from antiquity, gave them a cultural inferiority complex. Bostonian Charles Eliot Norton, upon arriving in England in 1868, found that the patina of age gave scenes in that country "a deeper familiarity than the very things that have lain before our eyes since we were born." Years later, as professor of art history at Harvard, Norton reflected on this experience in an article entitled "The Lack of Old Homes in America." He worried about the culture that was evolving in a nation of temporary abodes, "barren . . . of historic objects that appeal to the imagination and arouse the poetic associations that give depth and charm to life." Thanks to the culture of change, he said, "Boston is in its aspect as new as Chicago," and neither could offer anything to measure up to Norton's Old World standards.[25]

The national centennial celebrations in 1876 reinforced a growing awareness of American history which helped residents of the eastern states recognize and value what continuity did exist in their environment. In the Boston area this awareness was especially immediate, as people marked a succession of centennials of particular battles, parading through Lexington and Concord and Bunker Hill's Charlestown and feeling the evocative power of surviving places that had witnessed momentous events. The specifically architectural awareness promoted by exhibits at the Philadelphia Centennial Exhibition legitimized affection for remaining old buildings and helped launch the Colonial Revival school of architecture.

As the Colonial Revival style grew in popularity, the loss of old buildings became all the more disturbing. Now they were not merely quaint survivals but prototypes, their worth multiplied by all the progeny they might have spawned in the future. For the first time since Americans became architecturally self-conscious, they could imagine the possibility of a permanent community architectural identity. "When we have an opportunity of designing a building to be erected on some ancient site," wrote one correspondent to the Boston-based *American Architect and Building News,* "why not recognize the fact that the germ of a vernacular style was planted here 200 years ago, and, instead of ruthlessly rooting it out and substituting a neo-Grec or Jacobean mansion, take the tender sapling from its withered trunk, and replant it in its parent soil. . . ?"[26] In matters of taste, at least, old could be good.

One reason people were prepared to believe that old was good was the growing conviction that, in at least one important component of cities, change was indeed bad. That component was the private domestic environment, each family's home.

The Threatened Domestic Environment

Americans first acknowledged an exception from their approval of change in the urban environment in their vision of the ideal home, and even though their ideal relied upon material progress, it eventually became an important challenge to the whole culture of change.

By the middle of the nineteenth century, residential development in and around American cities was being shaped by what Gwendolyn Wright has called "the cult of domesticity."[27] The main axiom of this domestic ideology was separation of the workplace from the home. Houses were to be located in exclusively residential districts from which men would leave each day for workplaces such as offices, warehouses, and factories; the household was no longer to be a unit of economic production. Women and children therefore would be separated from work and protected from its effects. "The family," says Kenneth Jackson, "became isolated and feminized, and this 'women's sphere' came to be regarded as superior to the nondomestic institutions of the world." The cult of domesticity taught, in Jackson's words, that "the home ought to be perfect and could be made so." It needed to be perfect because the home and the nuclear family within it became more important as the basic building block of society, taking over moral, spiritual, and educational roles once filled by other community institutions. After the Civil War, says Wright, Americans set aside the quest for national salvation to seek instead "redemption for one's own family." Home life was considered the seat of all virtue; the stability of civilization rested upon the stability of the hearth.[28]

The house symbolized the family and its place in the world. "The good family and their suburban home became almost interchangeable concepts," says Wright.[29] "The suburban home, how it was furnished, and the family life the housewife oversaw, contributed to the definition of 'middle class,' at least as much as did the husband's income."[30] Houses were set on their own grounds, separated from neighbors at the sides and rear and set back especially from the street, surrounded by an ornamental space not meant to be productive like fields or kitchen gardens, nor utilitarian like urban courts or "yards" in the old meaning of the word. The new suburban yard recreated as a private retreat the nature that was being lost from the public landscape. It allowed the idealized domestic environment to extend outside the walls of the house and served, says Jackson, as "a kind of verdant moat separating the household from the threats and temptations of the city."[31]

Every part of this ideology isolated the home and family from cities and the changes that were going on in them. The idealized domestic environment put a boundary around the realm where change was normal or acceptable. Segregating home from work separated it not only from industrial nuisances but also from all the powerful economic engines of urban change. The domestic environment was instead a stable, permanent alternative to the city's tumult, "waiting like a refuge," says John Stilgoe, "in the storm of the late nineteenth-century urban frenzy." This was true in theory whether the family owned a gracious suburban villa that met the demanding requirements of the ideal or struggled to afford a simple cottage of its own. Families that were unable to buy into the physical expressions of the suburban ideal nonetheless tried to adapt rituals of the cult of domesticity to the less hospitable setting of urban housing. The lowest classes in their tenements experienced little stability in the physical environment, as the real estate market continued treating their homes as a transitional phase on the way to some more profitable land use, but settlement-house workers tried to socialize them to the domestic ideals of stability.[32]

American families did not necessarily become in practice any more settled or less migratory. Kenneth Jackson describes this paradox of a highly mobile population pursuing an ideal of rootedness, which was resolved, he says, by treating each particular house as "the temporary representation of the ideal permanent house": "Although a family might buy the structure planning to inhabit it for only a few years, the Cape Cod, Colonial Revival, and other traditional historical stylings politely ignored their transience and provided an architectural symbolism that spoke of stability and permanence."[33] The drive to express domestic permanence explains why the Colonial Revival and its kin, such as Mission Revival in California, received more widespread popular acceptance than anything American architects have done before or since.[34] In the best suburban developments this reassuring imagery extended to large-scale design that nestled the individual houses in an apparently timeless pastoral landscape.

These refuges and signs of permanence served as an increasingly important underpinning to the culture of change, a reassuring private stability which allowed people to face with equanimity the continual changes in their public environment. Within the city, the Back Bay development served this same purpose, allowing upper-class Bostonians, fortified in a precinct they believed secure, to hand over their old neighborhoods to business or to lower classes.

The problem was that the forces of environmental change did not respect the conceptual boundaries around them. Even the favored classes watched their private refuges overtaken. One universal threat was the very streetcars that allowed mass realization of the suburban ideal. Where neighborhoods grew on vacant land around a trolley line, homebuyers wanted to locate at least a block or so from the noisy tracks; when a streetcar company sought a line in an existing street of owner-occupied dwellings, such as Boston's Columbus Avenue or Marlborough Street, it could count on a vigorous opposition. Streetcars were not such a serious nuisance as elevated trains, but they were harbingers of further change, announcing the impending arrival of apartment houses and businesses, the metamorphosis of neighborhood character.[35]

Homeowners' insecurity was magnified by the idealization of the domestic environment, which made them sensitive to nuance and thus vulnerable to a broader variety of potential changes. "The very qualities that made the home so meaningful," says Gwendolyn Wright, "also made it precarious." A middle-class ideal that imitated country seats of the wealthy could never entirely measure up on an eighth of an acre, and so the suburban home relied on its neighbors' houses and lawns for much of the identity it sought to project. Real estate expert Richard Hurd asserted at the turn of the century that in residential areas "the erection of almost any building other than a residence constitutes a nuisance."[36]

Sensitivity to change was further reinforced by continuing belief in the inevitability of neighborhood decline, a deeply ingrained and tenacious idea still driving residential planning and the housing market well into the twentieth century, long after evidence was available to support a more optimistic view of the potential for environmental permanence. The infamous "redlining" maps that steered residential mortgage lending starting in the 1930s ostensibly showed the phases of neighborhood deterioration, based, says Jackson, on the assumptions that "change was inevitable" and "the natural tendency of any area was to decline."[37] Neighborhood stability, in this view, was only a respite from the inevitable and was therefore all the more important to maintain.

One of the periods in a neighborhood's life when it was most vulnerable to change was the early stages of development, while uncertainty remained as to what would fill its vacant lots or even whether they might be resubdivided. Subdivision lots were most often taken up and built upon during economic booms and lay dormant during busts; more or less complete development of a tract could take several cycles during which building patterns there might shift dramatically.[38] Buyers preferred, where possible, to avoid this uncertainty. Homeowners' insecurity translated into a powerful economic force. Marketing emphasized "established" neighborhoods, the character of which was already safely settled.

Developers of elite subdivisions, and later their middle-class imitators, took on an increasing share of infrastructure provision, installing utilities, paving roads, and planting trees and more elaborate landscaping, in order to reduce uncertainty about the neighborhood's ultimate character. This concern eventually drew land developers into the separate field of house building. In the early nineteenth century, subdividers often initially sold lots under conditions requiring prompt construction, so that early buyers' houses would help establish the value of the rest of the tract. By the 1890s developers sometimes built the first few houses themselves in order to control this critical determinant of neighborhood character.[39] In the middle of the twentieth century this trend would culminate in vertical integration of the housing industry, so that a single developer commonly took responsibility for subdividing and improving a piece of raw land, building all the houses on it, and selling them to the public.[40] Before this integration, sensitivity to neighborhood change ensured that homeowners and prospective buyers would remain skittish as long as any undeveloped lots remained nearby.

A steadily growing portion of the real estate market was nonspeculative, purchases by prospective residents who set the value of residential land not by its potential for but by its protection from change.[41] This new definition of value made the real estate industry ever more interested in the conceptual boundaries that exempted areas from the prospect of change. No place within reach of a metropolis was truly immune from change; like every historic structure, every valued neighborhood was potentially threatened. When intangible qualities of neighborhoods became a large part of their financial value, then their decline became not only a potential domestic trauma for their residents but also a significant economic waste for society as a whole.

Waste, Missed Opportunities, and the Need for Planning

The waste resulting from premature neighborhood obsolescence was "one of the most appalling losses in the economic life of the United States to-day," developer J. C. Nichols told the Eighth National Conference on City Planning in 1916.[42] Americans first began counting the costs of change in the nineteenth century, not through abstract concepts such as obsolescence but in the actual physical destruction of buildings long before their useful life was over. "We have been building up only to tear down a few years later," said Hugh O'Brien, Boston's mayor from 1885 to 1888.[43] As increasing environmental change forced people to recognize the economic waste in this process, some of them began to ask whether there might be better ways of making cities so that they would not need to be unmade so quickly.

Dislocation from environmental change showed up in numerous parts of the urban economy. Business districts shifted location, and residential neighborhoods fell from fashion, buffeting the finances of individual families and preventing the economic stabilization that could be accomplished through a system of long-term mortgage financing.[44] Infrastructure was provided haphazardly and then, like Boston's downtown hydrants during the fire, proved inadequate to its altered tasks. Cities paved streets only to have one new utility after another rip them up.

Boston provided one of the most direct examples of these costs in its continual struggle to cut traffic arteries through its tangled web of narrow seventeenth-century streets. "During the past twenty-five years," said Mayor O'Brien in 1885, "we have expended millions of dollars for widening and extending streets that could have been saved if some systematic plan had been adopted. . . . A vast amount of property in buildings has been destroyed by change of street lines and grades."[45] Street widening caused not only public costs but private disruptions as well; investments had to be made in uncertainty and sometimes amid the remnants of buildings that, while in theory "made whole" by municipal compensation, in practice were both a wasted asset in themselves and a drag on investment around them. The Boston Common Council street committee complained in 1860 that widening North Street in the North End had failed to improve business along its length because "new fronts have been placed [on] mere shells of buildings . . . disfiguring the appearance of the street."[46]

When American cities were smaller and simpler, such dislocations might have seemed an acceptable price for their vitality. But by the end of the nineteenth century some of them were growing to rank among the world's largest; surely urban fabric at this new scale could not be disposable. Historian Josef Konvitz speaks of cities' permanence as a problem beginning at the end of the nineteenth century, in that increasingly durable public works—transit lines, subterranean utilities, even paved streets themselves—no longer afforded flexibility in urban form. Elaborate new building types such as railroad stations, hotels, department stores, and elevator office blocks represented large investments that needed to be amortized over long periods and, unlike small older houses and warehouses, were not adaptable to unanticipated uses. The city planning movement arose in part as a response to this problem: if important parts of the environment were in fact permanent, then they ought to be planned as permanent.[47]

Planning for the future in this way required a new concept of progress. On his return to New York in 1855, Henry Tappan pointed out a fundamental criticism of the culture of change, a flaw in the notion of progress as Americans had applied it in their cities. The world's great cities, he said, progressed cumulatively as each generation built upon the best of those who had come before. The city should be "continually becoming dearer to us as it becomes more beautiful and contains more objects to render it worthy of our love." But New York grew by frenetically tearing down and rebuilding, indiscriminately destroying the best along with the worst. "If she goes on increasing and flourishing," asked Tappan, "must not all the works of the present and prosperous generation sink into insignificance, and leave not a trace behind . . . ?"[48] Americans had to figure out how to turn Tappan's criticism into a prescription, how to plan the best that would be kept as a foundation for what was to follow.

Bostonians drew these same philosophical lessons from their street widenings, because they would have been so clearly avoidable if previous city builders had exercised foresight. Nor was the problem limited to the old streets of the original peninsula; it was if anything more serious in the suburban wards of Dorchester and Roxbury, annexed in 1867, where many miles of new development relied on what only recently had been country lanes and farm roads.[49] At an 1870 meeting of the American Social Science Association, in Boston, Frederick Law Olmsted pointed out that

it is practically certain that the Boston of today is the mere nucleus of the Boston that is to be. It is practically certain that it is to extend over many miles of country now thoroughly rural in character, in parts of which farmers are now laying out roads with a view to shortening the teaming distance between their wood-lots and a railway station, being governed in their courses by old property lines, which were first run simply with reference to the equitable division of heritages, and in other parts of which, perhaps, some wild speculators are having streets staked off from plans which they have formed with a rule and pencil in a broker's office, with a view chiefly to the impressions they would make when seen by other speculators on a lithographed map.[50]

Such haphazard growth was setting the stage for a repetition of the same congestion and inefficiency the city experienced at its center, and the same expense and disruption in correcting them—which, said Olmsted, could never be accomplished as completely as if streets were laid out well in the first place. The traditional solution was to extend an urban grid over the countryside, as New York had done at the beginning of the century and many other cities did later, providing a neutral armature for whatever urban growth might bring.

Olmsted soon began arguing that such plans, intended to accommodate unlimited changes, were almost as wasteful as no planning at all. As the nation's most prominent landscape architect and prophet of the parks movement, a pulpit he had gained as co-winner of the 1858 design competition for New York's Central Park, Olmsted took on the even greater challenge of becoming the country's leading critic of the culture of change in the urban environment.

Olmsted formulated his most profound argument for environmental permanence by looking beyond the costs of actually changing land uses to count also the opportunity costs of trying to accommodate change by providing for every land use on every site. Grids might in theory be infinitely adaptable, but their one-size-fits-all urban fabric was in practice inappropriate for most of the uses to which it was actually put. A year after Olmsted's Boston speech, he made this argument in a plan for Staten Island, then a semirural suburb of New York. Most of the island would never be used for commercial or industrial purposes, he said, and designing it for these uses would only make it less suitable for its inhabitants.[51]

A few years later Olmsted had honed these arguments further, as David Schuyler describes.[52] In 1876, with engineer J. James R. Croes as his assistant, he reported a plan for parts of Westchester County that were about to be annexed to New York City as the Bronx. The Department of Public Parks, charged with laying out the new territory, spent several years wrestling with the difficulties of extending the Manhattan street grid, or something like it, over the rugged topography north of the city. Olmsted and Croes questioned the wisdom of this approach. While most people involved in developing the city considered the grid a great success, they said, its "inflexibility" increasingly brought problems:

If a proposed cathedral, military depot, great manufacturing enterprise, home of religious seclusion or seat of learning needs a space of ground more than sixty-six yards in extent from north to south, the system forbids that it shall be built in New York. . . .

The rigid uniformity of the system of 1807 requires that no building lot shall be more than 100 feet in depth, none less. The clerk or mechanic and his young family, wishing to live modestly in a house by themselves, without servants, is provided for in this respect no otherwise than the wealthy merchant, who, with a large family and numerous servants, wishes to display works of art, to form a large library, and to enjoy the company of many guests.[53]

The clerk or mechanic and his young family, as a result, could never hope to live in their own home in New York; the idealized domestic environment was denied to most of the city's population by the grid itself, the very instrument that was supposed to provide the ultimate in land-use adaptability.

"An attempt to make all parts of a great city equally convenient for all uses," concluded Olmsted and Croes, will also make them "equally inconvenient." They explained their alternative through the then especially powerful metaphor of the home: "If a house to be used for many different purposes must have many rooms and passages of various dimensions and variously lighted and furnished, not less must . . . a metropolis be specially adapted at different points to different ends."[54] If specific districts of the city could be built with a view to specific land uses, they could be laid out more appropriately for their intended uses, enhancing their functioning while at the same time saving money that would have been spent pointlessly adapting them for uses they would never accommodate. Topography, said Olmsted and Croes, ensured that Riverdale in the Bronx would become a commercial district "only by some forced and costly process," so why not lay it out in winding roads rather than straight blocks, which not only cost more to construct but marred the landscape's residential attractiveness?[55]

Such an approach required two innovations in real estate thinking. The first was "a certain effort of forecast as to what the city is to be in the future." Olmsted had already shown on Staten Island and in the Bronx his willingness to make such an effort; the workings of major topographic determinants were not mysterious. Such forecasting was after all the real estate speculator's stock in trade, but Olmsted stepped on the speculator's prerogatives by suggesting that projecting future land use was a matter not only of private but of public interest.[56]

The second innovation was to establish "permanent occupation" by intended land uses. Unlike Manhattan's grid, the curving streets that Olmsted proposed for Riverdale's suburban villas would never be good for anything

GENERAL PLAN
FOR SUBDIVISION OF PROPERTIES ON
BROOKLINE HILL

BELONGING TO

GEORGE A. GODDARD   LOTS 1-21   JOSEPH H. WHITE LOTS 184-173
GODDARD LAND CO.   "   22-160   ARTHUR HUNTER   "   174-228
MRS. L. S. ROGERS   "   161-181   JACOB W. PIERCE   "   229-296
                                                              "   183-291

else. This challenged the culture of change at its heart, the belief in limitless possibilities, as Olmsted acknowledged: "It may be questioned whether,
even in a locality as yet so remote from dense building and so rugged in
its topography, the demand for land for various other purposes will not, in
time, crowd out all rural and picturesque elements, and whether, for this
reason, it would be prudent to lay it out with exclusive reference to suburban uses?"[57] This was a delicate question. Olmsted pointed to London,
still the largest city in the world and growing in increments greater than
New York's, where similar picturesque suburbs were absorbed whole rather
than converted as the metropolis overtook them. He pointed also to the
considerable flexibility within such a district for incremental changes and
different building types that could be accommodated without altering the
district's permanent character. Despite these arguments, New York followed
few of Olmsted's recommendations, although Riverdale grew to be just such
a district as he proposed.[58] In 1881, Olmsted moved his office to Brookline
and continued addressing issues of environmental permanence in his plans
for the Boston park system and in other work around the country.

Olmsted explored his philosophy of the permanently differentiated city
through another medium, planning for private development of suburbs. He
defined "true suburbs" as places "in which urban and rural advantages are
agreeably combined with . . . prospect of long continuance."[59] Olmsted's
subdivision designs, like his proposal for Riverdale, used curvilinear layouts
that were intentionally unsuited to anything but individual residences and
that would resist conversion to other uses. The first of his suburban designs
to be constructed was Riverside, Illinois, begun in 1869. In an earlier un-
realized project for Berkeley, California, Olmsted felt himself excused from
the culture of change by the nature of his client, the brand-new College
(now University) of California, which was presumably less interested in
profit than in creating suitable surroundings for its campus. Olmsted therefore presented as one of the strengths of his plan its street layout, which
"would be inconvenient to follow for any purpose of business beyond the
mere supplying of the wants of the neighborhood itself." At his Fisher Hill
subdivision in Brookline, where construction began in 1884, the same logic
clearly governs the curvilinear street pattern, which avoids any convenient
connection between Boylston and Beacon Streets.[60]

Practical concerns were bringing real estate thought into line with such
reformers' ideas. Olmsted's extensively landscaped subdivision designs were
examples of the larger trend of developers taking on ever larger up-front ex-

FIGURE 2.2   *Frederick Law Olmsted's design for Fisher Hill, Brookline, 1884. Courtesy National Park Service, Frederick Law Olmsted National Historic Site*

penses. These costs included not only their provision of increasingly elaborate roads, utilities, and landscaping but also money they spent assembling and carrying large tracts of land that could only be brought onto the market over long periods. Stability of investment thus became important not only for the buyers but even more so for the developers of elite property, who had to be confident that their heavy initial investment would be returned in enhanced value over the years or even decades that might be required to complete sales. The people who later created such communities as Chevy Chase, outside Washington, D.C., says Kenneth Jackson, were "more interested in quality than in rapid growth." The financial strains of maintaining quality through lean times in Riverside, Roland Park, and the Country Club district of Kansas City made their respective developers keenly interested in protecting that quality against any threats of change.[61]

Similar worries plagued developers and investors in downtowns, where even more money was at stake. There the desire for stability arose not in order to finish selling off a project but from the need for longer times to recoup initial investment. As New York attorney William Seton Gordon explained in 1891, "While most changes are attended by an increase in the value of land, all have a tendency to lessen the value of buildings by disturbing the harmony assumed to exist at the first between buildings and neighborhood." For the tremendous investments being made in downtown buildings, this made accurate understanding of future land shifts increasingly important. Around the turn of the century the real estate industry sought a scientific understanding of urban change through increasingly systematic and quantitative appraisal methods. Investors hoped to defeat the disruptive power of change by correctly forecasting it.[62]

By the decades after the Civil War, theorists, city-building practitioners, and much of the public had found problems with the culture of change. People were displeased by the flux around them and were no longer reluctant to say so. If change in the urban environment was really a malady rather than a healthy fact of life, if at least some parts of cities ought to be permanent, then what could Americans do about it?

People in Boston and other cities tried actions of several sorts. They mobilized to prevent the destruction of buildings they valued as historic. They also mobilized to prevent encroachments on valued landscapes, and to create park landscapes meant to be permanent. They began exploring whether government's traditional role of promoting change could be reversed, using public powers instead to bring stability to the urban environment.

But first and most important, people sought private solutions, attempting to keep themselves and their families out of the path of change. They chose homes not for their speculative potential but as antispeculations, places they thought would retain their character, often suburban retreats. Developers sought to meet this demand, exploring private planning through deed restrictions. If people wanted permanence in their surroundings, and were able to pay for it, could they have it?

PART II

PERMANENCE

CHAPTER 3

❧❧❧

Selling Permanence

The making or unmaking of value in a community lies in proper restriction[s]
of land, and the more rigid and fixed they are, the safer and surer
is the land owner's investment.

—ALEXANDER S. TAYLOR

When Dr. Lemuel Hayward died in 1821 after a long career as one of Boston's leading surgeons, he left a mansion and an acre of garden behind it on Washington Street, between Bedford and Essex Streets, for eight heirs to share. The family decided to subdivide the garden as building lots. Fashionable new streets and row houses had been sprouting for years all around it. In the spring of 1823 a surveyor laid out the garden as nineteen house lots along a thirty-six-foot-wide dead-end "avenue," which soon came to be called Hayward Place. The heirs agreed to convey each lot with the condition "that no other building shall be erected or built on the lot except one of brick or stone, not less than three stories in height, and for a dwelling-house only."[1] The lots sold quickly, and the street was built up with what a resident later described as "large and elegant dwellings, . . . all of brick or stone," either occupied by their owners or "rented . . . to tenants at a high rent." Several of the heirs, including Dr. Hayward's son George, settled on the little street.[2]

Time passed, and Boston grew. Next-door to the former Hayward garden, "Rowe's Pasture" was built up. George Hayward became a prosperous surgeon in his own right and moved to Beacon Hill; his father's mansion came down to be replaced with a commercial building. By the early 1860s, forty years after Hayward Place was laid out, a busy horsecar line ran down Washington Street, its old houses either converted to businesses or replaced by big new mercantile structures. Business had spread onto side streets as far south as Bedford Street, the first big cross street north of Hayward. In the midst of all this, Hayward Place itself was still a quiet middle-class neighborhood, many of its houses occupied by their owners. By comparison with Peter Knights's samples of Boston's population, their lives were stable.[3] Elli-

MAP 4

nor Hayward, widow of one of the original heirs, still lived at number 13, and across the street at number 3 lived Samuel Parker, a retired customs inspector who had bought his house new in 1823.

Early in 1862, change turned the corner onto Hayward Place. The house next door to Parker's belonged to a Walpole resident, James Nightingale, who rented it that year to a Frederick Loeber, who lived nearby and owned a restaurant at the center of town on Congress Square. Shortly after Loeber rented number 2 Hayward Place, Parker heard workmen busy there. As he explained later, "It seemed, from the apparent preparation, that the changes might be more than what is usual in regard to dwelling-houses ordinarily," so he inquired and "to his great surprise and sorrow, he was informed by the workmen that . . . Loeber was going to convert the house . . . into a restaurant, or eating-saloon."[4]

Parker's neighbors were as unhappy about the change as he was, and once the restaurant opened they accused Loeber of

having large numbers of people in and about said premises, at all hours of the day and night, eating and drinking, and indulging in all kinds of merriment and loud and boisterous conversation, debate, and controversy, in the usual manner of allowing such establishments to be conducted in the large cities, and where the police have little or no power to repress or control the conduct of the class of persons collecting about restaurants, saloons, eating-houses, and other similar places of refreshment; and, in this way, . . . Loeber, as the natural and almost necessary consequence of applying the premises, . . . to the use aforesaid, has rendered the locality about Hayward Place almost wholly unfit for quiet and comfortable residences.[5]

Their description underlines the close relationship between dissatisfaction with environmental change and a more pervasive unease about the social changes that accompanied urbanization. The sense of losing control over society led to new demands put on spatial segregation of land uses as a means of ordering social relations. In the eighteenth century Dr. Hayward had built his mansion undeterred by the White Horse Tavern across the street, but now to the residents of his former garden Loeber's restaurant indicated the unraveling of civilized life.

Property and Permanence

In nineteenth-century America, with its reverence both for individual rights and for private property, it was perhaps inevitable that environmental permanence should be addressed first as a question of property rights. A man's home was his castle, and from that small part of the city he need fear no disturbing change. But if like the Hayward heirs he sold off parts of his garden for others to build on, did he have to relinquish all control over its future use? If buyers wanted "quiet and comfortable residences" insulated from change, was there no way to accommodate this market? Land conveyancers searched legal tradition for tools that could be adapted to these new tasks.

Restrictions in deeds, specifying permissible uses of land or forms of buildings, had been available as a legal tool for a long time. They appeared in Boston during the seventeenth century, and before 1810 they were used on Beacon Hill to specify front-yard setbacks, maximum and minimum building heights, and construction "of brick or stone" only.[6] Those writing such restrictions found many prototypes, which in the theory of the time could be grouped into two categories: *easements* and *covenants*. Easements altered the definition of what rights made up a particular piece of property; covenants modified the bargain by which the property was conveyed.

An easement establishes a relationship between two or more pieces of property. Party-wall easements, for example, set rules by which owners of abutting row houses share their common walls; rights of way allow access from one property across another. An easement "runs with the land": it fixes a relationship not between individuals but between pieces of land, no matter who comes to own them later. Ordinarily the relationship is permanent. The problem with easements was that they were not, in theory, adaptable to the new uses that Americans had in mind, such as prohibiting restaurants for the neighbors' benefit. English precedent, the ancestor of American jurisprudence, recognized only a limited set of easements, such as access, party walls, and riparian rights. Conservative English courts refused to enforce restrictions "of a novel kind . . . devised and attached to property, at the fancy or caprice of any owner," which would then run with that property "into all hands however remote."[7] They were nervous about the very permanence that made easements attractive.

Unlike easements, covenants were infinitely flexible, limited only by the imagination of the people writing them. A covenant, according to a contemporary definition, was an agreement, a branch of the law of contracts, the object of which could be anything not specifically illegal.[8] Massachusetts deeds in the first half of the nineteenth century included, for example, covenants to build row houses with facades "uniform, one with the others," to build only "dwelling-houses . . . or buildings for religious or literary purposes," and to put "a roof of slate or of some other equally incombustible material" on any building more than twelve feet high.[9] One special form of covenants, _conditions,_ if violated caused a property to revert to its original owner. Donations of land to religious congregations often included conditions requiring that a church be built by a specified time. Subdividers sometimes sold lots on condition that buyers erect houses within a certain period; this eliminated speculators and ensured that buyers would help establish the neighborhood.[10]

The problem with covenants was how and by whom they could be enforced, questions that in turn determined how long they remained effective. There was no doubt that a covenant, unless it stated otherwise, remained binding indefinitely between the individuals who originally signed it. The trouble began when properties changed hands. A covenant was of limited use if people could evade it by selling to others, but English precedent frowned on the assignment of contracts. This difficulty had been overcome by the invention of "real covenants," that is, covenants whose subjects "touched," or inherently concerned, a piece of land and therefore like easements would "attach" to it so that "he who has the one is subject to the other."[11] An early and common example was fence covenants, dividing responsibility for maintaining shared boundary fences. Conditions followed their own logic, the risk of forfeiture necessarily running with the land, but the reversionary rights vesting in the original owner personally and descending to his heirs, rather than attaching to any other piece of land he might happen to have owned. The presumption that covenants related individuals rather than pieces of property gave courts great latitude in deciding who could enforce them and whether they continued to run or expired with the sale of the property or the death of their original beneficiaries.[12]

The evolution of these legal tools was crucial to efforts at securing environmental permanence, but their importance was indirect. Legal evolution followed rather than led real estate practice, and practice was surprisingly independent of theory, at least until courts in the late nineteenth century began taking an active interest in restrictions. Nonlawyers, and even some lawyers, blissfully ignorant of legal subtleties, simply wrote in plain English what they meant to accomplish, in the innocent faith that courts would enforce it. Other more subtle lawyers drafted restrictions that they hoped would satisfy every school of thought. Either way, deeds left it to the courts to find the theoretical underpinnings for enforcing them, if it came to that.

The overwhelming majority of deed restrictions never made it into a courtroom. If a restriction was signed and then followed, or if it was violated without anyone suing, then its doctrinal correctness was irrelevant. The plain English of the restrictions succeeded or failed on its own, their evolution following a logic that came not from the theories of law but from the exigencies of real estate development. The courts that hammered out deed-restriction doctrine were guided by the principle of "reasonableness" and therefore were strongly influenced by prevailing practice and the expectations that had arisen from it.

In practice, deed restrictions at midcentury were used less to withdraw land from the potential for change than to shape change during a limited period of development. Deed restrictions could be used in pursuit of two distinct goals in the built environment: uniformity or stability. Uniformity was addressed through the specificity and stringency of the restrictions' substance; stability through their duration, their enforcement, and their potential for revision. In the early nineteenth century both uniformity and stability were new goals, and eventually both were widely pursued, but developers' most immediate aim was uniformity.[13] The residential subdivisions that first used systematic deed restrictions, such as Mount Vernon Street (1801) and Louisburg Square (1826) on Beacon Hill or Gramercy Park (1831) in New York, were designed as ensembles and used restrictions to ensure that the actions of independent builders would contribute to an overall composition.[14] The idea of such an ensemble—or at least its realization—was new on this continent and conflicted with the ordinary practice of uncoordinated individual construction. Deed restrictions resolved this conflict in a way more acceptable to Americans than the leasehold tenure of England or the strict public controls of France, where these design precedents came from. Uniformity was no threat to the culture of change. By creating a predictable product, restrictions rationalized the land-conversion process, making it more efficient and profitable.

Early restrictions at first glance seem to promise not only uniformity but stability; most of them before the 1860s specified no duration or expiration

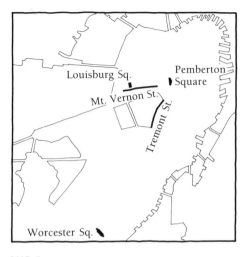

MAP 5

and therefore appear to be perpetual. This appearance is misleading. An examination of mid-nineteenth-century practice suggests that most of them
were conceived as applying only to the first generation of construction on
each lot.[15] Conditions in deeds from the city of Boston in 1859 on the South
End's Worcester Square, for example, referred to "the building which may be
erected."[16] This interpretation is reinforced by internal evidence in the restrictions themselves. First, many named existing buildings to be copied—
a common formula for construction contracts, but unreliable over a long
period during which the prototype might be altered or disappear. Five deeds
on Common (now Tremont) Street in 1811 contained the condition "that all
the said houses to be erected on said house lots . . . shall be as to the number
of stories and the height of them in conformity with the new block of houses
to the Northward thereof on Common street, unless all the proprietors of
the said five house lots should unanimously agree on some other plan, in
which their several houses shall be uniform, one with the others."[17] Second,
the requirement that a building be erected by a certain time implied applicability to that structure alone.[18] Finally, covenants were commonly put in the
form of conditions—violation of which would forfeit the property—making
it appear unlikely that they were expected to apply beyond a limited time.
Common sense boggled at the uncertainty that conditions could create in
real estate titles over a long period, and courts were thus very reluctant to
let them run indefinitely.

Bostonians at midcentury still looked to London for urban-design prototypes and probably modeled their deed covenants more or less directly on

the land-lease covenants that regulated building there. In the South End, for example, the city closely followed English practice, substituting the word *deed* for *lease*.[19] Leasehold covenants naturally applied only to the first structure on each lot, because tenants would negotiate new leases before rebuilding. Intentions about duration and enforcement of covenants were clear in the context of a well-defined landlord-tenant relationship but became ambiguous when the same terms were inserted into freehold deeds. Americans had not yet thought through all these ambiguities.

Like landlords enforcing their leases, it was subdividers or their heirs who enforced deed covenants or released buyers from their requirements. Neighbors within the plat had nothing to do with it.[20] Restrictions used in this way did not withdraw land from potential change indefinitely to protect purchasers, but only long enough to protect the developer while selling off the lots in a subdivision. Unscrupulous subdividers sometimes unloaded their last lots quickly, or even at an advanced price, by leaving them unrestricted.[21]

Marketing and description of subdivisions indicated a certain ambivalence about the purpose of deed restrictions. Lot purchasers were clearly meant to think of the restrictions as a benefit to themselves, not just to the subdividers. In 1835 the developers of Pemberton Square on the east slope of Beacon Hill aimed, they said, "to impose only such restrictions and obligations as will, in their opinion, subserve the interests of the purchasers." But when subdividers alone could enforce restrictions, or omit or even rescind them, then the protection depended on the developer's good faith — if indeed the developer could be found after the lots were all sold.[22] There is no indication that most homeowners expected their deed restrictions to provide any such durable legal protection. What long-term benefit they received was not from the restrictions themselves but from the character of the neighborhood that the restrictions helped create.

A different kind of long-term relationship was established when land was subdivided by a unit of government. From the 1840s to the 1860s, the city of Boston transformed the tidal flats along the neck into the new South End, selling thousands of lots of filled land. Most or all were subject to deed restrictions, specifying size, placement, and materials of buildings and restricting them to residential use for twenty years.[23] The municipality would be around indefinitely, and unlike private subdividers it would presumably be responsive to neighborhood concerns and interested in long-range land uses.

By the end of the 1850s, Bostonians were already beginning to look at deed restrictions with environmental permanence in mind. Restrictions were put to work for this end as the city began its expansion onto the Back Bay in 1857, an extraordinarily ambitious project which would take decades to complete. A three-member state commission administered it, from the beginning sub-

FIGURE 3.1   *Worcester Street in the South End. Courtesy Bostonian Society, Old State House*

jecting lots to dimensional restrictions specifying front-yard setbacks, minimum building heights of three stories, and maximum cellar depth to avoid drainage problems on the filled land. Back Bay use restrictions, unlike those in the South End, were perpetual. They offered an environment of long-term stability, evidently learning from and certainly competing successfully with the South End.[24] The existence of the Back Bay commission promised an effective means of enforcement, so buyers viewed the restrictions as durable protection. Even as development of the South End and Back Bay expanded the government's role in city building, it emphasized the extent to which that process was ordinarily a private one. The state acted not through its sovereign powers but by taking on the role and powers available to any subdivider.

Land developers, including the Back Bay commissioners, were beginning to impose restrictions that clearly aimed for long-term resistance to environmental change, rather than merely control of the initial development process. The Back Bay's unique combination of large-scale urban design, public ownership, and long-term institutional structure provided an unparalleled context for using restrictions this way. In ordinary development, however,

American practice and case law as yet gave little encouragement that restrictions could control change over any long period. Difficulties in enforcing them made them essentially unworkable for this new purpose, as demonstrated by the numerous restrictions imposed long ago and since lying dormant. Was there some way to make these deed restrictions enforceable not through the uncertain agencies of subdividers or their heirs but instead by the affected residents of a neighborhood?

Equitable Easements

The Supreme Judicial Court of Massachusetts provided an answer when it heard the complaint about Frederick Loeber's restaurant on Hayward Place. Samuel Parker and his unhappy neighbors early in 1862 called on Loeber's landlord, James Nightingale, who was sympathetic but found himself in a dilemma. His lease to Loeber recited the same provisions as the deed, limiting the property to a "dwelling-house," but Loeber interpreted that as allowing "any use he may choose" so long as he lived there.[25] As of 1862 the law offered two clear ways for this dispute to come to court. Nightingale could bring action against Loeber for violating his lease. Alternatively, the Hayward heirs could sue Nightingale for violating conditions in the deed. If they won, Nightingale would lose the house, and they would have to deal with Loeber themselves. But it was Parker and his neighbors who wanted relief, and neither of these courses of action was available to them.

This ordinary tale of nineteenth-century neighborhood life gained lasting significance when the neighbors' lawyers sued under a third untested doctrine. The deed, they said, contained not "conditions" but "restrictions" on the land, constituting "the organic law of that block of houses," enforceable by any neighbor who held property from the same subdivision.[26] Two years earlier, Associate Justice George T. Bigelow had endorsed this principle in another case, *Susannah Whitney v. Union Railway,* involving an 1851 Cambridge subdivision. Its restrictions specifically stated that any owner within the tract could enforce them, though the issue was unimportant because Whitney herself was not only a neighbor but also the original subdivider.[27] Bigelow's endorsement of neighbors' rights established no binding precedent but extended an invitation for some other plaintiff to come forward and test the principle. Parker became that test because he needed this doctrine; his deed did not state any right to enforce the restriction as a neighbor, yet unlike Whitney he had no other grounds upon which to sue. Bigelow had encouraged Parker's argument; and by 1862 Bigelow was chief justice.

The Supreme Judicial Court in 1863 ordered a permanent injunction against Loeber's restaurant. The case set important precedents in three distinct ways. First, restrictions could be enforced by any property owner within a subdivision; second, their duration could be permanent; and third, the word *condition* in an old deed could be interpreted not as a condition but as a restriction, so that courts could order violations corrected.

Parker's standing to bring the suit at all, said Bigelow, was "the most important and difficult question raised." Like a contract, which cannot be enforced by outsiders to the agreement, a real covenant bound only people between whom there was "privity of estate"—some transfer of property. But applying this rule in a subdivision produced strange results. A chain of transfers linked all the lot owners with the subdivider but not with each other. Each of them was a "stranger" to the transactions by which the subdivider imposed restrictions on every other lot. The subdivider, however, left the scene when he sold the last lot, and if he remained the personal beneficiary of the covenants, he had no direct interest in enforcing them. "In strictness, perhaps," wrote Bigelow, "the right or interest created by the restrictions . . . did not pass out of the original grantors, and now remains vested in them or their heirs. But if so, they hold it as a dry trust, in which they have no beneficial use or enjoyment . . . and [those] now holding the estates . . . are proper parties to enforce the restriction." Thus, as legal historian Lawrence Friedman puts it, Bigelow "vaulted over" privity of estate, making enforcement of deed restrictions practicable over long periods of time.[28]

Second, the court specifically addressed the restrictions' duration; the words *shall be* in the deed, said Bigelow, created "a permanent regulation."[29] Permanence had seemed legally elusive because of the rule against perpetuities. The rule traditionally applied to title, that is, to perpetual restrictions on selling property, or conditions that made ownership uncertain for unacceptably long periods. But trial lawyers regularly argued that permanent restrictions on the use or arrangement of buildings were perpetuities, and many courts looked askance at any covenant that was not limited in duration. The Massachusetts high court in 1829 accepted "partial and temporary restrictions" on land, "at least for a limited number of years," while a less sympathetic Illinois Supreme Court long afterward pronounced that "it is contrary to the well recognized business policy of this country to tie up real estate."[30] Opinions like these did little to encourage faith in covenants as long-term land-use controls. Bigelow had earlier explained that restrictions without time limits did not violate the rule against perpetuities because they could be released at any time by their beneficiaries.[31] By enforcing the Hayward Place restrictions after forty years, Bigelow made clear that in Massachusetts, people could freeze change in the built environment for as long as they liked.[32]

Finally, in addition to making restrictions enforceable by neighbors, Bige-

FIGURE 3.2 *Hayward Place from the corner of Washington Street, 1904. Society for the Preservation of New England Antiquities*

low provided real relief to them by interpreting conditions as restrictions. Conditions not only created awkward uncertainties as to title; they also did nothing to correct the practical problems they addressed. If an offending building caused forfeiture of a property, the result was new ownership of the same offending building. Bigelow simply assumed without comment that the Hayward Place covenants were restrictions, affecting the use of land rather than its ownership. Subdividers even before *Parker v. Nightingale* had begun addressing this problem by imposing "conditions" that "shall not work a forfeiture."[33] After *Parker*, courts began deliberately reinterpreting conditions as restrictions in order to enforce them over long periods of time.[34]

Justice Bigelow's decision had more lasting effect on the legal landscape than on the landscape of Boston. Not only did change continue, but so also did acceptance of change. Commerce continued spreading around Parker and his neighbors. The First Church, whose Chauncy Place building was within the same city block as Hayward Place, decided in 1865 to find a new location because tall commercial structures around it had darkened its interior. Parker died, and several of his co-plaintiffs moved away. For the residents of Hayward Place, Justice Bigelow's proclamation that their restrictions were "a permanent regulation" was apparently too strong medicine;

BOSTON PROPER.

Note.– Extension not adopted.

L-1084

they simply wanted Loeber's restaurant out. In 1869, just five years after the state's high court bestowed residential permanence upon them, Hayward Place's owners—including some of the original plaintiffs—petitioned the city of Boston to extend the street through so that it could become a business thoroughfare. The following year they signed mutual releases of their restrictions, "it being deemed for the best interests of all concerned, that said condition and restriction should be waived, so that . . . Hayward Place, and the houses thereon, may be used for business purposes, we the undersigned, owners . . . waive all of said conditions and restrictions, . . . so that each several owner may use his or their respective estates entirely independent of any other owner."[35] Two years later the Great Fire swept away all the new mercantile buildings to within a block of Hayward Place, and the flood of commercial refugees seeking new quarters swamped what remained of the little neighborhood.

Parker v. Nightingale launched in America the branch of property law variously known as deed restrictions or covenants, equitable restrictions, or equitable easements. While the real estate industry and the public called them restrictions, the lawyers' term *equitable easements* best embodied both what was new and what was powerful about them. They were "equitable" because judges ruling on them would act technically as courts of equity rather than courts of law and could therefore order that violations be abated, rather than leaving them in place and merely awarding damages. They were "easements" because they established relations between property rather than between people, so that legal action could be initiated not only by subdividers but by neighbors, who most cared about violations.

Equitable easements took a while to filter into practice, partly because courts took time to work out the details of the new doctrine. On the Back Bay, residents wanted the protection promised by this tool and were too impatient to wait for the courts. In 1866 they secured an act from the legislature that accomplished the same result by empowering them to sue the Back Bay commissioners to enforce their restrictions; three years later the Supreme Judicial Court declared that owners in the Back Bay already had a right to enforce their own restrictions, under the *Parker* doctrine.[36]

In the emergence of new legal doctrines like that of equitable easements, the conservative momentum of the law is maintained by judges' reluctance to reverse precedent explicitly, relying instead on finding rules to "distinguish" cases from earlier decisions that they do not care to follow. In *Parker v. Nightingale*, Bigelow thus did not change the definition of deed restrictions

FIGURE 3.3 *Plan accompanying petition for extension of Hayward Place, 1871. Engineering Department, City of Boston*

but articulated a category that supposedly had existed all along: restrictions imposed for the mutual benefit of a group of owners, and therefore enforceable by any of them. By what rule would courts, and property owners, know when a set of restrictions belonged to this new category? The *Parker* decision stressed the common "scheme or joint enterprise" expressed in the restrictions, upon which all the Hayward Place owners had relied.[37] The "general plan," as it was called in subsequent decisions that further elaborated the concept, was a reification of binding shared assumptions about a neighborhood's enduring form and character.

Courts were initially cautious in recognizing the existence of such plans. The kind of arbitrary control developers had often exercised while selling off a subdivision was not enough to make restrictions enforceable afterward by the purchasers. In the decade after *Parker,* the Massachusetts high court recognized plans conferring mutual enforceability only in the Back Bay and Beacon Hill.[38] But as popular expectations grew that restrictions would be enforced, courts had an easier time discovering such plans. The restrictions imposed in any residential subdivision developed in a reasonably coherent manner created equitable easements.[39] As the body of case law matured into a predictable set of rules, land developers could follow these rules in their deeds. By 1895 the "natural" assumption, according to the Supreme Judicial Court, was that any restrictions were intended as part of a general plan.[40] The burden of proof had shifted in favor of permanence.

Given the commercial context of American real estate development, equitable easements were most clearly accepted when courts decided they were worth money. Justice Bigelow suggested this possibility in the *Parker* decision where he noted that purchasers might pay a premium for restrictions. In 1890 the Supreme Judicial Court recognized expectations of permanence under restrictions as a compensable property right. The city of Boston in 1886 had taken one side of Pemberton Square for a new courthouse site. When the square was developed in 1835, it was "mutually agreed, in the strongest and most unmistakable terms," according to the court, that certain areas "shall remain forever open," including the front ten feet of the courthouse lots. The city blocked Nathaniel W. Ladd's view of the square by building to the front line of the lots but claimed that equitable easements, unlike ordinary easements, were not property interests for which Ladd had any right to compensation. Wrong, wrote Justice Oliver Wendell Holmes Jr.: "If the plaintiff has an easement, the city must pay for it."[41]

In some other jurisdictions, an economic viewpoint governed interpretation of deed restrictions from the beginning, but that worked against securing permanence in the environment because it suggested remedies through paying damages rather than correcting violations. The problem, as Andrew J.

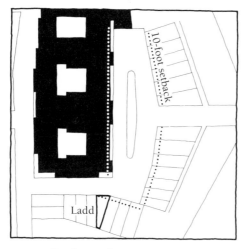

MAP 6   *Pemberton Square*

King points out in a study of restrictions in Illinois, was that "a change in neighborhood usually indicated that business or multi-family use now predominated. Normally land values would rise, and the plaintiff could show no recoverable monetary loss." Environmental permanence was not an economic but a cultural goal. Compensation "would be an unsuitable remedy" for an encroachment beyond the building line on Commonwealth Avenue, decided the Massachusetts high court in 1891. "The injury is not one easily measurable by money."[42] Strictly economic theories of land use, which did not reckon neighborhood character independent of its financial value, could not account for complaints about neighborhood change and could do little to answer them.

Massachusetts judges, like other affluent Americans who were moving to restricted subdivisions, did want an answer to neighborhood change. Their decisions increasingly reflected a preference for permanence. Justice John W. Hammond, upholding restrictions in a 1911 case, summed up the Massachusetts judicial attitude. "If, in these days of noise and bulging, intrusive activities, one who has been in confusion all day desires to have a home where, awake or asleep, he can pass his hours in quiet and repose," he wrote, "there is no reason of public policy why, if he can get it, he should not have it.[43]

"A Permanent Residential Restricted Neighborhood"

While lawyers and judges worked out what legal tools would be available for the private control of neighborhood change, thousands of large and small subdividers were figuring out how to respond to this new market preference. Some form of land-use and building-line restrictions became common even in unpretentious subdivisions.[44] Restrictions spread nationwide even to places where neither courts nor custom had favored them previously; Illinois subdividers used them throughout the late nineteenth century, even though courts refused to enforce them there until 1902.[45] Everywhere their use became more self-conscious; developers began to treat restrictions as a marketing tool.

Early restrictions regulated buildings' construction and position on the land; restrictions on permissible uses gradually became common and eventually became the most important application of the tool. Regulation of siting and dimensions fit the early idea of applying restrictions to a single generation of building, though they could also serve over the years to keep alterations and reconstruction in conformity with their surroundings. Land-use regulation inherently applied over a period of time, whether finite or permanent. The first generation of use restrictions focused on the activities to be excluded, accepting the nineteenth-century pattern of mixed land uses but seeking a benign mix. A particularly thorough version in Cambridge in 1850 forbade owners to build structures "which shall be used for the trade or calling of a butcher, currier, tanner, varnish-maker, ink-maker, tallow-chandler, soap-boiler, brewer, distiller, sugar-baker, dyer, tinman, working brazier, founder, smith, or brickmaker, or for any nauseous or offensive trade whatsoever; nor occupy such lots for these or any other purposes which shall tend to disturb the quiet or comfort of the neighborhood."[46]

Soon mixed use itself began to seem a problem, and restrictions focused not on what would be prohibited but what would be allowed, at first simply by limiting land to residential use. Developers soon found that there was a market for unmixing uses even further by separating social classes. They restricted subdivisions to ensure a certain class of occupancy by limiting them to single-family houses, by setting a minimum construction cost for them, and in many parts of the country by limiting the race, religion, or ethnicity of their owners or occupants.[47] Almost as important as class were the visible signs of class, and provisions for design and landscaping, together with prohibitions of such activities as outdoor drying of clothes, made for ever more elaborate restrictions.

Developers could best project an elite character for their subdivisions by combining a future assured through restrictions with a visible past offering a patina of environmental continuity. J. C. Nichols, developer of Kansas City's Country Club district, explained in 1916 that good subdividers practiced "preservation . . . of the interest and charm, the historic feeling, the peculiar individuality of property." Near Boston, this combination of preservation with prospective permanence was "The Vision" described in a brochure for the new deed-restricted community of Westover: "Here is a compact area of nearly a thousand acres of virgin territory of striking natural beauty, which has been preserved for a notable undertaking—*the planning and building of a complete village of small estates, where every home shall have a perfect setting and a protected privacy, in harmonious and artistic surroundings, which shall grow more beautiful through succeeding generations.*" Other developers provided this appearance of continuity not with any actual historic features of their sites but through design controls requiring traditional styles of architecture. Oak Hills Village in Newton "could not be thoroughly New England unless the houses within its gates were typically New England," said one description of its architectural restrictions. "Modernity appears only in the conveniences that are inside the dwelling."[48]

While restrictions grew in complexity, the "restricted neighborhood" came to be treated as something of a commodity, a standardized product that could be traded without further description. Real estate advertisements used the word *restricted* to telegraph an image of exclusivity and stability while rarely bothering to elaborate on the substance of the restrictions.[49] Specifics were more common in advertisements for moderate rather than high-prestige developments, addressing resistance among people who might fear that their intentions would be restricted against. An 1897 advertisement for a Devon Street subdivision in Dorchester offered "small, choice building lots . . . restricted to one or two family houses"; the message was that duplexes were not prohibited.[50] For elite projects, on the other hand, advertising copywriters could rhapsodize about picturesque settings and use a phrase such as "carefully restricted" to say all they needed.[51] The Norton Estate in Cambridge near Harvard was designed in 1887 by Charles Eliot, an Olmsted apprentice and son of Harvard College president Charles William Eliot, and it included restrictions elaborate for the time. They permitted single-family dwellings only, to cost at least $4,500 above the foundations, specifying large setbacks not only for front yards but also at the sides and rear of lots, and regulating the heights of fences. Advertisements for the lots expressed all this as a "carefully protected neighborhood."[52]

"In some localities," found Helen C. Monchow in a 1929 study of deed-restriction practice, "subdividers literally sell the restrictions themselves." Many developers distributed pamphlet explanations of their restrictions, written partly as aids to their administration and partly as marketing tools. Developers became among the most vocal critics of change in cities because in their restricted subdivisions they were selling the remedy. We have a remarkable window on the developers' view of their product; in 1917 some of the biggest subdividers in the country began an annual "Conference of Developers of High Class Residential Property," with a stenographer keeping a verbatim transcript. At the second conference John Demarest, who was developing Forest Hills Gardens in a suburban area of New York City, brought up the marketing of restrictions. Salesmen needed to be "properly couched in the real pathetic situation that has been created" in old urban neighborhoods, "sections that we find all over the city, sections that have been destroyed and ruined practically by reason of lack of restrictions," Demarest said. "It could be made a very impressive sales argument as distinguished from rattling off, 'We restrict against this and we restrict against that.' . . . Your restrictions are unquestionably one of your best selling assets, if they are properly presented."[53]

At the same conference Harry Kissell described how he presented the benefits of his Springfield, Ohio, restrictions: "That can be illustrated by going into one of the finished residential parts of town where they have built a billboard up against a good house and I took a picture of that and in the advertisement I said, 'This can not happen in Ridgewood,' and then we took pictures of houses jammed into lots, and so forth, with no air spaces, and we said, 'This can not happen in Ridgewood,' and then we took pictures of unsightly alleys and said, 'This can not happen in Ridgewood.'" "You could say," added Demarest, "that if they had not come in and damaged that section of the City they could still have remained in those magnificent surroundings that they created years ago."[54]

Subdividers found that buyers responded not only to the substance of restrictions but to their duration. "The making or unmaking of value in a community," wrote longtime Cleveland developer Alexander S. Taylor in 1916, "lies in proper restriction[s] of land, and the more rigid and fixed they are, the safer and surer is the land owner's investment." Monchow concluded that "the more highly developed the subdivision, the longer the terms of the restrictions."[55]

Marketing reflected this emphasis on duration. Restrictions on the lots in one Boston subdivision "will always keep them strictly first-class estates," assured one ad in 1896. "A great opportunity to build in a permanent residential restricted neighborhood," said another almost thirty years later. J. C. Nichols, inverting C. E. Norton's lament about the lack of old houses in America, explained that restricted subdivisions held the ancestral seats of the future. Nichols emphasized "the traditions that gather around a family where you know that their home is placed where it is going to be permanent in the history of that family. I often refer to how the old homes in England were the nuclei of strong family life." As William C. Worley points out in his study of Nichols, resales were competition, so subdividers had a direct interest in these sentiments. Outside Cleveland, the Van Sweringen brothers developed Shaker Heights in the teens and twenties, with restrictions running to the year 2026, more than a century. "No matter what changes time may bring around it," said one of their advertisements, "no matter what waves of commercialism may beat upon its borders, Shaker Village is secure, its homes and gardens are in peaceful surroundings, serene and protected for all time."[56] Such ostentatiously long duration made no sense in terms of rational planning or economics, but developers looked beyond economic rationales to emotional appeal. They were selling something more than economic accordance between building and location; they were selling permanence.

*P*ermanence was a new product for the real estate industry, which previously had thrived on change. But change had come so thoroughly and so rapidly in Boston and other cities that it created a market for a respite. Developers responded with private planning. In two generations, Americans effected a major modification of traditional property rights which was accepted by buyers and the courts only because the alternative had caused such deep dissatisfaction. New neighborhoods became more stable. But deed restrictions offered only prospective permanence, extending new parts of the city into the future. For unwanted change in the old city, Bostonians needed other solutions.

CHAPTER 4

❧

Preservation

*Why does Boston differ from Chicago? Why do we differ here from
Cincinnati? . . . If in addition to the loss of the house where Benjamin Franklin
was born, the old Hancock residence, and the Brattle Street Church, you shall
add the Old State House, which has already been desecrated and half its
sanctity destroyed, the Old South, and Faneuil Hall, then what have you,
Bostonians, left in any sense different from any city that has sprung
up within the last twenty years?*
— REV. WILLIAM H. H. MURRAY

*These monumental buildings are Boston's ancestral jewels, held in trust by us,
to be handed down to our posterity.*
— REV. JAMES FREEMAN CLARKE

Even in the mid-nineteenth century, people found the disappearance of
prominent old buildings disturbing because they believed, despite the culture of change, that at least some of them were supposed to be permanent.
Ideas about environmental permanence were tied up in attitudes about
social and institutional stability, and instability was uncomfortable. Growing antiquarian sensibility allowed people to appreciate buildings and scenes
of great age even while applauding the progress that was relegating them to
memory. These conflicting ideas did not get sorted out, because they were
seldom translated into action. Starting around the time of the Civil War,
however, the combination of increasingly pervasive urban change together
with an increasing awareness of history forced Americans to recognize these
contradictions and to consider, at first tentatively and unsuccessfully, what
to do with old but valued pieces of the urban environment.

The Place of Old Buildings

Nineteenth-century Americans' earliest historical awareness had to do with people and events, which they associated only sometimes with places and seldom with actual remaining structures. Thus in 1826 Bostonians could propose demolishing their Old State House to erect a statue commemorating the events that had occurred in it. History in the environment meant not antiquities surviving from earlier periods, but monuments erected by the present generation. Perhaps the most conspicuous in the nation and one of the most admired was the Bunker Hill monument in Charlestown, a 221-foot granite obelisk built between 1825 and 1843. Not until the end of the century did citizens begin to express regret that the monument's construction had effaced the revolutionary battle's last remaining actual traces.[1]

As for the permanence of monuments and monumental buildings themselves, Bostonians' thoughts throughout most of the nineteenth century were innocently simple and strangely contradictory. While they expected the city to change, they had high hopes for the durability of their institutions, and the structures that symbolized them should therefore endure. Samuel Adams, laying the cornerstone of the Massachusetts statehouse in 1795, hoped that it might "remain permanent as the everlasting mountains." At the Second Baptist Church dedication in 1811, Rev. Thomas Baldwin said, "We placed no inscriptions under [the cornerstone]; our hopes were, that the building would stand, till the Arch-Angel's trumpet shall demolish the universe." The owner of a Trinity Church tomb in 1871 recalled of the bodies lying under the building that "when they were interred there, it was supposed they would not be removed until the general resurrection."[2] While the durability of institutions was loosely expected to ensure the permanence of the buildings they occupied, it did not necessarily follow that protecting the buildings was a particularly high priority. When churches discovered conflicts between their roles as custodians of souls and as custodians of buildings, it seemed obvious that buildings would have to suffer.

Governments, like churches, were custodians of public landmarks, and their future seemed assured by permanence of use. But like churches, government functions could move, and unlike most churches they could do so without directly consulting their constituencies. Even on the same site, permanence of use did not necessarily yield permanence of structure; by the 1860s the legislature was considering replacing the "everlasting" statehouse. Or the government might make a bad custodian, as for example when city workers sometime in the mid-nineteenth century rearranged headstones in the Granary and King's Chapel burial grounds. Whether their purpose was symmetry of appearance or ease of maintenance, the effect, in Oliver Wendell Holmes's words, was that "nothing short of the Day of Judgement will tell whose dust lies beneath any of these records, meant by affection to mark one small spot as sacred to some cherished memory."[3]

Boston had long held as permanent certain prominent features of the urban environment. The original city charter in 1822 specifically prohibited selling the Common or Faneuil Hall. These two places gave Boston's citizens prototypes for thinking about environmental permanence. When the city applied street numbers to Tremont Street and its graveyards in 1850, the Common was exempted from the system.[4] Even as Bostonians withdrew things from prospective permanence, they were drawing the line somewhere. But enumeration of these two properties served to devalue all the others that were not on the list. This exclusion was nearly fatal to the Old State House, which the city treated as an income source, renting its rooms to businesses that disfigured its walls with advertising signs in what one modern preservationist has called "adaptive abuse."[5] Its appearance was both an embarrassment and a puzzle: was it an historic shrine or a run-down commercial building?

Even for the Common and Faneuil Hall, the policy of permanence was incoherent. They were fixed landmarks in that they would not be sold and presumably would not be destroyed, but neither of them was particularly well cared for. Until well into the nineteenth century the Common was a pasture and remained scruffy. Later it served as a dumping ground for snow cleared from the streets, with all the unsavory stuff cleared with it. Faneuil Hall had been built as a combination market and meeting hall, and the municipal government treated it too as an economic asset, managed as an income-producing part of the marketplace complex. This ambivalent treatment was partly deliberate. There was simply no category for preserved things; preservation was not in itself a land use, so the existence of the Common and Faneuil Hall depended on maintaining their functions. Many controversies about the Common, as we will see, grew out of the fact that it was not clear exactly what its use was.

Bostonians' ambivalence about the permanence of public buildings became especially evident as they moved their institutional occupants onto the new Back Bay. This district was conceived as a civic showpiece, a special case. Many of the people steering institutions there felt they were heading for safety, to a place that would be immune from the rapid changes that had driven them from other localities. Even as church proprietors embraced the culture of change to explain and excuse their abandonment of beloved downtown structures, they erected extraordinarily elaborate buildings which were clearly not intended to be transitory. They, like the upper-class families who were their members, patrons, and neighbors, sought per-

86

manence. Rev. Phillips Brooks concluded his dedication prayer for the new Trinity Church, "And so make this church the Church of the Trinity forever," and the structure was as much as possible adequate to the task. Even more than the ideal family home, public buildings like H. H. Richardson's Brattle Square and Trinity Churches were meant, in historian Alan Gowans's words, "to stand for and from eternity."[6] American cities could have prospective permanence, even if they could not have the visible retrospective permanence of the Old World.

The New World had its own antiquities, including the spectacular pueblos of the Southwest and the enigmatic mounds of the Midwest, and Americans' unsatisfied yearning for environmental antiquity led to their appreciation and exploration, and eventually their protection. Charles Eliot Norton and other Bostonians led in this movement by organizing the Archaeological Institute of America in 1879.[7] These indigenous ruins helped satisfy a longing for ancient traces on this continent, but from the everyday environment of American cities they seemed even more foreign than European castles.

In Europe, where old buildings were both more numerous and more ancient, a preservation movement had been growing from the beginning of the nineteenth century, and as the second half of the century began, a preservationist debate was raging there. European architects "restored" a tremendous number of surviving historic buildings, but restorers like Sir Gilbert Scott in England and Eugène Viollet-le-Duc in France were not shy about improving on history. Scott's alterations of medieval cathedrals involved such thorough reconstruction that they became essentially works not of preservation but of nineteenth-century revival architecture. Viollet-le-Duc advocated restoration to a hypothetical "condition of completeness which could never have existed at any given time."[8] These men thought of historic structures as monuments, not artifacts, valuing them mainly as symbols rather than as objects surviving from the hands of original makers. Their restoration efforts were guided more by stylistic theories and beliefs about periods of significance in each building's history than by actual evidence from the surviving fabric.

On the other side of the debate was English art critic and social theorist John Ruskin, who valued old structures for age itself. "I think a building cannot be considered as in its prime until four or five centuries have passed over it," he wrote in *The Seven Lamps of Architecture,* published in 1849. Restoration, therefore, was "a Lie": "You may make a model of a building as you may of a corpse, and your model may have the shell of the old walls within it as your cast might have the skeleton, with what advantage I neither see nor care; but the old building is destroyed."[9] Ruskin saw buildings mainly as artifacts. He valued them for their authenticity and thus found them irreplaceable even in the smallest part. Their symbolic significance was secondary, and in any case symbolism too was cumulative, so that the idea of restoring to an earlier period of greater significance was a contradiction in terms. Because the unarrested aging process would eventually destroy buildings, Ruskin's views did not allow for literal permanence, but he aspired to a durable architecture that would undergo decay only at the scale of geologic time.[10] For existing antiquities, Ruskin had simple advice. "Take care of your monuments," he wrote, "and you will not need to restore them."[11]

William Morris, a disciple of Ruskin, in 1877 founded the Society for the Protection of Ancient Buildings. The society, which Morris nicknamed the "anti-scrape" movement, aimed "to put Protection in place of Restoration." Fifty years of restorers' "knowledge and attention" to Britain's old buildings, he said, "have done more for their destruction than all the foregoing centuries of revolution, violence and contempt."[12] What exactly did Morris aim to protect? "Anything which can be looked upon as artistic, picturesque, historical, antique or substantial: any work, in short, over which educated, artistic people would think it worth while to argue at all." Or as one contemporary critic said of the group's inclusive goals, it wanted "to preserve what is left of the past in the most indiscriminate way; whether good or bad, old or new, preserve it all."[13]

Americans followed these European debates. "All over the country," says Gwendolyn Wright, "people of every class, from the mechanic to the dowager, had become familiar with the aesthetic and social theories of John Ruskin." His ideas informed building for permanence in the newly made city, such as the monumental buildings of the Back Bay. But Americans only slowly came to see Ruskin's prescriptions for antiquities as having anything to do with their own environment. European ideas formed an intellectual background, but only a distant one, as Americans recognized their historic landmarks and worked out what to do with them.[14]

Before the Civil War, Americans began to develop their own sense of local antiquity. Publishers offered more urban guidebooks as cities grew larger and as railroad extensions made it easier for strangers to visit them; most of these books included antiquarian notes among their descriptions. In 1851 two Boston guides appeared devoted to the city's old landmarks: Nathaniel Dearborn's *Reminiscences of Boston* and J. Smith Homans's *Sketches of Boston, Past and Present*. Three years later Samuel G. Drake published his *History and Antiquities of Boston*, the first in a popular series. Donald J. Olsen finds in London during the same years a similar growth in popular antiquarianism, which showed "a widespread eagerness to see behind the commonplace present to a romantic past."[15]

Bostonians' antiquarian awareness included the homes of heroes, such as

FIGURE 4.1 *"View of the Old Building at the Corner of Ann St.," an 1835 print of the Old Feather Store. A glimpse of modern Quincy Market in the background provides a contrast with the new and reminds us that we are in a rapidly growing city. Boston Athenaeum*

John Hancock's house on Beacon Hill, and the sites of heroic events, such as the Battle of Bunker Hill, but it also encompassed landmarks valued solely for hoary antiquity. The places with heroic associations—almost all dating from the revolutionary era—fit within the European tradition of seeing ancient structures as monuments, but the second category followed instead the Ruskinian tradition of viewing old buildings as artifacts. One such landmark in Boston was the Old Feather Store, a medieval-looking seventeenth-century house next to Faneuil Hall. At least six different views of the building were published between 1825 and 1850, and another four appeared during the 1850s; it was "quaint," a curiosity. The Old Feather Store was demolished in 1860 to widen North Street; its imminent demolition prompted early efforts at photographic documentation but no serious attempt at preservation.[16] Antiquarians' customary response to the passing of landmarks was regret rather than resistance.

Preservation, in James Marston Fitch's definition—"curatorial management of the built world" — did not exist in American cities, and the absence of this concept no doubt unfavorably colored people's impressions of old buildings.[17] Like the Old State House, such structures were adaptively re-used, but the reason was almost always economy. Adaptations were often mean, and the idea of a lavish restoration was inconceivable. Substantial money would be put into an old building only in order to make it look new.

The embryonic preservation movement in America before the Civil War focused exclusively on places with historical associations. In 1847, residents of Deerfield in western Massachusetts organized to save the Old Indian House with its hatchet-scarred door recalling a 1704 attack on the settle-ment. They failed to preserve anything but the door itself.[18] In 1850, New York State bought the Hasbrouck House in Newburgh, George Washington's headquarters during the final years of the Revolution, and opened, according to preservation historian Charles Hosmer, the "first historic house museum in the United States." In 1856 the state of Tennessee purchased the Her-mitage, Andrew Jackson's estate outside Nashville. Near Boston, the Essex Institute in Salem began before the Civil War to take an interest in preserv-ing buildings.[19]

By far the most important antebellum preservation effort was the nation-wide campaign to buy Washington's home, Mount Vernon. By the 1850s, Americans had come to treat it as a national shrine, and they were puzzled and offended that Washington's descendants, who still owned it, were not receptive to their pilgrimages. Southerner Ann Pamela Cunningham in 1853 began campaigning to save it from becoming "the seat of manufacturers and manufactories" or, as was more likely, a resort hotel. She organized the Mount Vernon Ladies' Association for the purchase and "perpetual guardian-ship" of the building.[20] In 1856, as she expanded her organization nation-wide, she was joined by former Massachusetts senator Edward Everett, who had been instrumental in the erection of the Bunker Hill monument. Everett was motivated by reverence for Washington as well as a perception that the Mount Vernon campaign could help the cause of national unity. By 1859 this early women's organization had succeeded in raising the enormous sum of $200,000 and buying the property. Caring for it through the Civil War and the years that followed would prove an equally formidable task.[21]

All of these places had in common associations with heroic figures or his-toric events. There was little discussion of their architecture or of whether or how they would be restored. Their primary role was to serve as cultural symbols. In this they competed with the sculptural and architectural monu-ments Americans were increasingly making.

All the structures preserved before the Civil War stood in rural areas or small towns. There was little organized preservationism within cities. The

FIGURE 4.2 *Hancock House, photographed by Edward Lamson Henry, c. 1863. Society for the Preservation of New England Antiquities*

greatest exception was Independence Hall in Philadelphia, bought by the city in 1816 to save it from destruction by the state, but like the Old State House in Boston, its status remained in doubt for decades to come.[22] Most urban antiquarians little thought that they could or should influence the physical evolution of the city. Historic structures just happened to remain, and it would have seemed strange and impractical to try to save them.

Bostonians first seriously questioned this, and learned about the practical and philosophical difficulties of preservation in the city, in an unsuccessful effort before and during the Civil War to save John Hancock's house. Hancock planned to bequeath his house to the commonwealth, but died in 1793 before he could act on his intention.[23] The estate instead passed to his young nephew, also named John Hancock, and it was the death of this nephew in 1859 that precipitated the house's crisis. "I hope," he wrote in his will, "the estate may not be sold, but retained in the family," and he directed that it "not be sold till four years after my decease," perhaps hoping the delay would lead his heirs to some durable arrangement for keeping it.[24] Instead, they immediately offered it to the commonwealth for $100,000. Governor Nathaniel P. Banks recommended the purchase as an official home for the state's governors. The legislature approved buying the house, but with evident ambivalence. It required unanimous action by a committee of eight state officials, who were also to report "a recommendation as to the uses to be made of said estate in the future," with the stipulation that "it shall never be used as a residence for the governor."[25] The purchase was not consummated, and in 1863, immediately after the four years had passed, two men bought the land beneath the house for $125,000.

Charles L. Hancock, the estate's administrator, offered the structure itself, together with its valuable furnishings and portraits, as a gift to the city, to be removed from the site.[26] The city council appointed a committee headed by Thomas C. Amory "to consider the propriety of some effort on the part of the City Government for the preservation of the Hancock House," which planned to save the house by moving it.[27] The least expensive destination would be across the street onto the Common, but Amory's committee did not wish to establish the precedent of a building there. If located on the Common or in the Public Garden, the house might be reused as a caretaker's residence; elsewhere it could become "an historical cabinet." Individuals quickly pledged $6,000 and were expected to provide double that toward the estimated $17,000 cost of the move, but the effort faltered when the council learned that its estimate was low.[28] Demolition began in June for two modern mansions to replace the single historic one.

As a last resort, Bostonians looked to the new owners themselves. "It is not often," said a large handbill, "that an opportunity is given to men of wealth to earn a title to public gratitude by an act of simple self-denial." The poster pointed out that although "they have made an honest purchase, and of course may plead that they have a right to do what they will with their own," they "must at any rate be prepared to hear, during the whole of their lives . . . the frequent expression of public discontent. Argument may show them blameless, but sentiment will ever condemn the proceeding" of demolishing John Hancock's house.[29] This was an appeal to the old notion of wealth bringing a responsibility to the community. It did not work.

Public sentiment relied on prominent families, like institutions, to main-

BOSTONIANS!

SAVE THE

OLD JOHN HANCOCK MANSION

THERE IS TIME YET, ALTHOUGH THE WORK OF

DEMOLITION HAS COMMENCED

It is a question of some perplexity to decide how far it is wise or proper for the city government or for individuals to interfere to prevent the act of modern vandalism which demands the destruction of this precious relic; for that it is destroyed, in effect, if removed, we conceive admits of no question. Will it, or will it not, be a mitigation of the public disgrace to establish the house itself elsewhere as a perpetual monument of the proceeding.

Without wishing in the least degree to discourage the public spirit and the patriotism of those gentlemen in the City Council who are seeking at this moment to do the best thing they can for the prerservation of the house, we still think it right that one preliminary appeal should be made to the present owners. They are gentlemen of wealth, they have made an honest purchase, and of course may plead that they have a right to do what they will with their own. It is with full recognition of their rights in this respect, and withal in the utmost kindness to them, that we would admonish them how dearly is purchased any good thing which costs the sacrifice of public associations so dear and so noble as those that cluster around the Hancock House.

These purchasers must at any rate be prepared to hear, during the whole of their lives and that of their remotest posterity, so long as any of them may live in the elegant modern palaces which shall supplant the ancient structure, the frequent expression of public discontent. Argument may show them blameless, but sentiment will ever condemn the proceeding in which theirs will be perhaps the most innocent, but nevertheless the most permanent part. It is not often that an opportunity is given to men of wealth to earn a title to public gratitude by an act of simple self-denial. Such an opportunity falls to the lot of the purchasers of this estate. *Published by ...*

FIGURE 4.3 *A large handbill printed in red ink as the last gasp of the effort to save the Hancock House, June 6, 1863. Society for the Preservation of New England Antiquities*

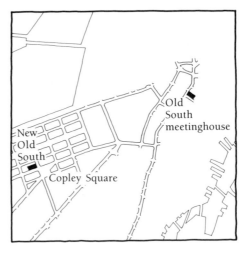

MAP 7

tain their landmarks and historic shrines. In this view the crisis of the Hancock House ought to have been resolved sixty years before it happened, for Hancock's heirs should have honored his intentions and given his home to the commonwealth. That they did not was thus no failure of the system but a failure of character in individuals. Bostonians instinctively turned to a new set of individuals as an alternative to public action.

The Hancock House episode was a pivotal event in the history of American preservation. Both the state and city governments took actions recognizing that preservation could be a legitimate aim of public policy and a legitimate object of public expenditure. Private individuals too assumed financial responsibility for preservation, bringing the Mount Vernon precedent to the urban environment. Finally, translating public policy and individual responsibility into effective action posed not only practical difficulties but also the problems of assigning a use to a building that had left the utilitarian realm to become instead "an historical monument."[30] Although the Hancock House effort failed, its failure was a catalyst. Bostonians had gone beyond regretting the loss of urban landmarks to try saving one. In later years they would find energy in the realizations both of how close they had come to succeeding and of how great was their loss.

Historic Monuments

In the years after the Hancock House fell in 1863, Bostonians experienced further losses of prominent old buildings, mostly as churches migrated to the Back Bay. Brattle Square Church acquired its new site in 1867; Trinity Church in 1870 began preparing to move, although the congregation still held services in its downtown building until the Great Fire consumed it in November 1872. Both these moves aroused opposition, but both went ahead anyway. "For the last few years nearly all of the older churches have been on a stampede after their worshippers," said the *Christian Register* in 1871. "Soon the Old South will be the only reminder, in the heart of the city, of the church edifices of a former generation."[31] The greatest American preservation effort of the nineteenth century, the one that brought preservation to the cities, began when the Old South Church decided that it too would follow its worshipers to the Back Bay.

The Old South dated from 1729, a large brick barn of a building whose plainness made it fit the old Puritan term *meetinghouse* better than *church*. The provincial town used it for public meetings too big for Faneuil Hall, and so it had a unique revolutionary-era role as the site of famous orations and gatherings such as the one that launched the Boston Tea Party.[32] It was said to be the second richest church in the United States, after Trinity in New York. It was this combination of great age, social prominence, and especially historical importance that made the Old South meetinghouse seem a special case, its preservation worthy of extraordinary measures.

The effort to preserve the Old South went through three phases of successively widening scope. First, a faction within the church sought to block the decision to move. Then, opponents both within and outside the church challenged its right to make such a move, in effect trying to force the congregation to take responsibility for preserving the building. Finally, preservationists campaigned to save the building independently of the congregation.

The Old South's organization was typical of Protestant churches of the period. About 350 individuals were listed as members of the church. Anyone could attend Sunday services and, member or not, paid "pew rent." The only exceptions were the forty-five or so pew proprietors, who made up the voting membership of the Old South Society, the corporation that for civil purposes was the church. These proprietors had each paid a substantial fee for their right and paid a quarterly "pew tax" as well; they were the more well-to-do among the congregation. A powerful "standing committee" controlled admission to pew proprietorship and also managed the society's million dollars or so of assets. These officers, said a contemporary observer, "are chosen mostly from a class of men who can afford to live on the Back Bay," and in the early 1870s ten of eleven did, while of the congregation as a whole less than a quarter lived there.[33]

One embarrassing hour in 1865 convinced many in the society that it was time to leave the old meetinghouse. A national synod of Congregationalists met in the Old South that year, but traffic noise from Washington Street drowned out the proceedings. After the very first speaker, the participants resolved to remove to a quieter location, to the horror of their hosts.[34] The following year a committee of the church's proprietors described its neighborhood: "Business presses on all sides; and the air around this locality is corrupted by cooking and eating houses, and other establishments about us. Washington Street has become so crowded and unpleasant that it is hardly a suitable place for females to walk in the evening."[35]

In 1869 the congregation bought a lot in the Back Bay at Copley Square. The pew proprietors approved, 14 to 6, this purchase of land "sufficient for a house of worship," yet they almost unanimously affirmed that they did not by this action "contemplate the sale or removal of the Old South Meetinghouse."[36] How could these two votes be reconciled? Together they were a compromise that meant different things to different people. For the majority it was a matter of timing. A new church would be built on the lot, and the fate of the old meetinghouse would be decided then. From the beginning, the society's building committee made provisions for a complete replacement of the old structure on the Back Bay, even though they constructed only a chapel at first. The minority, said one of its members, viewed the purchase merely as "a precautionary measure."[37] Several alternatives seemed possible. Perhaps the Back Bay chapel might be operated as a sort of satellite facility for the congregation, like the Beacon Hill chapel it replaced, or like the church's Sunday School in the West End. Perhaps the society would partition, one half to remain in the original meetinghouse and the other to worship on the Back Bay. They knew that the church's charter prohibited selling or leasing the meetinghouse property, in accordance with the 1669 gift by which the society had acquired it.[38] They questioned the religious efficacy as well as the fairness of catering to the richest quarter rather than the bulk of the congregation and the large transient downtown population, which the Old South's location and financial resources made it uniquely able to serve.

Several of the preservationist minority were already at odds with the rest of the proprietors. Publisher Uriel Crocker and his son Uriel H. Crocker had questioned the church's financial management, and in 1857 the younger Crocker was deposed as an officer of the society. During the next fourteen years he came repeatedly before the Supreme Judicial Court arguing against the Old South. The first suit, heard between 1859 and 1866, charged that the society had diverted money from its poor-relief funds to general support of the wealthy congregation. Crocker won, although the court did not find the amounts involved as large as he claimed. During this period he evidently found it uncomfortable to worship at the Old South and temporarily joined the West Church. After he won the decision against Old South's management, the society in 1870 took the unprecedented step of expelling him and confiscating his valuable pew rights. He sued and lost.[39] Like the issue of preserving the old meetinghouse, this earlier acrimony involved a perceived failure of the society in its duty to the community.

Despite the charter's prohibition of selling the old meetinghouse, the Old South standing committee informally entertained offers for the property. The Boston Board of Trade in 1869 proposed a Union Merchants' Exchange for the site. In April 1872 the society voted to ask the legislature for authority to dispose of the property, but they were too late for action in that year's session.[40]

That November the Great Fire destroyed the city around the Old South, and firemen worked hard to keep the flames from the meetinghouse itself. Many of the church's proprietors, wrote historian Charles Francis Adams in the *Nation*, "by no means regard this as a matter for felicitation," as they saw the smoking ruins of nearby Trinity Church end opposition to that congregation's relocation. They found another way to take advantage of the fire. The city commandeered the Old South to quarter troops guarding the "burnt district," and several burned-out businesses sought to use the meetinghouse as temporary accommodations when it became available. Almost as soon as the fire was out, the standing committee announced that the post office wanted the Old South as emergency quarters; this use was perhaps the most essential the committee could have proposed, and the one best calculated to win legislative approval. The petition to the legislature was not limited to post office use, however, or to leasing the property; the society asked for the removal of all restrictions on its disposal.[41]

The campaign had now entered its public phase. A hundred of the church's members and nineteen of its proprietors—only twenty-one had voted for the post office lease—asked the legislature to deny the request, as did other opponents from all around New England. Many of their arguments still involved interests within the religious society itself, and one legislator wondered whether "the Lord could not afford to own a respectable corner lot."[42] But the campaign also considered the meetinghouse as an historic monument, and the Old South Society as a custodian in the larger public interest. "Here are some twoscore persons," wrote Charles Francis Adams of the pew proprietors, "who, by mere accident, find themselves the trustees of an edifice of first-class historical interest. Instead of jealously guarding and preserving it, they are wholly unable to see anything but the inconvenience to themselves and their families of attending religious services in it once a week."[43]

The standing committee vehemently objected to this view of their responsibility. There was "no sense in having such a sentimental veneration for bricks and mortar," testified Deacon Charles Stoddard, "for even if the British did do something or other in the church, that was nothing to do with the work of Christ." Stoddard fought the placing of an historical tablet on the wall, and Rev. Jacob H. Manning, who previously had encouraged historical appreciation of the building, now told his congregation that it threatened to "bring us into bondage."[44]

The Old South's defenders did not describe the building as an architectural or visual landmark. They almost ostentatiously disdained its appearance. As the *Globe* reported, "No enthusiasm for the preservation of the old structure could ever throw a glamour of beauty about the severely plain, rectangular building, its curious spire, or the odd-looking weather vane which surmounted it. Only historic associations could make the structure so interesting to the people of New England and of the nation." "They say the Old South is Ugly!" said reformer and orator Wendell Phillips. "I should be ashamed to know whether it is ugly or handsome. Does a man love his mother because she is handsome?"[45]

At the same proprietors' meeting that approved the post office lease, the society also voted to offer the meetinghouse for sale to the Massachusetts Historical Society for its appraised value. The historical society's executive committee answered that it could not possibly afford the building, although it would be happy to act as a custodian if someone were to contribute the purchase price. Individual members of the majority offered $25,000–$35,000 toward the cost, out of a personal responsibility that they did not feel the church as an institution shared.[46] But neither the historical society nor anyone else attempted to raise the additional hundreds of thousands of dollars that would have been necessary to meet the terms of this offer.

The legislature approved not the complete release the society sought but only the actual two-year lease to the U.S. government for the post office. In the spring of 1873 the Old South moved services to its Copley Square chapel, voting that "for all purposes it shall be the meeting-house of the Old South Church."[47] Over the objections of its preservationist pew holders, the society began constructing a $450,000 church there. Then, in 1874, when the post office lease was half over and the new church was rising in the Back Bay, the society renewed its application for a complete release to dispose of the building. The legislature passed the contentious issue to the Supreme Judicial Court.[48]

In the summer of 1875 the court heard arguments on the society's right to sell the meetinghouse. A preliminary decision in October of that year seemed to favor the building's preservation; the court held that a majority vote of the proprietors was not alone sufficient for its sale and destruction, but that the society also had to demonstrate that the minority's interests were not unrea-

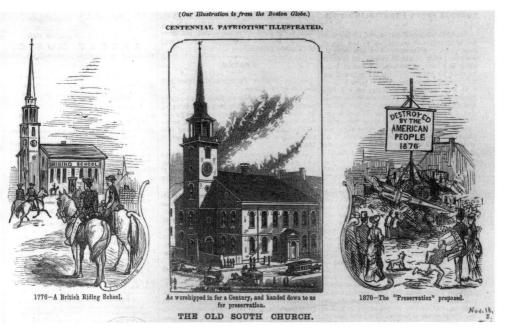

FIGURE 4.4   *"The Old South Church,"* Boston Globe *cartoon, June 24, 1876. Courtesy Boston Public Library, Print Department*

sonably compromised by the action. Once again the issue would be treated as a matter internal to the Old South Society. The congregation dedicated its new church in December 1875.[49] The following spring the court heard the second half of the case. The justices, noting that the law did not permit them to take into account "regrets . . . at the probable removal of a building surrounded by so many patriotic and historical associations," on May 8, 1876, granted the Old South Society permission to dispose of its meetinghouse.[50]

As soon as the decree was finalized, the society advertised for sale "all the materials above the level of the sidewalks. . . . The spire is covered with copper, and there is a lot of lead on roof and belfry, and the roof is covered with imported old Welch slate. 60 days will be allowed for the removal. Terms cash."[51]

On Thursday, June 8, 1876, auctioneer Samuel Hatch, who had earlier presided over disposal of the Hancock House, announced in the Old South that "this ancient structure has done its work. Time is no respector of persons or of buildings," and then he opened bidding, which reached only $1,350. On Saturday the purchaser began dismantling the steeple of the meetinghouse as salvage.[52]

The following day, the third and most extraordinary phase of the Old

South preservation effort began as George W. Simmons & Son, proprietors of Boston's "Oak Hall" clothing store, secured a seven-day delay in the demolition. Simmons hung from the steeple a banner reading:

THE ELEVENTH HOUR!

MEN AND WOMEN OF MASSACHUSETTS!

Does Boston desire the humiliation which is to-day a part of her history since she has allowed this memorial to be sold under the hammer?

SHALL THE OLD SOUTH BE SAVED?

We have bought the right to hold this building uninjured for seven days, and will be conditionally responsible for raising the last $100,000 to complete its purchase.

G. W. Simmons & Son, Oak Hall, Boston.[53]

At noon on Wednesday, June 14, Bostonians crammed the building for a mass meeting at which Wendell Phillips, according to one of his listeners, "spoke as if pleading for the life of one condemned unjustly."[54] Now the issues were secular. Phillips invoked the national centennial and challenged the idea of monuments that had prevailed among Bostonians for generations: "The saving of this landmark is the best monument you can erect to the men of the Revolution. You spend $40,000 here, and $20,000 there, to put up a statue of some old hero. . . . But what is a statue of Cicero compared to standing where your voice echoes from pillar and wall that actually heard his philippics? . . . Shall we tear in pieces the roof that actually trembled to the words which made us a nation?"[55]

The meeting appointed a committee, chaired by Governor Alexander Rice, to appeal for funds and negotiate the building's preservation. The committee obtained a month's extension on the structure's stay of execution and asked the Old South's standing committee for a lease on the underlying land and an agreement to sell it for a value to be fixed by appraisal, as in the offer to the historical society. The church's officers responded on the day before demolition was to resume. They withdrew the historical society offer; the price of the land was $420,000, to be paid in cash in two months. They expressed skepticism that the preservation committee would raise it and required that the committee agree in writing "that if at the expiration of the time above fixed . . . you are unable to purchase the property on the terms proposed, you will not ask us for any further extension of time."[56] They pointed out that they had generously refrained from asking any rent for the building in the interim. "The society," wrote the *Commonwealth,* "does not mean that two edifices bearing the name of 'Old South' shall stand at the same time in the city of Boston—one to be a continual reminder of the unpatriotic course of the controllers of the other!"[57] Clearly the Old South Society was unwill-

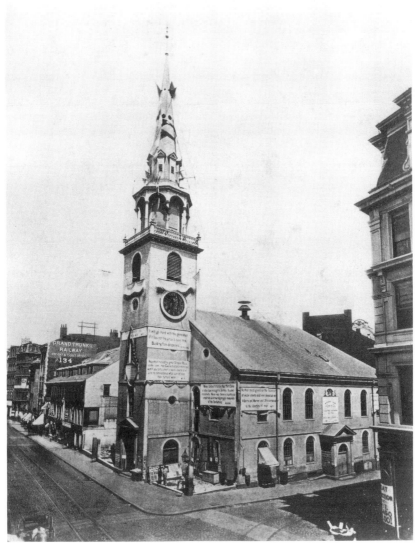

FIGURE 4.5   *The Old South meetinghouse during fundraising efforts, photographed by J. W. Black and Co., 1876. Society for the Preservation of New England Antiquities*

ing to become the de facto funder of the building's preservation by holding it off the market indefinitely.

Despite the roster of male speakers and committee members, it was the women of Boston who did most of the work toward saving the Old South.[58] Women canvassers carried out most of the fundraising, which totaled $60,000 in its first month. While the preservation committee wrangled over the land, twenty women on July 19 spent $3,500 to buy the structure itself from the salvage contractor. They engaged architects to prepare plans for moving and reconstructing the building, if necessary. They proposed to acquire as its new site a vacant lot at Copley Square, opposite the new Old South Church.[59]

Purchase of the structure energized the preservation effort, but the sum of money required was enormous. Preservationists appealed to the city for financial assistance, but the society's short deadline fell before the city council would reconvene in the fall.[60]

The Old South was rescued by one woman. The building's purchase, and the contingency planning for moving it, had been organized by Mary Hemenway, whose husband, Augustus Hemenway, perhaps the richest man in New England, had died just a month before, leaving an estate valued at $15 million. She had long been active as an educational reformer and philanthropist; in later years she would fund archaeological exploration of the American West. Shortly before the standing committee's immovable deadline, she anonymously offered $100,000 to the preservation effort. This offer, together with a $225,000 mortgage previously arranged with the New England Mutual Life Insurance Company and a reduction in the price to $400,000, meant that the Old South was saved, at least for a while.[61]

A trustee for the preservation committee took title to the property on October 11, 1876. The Old South Society, which had not been so concerned about the building's future when it was sold for salvage, was considerably more concerned now that it appeared it would continue to stand. The sale was subject to the conditions

that said building shall not at any time during the period of thirty years . . . be used for any business or commercial purpose, and shall be used during said period for historical and memorial purposes only, and that it shall not at any time during said period be used for any purpose whatever on Sunday, . . . and in case of breach of the foregoing conditions or any of them, said building shall be forfeited to said Old South Society in Boston, and said Old South Society in Boston reserves the right to enter for breach of condition and enforce said forfeiture, and take down and remove said building.[62]

The church, its attorneys later explained, had no objection to selling the building to the Massachusetts Historical Society without such draconian conditions, but "it was a very different question whether it should pass into the control of men who, by reason of successive defeats in the Courts or other reasons, had become unfriendly to the interests of the Society."[63]

The preservation committee asked the 1877 legislature to incorporate a tax-exempt "Old South Association" as a permanent custodian for the building. The incorporation bill gave the association eminent-domain powers, specifically to remove the odious conditions in its deed. Some legislators claimed that this was a high-handed breach of contract, and that historic preservation was not a public purpose for which eminent domain could legitimately be used. The bill passed by 176 to 30 after John D. Long, past speaker of the Massachusetts House and one of the charter directors of the association, explained that, far from being a contract freely entered, the society's terms were nothing short of ransom. "As they have not done equity," he said, "they have no right to expect equity." Long urged his former colleagues to pass the bill in order to end the "miserable squabble" that had now occupied the city for years.[64]

The Old South campaign was not at an end. The building was still encumbered by a $225,000 mortgage. The preservation committee in 1877 sought, along with eminent domain and tax exemption, a state appropriation of $25,000, but 241 petitioners, many of them business firms, opposed the expenditure because of the need for "strict economy" in that depression year. As far as can be discerned, not a single woman signed this remonstrance, although at least one of the petitioners was the father and two were husbands of women on the preservation committee.[65] The legislature dropped the appropriation before passing the bill. The following year the Old South Association came back to ask $50,000. During the two years of deepest depression Americans had yet experienced, more than fifty thousand people from around the nation had contributed over $230,000 to the preservation effort. A succession of fairs, balls, and other fundraising events for the Old South were raising diminishing amounts of money while hurting the rest of Boston's charities. "We ask this aid," said lawyer George O. Shattuck for the association, "because we need it." Opponents cited not only the state's fiscal condition but also the danger of setting a precedent for historic preservation as a new category of public spending. The legislature voted $10,000, to be paid only when the remainder of the money had been raised from other sources.[66]

The preservation of the Old South had to overcome not only practical but philosophical difficulties. When Bostonians set out to save it, they had little coherent idea of what to do with it. It was to be an historic monument, like the Bunker Hill column, but unlike a column or a statue the meetinghouse was a usable structure, now without an assigned use. At the first mass meeting in 1876, Wendell Phillips suggested it become a "mechanics' exchange," in recognition of the role of the workingmen of Boston during the Revolution. Rev. William H. H. Murray of the nearby Park Street Church said, "I would, had I my wish, make this building a Westminster Abbey," complete with busts of American patriots. A group of Boston antiquarians began

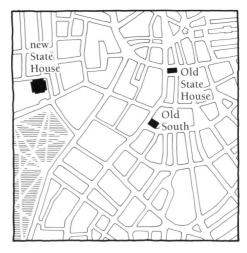

MAP 8

preparations for an historical museum that they hoped would occupy the building, although nothing immediately came from the effort.[67]

Instead, fundraising itself became the building's use. The Old South Association continued for years arranging festivities and exhibitions, slowly paying down its mortgage. Twenty-five cents gained admission to a rotating exhibit of revolutionary relics, described for the *New York Graphic* by one British visitor: "Pewter plate General Washington once ate from. Verified by inscription on plate. . . . A wasp's nest. One of Lady Washington's old shoes. Buttons off Washington's coat never sewed on by Lady Washington. . . . Silk banner inscribed 'The Hero of Tippecanoe.' No explanations. Boston children leaving with impression that this relic of the Harrison campaign of 1845 [*sic*] was carried during the revolution. . . . Nut crackers of the times which tried men's souls."[68] The Old South had become a "side show," complained the *Boston Globe*. "There is still room, however, for a fat lady." In time its uses came to be more genuinely educational, with the beginning in 1883 of an historical lecture series later endowed by Mary Hemenway.[69]

The greatest significance of the Old South campaign was that, despite overwhelming odds, it worked. The building occupied some of the most valuable real estate in America; its owners were hostile to its continued existence; demolition had actually begun before the preservation effort got under way. Yet it was saved. Here was a case, given tremendous nationwide attention, where for one part of the urban environment change was not the answer. Permanence was, and a community took action to achieve it. If the Old South could be saved, anything could.

One of the first significant by-products of the Old South's preservation was to alter the context for debate about the future of the nearby Old State House. Most Bostonians agreed that the Old South was the more important of the two. As demolition of the Old South began, one scheme called for commemorating it by reerecting its clock in a tower "on the site of the Old State House," according to the *Globe,* "when that crumbling structure shall have been removed." Once the Old South was out of danger, however, the *Evening Transcript* noted that the Old State House "does not require redemption from other hands, but is already the property of the people, and therefore can easily be preserved." [70] The two cases involved very different issues. The claims against the Old State House were not financial but functional; it stood in the middle of what its detractors thought should be an unobstructed wide street. In addition, while the Old South's proprietors had maintained it more or less faithfully, the Old State House raised curatorial issues of material integrity and restoration.

Even for Boston, the Old State House was old indeed. Its exterior walls dated from 1712; the rest of the building had been rebuilt after a fire in 1747. It was the seat of government in Massachusetts until 1798, when that function was transferred to the new statehouse on Beacon Hill designed by Charles Bulfinch. For some years it deteriorated in commercial tenancy, leading to the 1826 proposal for its removal; instead, the city renovated it for use as a city hall from 1830 to 1841, after which it was again crammed with as many as fifty tenants.[71] The Old State House in its heyday had been an imposing presence at the head of present-day State Street, appropriately ostentatious for the representatives of empire in one of its most prosperous colonies. By the early 1870s a contemporary observer argued that

its external and internal appearance has been so changed that it would be a mistake to allow sentimental considerations to delay its demolition, for the climax of incongruity was capped when after every vestige of its original internal arrangements had yielded to the encroachments of business, a French roof was put on the sturdy old Britisher. . . . When a historic memorial is so altered that its identity is lost, the lover of the past is repelled by the attempt to combine essentially inharmonious characteristics, and would prefer demolition to disfigurement.[72]

In 1876 the building's leases expired, and the Board of Aldermen ominously referred the question of their renewal not to the Committee on Public Buildings but to the Committee on Streets. Alderman John T. Clark, who had presided at the Old South preservation meeting on June 14, voted less than two weeks later in favor of demolishing the Old State House. "If the Old South stood in the way of a necessary improvement of the public street," according to a newspaper account of his comments, "he should be in favor of its removal." A resident of Chicago, feeling that city's acute short-age of structures more than five years old, suggested buying the building and reerecting it there. The Boston city council decided, mainly for finan-cial reasons, merely to remove a portico that projected most seriously into the traffic, and to renew the tenants' leases for five years.[73]

Those five years encompassed the whole public phase of the Old South campaign, and by the time they had passed there was little chance of the newly preservation-conscious city letting this other conspicuous landmark fall. William H. Whitmore, city registrar and commissioner of public records, had worked on the Old South effort and devoted himself next to saving the Old State House. In 1876 he had requested that his department be moved to it, but the request was ignored.[74] In 1879, as an indirect offshoot of earlier efforts to organize an historical museum in the Old South, Whitmore helped organize the Boston Antiquarian Club, later renamed the Bostonian Society. Its first president, Samuel M. Quincy, said that it aimed "to aid the histo-rian in his work, and in preserving intact the monuments of past times"; it quickly resolved to fight for the Old State House.[75] Whitmore, meanwhile, won election as the Common Council's president, and in 1880 he persuaded his fellow councilmen that the Old State House should join Faneuil Hall and the Common as an inviolable property of the municipality. The Board of Aldermen did not concur, so this request did not come before the legis-lature, but opposition had more to do with avoiding state interference than with any remaining desire to get rid of the building.[76]

At the end of the new leases in 1881 Whitmore sought to eject the tenants in order to use the building for municipal offices. He secured a $35,000 ap-propriation to restore it, which he cheerfully admitted was his main goal. "I hope that in the course of another ten or twenty years our successors will go beyond that," he said. "I hope the time will come when public convenience will allow the removal of the public offices from the building. . . . When that time comes I feel sure that the greatly enlarged city of Boston will thank us for having preserved the opportunity for it to establish a city museum."[77]

Some downtown real estate interests sought to reverse this decision so that the building could be removed as a traffic improvement. Their cause was lost when the largest landowners in the area, including the owner of the Sears Building across the street, sided with the preservationists. But Whit-more's plan was more vulnerable to criticism on economic grounds, espe-cially after a bank offered to restore the building at its own expense and pay the city more rent than it had been receiving. The Board of Aldermen and even Whitmore's own Common Council reversed themselves to favor this private-sector form of preservation. One newspaper endorsed it pre-cisely because it was private. "There is nothing about the appointments of

FIGURE 4.6 *Old State House, 1876. Signs cover much of the building's exterior. A mansard roof has been added to increase rentable space. A portico added in 1830 projects into traffic. Society for the Preservation of New England Antiquities*

FIGURE 4.7 *Old State House after 1881 restoration, photographed by Wilfred French. Society for the Preservation of New England Antiquities*

a first-class banking house," wrote the *Globe*, "that could in any way offend the most fastidious sense, and this cannot be said of some of the city departments which it is proposed to locate there."[78] Whitmore denounced the bank's plans as tantamount to destroying the building. He eventually won a compromise in which the city would lease the building's lower floors but would restore the exterior and the upper-story assembly halls "as memorial halls, to be always accessible to the public."[79] The Bostonian Society was granted possession as custodian of these rooms.

Restoration of the Old State House, by city architect George A. Clough working under Whitmore's direction, aimed to bring the building's exterior and interior "as nearly as possible to their appearance when used by the Legislature."[80] This was exactly the brand of restoration that Ruskin opposed as a "lie," and Bostonians made similar objections. "So far as the interior is concerned we cannot make it a relic," said one Common Council member. "We can only make an imitation. It will be a spurious relic."[81] When the project was completed in 1882, Whitmore's report confirmed this: "The anti-quarian part" of the work, on the second floor, "has cost considerable money, but there every part of the finish had to be constructed afresh."[82] The res-toration became the subject of bitter debate for years after its completion. A recent preservation report on the building concludes that by this work, "the entire interior of the building was restored faithfully—back to the 1830 reconstruction" for a city hall that Whitmore and Clough mistakenly iden-tified as its original form.[83]

B oston's greatest contribution to American preservation was saving the Old South Church. It was the first time Americans challenged the culture of change head-on and won. Mount Vernon, by contrast, was a movement not to protect a structure from imminent destruction but to ensure the perma-nence of a shrine, and its significance lay in the selection of a genuine relic building as an appropriate monument. But at the Old South, preservationists faced the American condition at its most virulent in the congregation's stead-fast preference for new rather than old, combined with the tremendous prac-tical pressures for change expressed in the site's land value. The success of the private effort to save the Old South, coming after the failure of both state and city governments to save the Hancock House, set a precedent of privat-ism that defined the New England preservation movement for generations.

Both the Old South and the Old State House were saved for their historical associations rather than their architectural qualities; they were monuments rather than landmarks. Each presented awkward conceptual problems of future use. They were exceptions from the utilitarian calculus by which the culture of change still prevailed in the business center around them, even if it was losing its hold in some residential neighborhoods. The Ruskinian pre-mium on visible antiquity was not an important motivation for saving these buildings; neither of them was valued yet for its contribution to the visible cityscape. Another contemporary preservation cause, however, had every-thing to do with the appearance of the city, in the protection of the city's old public landscapes, its burial grounds and especially its Common.

CHAPTER 5

❦

Parks and the Permanent Landscape

The object of a park is to secure to the dwellers in cities the
opportunity of enjoying the contemplation of such objects of natural beauty
as the growth of the city must otherwise destroy.
— H. W. S. CLEVELAND

Government powers, long used to encourage environmental change, first helped achieve environmental permanence through the parks movement. Parks were not about history or old buildings, but they were very much about conferring permanence on valued pieces of the environment. Parks advocates responded to disappearing green spaces—estates and gardens, and burial grounds, with their historical associations—within big cities, and disappearing rural landscapes and views around them.

The Parks Movement

Massachusetts incubated many of the ideas that produced the American parks movement. Emerson, Thoreau, and other Transcendentalist writers voiced a new appreciation for nature in fast-urbanizing society. Gentlemen farmers around Boston vied with one another in cultivating their estates and in 1829 organized the Massachusetts Horticultural Society. Some of these same people founded Mount Auburn Cemetery, which became a model for park design. Chicago landscape architect H. W. S. Cleveland, who had moved there from Boston, cited Boston's suburbs as the model landscape that parks ought to emulate. Horticulturalists in town established the Public Garden in 1839 next to Boston Common, and twenty years later Boston voters overwhelmingly dedicated it to remain forever open, excepting only greenhouses or a possible city hall.[1] With the Common and the Public Garden and beautiful rural suburbs close to town, Bostonians enjoyed an intimate relationship between city and country.

New Yorkers, by contrast, saw Manhattan's picturesque landscape erased by the urban grid as their city raced up its narrow island, and this urgency led them to act first in translating these ideas into parks. In 1857, work began on Central Park, which was then a sorry wasteland of shanties, rocks, and rubbish heaps. New Yorkers sought not to preserve this existing landscape but to replace it with a landscape that would remind them of others they were losing. While H. W. S. Cleveland was still in Boston, he and his partner Robert Morris Copeland wrote "A Few Words on the Central Park," urging the importance of following a master plan in its development.[2] The city's parks commissioners announced a competition to provide this plan, and in 1858 they awarded first prize to Frederick Law Olmsted and Calvert Vaux.

Central Park launched Olmsted and Vaux's partnership, and it launched a national movement for urban parks. Olmsted through his writings gave the movement direction by defining for Americans what a park was.[3] Public-health reformers were already advocating parks as necessary "lungs of the city," which would reduce infectious disease by purifying the air. Olmsted added another therapeutic purpose: where nerves were jangled by the city's fast pace, parks would soothe them by offering in its midst an atmosphere of spaciousness and repose. Parks were designed landscapes meant to look undesigned, deliberately arranged to exclude the geometry and bustle of the city. This distinguished them from all the public grounds that Americans already knew. Parks were not formal gardens, not places for militia exercises or organized athletics, not sites for monuments or public buildings.

During the years after New York City created Central Park, Brooklyn, Philadelphia, Chicago, and Baltimore all established "country parks," but Boston was slow to follow. The Public Garden and the Common together were all that fit on Boston's little peninsula; there was no scope for a large urban park until the city annexed Roxbury in 1868 and West Roxbury, Dorchester, and Brighton in 1874. With these annexations came agitation for parks. In 1869, real estate lawyer and future city councilman Uriel H. Crocker, who would soon help save the Old South, proposed a metropolitan park system extending into towns not yet annexed. He sought to preserve remaining scenery in Boston's "beautiful suburbs," where, he said, "we should endeavor to secure the lovely spots for the benefit and enjoyment of the people before they are built upon, and their natural beauty destroyed."[4] Boston's parks advocates thought of parks together with street and other infrastructure planning as just the most urgent phase of a comprehensive effort to knit newly annexed territory together as a great city.[5] They reminded Bostonians of the street widenings, so expensive after the city had grown, that would have been so easy beforehand. In 1870, Crocker drafted and the legislature passed an act that would allow Boston to develop parks even outside its borders. The act required two-thirds approval of the city's

FIGURE 5.1 *Boston metropolitan park system proposed by Uriel H. Crocker, 1869. It aimed to secure permanently a variety of existing rural landscapes in Boston's suburbs. Boston Public Library*

electorate to take effect, and it won a respectable but inadequate 63 percent. The project's revival was postponed first by the fire and then by the Panic of 1873. In 1875, voters approved a new measure limited to the now much expanded city, and the mayor appointed as parks commissioners Charles H. Dalton, William Gray Jr., and T. Jefferson Coolidge.[6]

In 1876 these commissioners reported their plan. In concept though not location it was much as Crocker had proposed: an interconnected system

FIGURE 5.2 *Jamaica Pond, from* Ballou's Drawing Room Companion, *1855. Society for the Preservation of New England Antiquities*

stretching out from the Common and the Public Garden, an "emerald necklace" (as it was later called) of parks linked by parkways. An embankment along the Charles River and a park on the Back Bay mud flats would be entirely artificial creations, but the biggest parks, Jamaica Pond and West Roxbury Park, were chosen to preserve existing landscapes, like the parks in Philadelphia and Baltimore. West Roxbury (later renamed Franklin) Park included nearly five hundred acres within the city where, the commissioners said, "the natural features have remained uninjured." Jamaica Pond already served informally for recreation, especially in winter, and it was surrounded by the sort of country estates that exemplified the word *parklike*. Two unsightly icehouses had appeared among them, and "unless the city takes possession of the entire shore," wrote the commissioners, "the rural character of the scenery will probably be hopelessly destroyed within a few years."[7]

This ambitious plan frightened skittish city governments during the depression years, even though citizens petitioned for it and approved it at every turn. Eventually the whole system was adopted piecemeal by a succession of city councils, the land mainly acquired by 1883. Frederick Law Olmsted informally approved the commissioners' site selection, and in 1878 they took him on as their landscape architect. Olmsted considered Boston's parks the most important project in his office, which he moved in 1881 from New York to Brookline.[8]

Park landscapes, whether preserved or newly constructed, aimed at a look

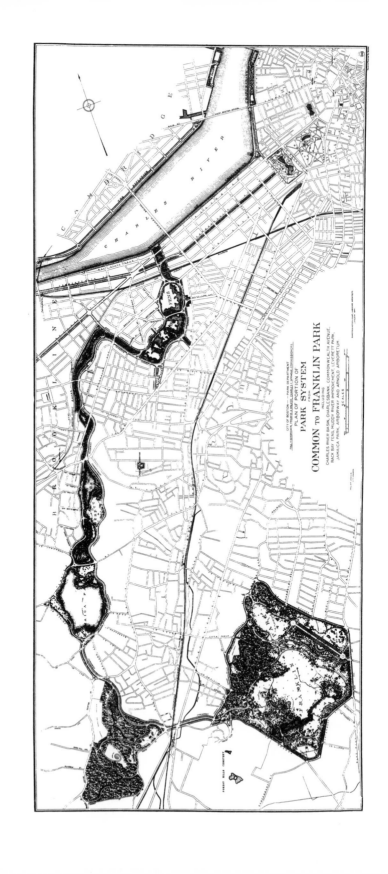

CITY OF BOSTON — PARK DEPARTMENT
FREDERICK FRANKLIN & PRIVATE CHARLES T. SPRAGUE, COMMISSIONERS

PLAN OF PORTION OF
PARK SYSTEM
FROM
COMMON TO FRANKLIN PARK

INCLUDING

CHARLES RIVER BASIN, CHARLESBANK, COMMONWEALTH AVENUE,
BACK BAY FENS, MUDDY RIVER IMPROVEMENT, LEVERETT PARK,
JAMAICA PARK, ARBORWAY AND ARNOLD ARBORETUM.

of timeless age, and both their construction and the movement's politics aimed at actual permanence. Once parklands were secured, "considerations of stability and endurance" governed how they should be treated, Olmsted told the American Social Science Association in 1880. He concluded by exhorting his listeners to "make the park steadily gainful of that quality of beauty which comes only with age." In 1886, writing about Franklin Park, he cited "the element of lastingness" as a central principle of park design, saying that "as a rule, the older the wood, and the less of newness and rawness there is to be seen in all the elements of a park, the better it serves its purpose. This rule holds for centuries—without limit."[9]

Boston Common

Boston Common was the only part of the park system that had been around for centuries. It was a truly permanent feature of the city, more permanent than any structure or street or other public space. Actually getting rid of the Common was unthinkable, yet in the late nineteenth century, Bostonians found an increasing need to defend it. The threats came from differing definitions of what the Common was, the essence that was to be presumed permanent.

The Common's presumed permanence, in legal terms, dates from a 1640 town-meeting vote that "there shall be no land granted either for houseplot or garden to any person out of the open ground or common field." When the 1822 city charter excluded the power to sell or lease the Common, contemporary legal opinion held that it merely recognized a status that already existed because of this vote and two centuries of dedication to public use.[10] But what public uses?

The seventeenth-century Common was a pasture for cows and sheep, and sometimes a site for executions and for burials. In the eighteenth century, militias drilled and revivalists preached there as the cows looked on. From 1768 to 1776 the British troops who occupied Boston mainly occupied the Common. The town selectmen in 1769 appointed the first committee "for the preservation of the Common" because of the troops' wear and tear on the pasturage; later they multiplied the damage by throwing up earthen fortifications. Early-eighteenth-century townspeople had inaugurated a more urban use of the Common by planting a "mall" along Tremont Street, a double row of trees where "every afternoon, after drinking tea, the gentlemen and ladies walk," according to an English visitor.[11] The occupying troops cut these trees

FIGURE 5.3 *Frederick Law Olmsted's Boston park system: the "emerald necklace."* *Courtesy National Park Service, Frederick Law Olmsted National Historic Site*

for firewood, but Bostonians planted new ones so that by the 1830s each perimeter street had its own mall. A guide published in 1821 included a table by which proto-joggers could calculate their speed "by the time taken to pass the long Mall" on Tremont Street.[12] As paths and trees began to invade the Common's interior, they conflicted with earlier uses; the militia were confined to an ever smaller treeless plain, and in 1836, "dangerous accidents having occurred to promenaders," the anachronistic cows were banished.[13] By the 1860s, open tracts saw more baseball games than militia drills. The Common hosted open-air meetings, fireworks, festivals of every sort, and from 1863 to 1882 even a "deer park"—a sort of petting zoo.[14] It was, in other words, a thoroughly miscellaneous urban public ground shaped in the years before American cities self-consciously built parks.

The presumed permanence of park landscapes conflicted with the Common's tradition of continuing adaptability. The parks movement provided a coherent definition of urban open space, but its definition excluded many of the Common's past functions. For more than two centuries it had been an open-ended community resource. It was space available for the new game of baseball, but it was also available for exhibits of industrial products in the early nineteenth century and for army recruiting centers during the Civil War. If the Common's essence was its common-ness, then such uses were no less appropriate than promenading. The Common was set aside, the editors of the *Globe* said in 1877, to be employed "for public uses. To hold that these employments are to consist in walking, playing and breathing upon it would be to greatly restrict its benefit."[15] But if the Common's permanent essence was open space as defined by the parks movement, then its uses should indeed be restricted to "walking, playing, and breathing."

As the city grew in size and density, the inherent conflict between the Common's roles as open space and as available space grew in intensity. More new uses arose that could not be accommodated elsewhere. In 1863 the city council considered but rejected moving the John Hancock House there, noting that "there are prejudices, perhaps well grounded, against erections of any description on the Common." Temporary structures were a more difficult issue. The promoters of a "Peace Jubilee" after the Civil War sought and received permission to erect a temporary "Coliseum" on the Common, but vehement protests led them to build on the Back Bay instead. After the fire there was even opposition to the city council's offer to accommodate merchants on the malls while they rebuilt, and no businesses took advantage of it.[16]

These conflicts reached a crisis in 1877, in a proposal for a temporary exhibition hall for the triennial industrial exhibition of the Charitable Mechanic Association, a venerable fraternal organization that had promoted

Massachusetts industry since the eighteenth century. The mechanics' exhibitions had outgrown their traditional sites in Faneuil Hall and Quincy Market; the example of the Philadelphia Centennial Exhibition, together with the desire to spur the economy at the depths of a depression, led to an ambitious scheme for a six-hundred-foot-long crystal palace on the Common's playing fields. "It was for such purposes that the Common was kept," said Edward Everett Hale, a staunch defender of Boston traditions. "I do not see the distinction between putting a canvas tent on it for a week, and showing azalias [sic] under it, and making a tent . . . of iron and glass, and keeping it up a month." The mechanics' proposal fell squarely within the tradition of treating the Common as available space. As the association's representative explained it, "We simply want to have the use, for a short period, of a small portion of a large tract of unused land." To serve the city as it was meant to, explained another member, the exhibition hall needed to be located in a convenient and central place, and "this is altogether the most central place of any that I know of." [17]

Among the project's opponents, led by William H. Whitmore, were many people who had worked to preserve the Old South. They invoked that effort partly out of exhilaration at its recent success, momentum that they hoped to borrow for this new cause, but also because they thought of the two issues as kindred. Like the Old South, one said, the Common was a place of "old and sacred memories." [18]

Early in March the Common Council rejected the association's proposal, on the motion of Uriel H. Crocker, the parks advocate and Old South preservationist. The mechanics, like the Peace Jubilee organizers before them, found space at the Back Bay frontier. The Common's defenders had petitioned the legislature, for good measure, and two months later this effort brought "An Act for the Preservation of Public Commons and Parks." The act provided that no building larger than six hundred square feet could be erected in any public common or park in Massachusetts without the legislature's permission, and thus converted this specific threat in Boston to a general statewide affirmation of the permanence of parks. [19] The Common's essence, it was decided, was open space, and no further serious attempts were made to place substantial buildings there.

A more utilitarian demand threatened the Common, however, and was not so easily deflected. If it was space available for community needs, many people thought there was no more pressing need than access. Increasing concentration of business downtown and the need to move tens of thousands of people in and out of it every day strained transportation facilities, more acutely in Boston than in other cities because its streets were narrow and access constricted by arms of the harbor, Beacon Hill, and the Common.

The Common's irregular shape obstructed what would otherwise have been the longest straight street in Boston, connecting the city's most populous neighborhoods and suburbs with the heart of downtown from Columbus Avenue to Tremont Street. The extension of Columbus Avenue across the Common remained a vague threat never seriously attempted, however, and a more modest corner cutting was easily defeated in 1872.[20]

Streetcars from all these southwesterly directions ran around the perimeter of the Common to come together on its Tremont Street side. There they formed "blockades," or traffic jams, exacerbated by the uncoordinated operation of competing companies on the same tracks. Many Bostonians who opposed streets across the Common thought widening Tremont Street reasonable, and perhaps even prudent to forestall more radical solutions. "Nobody's morning or evening walk would be much curtailed," wrote one; "nobody's enjoyment of the grounds at all diminished."[21] But when the councilors in 1874 held hearings on the idea, they found intense opposition. Some Bostonians even insisted that any widening should come from the buildings on the other side of the street; others made early proposals for placing the streetcars underground in a subway. "We are almost prepared to declare," the Globe's editors wrote hysterically, "that any man who should propose a diversion of any portion of the Common from the uses to which it has been set apart should do it with a rope around his neck and a committee of citizens at the other end!"[22] The proposal died when that year's council election returned a majority pledged to defeat the scheme.

The Common's defenders consolidated their victory the following year in two ways, one big and one small. The big measure was structural reform to raise the threshold for change. "What we want," said the Globe editors during the Tremont Street battle, "is an insurmountable safeguard that no committee, present or future, and no organization or body of men can get over, giving us assurance that these grounds can *never* be thus desecrated."[23] They got it in an 1875 act of the legislature providing that neither streets, street railways, nor a subway could be placed in any Massachusetts common or park more than twenty years old except by approval of the city's voters.[24] Years later the structural impediments to change on the Common, which already included city charter provisions, legislative acts, and the vague doctrines of long-term public dedication, would be reinforced still further: in 1908 George F. Parkman left $5 million to the city as an open-space endowment, contingent that "the Boston Common shall never be diverted from its present use as a public park."[25]

The small consolidation of the 1874 victory involved the physical boundary between Tremont Street and the Common. The old fence there was removed during the hearings on street widening, and while some parks advocates favored this new openness, under the circumstances it made the Common seem less defined and more vulnerable, as if the streetcar tracks might some night creep onto the mall. The newly preservationist city council proposed a massive granite curb but was persuaded instead to use cast-iron fencing, set in existing postholes to avoid trenching across the roots of trees.[26] This careful measure originated with Uriel H. Crocker's brother and law partner, George G. Crocker, a young former state legislator who had taken up the fight to preserve the Old South after his brother had left, and who years later would become even more important to the fate of the Common.

A decade later streetcar blockades had worsened, prompting another attempt to solve them on the Common. In 1887 the West End Street Railway petitioned the legislature to authorize tunneling under Beacon Hill and elsewhere, or, as an alternative, to permit on the Tremont and Boylston Street malls of the Common what we call today a transit mall. Horsecars would join pedestrians there, separated from other traffic, on tracks "to be laid as an experiment only—not to become permanent unless it shall be voted by the citizens of Boston at the next city election."[27]

Instead of constructing a tunnel or a transit mall, the West End alleviated congestion by consolidating all Boston's streetcars under one ownership and coordinating operations. But by the early 1890s increasing traffic showed that this had been a temporary solution. Mere street widenings, as difficult as they would be to accomplish, would not be enough. Lengthening commutes pointed toward the more radical solution of supplementing streetcars with some form of rapid transit. Boston suburbanites familiar with New York or Chicago thought enviously of sailing above traffic at twenty or thirty miles an hour on those cities' elevated railroads. But elevateds would not work well in Boston's narrow and twisting streets. Some suburban residents proposed running an elevated instead across the Common or above the Tremont Street mall. They told the legislature's rapid-transit committee, reported the *Evening Transcript,* that "the sentiment which was formerly attached to the Common had to a great extent died."[28]

They discovered, however, that affection for the Common was alive and well. Protests rained on the legislature from as far away as Virginia, and once again women took a particularly active preservationist role. Mayor Nathan Matthews proposed a compromise route above Tremont Street, which would then have to be widened at the expense of the mall. The West End company, already reviled as a monopoly, intensified the protests by proposing several subways trenched across the Common to meet at a subterranean switching yard for which four acres would be excavated. The legislature instead seized on an "Alley Route" away from the Common where a new street, just wide enough to hold the elevated railroad, would be carved from the backs of building lots half a block east of Tremont Street. Cutting a slot through the most valuable property in the city, however, would be astonishingly expensive. Mainly for this reason, Mayor Matthews and the good-government Citizens' Association opposed the idea, and it was defeated at a city referendum in November 1893.[29]

The Citizens' Association instead wanted to route streetcars into a more modest subway skirting the Common along Boylston and Tremont Streets. After the defeat of the elevated the city turned to building this subway, the first in the nation to be completed.[30] The comparative ease of excavating under parkland, together with potential business disruption while streets were dug up, led the transit commission to plan its subway not under the streets themselves but under the adjacent malls of the Common, with the loss of hundreds of trees. Citizens' Association organizer George B. Upham, later called "the father of the subway," understood that it would inevitably run under the malls but felt that it would "prove a safeguard to the Common as it would prevent a demand for a larger portion of it."[31] Many of Upham's followers had not understood this compromise. "We have been fooled and bamboozled," wrote one. "We thought by a subway under Tremont [Street] we were to save the Common, but we are really to have a worse injury to it than to have tracks on the mall under the trees." Others pointed out that the decision was a purely economic one, to avoid the expense of excavating and relocating utilities in the street. "We are constantly paying enormous sums," wrote "M.P.L." to the *Boston Daily Advertiser,* "for acquiring bits of nature which if not purchased just then will be destroyed. Does not Boston Common come under this head?"[32]

Most of the Common's defenders no longer insisted that it was inviolable; they simply did not want it to look bad. A remarkable amount of debate addressed the fate of individual trees under various proposed subway alignments. In May 1895 several hundred friends of the Common signed a petition requesting that no permanent subway structures be located above ground there, and that all subterranean structures be located at least twelve feet from the surface, leaving room for tree roots. In return, they were willing to let the transit commissioners decide how far the subway would extend beneath the Common.[33] "Almost everybody," wrote the staunchly preservationist editors of the *Evening Transcript,* "believes the commission to be thoroughly imbued with Boston notions as to the indispensable duty of preserving all the best features of the Common."[34]

The transit commission's five members were well chosen to inspire confidence in their sensitivity to the Common. Among them was Charles H. Dalton, former chair of the parks commission, and Thomas J. Gargan, a

FIGURE 5.4 (TOP) *Subway excavations under the Tremont Street mall of the Common, 1896. The Bulfinch statehouse dome and the Park Street Church spire are visible on the skyline. Courtesy Bostonian Society, Old State House*

FIGURE 5.5 (BOTTOM) *Subway excavations under the Tremont Street mall of the Common, 1896. Courtesy Bostonian Society, Old State House*

former legislator and city councilman who had actively fought the Charitable Mechanics' building. The commission elected as its chair George G. Crocker, who had worked so hard twenty years earlier preventing damage to the Common's trees by a curbstone. Crocker wedded preservation with pragmatism. The commissioners worked with George B. Upham and with Charles Sprague Sargent, director of Harvard's Arnold Arboretum, to protect trees. When it became clear that the Boylston Street excavations would disturb a long-discontinued burial ground, the commissioners called upon Dr. Samuel A. Green, an official of the Historical Society and former mayor, to arrange both respectful reinterment of the remains and an historical investigation of the site.[35] They engaged landscape architects Olmsted, Olmsted, and Eliot to make the subway excavations an occasion for restoring the entire Common, hoping, in the commissioners' words, to provide Bostonians "some compensations for the sacrifices they have made in having the subway built under the Boylston and Tremont street malls" and "permanently add to the beauty and salubrity of the Common." By most accounts they succeeded. Several years later George B. Upham founded the Boston Common Society to lobby for its continuing care, and Crocker, Dalton, and Gargan all worked as members of its executive committee.[36]

Boston's Common was initially valued, like the Old South and the Old State House, as the site of historic events. One defender in 1877 mixed up places with people as equivalent reference points in history, "names that would cause the blood of every true Bostonian to thrill. Those names were George Washington, Adams, Hancock, Otis, Faneuil Hall, the Old South, and last, but not least, Boston Common." On this mental map of history the Common was not merely a single point but a whole symbolic landscape where every hill and every tree had its own meaning. Even as late as the 1890s many Boston men could remember playing there as boys amid still recognizable earthworks thrown up by British troops.[37]

Debate gradually came to revolve around the Common's role not as a symbol but as a visible piece of the urban environment. In the 1870s, as preservationists deprecated the Old South's architecture, the *Globe* similarly dismissed the Common's appearance: "Nobody affects to believe that this precious spot of historic ground has high pretensions as a city park."[38] But as the "emerald necklace" of parks took shape during the next decades, the Common was its heirloom jewel. Newly created parks were infused with some of Boston's traditional reverence for the Common, and the Common itself was absorbed into the ethos of the parks movement. During construction of the subway, public opposition centered not on the symbolic issue of disturbing an historic burial ground but on the visual issues of damaging trees or erecting inharmonious structures on the Common.

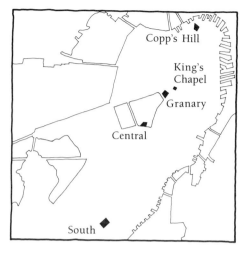

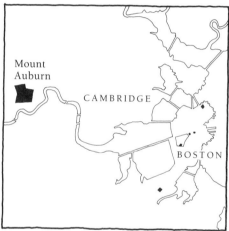

MAP 9 (TOP)   *Boston burial grounds*

MAP 10 (BOTTOM)

Burial Grounds

Boston's treatment of its old burial grounds clearly showed the shift from preserving historic monuments to preserving visual environments. The ancestral symbolism of the graveyard could be antithetical to environmental permanence when it was served by removing remains to fashionable new cemeteries. By the end of the century, however, burial grounds were treated

FIGURE 5.6 *King's Chapel burial ground around the turn of the century: graveyard as little park. Courtesy Bostonian Society, Old State House*

as little urban parks, all the more satisfying because their old stones gave a sense of temporal depth.

Burial of the dead in "rural cemeteries" was among the earliest special cases of permanence in the environment, as urban Americans sought resting places that were indeed final. Bostonians in 1831 began creating Mount Auburn Cemetery in Cambridge, "secure from the danger of being encroached upon, as in the graveyards of the city."[39] Mount Auburn became the prototype for a national rural-cemeteries movement, the suburbanization of the dead. Like suburbs for the living, which were taking shape around the same time, they were an admission that distressing change could not be avoided in the city.

Rural cemeteries were a new landscape type. Their sites were chosen to ensure permanence and their designs to express it. A landscape could express permanence by looking as if it had lasted a long time, implying that it would last into the future. Cemetery designers sought this appearance of continuity even where they were making new landscapes. Mount Auburn really was an old and valued Cambridge landscape adapted to a new purpose, and thus an early instance of landscape preservation. Before urban parks, the semipublic landscapes of rural cemeteries became popular places for country drives, picnics, and contemplative strolls.[40] These unanticipated and sometimes unwelcome demands helped give rise to the parks movement, and early park designers looked to cemeteries as prototypes.

The rural-cemetery movement anticipated the disappearance of urban burial grounds, and so made their disappearance easier and more likely. By the Civil War, suburban cemeteries had become the norm, from elite Mount Auburn to Brookline's modest Roman Catholic Holyhood and other towns' public cemeteries. Many families who already owned plots in city graveyards relocated ancestral remains to these attractive alternatives. Boston's municipal government in 1857 purchased suburban Mount Hope Cemetery with the idea of aiding this process. The city's cemetery trustees hoped that income from redeveloping old urban burial grounds would endow Mount Hope's perpetual maintenance. Like other purveyors of suburban real estate, they put a price on permanence and coupled it with social distinction. The poor, buried for free, entered through a separate gate into a little corner of the cemetery laid out in a citylike grid, where "after the lapse of a certain number of years," the trustees explained, "the same spaces for burial may be used again and again."[41] Paying customers got deed-restricted perpetual lots, in a landscape of curving lanes.[42]

Mount Auburn and its younger cousins changed expectations about places of interment, and Boston's management of its old urban burial grounds came to reflect these new ideas. Even if graves there were ultimately to be relocated, propriety demanded in the meantime that they be planted and groomed. Imitating rural cemeteries solved some of the problems that had given rise to the movement. Gloomy and dusty urban burial grounds blossomed into places of restful contemplation for visitors and pleasant amenities for passers-by. Mayor J. V. C. Smith in 1855 asked for such improvements at the South Burying Ground, including the removal of fences and walls that blocked access and views, calling this the "equivalent to giving a third spacious square" to the South End.[43]

This new treatment transformed perception of the burial grounds, but as with preserved old buildings it also brought some confusion about their purpose. Nineteenth-century eyes found graveyards, once landscaped, easier than the Old South or the Old State House to value for their visual qualities. Viewed through the lens of the parks movement, "the ancient tombstones still standing there, with their quaint epitaphs," became a "chief attraction"

FIGURE 5.7 *King's Chapel and its burial ground, c. 1870s. Society for the Preservation of New England Antiquities*

of these little open spaces, offering temporal insulation from the city around them. But any recreational use, and even their mere location downtown, seemed disrespectful in light of new sensibilities about death and mourning that demanded privacy.[44] And while new cemeteries and parks both implied permanence, the burial grounds' custodians still saw both their landscape and their historic relics as incidental to their utilitarian function of receiving the dead for eventual reinterment elsewhere. Latent confusion over the graveyards' future reached a crisis in the 1870s.

When the Boston Board of Health was established in 1872, it took over responsibility for the city's burial grounds. From their offices in a basement next to city hall, board members looked directly up at King's Chapel burial ground, and every time they felt damp or chill they wished something else were on the other side of the wall. Health officials spent as little as they decently could on maintaining the burial grounds. "Sooner or later," they wrote, "the remains of those buried in these cemeteries will be removed, and the ground used for other purposes," confirming the message of the street numbers assigned there a generation earlier. In 1877 the board calculated the value of Granary and King's Chapel graveyards as $1.2 million

land

and noted that this was more than ample to replace them with a fine rural cemetery and "keep [its] grounds perpetually in order." The city was then seeking sites for a new courthouse and a city hall extension, and the board suggested that these two burial grounds might be available.[45]

This tactic backfired. Public health discouraged further interments in the center of the city, whether the burial grounds remained or not, but people now assumed that the board's motive was redevelopment. When the board in 1879 proposed discontinuing further use of downtown tombs—burials in ordinary graves had ceased long before—tomb owners asserted their right to continue using them, many making clear that they did so only because this seemed the graveyards' strongest defense.[46] "There is no practical use likely to be made of the tombs," testified one owner, whose family all had lots at Mount Auburn or other cemeteries, but "desire to maintain these grounds as monuments to the memory of our honored predecessors." "If the order passed," said another, "the next thing would be to remove the remains in dump carts."[47] The members of Board of Health quickly disavowed any such intentions, but it was too late.[48] They had provoked a new preservation campaign.

Upstairs from the Board of Health the building's owner, the Massachusetts Historical Society, looked out on the burial ground. "We seem to have been stationed here as the special guardians of this old Graveyard," said society president Robert C. Winthrop. Like Westminster Abbey, he said, "this is by no means a mere question for the descendants of anybody. Its interest reaches far beyond any personal sentiment or family pride. . . . This time-honored Graveyard goes back in history a hundred years behind the Old South or Faneuil Hall, and is . . . the most historical and sacred spot within our limits. . . . It should be preserved, as by a solemn consecration, for all generations."[49]

History could not address the public-health arguments against the burial grounds, but the parks movement provided an answer. "I do not believe that any evil consequences happen from the very rare interments in King's Chapel Burial-ground," wrote Dr. Oliver Wendell Holmes Sr. "On the contrary, I believe it has a positively beneficial influence, as an open breathing-space in a crowded part of the city." The Athenaeum overlooked the Granary burial ground, and trustee Francis Parkman found it "a positive advantage in supplying light and air."[50] Winthrop thought of the Historical Society's preservation effort partly as protection of its real estate investment by defending adjacent open space.

The city council did not close the tombs. The Historical Society took no position on further interments but asked the legislature for "permanent preservation of [the state's] ancient burial grounds." The Boston city coun-

FIGURE 5.8 *The Granary burial ground and Tremont Street, 1894. Courtesy Bostonian Society, Old State House*

cil supported this request, and the legislature responded in 1880 with an act preventing any century-old graveyard from being put to another use without legislative approval.[51] Like the Commons and Parks Acts, this erected a higher procedural barrier to change, again transforming a Boston preservation controversy into a statewide protective measure.

Bostonians clearly wanted the burial grounds as permanent features of the city. What was to be permanent might be a monument to historical figures resting there, but increasingly it was just a familiar and welcome oasis of greenery in the city. "The day will come," said a councilman in 1879, "when all such places will be made into public parks." The city began the process when it planted them in the 1850s and opened them for the first time to the general public.[52] William H. Whitmore, who defended Boston's burial grounds, nonetheless suggested during the transit debate in the 1870s that streetcars might loop around the perimeter of the Granary, where they need

128

not disturb its visual qualities. "Very few persons" cared about the graves, he said, but his plan contemplated "leaving of course the front of the enclosure as it is at present," and he showed that it could be accomplished "without destroying any trees."[53] There was no controversy when the subway in 1895 relocated graves from the Central Burying Ground under the Common, not because the remains there were less aristocratic than those in King's Chapel or the Granary—the plebeian South Burying Ground was successfully defended from further disruption starting in the 1880s—but because the disruption was subterranean; with or without graves, it would remain open space.

Wilderness and Scenic Preservation

Some of the same eastern urbanites who fought to protect open spaces in cities also worked for the permanence of wilderness and scenic areas elsewhere in the country. Learning from the mistakes that required expensive re-creation of nature in urban parks, they urged saving natural wonders before they were violated. The movement began with Yosemite and Yellowstone, extraordinary places in the West, but it came back east to the Adirondacks and Niagara Falls in New York, and then to urban regions, starting around Boston.

No wild landscape anywhere in the world was set aside as a park before Yosemite. The federal government in 1864 ceded the land to California to create the first state park. Frederick Law Olmsted, then living near Yosemite managing a mining company, was appointed president of the state park commission and wrote a plan articulating for the first time the idea of wilderness reservations. Unique natural landscapes, Olmsted thought, rightfully belong to all the people and must be held in trust for future generations. The first priority in managing the park, therefore, was "preservation and maintenance as exactly as is possible of the natural scenery."[54]

This philosophy soon produced the unprecedented innovation of national parks, but not through Olmsted's report, because California declined to publish it. The idea continued to arise, as Olmsted put it, through "the workings of the national genius";[55] it arose around a campfire in the Yellowstone Valley in the Wyoming Territory in 1870. An official exploration party, awestruck at the landscape, resolved when they reported to Congress to urge setting it aside for posterity. Yellowstone lay in no state, so Congress in 1872 made it the world's first national park. Secretary of the Interior Lucius Q. C. Lamar a few years later called it one place that "shall stand while the rest of the world moves."[56]

Back in New York and working on parks in Buffalo, Olmsted by 1869 was thinking about protecting nearby Niagara Falls from inappropriate development. He outlined an international park around the falls, but the idea lay dormant for a decade. In 1879 he began working on the problem with the governments of New York State and the province of Ontario. Any Niagara park would have to be created not by reserving public lands but by taking private property, some of it developed and expensive, and some of its owners hostile to the plan. Olmsted worked with Charles Eliot Norton orchestrating a national campaign that brought about establishment of the Niagara Falls state reservation on the New York side in 1885.[57]

The same year, the New York legislature also set aside the Adirondack Forest Preserve, the other great eastern reservation of natural scenery. W. H. H. Murray, pastor of Boston's Park Street Church and defender of the Old South, had publicized the Adirondack landscape in his *Adventures in the Wilderness: or, Camp-Life in the Adirondacks,* published in 1869. Once people valued the mountains' wildness, they sought to protect it. Indiscriminate logging threatened not only scenery but also watersheds and future timber supplies. Modern forestry was emerging at this time as both a science and a conservation movement. Olmsted helped Charles S. Sargent begin publishing *Garden and Forest,* a national forum for the new fields of forestry and landscape architecture. Olmsted and Sargent joined in the cause of preserving the Adirondacks. They sought to protect the forest not as a wilderness shrine but as a resource to be used, an economic resource as well as a visual and hydrological one. These early conservationists sought what would today be called sustainability: the Adirondacks were to be not a park but a "preserve" where logging would be managed responsibly, so that it could continue permanently and could be compatible with visual and recreational values. Much of the Adirondacks already belonged to New York State, so the preserve began like Yosemite and Yellowstone as a reservation from public property, a change not in ownership but in mission. Logging abuses and timber theft broke down that multiple-use mission, and the legislature in 1892 converted the reserve to a park. In 1894 the state constitutional convention unanimously adopted, and the voters approved, an amendment guaranteeing that the park "shall be forever kept as wild forest lands."[58]

Back near Boston, continuing suburban growth threatened landscapes, and spurred preservation efforts, at ever-larger scales. The early push for metropolitan parks around Boston was satisfied for a time by annexations that brought some of the suburban landscape under municipal control. But as the metropolis grew and the likelihood of annexation receded, some of the same Massachusetts residents who worked for the permanence of landscapes around the country returned the parks movement to its original regional scope.

FIGURE 5.9 *The Waverley Oaks, c. 1900. Society for the Preservation of New England Antiquities*

This new generation of park activism was led by Charles Eliot, son of the president of Harvard and student of his father's cousin, Charles Eliot Norton. Eliot apprenticed as a landscape architect in the Olmsted office and then went into practice for himself in 1886.[59] He publicized the profession and wrote about the process of suburbanization by which, he said, developers consumed the natural features that had made their localities attractive.

When *Garden and Forest* editorialized about threats to the Waverley Oaks, a stand of ancient trees outside Boston, Eliot proposed a private association to hold "surviving fragments" of "the primitive wilderness of New England . . . just as the Public Library holds books and the Art Museum pictures— for the use and enjoyment of the public."[60] Eliot set out to create this organization. Through the Appalachian Mountain Club he arranged a meeting of "persons interested in the preservation of scenery and historical sites in Massachusetts." A hundred people gathered at the Massachusetts Institute of Technology on May 24, 1890, to hear Eliot invoke the Old South and other preservation successes and suggest that more such efforts would be elicited by creating a statewide umbrella organization as a guardian for the resources they saved. He saw this private group as a demonstration of what he hoped would become a government role.[61]

The 1891 legislature chartered the Trustees of Public Reservations, a private, tax-exempt organization for saving "beautiful and historic places." The first trustees included Olmsted and Sargent; they were later joined by Augustus Hemenway, whose mother had saved the Old South. They elected Senator George F. Hoar their president and Charles Eliot their secretary and immediately began arrangements to accept their first donation, a small piece of the vast Middlesex Fells woodland north of Boston that had long been proposed as a park. Another donor tried but was unable to purchase the Waverley Oaks.[62]

Eliot quickly turned the new organization to his larger agenda of public action. He brought together local parks commissioners in December 1891 to revive the idea of a metropolitan parks system, reminding them that greater Boston "yet allows its finest scenes of natural beauty to be destroyed one by one, regardless of the fact that the great city of the future which is to fill this land would certainly prize every such scene exceedingly, and would gladly help pay the cost of preserving them to-day."[63] At the request of these parks boards and the trustees, the legislature in 1892 appointed a temporary commission to plan metropolitan parks. This commission worked with Eliot as its landscape architect to draw up a system of open spaces for suburban Boston, encompassing all the stream valleys and as much as possible of the seashore and hilltops as well as major woodlands such as Middlesex Fells. The 1893 legislature approved this innovative plan and established a permanent Metropolitan Park Commission to carry it out. That same year Eliot joined the Olmsted firm as a partner, bringing the regional parks into the same office where he had apprenticed on the Boston park system, now nearly complete. Eliot's metropolitan parks extended Olmsted's ideas to a new scale.

The Metropolitan Park Commission complemented the Trustees of Reservations, as Eliot explained it.[64] Metropolitan parks, like most parks, were located and developed with a view to human use, a system shaped by both the urban and natural geography of the Boston area. The trustees, on the other hand, preserved places as found, their reservations selected for intrinsic qualities independent of location, with only minimal intervention to make them accessible. The main distinction between the two was practical: while the trustees warned that they did not "possess either the money or the authority to snatch real estate out of the hands of anybody,"[65] the Metropolitan Parks Commission had both money and authority. During its first nine

MAP 11   *Metropolitan parks system, 1901 (including linked local parks)*

years, the commission spent $5 million on land, and as one of its first acquisitions it snatched up the Waverley Oaks. The trustees after 1893 focused their efforts outside the metropolitan district.[66]

Charles Eliot died in 1897 at the age of thirty-seven, of spinal meningitis contracted during fieldwork on the parks in Hartford. Boston's metropolitan park system of more than nine thousand acres was mostly secured at the time of his death, largely through his efforts.[67] The Trustees of Reservations grew more slowly, with four properties in 1897 and ten by 1930. They soon inspired similar land trusts. British preservationists cited the Massachusetts group as a model for their National Trust for Places of Historic Interest or Natural Beauty, founded in 1893 (it was in turn the model for this country's National Trust for Historic Preservation in 1949). New York State in 1895 chartered the Trustees of Scenic and Historic Places and Objects, which worked for the establishment in 1900 of the Palisades Interstate Park to preserve the cliffs across the Hudson from New York City.[68] The organization renamed itself the American Scenic and Historic Preservation Society in 1901; it continued to limit its landholdings to New York State but became active in historic and landscape preservation issues nationwide.

These groups embodied the connection between parks and preservation. The outdoors was intertwined with history for Eliot; in his youth he hiked the countryside around Boston with Drake's *Historic Mansions of Middlesex* as his guide. Visiting England, he took an interest in the protection of commons and footpaths, ancient landscapes whose very identity was historically defined.[69] But preservation for Eliot and the trustees was mainly about landscapes rather than architectural landmarks. "Massachusetts," they wrote, "possesses no such richly historical treasures" as England.[70] In the trustees' eighth year they acquired a field in Milton that had belonged to eighteenth-century governor Thomas Hutchinson, but they turned down several historic buildings and did not obtain one until 1928.[71] American Scenic more thoroughly covered the whole range from landscapes to architecture, and from wilderness to the center of the city.

The parks movement was one of the earliest organized responses to environmental change, and it was the first to use government powers in pursuit of environmental permanence. Parks and preservation were related in motive and in mechanism: scenic and historic resources both were valued and ideally permanent; both were threatened and needed to be saved. American Scenic asserted a third relationship, that topography molds history, and scenic and historic resources thus were linked organically from the beginning. The first preservationist interest in the Common and burial grounds was nominally historic, but eventually it became clear that people valued these places for a sense of age that was independent of specific historic events or personages. The precedent of permanent landscapes in cities helped Americans invent the idea of permanent landscapes elsewhere, protecting wilderness before it was disturbed. The value of these places had little to do with human history. The Trustees of Reservations and the American Scenic and Historic Preservation Society show that the line between historic and visual motives for preservation was not important to contemporaries, who simply found value in the landscape and worked to make it permanent.

CHAPTER 6

❦

From Monuments to Landmarks

The interest in Park Street Church is not due to great antiquity or wealth of historic associations, like the Old South Church. . . . The chief interest lies in the fact that the church is an impressive architectural monument, situated at a strategic point in the landscape of the city and constituting a beautiful and time-honored feature of Boston, indissolubly bound up with the very thought of Boston in every mind.

— PRESCOTT F. HALL

The ahistorical brand of preservationism that emerged around issues of open space in the city quickly came into play toward buildings, too. People began to treat them not as historic but as architectural monuments—landmarks—defining their significance by their visual importance. The fulcrum for this shift was the Massachusetts statehouse, on Beacon Hill facing the Common, designed by Charles Bulfinch and completed in 1798, the building that superseded the Old State House and later won Bulfinch the commission for the capitol at Washington. The 1808 Park Street Church at the same end of the Common was even more a landmark, since its significance tilted still more toward the visual than the historical.

The Bulfinch Front

The Bulfinch statehouse was the subject of the country's first major preservation controversy in which architectural history was more important than political, military, or religious history. It was the first one in which architects took a leading role. It also revealed latent conflicts between preservation and some of the kinds of permanence that people sought. It did not pit preservation against utility, but rather one kind of permanence against another.

The last time Massachusetts had focused its attention on enlarging its capitol was immediately after the Civil War, and immediately after the demise of the Hancock House. Between 1864 and 1867, five legislative committees

FIGURE 6.1 *Bulfinch statehouse. Society for the Preservation of New England Antiquities*

considered the problem, the final one commissioning architects Alexander Estey and Gridley J. F. Bryant—who had designed an earlier extension behind the building—to prepare three alternative schemes: a textbook triumvirate of preservation, replication, and demolition. "Plan No. 1" preserved the Bulfinch building, with short wings added to meet the state's "most pressing wants." "Plan No. 2" added to these wings an expansion of the House chamber by extending the front twenty-five feet forward. The Bulfinch facade would be reconstructed there "as far as it could be done with consistency," making, as Bryant explained, "only such changes . . . as the additional importance and character of the building seemed to require": a bigger, improved copy. "Plan No. 3" called for demolishing the Bulfinch building to construct a new statehouse on the same site. Legislators chose preservation, but only for financial reasons. They rejected even Bryant's minimal Plan No. 1 in favor of an economy scheme of interior rearrangement by which they hoped "the necessities of the government will be met for a series of years, . . . until the people shall demand and authorize the erection of a new building." As they anticipated, their short-term approach kept the statehouse usable for only a decade or so.[1]

When the question next came up in the mid-1880s, circumstances had changed. The government had grown, squeezing departments out of the statehouse to scattered rented spaces, an arrangement Governor Oliver Ames described as "not only expensive but inconvenient." The state tried consolidating offices in the immediate vicinity of the capitol, but in this old neighborhood it could only rent or buy what one suburban newspaper called "disused tenements."[2] Neither these buildings nor any modest changes to the existing statehouse could possibly accommodate the growing apparatus of government. The economy had changed, too. Instead of the burden of Civil War debt and postwar inflation, Massachusetts enjoyed a prosperity that encouraged greater architectural ambitions.

One more changed circumstance complicated these ambitions: success in saving the Old South and the Old State House. These successes made newly poignant the memory of the Hancock House, which began to achieve mythic status as the preservation movement's martyr, a nineteenth-century equivalent of New York's Pennsylvania Station: Massachusetts would shortly decide to recreate the Hancock House as its pavilion at the 1893 Chicago Columbian Exposition.[3] Expanding facilities next door at the statehouse would not be so simple as demanding "a new building." But if the eighteenth-century capitol remained, how could it accommodate a twentieth-century government?

Various schemes were revived for adding wings to the Bulfinch building, but any such plan had problems. Creating enough space this way would require radical rearrangement of the existing interior. It meant clearing the most densely built and expensive of the adjacent blocks. It was also perceived as a grave threat to the old landmark, in part because land acquisition for wings would be identical to that for a wholly new structure, but also because of what such extensions, if actually constructed, would do to the building's proportions. Governor Ames, who in his private life was an important architectural patron of H. H. Richardson, explained that wings would "give us an unshapely and inartistic structure in place of one that is symmetrical and in good taste."[4]

The Bulfinch building's appearance might be enhanced, on the other hand, by new state offices in separate buildings designed to give it a deferential setting. One legislator proposed a "handsome colonial building, subordinate in appearance to the State House."[5] Detached buildings, however, would do nothing for the cramped legislative chambers themselves. In addition, the most eligible sites for such buildings were the same as any wings would occupy, making this plan equally costly.

There were many reasons for looking north to the less expensive land behind the building, where construction would have the smallest visual impact. The statehouse backed onto Mount Vernon Street, the elite spine of

FIGURE 6.2 *Detail from bird's-eye view of Bulfinch statehouse and its neighborhood, H. H. Rowley & Co., 1880. To the left is the Common, in the foreground Park Street Church and the Granary burial ground, and on the right behind the statehouse the Beacon Hill reservoir.*

Beacon Hill, although the houses immediately across the street were small and unprepossessing. Closing this street was the only way the building could extend rearward "in one solid mass," but it would involve heavy damages unless the plan created some satisfactory new approach to Beacon Hill.[6] A tempting solution beckoned from beyond the little houses on Mount Vernon Street: the vacant full-block "reservoir lot," which the city of Boston was holding off the market impatiently while the state deliberated how to expand its capitol. But the reservoir lot shared either the difficulties of closing Mount Vernon Street or else the inconvenience of a detached office building—until the state began exploring the possibility of bridging the street to make the new building an "annex" to the existing statehouse.[7]

Not everyone had become a preservationist. Many still felt that a proper capitol was a new capitol, on Beacon Hill or elsewhere. The whole question was first formally raised by an 1885 petition "that the Commonwealth procure a new State House in some other location," so that the Bulfinch building could be reused as a new Suffolk County courthouse. Among the "other locations" mentioned were the Back Bay, Parker Hill (the same eminence to which the city had removed its Beacon Hill reservoir), and the city of Worcester. People who wanted a new capitol elsewhere provoked a debate over permanence and sacredness of site, like the earlier debates about migrating churches, but even they usually assumed permanence for the old structure. For all the nervousness about threats to the building, few people were willing to advocate destroying it, and accounts announcing a danger of "having the work of Charles Bulfinch removed or remodelled" were making a rhetorical warning about remodeling as much as a real warning about removal.[8]

The legislature in 1886 approved the concept of enlarging the statehouse, but only after amending the measure to require "that the present state house, and particularly the southern front thereof, be substantially preserved."[9] After two more years of planning, the state took the reservoir lot to extend the statehouse northward, and Governor Ames announced a competition to design a "State House Annex," with instructions stipulating that "the architectural design is to be in harmony with the present building," and required drawings "showing method of connecting proposed building with State House."[10] Charles Brigham's winning design made the connection by two bridges across Mount Vernon Street, but it was modified before adoption so that the annex itself spanned the street, fusing with the Bulfinch building in a single mass.[11] This change would loom important later, but it attracted little attention at the time. Three statehouse construction commissioners were appointed to build it.[12]

The commissioners were not sympathetic to the Bulfinch building, an attitude that became especially clear a few years later when their new building stood nearly complete beside it. They hesitated to begin dismantling the old wall to connect the two, they said, because "once inside of it, it would be difficult to know where to stop."[13] Commissioners and legislators faced an aged and comparatively uncomfortable building next to spacious quarters they could see rising. In 1893 the commissioners blandly revived the question "whether the whole State House should not be made new":

When the extension already authorized is completed, practically nothing of the old part will be left. . . . It is some hundred years old. Its outer walls and wooden finish will not be in keeping with what, while called an extension, will really be five-sixths of the whole building. The dome is of wood, subject to the impairment of age, and should be of iron. It is hardly possible that many years will pass before, in any event, this old and most conspicuous part, facing Beacon Street and the Common, will be made new and of equal quality with the rest.[14]

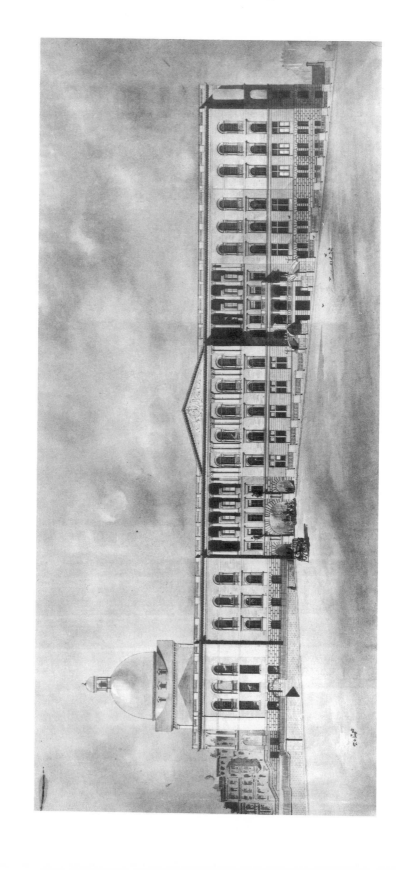

This remarkable passage reveals a paradoxical conflict between permanence and preservation. The ideal of permanence had triumphed so far that the commissioners sought a hermetic permanence of materials not "subject to the impairment of age." They were building "not for a day or a hundred years," they said, so "such should be the durability of material and solidity of construction, as to insure a building that will stand for centuries."[15] They could not find this perfection in old buildings.

Bostonians assumed that they had won preservation of the Bulfinch statehouse, but in fact the battle had not yet been fought. Those who would get rid of the Bulfinch statehouse invoked both lines of argument favoring change, the first of which equated age with corruption. The building was so well liked that its detractors limited this argument to corruption in the literal sense of the word: it "consisted mainly of a wooden dome, badly rotted," said the *American Architect,* "and covered with a tin roof, which . . . would fall down from decay before long any way." The physical condition of the building would appear to be a factual question, but somehow this question seemed impossible to answer. Even after an independent commission of experts investigated it in 1895, legislators were left to choose between wildly different opinions.[16] Architect William G. Preston described it as a structure of "good old handmade bricks, made honestly in the old times, hard and red and laid in mortar; and the mortar was solid and hard. . . . Those great walls four feet thick, made honestly, would certainly . . . carry an eight story building without any strengthening." But Charles Brigham called one of those same walls "the most decrepid [sic] piece of brick construction that you could very well find."[17]

Both sides agreed that parts of the building—in particular the dome—had deteriorated, and their disagreement is best understood as a philosophical question: was a hundred years' inevitable aging to be accepted as normal, a healthy subject for restoration, or was it to be seen instead with the disgust connoted by descriptions of decay and decrepitude? As a practical matter, the building's rehabilitation presented no insurmountable difficulties, "so that if the building is to be destroyed," said Clement K. Fay, attorney for the Boston Society of Architects, "it will not be because it cannot be saved, but for some other reason."[18]

The second argument for change—faith in material progress—provided that other reason for those who wanted to take down Bulfinch's statehouse, and gave rise to its own conflict between preservation and permanence. If environmental permanence was a desideratum, should it be permanence of

FIGURE 6.3 *Statehouse annex design, Charles Brigham. Courtesy Boston Public Library, Print Department*

FIGURE 6.4   *Rear wall of Bulfinch statehouse during preparations for connecting the annex (at left). "Once inside of it," said the construction commissioners, "it would be difficult to know where to stop." Courtesy Bostonian Society, Old State House*

what was there now, or of something new and better? A still-vital faith in progress suggested that there ought to be one last wave of change, making an environment worthy of permanence. Worthiness was a central issue in this era when many American states built new capitols intended as their respective emblems. This capitol especially, serving a rich and cultured commonwealth from its pride of place on Beacon Hill, the social and topographic pinnacle of the city, should be its architectural pinnacle as well.[19] Could Bulfinch's "good old handmade bricks" bear this tremendous symbolic weight?

This question made the statehouse, more than any other preservation controversy so far, a design issue, and a potentially troubling one for the architecture profession. Historian Charles Francis Adams thought it "a curious and somewhat saddening fact" that after almost a century "the Old State House on Beacon Hill still remains infinitely the most dignified and most imposing, the most characteristic, the most perfectly designed and agreeable architectural effort we can boast."[20] Did architects really want to agree that their profession's best work had been done in a previous century? Architects and their patrons could ask this question seriously because they were increasingly rejecting eclecticism and searching for academically correct roots. Bulfinch's simple Georgian lines were just the antidote for Victorian excess, and Charles A. Cummings, the head of the Boston Society of Architects, denounced as "false progress" the prospect of replacing them with what one newspaper feared would be "some architectural phantasy of the newest new school."[21] The Colonial Revival had been taking hold in New England for more than a decade and was beginning to spread elsewhere, and its practitioners grew increasingly rigorous in their adherence to its canon. This led to preservation arguments based not merely on architectural quality but on significance to architectural history, as when one defender explained that Bulfinch's building was "the prototype of nearly all the legislative buildings which have been erected in this country since[,] . . . a type which is quite unique to this country."[22]

Architects led the fight to save the Bulfinch statehouse, a first for the profession in this country. They had been conspicuously silent about both the Old State House and the Old South Church, the replacement for which was designed by the same Charles A. Cummings who now defended the Bulfinch building. "Where was his well-developed 'historical sentiment' at that time?" asked one skeptic.[23] If architects had earlier identified their interests with those of clients who commissioned new buildings, now their sympathies clearly lay with Bulfinch as their predecessor, and the emerging profession of restoration architecture demonstrated that preservation too could pay.

In 1894 the Boston Society of Architects set up a statehouse committee which promoted preservation in two ways. First, it answered doubts about the building's condition and proposed practical methods to preserve it. One member of the committee seized for their cause the mantle of progress by claiming that the building's preservation had only recently become feasible, because "principles of construction have undergone such revolutionary changes, that what would have been impossible twenty five or fifty years ago is now made comparatively a simple problem of the use of steel construction."[24] Second, the architects educated the public, and the legislators, about the quality of the building's design and its place in the history of American architecture.

This involvement by architects, and this focus of public attention on architecture, was part of a more general trend toward seeing preservation questions in terms of visual issues, such as affection for views of the statehouse and its dome. Such concerns were not heard so much during the controversies over the Old South Church and the Old State House, which were treated as historic memorials; the visual emphasis had its precedent instead in defense of the old burial grounds and the Common.

Ironically, this visual focus worked against the Bulfinch building, leading to the strangest episode of the story, an officially endorsed plan to replace the Bulfinch statehouse with a replica—eventually a larger-than-life replica, as Bryant had proposed twenty-five years earlier. The commissioners, acknowledging the building's architectural significance, "recognized of course that no change would ever be permitted in the now historic and always admirable" design, but their version of permanence did not encompass the materials in which the design was realized.[25] As Commissioner William Endicott Jr. asked, "Will a proper appreciation of Mr. Bulfinch require that the building should be carried forward in pine wood and lathe [sic] and plaster finish until it shall burn down? Is it not a truer loyalty to put the idea of Mr. Bulfinch into enduring materials and pass it down the centuries?"[26] At a hearing before the legislature's statehouse committee, Endicott explained that the commissioners' plan would "preserve the structure in new material." "To this Mr. Fay remarked, 'I fail to see how you can preserve the building by substituting a new structure.' 'We desire to preserve the idea,' answered Mr. Endicott."[27]

Did Charles Bulfinch produce an "idea" or a particular tangible object? Was his statehouse a sort of Platonic ideal, a soul that might be reincarnated in a new body? A puzzled Commissioner Endicott attempted his own analysis of these questions. "The devotion of the architects to Mr. Bulfinch," he wrote, "simmered down, seems to be one of two considerations: it must be either the dimensions and form of the wall or the bricks themselves." He thought he had a solution: he wondered if architects would favor "a new structure, as proposed by the commissioners, of the same outlines and dimensions as the present one, provided the bricks of the present building shall all be used in interior brickwork of the new. It would seem that this should satisfy them in both respects." It did not satisfy them, but Endicott had hit upon a fundamental dichotomy between a visual concern for preserving "form" and an archaeological or art-historical interest in preserving "the bricks themselves." Representative John E. Tuttle, a Boston real estate broker who had worked to protect the Common, saw only a visual issue and thus favored the commissioners' plan: "I consider it a great tribute to the Bulfinch style of architecture that we should attempt at this day, a hundred years later, to . . . reproduce it." Testifying before Tuttle, Francis A. Walker, president of the Massachusetts Institute of Technology, argued the opposite view in terms directed at Endicott, a trustee (and soon president) of the Museum of Fine Arts. "Anybody can make a copy," said Walker, but "it takes a master to make an original."[28]

This new awareness of the city as a visual experience also led to the project of honoring the statehouse by clearing two blocks east of it to extend its park setting. Far from enhancing the building, however, the demolitions carried out in 1894 gave new impetus to the idea of replacing it. "When the buildings on the east side were cleared away," reported the *American Architect,*

and people had a chance to see the east front, it was at once plain that things had, behind the high fence, arrived at a very dubious stage. Taken as it stands, the east front seems to suggest nothing so much as that it was the designer's original intention to do away absolutely with the old building and to repeat at the south end the treatment employed at the north. Doubtless this may not have been the architect's real intention, for it could hardly have been known at the time the design was prepared that a park was to be made on the east side which would expose that part, instead of leaving it to the seclusion of a narrow street.[29]

The painstakingly created views revealed "a building five hundred feet long with a dome at one end"; "a tender too large for the woodburning locomotive that was trying to pull it up hill"; an enormous tail for a "little dog."[30] The construction commissioners saw the problem and decided to get a bigger dog.

The commissioners' 1893 report had recommended that "the front should be rebuilt, preserving its present proportions," but after the unfortunate proportions of the whole became apparent, they asked the next legislature to authorize a reproduction "with the proper increase of width and height."[31] "Bulfinch originally intended a wider front," Long claimed, "and there is some reason to believe that he contemplated with it a higher dome accompanied by a colonnade." The commissioners, he said, had no intention "of recommending any other change than the conservative one above suggested."[32]

Although the legislature's statehouse committee approved this plan, five of its eleven members dissented, including its chair. Their minority report admitted that the existing building needed work. But, they said, "the way to preserve the State House is to preserve it." Only this promise had allowed the project to go ahead. "The annex was built to preserve the State House and to harmonize with it. We are told, now, that the State House must be

destroyed and rebuilt so that it may harmonize with the annex." The commissioners proposed "to preserve the 'idea' of the State House by destroying
the State House itself." The minority offered instead a bill providing for "so
thorough a repairing and fireproofing of the present structure that the question of its preservation will be permanently solved." "The State House can
thus be put into a condition almost unexampled among historic buildings
for safety and solidity and we desire to repeat that this is the only kind of
preservation that is worthy of the name. Reproduction of colonial architecture never can retain the quaintness and beauty of the original. If the State
House is once destroyed it is destroyed forever, and putting up a new building of stone and iron does not put it back again."[33]

Finally, the minority disagreed that building a new front would improve
the appearance of the complex as a whole, and they argued that even on these
grounds preserving the original was preferable, since "it will serve to emphasize the fact that the State House and annex are in reality two buildings, the
former having been specially preserved for the people, and the union of the
two will not be subject to the strict criticism to which one modern building
would be exposed."[34] This discussion of the proper relationship between
new and old building fabric showed the sophistication of public discourse
resulting from Boston's two decades of successful preservation efforts.

If the statehouse was to be preserved, the scale of the project would raise
daunting details of restoration, and public debate extended even to these
details. As Alden Sampson said of the Bulfinch building, "Its very faults are
not without interest." For example, the facade's columns, modeled on ancient Greek construction of stone, had been executed instead in wood, each
one turned from a single tree trunk. Would not Bulfinch's intentions be best
respected by making them of stone, as he presumably would have done had
it been available? So argued architect and preservation advocate William G.
Preston, echoing Viollet-le-Duc's philosophy of restoration to "a condition of
completeness which could never have existed at any given time." Counter-
arguments followed the Ruskinian "anti-scrape" philosophy that favored not
restoration but preservation as found. Even if Bulfinch would have preferred
stone, which preservationists were by no means willing to concede, "he got
the value out of wood," said H. C. Wheelwright. "The things that he did
have a value that nothing we do in the more complicated days of the present
can equal."[35]

The Bulfinch statehouse preservation campaign also brought an expansion of what, for Massachusetts, would be considered "historic." The term
had previously applied almost exclusively to the state's heroic period, the
Revolution. "There is nothing particularly historic about our present State
House," editorialized the *Herald*. "Most of the great events in our local his-

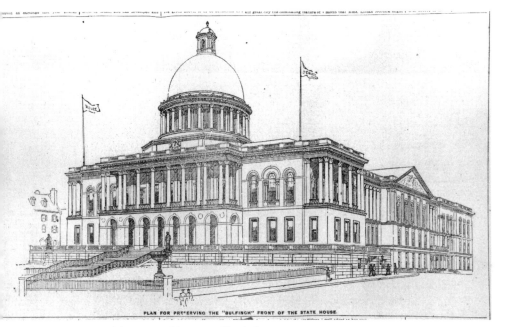

FIGURE 6.5 *A bigger and better Bulfinch front, as drawn by architects Albert W. Cobb and Warren A. Rodman, 1895. Boston Public Library*

tory took place before it was built."[36] Now history leaped forward, as the building's defenders found its significance in the comparatively recent Civil War and the administration of "the great war Governor," John A. Andrew.[37] "We cannot know how precious everything connected with that War" will be, said Edward Robinson, secretary of the Boston Art Commission, "two hundred years from now." Civil War veterans for years had claimed the mantle of history with monuments and reunions at their battle sites, and now the time horizon of historical significance encompassed living memory on the home front, too. Some preservationists even tried to transcend heroic and martial sensibilities with a more continuous view of history. The Old State House had seen only fifty years in the life of the colony, pointed out Henry Lee, but this one "witnessed the first hundred years of the history of the State. It is all the history there is."[38]

Finally, this building raised in yet another way the question of use. As at the Old State House, there were plenty of potential *uses,* but what was the *purpose* of preserving it, and what use would accomplish it? Former governor John D. Long, chairman of the construction commission, could accept preservation itself as a legitimate use for a building; he had been one of the incorporators of the Old South Association in 1877 and was instrumental

in guiding that controversial incorporation through the legislature. He remained one of the association's directors even as he was trying to tear down the Bulfinch statehouse.[39] The Old South was a monument, and nothing else; for Long this took it out of any utilitarian calculus. He had difficulty seeing the statehouse in the same way, as when Fay, for the Boston Society of Architects, pictured it becoming "not an office or administration building full of busy offices, but rather a show building, an historical relic, . . . not . . . to be used as a beehive of industry, but as an impressive entrance to a building that may be put up behind it or on each side." "The whole nutshell lies just here," replied Long. "We had supposed that the scope of our duty was to regard this as a building, the main purpose of which was utility as a State House." If that was the purpose, he said, "it is a great deal better to tear it down."[40]

Each year the statehouse committee agreed with Long, and each year the full legislature granted the building a reprieve. By 1896, with the annex awaiting connection and the old building more or less damaged by the work behind it, some action was becoming imperative. After a series of public hearings dominated by preservationists, the statehouse committee nonetheless voted again 6 to 5 in favor of demolition and reconstruction, bringing this story to its crisis. Preservationists and architects made the "Bulfinch front" a nationwide cause and a statewide political fight. State representative Alfred Seelye Roe of Worcester addressed mass meetings at Faneuil Hall and the Old South meetinghouse, establishing a rhetorical equivalence among the three monuments. The building's opponents in the legislature complained, to Roe's evident glee, about organized campaigns by which their constituents bombarded them with letters and petitions.[41]

The campaign extended beyond Massachusetts' borders to include agitation around the country, especially in Chicago. Chicagoans proposed buying the building and reerecting it in Illinois. Their earlier threats to move the Old State House there had seemed mere braggadocio but looked more serious now because in the meantime, Chicagoans had scoured the country for historic buildings they could bring to the 1893 World's Columbian Exposition, including an unsuccessful attempt to snatch Hawthorne's birthplace from nearby Salem. Their efforts stimulated preservation in the East in the same way that American raids on European historical patrimony catalyzed preservation there.[42]

Preservationists won in the full legislature in the last days of the session, when it approved a bill submitted by Roe, providing for preservation of the statehouse and ensuring the necessary sensitivity to artifact by taking the

FIGURE 6.6 *The Bulfinch front and the completed statehouse annex after demolition of structures to the east, 1903. Courtesy Bostonian Society, Old State House*

restoration out of the commissioners' hands. It would be supervised instead by Governor Roger Wolcott, together with the president of the Senate and the speaker of the House, "friends" of the Bulfinch building, said Roe, and calculated to outrank the eminent commissioners.[43] These three consolidated the victory by selecting as architects Charles A. Cummings, Robert D. Andrews, and Arthur G. Everett, each of whom had been active in the preservation campaign. Work was finished in time for the centennial of the building's original opening, "fresh from the hand of the rehabilitator, old yet new," said Roe at its rededication. "The results surround us. *Esto perpetua.*"[44]

Brimstone Corner

The Bulfinch statehouse brought together two strains of preservation: one venerated historical significance and had saved the Old South and the Old State House; the other valued broader visual, functional, and sentimental significance and had prevented encroachments on burial grounds and the Common. At the statehouse, preservation was more about architecture than history, and it was about architecture evaluated not so much in an academic framework as for its contribution to the cityscape. Across the short side of the Common, next to the Granary burial ground, was Park Street Church, subject of a controversy that flared and then fizzled during two years beginning late in 1902, following close upon the Bulfinch statehouse campaign and further extending the directions it set. Preservationists who focused on Bulfinch's architecture were confident that the statehouse was also of the greatest historical and symbolic significance, a monument in every sense of the word. The Park Street structure, on the other hand, was still more recent and of what even its defenders admitted was limited historical value, but it was a familiar and beautiful building at the most prominent corner in the city.[45] It was a landmark, not a monument. Park Street Church produced the best articulation yet of an aesthetic basis for preservation, and of a philosophical kinship between preservation and the parks movement.

The Park Street Church debate was prefigured in different ways by two episodes, each of which was resolved before it could become a real controversy. The first had happened twenty years earlier, when Back Bay residents in 1881 campaigned to preserve the new Brattle Square Church on Commonwealth Avenue, or at least its spire, as the defunct congregation's assets were liquidated. When an auction of the property was announced, J. Montgomery Sears led other Back Bay residents in organizing to save the H. H. Richardson building, then just nine years old. They did not want to see, in the *Evening Transcript*'s words, "our most magnificent avenue . . . bereft of its most conspicuous ornament." The appeal quickly brought pledges of $30,000, but the

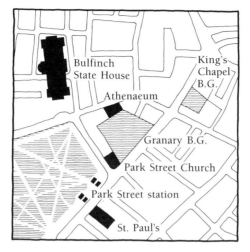

MAP 12

organizers expected the building to sell for $150,000, and so they abandoned the effort. Sears attended the auction out of curiosity, and when bidding ran to only half the anticipated sum, he stepped in and bought the property himself for $81,000, with "a vague idea of utilizing it as a public hall or music hall, or in some other way preserving it."[46] He offered it at cost to any religious body, or at a slight advance to anyone else who would preserve at least the tower. Lest potential allies think this his own private philanthropy, he threatened five weeks after he bought it to demolish the whole thing if a purchaser did not come forward within two months, and two months after this deadline passed he advertised for removal of the building as salvage. George B. Chase, a member of the Old South Preservation Committee, organized a campaign to save the tower alone. He had obtained pledges for most of the money, and assurances that the city would fit up and maintain the steeple as a clock tower, when the First Baptist Church bought the building and thus ended the question.[47] This six months of sporadic effort was significant for what it reveals about contemporary attitudes toward preservation. Some of the Brattle Church neighbors drew from the Old South and Old State House campaigns the same lesson they took from their successful Back Bay deed restrictions: that they need not accept change in any part of the environment they valued, whether or not it had already achieved the semblance of permanence through longevity. The Brattle Church tower took its value not from history but from its place in a larger scheme of urban design.

The second episode involved St. Paul's Episcopal Church, and it started immediately before the Park Street Church controversy and in just the same

FIGURE 6.7 *Commonwealth Avenue from Berkeley Street, 1885, showing the Brattle Square Church tower. Society for the Preservation of New England Antiquities*

way. A few steps away from Park Street, St. Paul's faced the Common on Tremont Street, a granite and sandstone Greek temple built in 1819 to the designs of Bulfinch's disciple Alexander Parris. In 1901 a real estate syndicate, after negotiating with the congregation's treasurer, offered $1.5 million for the church property. The proprietors, uneasy about removing the last Episcopal church from the center of Boston, declined this princely sum. The following year a new offer matched that amount and added a $5,000 individual bonus for each of the forty-one proprietors who would vote in favor of the sale. Such blatant bribery evidently offended; this time the vote against selling was "practically unanimous."[48]

Later in 1902 a different syndicate headed by developer John Phillip Reynolds Jr. approached the "prudential committee" that managed the worldly business of Park Street Church across the street. Although its lot was only half the size of St. Paul's, the Reynolds syndicate offered $1.25 million for it. Park Street was an evangelical congregation, born in the religious revival of 1808, and so its site had come to be called Brimstone Corner. Attendance had fallen off over the years, and in 1895, with chronic annual deficits, the church society rented out part of its ground floor as stores. Two years later, while the congregation was drifting without a minister and its debt increasing, the society renewed the store's leases with a new clause "in case of the sale of the Church," for the first time acknowledging this possibility. The deacons brought back a previous pastor, Dr. John L. Withrow, and then determined in 1898 that "the church should be kept in its present edifice."[49] A few years later, with their finances unimproved and their mortgage coming due, they were not so sure. The developers' offer, said Withrow, was "the Lord's doing."[50]

Some members of the society wondered whether moving to the comfortable Back Bay and taking refuge in an endowment might be too big a departure from their evangelical mission. Framing the question in this way tilted the answer toward preservation, but the practical businessmen who served the church as officers and deacons saw it differently. The society's property already constituted an enormous endowment which could both pay for a new church and support substantial missionary work; the question was whether to devote it to religious purposes or keep it locked up in architecture. "Are we right in allowing so vast a sum to lie hid in a napkin," asked Withrow, "when the income of it would do so much?"[51]

Withrow announced the syndicate's offer before services the first Sunday of December 1902. The deacons set two meetings, the following Thursday and Saturday, for the pew owners and then the society as a whole to vote on the sale. Women pew owners and congregants were excluded from voting, according to an old rule. The male members of Withrow's flock followed him and then in a unanimous vote affirmed the congregation's harmony in its decision. Ten days after the deal was first publicly proposed, the signed agreement was recorded in the registry of deeds.[52]

The sale quickly aroused opposition, spontaneous at first, but soon organized by attorney Prescott F. Hall and Dr. L. Vernon Briggs, who hosted a meeting at his Beacon Street home on January 14, 1903, to coordinate "the different efforts now being put forth by many persons." Briggs announced that $100,000 had been pledged already to save the church; the public later learned that this came from two individuals offering $50,000 each.[53] The Committee for the Preservation of Park Street Church was organized at that meeting, its membership entirely unconnected with the congregation, and it soon announced total pledges of $200,000 and then $300,000.[54]

Like the Bulfinch statehouse, Park Street Church was valued not as an historic site but as a work of architecture, "the finest of the few Wren [style] spires left in America." While the Boston Society of Architects did not take action as an organization, individual architects were again prominent in the preservation effort. The building was valued not only for the details of its design but even more for its particular combination of architecture and location, making it a landmark that admirers said was "seen by more people to-day than any other building in the city."[55]

FIGURE 6.8 *Park Street Church, with Park Street subway entrance in the foreground, photographed by Henry Peabody, 1906. Society for the Preservation of New England Antiquities*

Brimstone Corner had always been visible, but its prominence increased markedly with the 1898 opening of Park Street station in the Common across from the church, the new subway's most important stop. More than thirty thousand people a day, who in the past might have stepped off a streetcar anywhere along Tremont Street, now emerged blinking in the daylight to the sight of Peter Banner's graceful steeple. This was not lost on the developers who offered fortunes for Park Street Church and St. Paul's, also across from this station. The Park Street site, said the syndicate's agent, "is the most conspicuous in the whole city, and there can be no more advantageous position for a retail establishment." While the corner's new place on Bostonians' mental maps increased the property's commercial value, it also made the church's preservation seem more important. The subway in large part made the issue. "It is essential that a monumental public building of some kind stand on the site of Park Street Church," wrote the preservation committee; the church "already stands there, and it will cost less to retain it than to build another monument in its place."[56] "If some one thinks that his instinctive protest is wholly on account of the edifice, and not partly against the desecration of the site," said one letter to the editor, "let him ask himself if his feeling for the church would be the same if it were situated, let us say, on the corner of Washington and Boylston Streets. Or, to put it another way, would not his regret be much less keen if he could be assured that the church would be replaced by some noble work of art or by a beautiful building devoted to public enlightenment?" According to the building's defenders, Columbus Avenue, the main artery of the South End, had been laid out to create a vista terminating at Park Street Church, one of the only intentional vistas in Boston.[57]

Preservationists' concern was fueled by the church's proximity to other landmarks that had been successfully defended over the past generation. As the preservation committee conceived it, much more than this single building was at stake. The accomplishments of those who had preserved the Bulfinch statehouse, the Granary burial ground, and the Common would all be tarnished, possibly even reversed, by the demise of Park Street Church. The church was "the beginning of the noble approach to the State House," an effect that would be "ruined," said architect John L. Faxon, if it were replaced by a tall structure. The Granary burial ground, according to preservation committee organizer Prescott F. Hall, could become "merely a well or backyard for office buildings." Most important, the church shared in and perhaps contributed to the sanctity of the Common. "A monument on this corner constitutes a part of the beauty of the Common," wrote the preservation committee. "If you do not have a monumental building on this corner, you weaken the hold on the Common, and make it easier for the projected extension of Columbus Avenue and Commonwealth Avenue across the Common." The committee tried, through these arguments, to increase the spatial scale of the building's significance: "It stands at the head of the Common, and as such, it also stands at the head of our city park system."[58]

Park Street Church was associated with the park system not merely by proximity; these preservationists, like the Trustees of Reservations and the American Scenic and Historic Preservation Society, argued the fundamental kinship of the parks and preservation movements. Joseph Lee, one of the committee's founders and a nationally prominent recreation reformer, wrote of Park Street Church:

We are spending, and rightly spending, through our City and Metropolitan Park commissions millions of dollars for the sake of preserving or creating beautiful scenery in suburban and out-of-town sections. But the real beauty of a city—the beauty by which it must live in the hearts of its citizens—is not rural but civic beauty; not the beauty of the scenery by which it is surrounded, but the beauty and appropriateness of its own public and business structures and of the civic centres of which they form a part; not the beauty of the woods and fields that you can visit when you leave the city behind, but that which is found in the city itself, in the place where its citizens live and do their work, where its business and social life are carried on.[59]

Prescott F. Hall said that "there is as much reason for the preservation of a unique building like Park Street Church as there is for preserving notable natural features in the State," and he concluded that the commonwealth of Massachusetts ought to do both.[60]

These people looked to the government not merely because of the philosophical rationale of the park analogy but also for pragmatic reasons. The $300,000 total pledged was more than had been collected by any preservation effort in the nation since the Old South, yet it was only a fraction of what Park Street Church would cost. Unless some individual of enormous wealth took an interest in the building, only the government had the money to save it. Only the government could forcibly intervene once the agreement of sale was signed, though Reynolds's syndicate was cooperative enough that such force seemed unnecessary. The state was spending millions and using its sovereign powers for projects that appeared related—a park system, construction and restoration a block away at the statehouse, and reshaping its environs on Beacon Hill. The committee almost immediately resolved to attempt a legislative solution. Offering its pledges as the nucleus of the purchase price, it sought state acquisition of the building either as an addition to the metropolitan park system or for conversion to state offices.[61]

The office-conversion idea reflects these preservationists' strong, clear commitment to adaptive reuse of the building. It was not meant as an historic shrine. The committee was interested solely in the church's exterior and was willing to sacrifice the interior to save it. While some members would have liked to see the building used for assemblies—"an uptown Faneuil Hall"—they also explicitly advocated and worked out the real estate arithmetic of cutting the interior into stores and offices.[62]

Purchase by the state was a long shot. No building in Massachusetts had yet been purchased by local or state government for the purpose of preserving it. Though no one opposed preservation at the legislature's hearings on February 27, it quickly became clear that the state would not commit the resources to save Park Street Church. At the same time, it was also becoming clear to real estate and finance people on the preservation committee that tight money markets made the development unlikely.[63] Early in March the preservationists met at the Parker House to consider these changed circumstances.

The first new approach was an offer of a $350,000 endowment for the Park Street Church society on condition that it remain in its building. This strategy recognized that the largest available sum that could be applied to preserving the church was the expenditure the congregation could avoid if it did not have to buy a site and construct a new building. The endowment offer was, in effect, an effort to separate issues for the society's members—allowing them to decide whether they wanted an endowment separately from whether they wanted to move. A member of the congregation said at the legislative hearings that the society "does not need all the money and it may be shamed into turning part of it back towards saving the church."[64] But just as at the Old South, it was difficult for a religious body to decide explicitly that architectural preservation was a legitimate use of its resources. Sentimental considerations indeed led many congregations to preserve old buildings that could have been translated into endowments for other purposes, but they most often did this by avoiding asking the question out loud.

The members of the Park Street Society replied that they would accept such a condition only for an endowment of $600,000 or more. That the church responded at all was a tacit acknowledgment that the sale would not be consummated. The answer embodied the same spirit of rationality in which the offer was made. They could net $600,000 by moving; in effect, they refused to donate any substantial portion of their asset to this extraneous cause. To the public at large, however, it appeared that they were being greedy, even that they were holding the building for ransom.

A second proposed preservation strategy was purchase by a "Civic Memorial Corporation," to convert more of the building to income-producing uses and lease most of it back to the church. This corporation was conceived in the tenement-reform tradition of investment philanthropy; unlike housing schemes, whose promoters felt an ideological need to offer competitive 5, 6, and even 7 percent dividends, this one proposed a 2 percent return, emphasizing philanthropy over investment. This plan too would tap the society's assets, in the form of rents, interior space to be converted, and even direct reinvestment by the society in the Memorial Corporation's bonds. Individual church members also indicated some interest in making such an investment, at least half of which would in effect be donated.[65]

On April 1, 1903, the developers' option officially lapsed; the syndicate backed out of the deal. Newspapers announced that the building was saved and contributed to a perception that the congregation would now cooperate in preserving it, though the church's leaders said nothing to indicate that it was not still on the market. The Civic Memorial Association plan was not successfully negotiated, and at a June 30 meeting—from which women were again excluded—the congregation, amid hard feelings, voted to seek another buyer.[66]

By the following spring the prudential committee had sifted the options down to two, neither of them as financially attractive as the aborted sale had been. One was a proposal by the *Boston Herald* that the church build a five-story headquarters for the newspaper, which it would rent for $52,000 a year on a twenty-year lease. The other, a less complicated version of the preservation committee's plans, called for the congregation itself to convert more of the ground floor to commercial use while keeping the church in place upstairs. The prudential committee recommended the *Herald*'s proposal.[67]

Preservationists began a new kind of lobbying campaign, aimed not at any public body but at the church members themselves, the group best able to save the building and presumably having the greatest affection for it. The lobbying proceeded along several lines. Preservationists cited financial analyses showing that renovation would produce more income than new construction. As with the endowment offer, this helped to separate issues for the society; if financial security and preservation were not mutually exclusive, then a decision to destroy the building required a more compelling rationale. The preservationists brought into question the financial wisdom of accepting the *Herald*'s proposal, in particular. A newspaper plant was a specialized property that would be obsolete at the end of the lease, they said, leaving the church without an income. Finally, they aimed to tap the congregation's sentiments to save the building: reverence for the building itself and the congregation's own history in it, and also the same sort of prickly pride that had saved St. Paul's. The *Herald* had begun claiming that the popular press was an appropriate successor to the evangelical pulpit. "Shall the church assent to this humiliation?" asked preservationists.[68]

The congregation supported its deacons' recommendation, endorsing the *Herald* deal 68 to 59, but this was a big change from the earlier sale's near-unanimous support and indicated the effectiveness of the preservationists' arguments. Their lobbying continued, and two weeks later, when pew owners met to take final action, the deacons withdrew the proposal without putting it to a vote.[69]

Dr. Withrow, unlike Rev. Manning at the Old South, chose to interpret the preservationist interest of the congregation and the community as a hopeful sign for the church's religious future; at the beginning of 1905 he urged the society to find him a young associate who could work to make the church prosper again at its old location. He may have heeded the *Boston Journal*, which asked, "If Park Street Church cannot make a success on 'Brimstone Corner,' which has been advertised all over the country, where in the city can it make a success?"[70] For a church committed to reaching out for new believers, perhaps the most conspicuous corner in the city was after all the place to be. By the end of the year the congregation found its dynamic new minister in Dr. Arcturus Z. Conrad, and Park Street Church continued to fulminate at Brimstone Corner. Conrad quickly seized on the preservation committee as a potential ally. He appealed to these citizens, strangers to his congregation, to help him keep the church at its traditional location. He asked $10,000 for painting and restoring the building. Conrad acknowledged that he was not in a position to guarantee that the church would remain, but he promised personally that if it moved despite their aid, the money would be returned. Within a few weeks he had his $10,000. By the building's 1909 centennial, six years after the deacons turned down $350,000, they were plaintively appealing to lift a debt of $35,000 and seeking to raise an endowment of $100,000, which they would accept, they said, "on the condition of the continuance of worship at the present location." They did not raise the money for many years. Conrad, who succeeded Withrow to the pulpit, neutralized any implied threat of removal by treating the church as if it were his associate minister: "The building itself is eloquent. . . . Our Church building works with us and for us . . . . This temple is religion in brick and mortar. . . . [A] sentinel of God on this conspicuous corner of Boston Common . . . it preaches."[71]

Preservationists' role in saving Park Street Church is not easy to gauge, because unlike their counterparts at the Old South, they achieved their aims indirectly, and mostly out of the public eye, through the internal workings of the congregation. A similar private drama played out during the same years on the other side of the block among the proprietors of a different kind of institution, the Boston Athenaeum.

The Athenaeum was at the heart of Boston's elite Brahmin society, a private library founded in 1807. In 1849 it moved into a Renaissance palace on Beacon Street a block from the Bulfinch statehouse, backing onto the Granary burial ground across from Park Street Church. The trustees in the 1870s flirted with a move to the Back Bay, and they took up the question seriously in 1901 as tall new office buildings began to cut off their light. They described fire dangers in the old building and the financial advantages of selling it to developers, and the Athenaeum's membership voted 4 to 1 for moving.[72] The trustees bought a site facing the Public Garden at the corner of Newbury Street and prepared to build a new, bigger Renaissance palace there. But leases on the new site delayed action for two years, during which library members began to have second thoughts.

The Athenaeum's membership included activists from every preservation campaign since the Old South, and a group of them led by Katherine Pea-

FIGURE 6.9 *The Athenaeum gutted in the renovations of 1913–15. Boston Athe-*
naeum

body Loring and the poet Amy Lowell started a new campaign among their
fellow proprietors. They pointed to the Athenaeum's associations with Boston's literary Golden Age, and the personal associations the quirky structure
held for two generations of Boston's elite. But many advocates of the move
were also active preservationists, like Charles A. Cummings, who had just
finished restoring the Bulfinch statehouse across the street. The statehouse
at a hundred years old had been called too young to be historic, and there

was discomfort even among the Athenaeum's friends at ascribing historical significance to a building half that age. Percival Lowell defended it as "an heirloom from the past upon which the moss and lichen of affection is just beginning to grow." The *Evening Transcript* pointed out that many of the new buildings around the Athenaeum held other institutions drawn there through "a reliance upon its permanence." Eventually preservationists benefited from the same development slump that saved Park Street Church, as the trustees realized that selling the old building would not pay for a new one. The proprietors narrowly reversed their vote for moving, and in 1904 they began renovations. Seven years later Charles Francis Adams, calling the irreplaceable collection's still-flammable housing "a breach of trust little short of criminal," shamed his fellow proprietors into gutting and rebuilding a fireproof replica of the interior within the old walls. Its steel structure supported two additional floors, set back from the facade to preserve the view from the street.[73]

The Bulfinch statehouse, Park Street Church, and the Athenaeum were high-water marks of preservation as a movement to resist change in the urban environment. They took significant new directions, to which the movement would return later in the twentieth century. The chronological threshold for preservationist attention advanced until at the Athenaeum it encompassed not only history but preservationists' own lifetimes. Architects at Park Street and the Athenaeum continued in the roles of preservation experts and advocates that they first took at the statehouse. The Park Street preservationists embraced adaptive reuse; they cared only for the church's exterior. All three campaigns were not about historic events but about architecture and urban views—not monuments but landmarks.

A City Worthy of Permanence

When these preservationists concerned themselves with the place of landmarks in the visual structure of the city, they fit into the contemporary "City Beautiful" movement. This early advocacy of city planning grew out of a generation of concern with environmental stability; as people began to realize that constant change was not the inevitable fate of all urban fabric, the design of those portions that would not change became a more serious matter. They sought what Charles Zueblin, president of the Chicago-based American League for Civic Improvement, called an "art of permanent city making."[74]

City Beautiful proponents called for an architectural treatment of the whole city, or the largest possible pieces of it. Not merely buildings but groups of buildings, whole streets and districts, should be consciously designed as harmonious wholes in an architecture of ensemble. City Beautiful planning was Baroque planning; instead of the infinite adaptability of the grid, the city's form would embody an order and symmetry that was inherently permanent and would express the city's enduring civic and cultural structure. The City Beautiful usually wore neoclassical styles, which seemed so permanent both in their solid simplicity and in their ancient origins. Zueblin and others traced the City Beautiful to the neoclassical "White City" of the World Columbian Exposition at Chicago in 1893. Americans returned from Chicago with critical eyes for their hometowns and a new awareness of the possibilities of environmental orderliness at a large scale. William H. Wilson, in his recent study of the movement, emphasizes more complex origins, and early successes that helped create public receptivity for the White City's aesthetic. Among these were Olmsted's and Eliot's Boston park systems and the Back Bay. On Commonwealth Avenue, buildings of the greatest individual exuberance fit together harmoniously as a larger whole. Nearby Copley Square was "the best evidence of the quality of public life" in Boston, wrote Zueblin, where thirty years' assembly of cultural and religious buildings culminated in the Boston Public Library, whose 1888 design by C. F. McKim was the national debut of monumental neoclassicism.[75]

Preservation figured prominently in City Beautiful thinking. Charles Mulford Robinson, whose writings helped define the movement, listed its "architectural obligations." The first was to "save what is good from the legacies of earlier days." This obligation, he said, "takes no account of either sentiment or history," only of aesthetics, and his main example of this sort of preservation was Boston's Bulfinch statehouse.[76] But preservation was one principle among many. The statehouse fight also showed that a city worthy of permanence could be hostile to preservation when new civic ambition shone brighter than the lights of the past. If Bulfinch's old dome was not good enough, many legislators were eager to build a better version for the ages.

Clearing a park around the Bulfinch statehouse was an early example of another City Beautiful conflict between preservation and permanence: in most American cities, Baroque public spaces implied a lot of rebuilding. Boston, like most cities, shied away from massive public reconstruction of its historic core, making the City Beautiful around its edges instead. A new dam—the posthumous culmination of Charles Eliot's metropolitan park system—created the Charles River Basin, with the Esplanade on Boston's shore and the Embankment and new MIT campus on Cambridge's side; along the Fenway, the new Harvard Medical School campus seemed to Eliot's colleague Sylvester Baxter "like a fragment of the memorable White City." The White City aesthetic could be wedded with historical sensibilities by centering new public spaces on existing landmarks like the Bulfinch statehouse, but that meant demolishing other old buildings around them. In

Paris, Baron von Haussmann had called this *dégagement*—disengaging historic monuments from the urban fabric to make them more visible, as he did in the 1850s and 1860s by leveling the blocks around Notre Dame. The Boston *Real Estate Record and Building News* in 1893, the year of the Columbian Exposition, proposed new squares around the Old State House, the Old South, and Christ Church (the Old North). These landmarks would be rendered all the more visible when they were linked by new avenues, including one opening a vista of the Bulfinch statehouse. It would have required tearing down Park Street Church.[77]

These proposals and the statehouse park support historian Jon Peterson's observation that the City Beautiful took its impetus less from design professionals than from a grass-roots impulse for civic adornment. Politicians came up with the void around the capitol; the architect of the annex opposed it. As a gesture of respect for a building, clearing its neighborhood was dramatic. But the statehouse, its park, and the newly exposed buildings around it were not parts of any larger plan. The ensemble did not work. In 1899, with both the addition and the Bulfinch restoration completed, the legislature's statehouse committee published an elaborate rendering of the Bulfinch building with symmetrical wings facing the Common.[78] Wings would hide the annex and allow the Bulfinch facade once again to read as the front rather than one end of the building. The capitol was eventually expanded in this way between 1914 and 1917, by architects Robert D. Andrews and R. Clipston Sturgis, in a corrective second essay at making this landmark the focus of a larger urban composition.

An inclusive view of preservation's proper concerns was articulated by English architect Charles R. Ashbee, a leader of the Arts and Crafts Movement and a member of the governing council of Great Britain's National Trust for Places of Historic Interest and Natural Beauty. This offshoot of the Trustees of Reservations had flourished, and in the fall of 1900 it sent him in an effort to organize an "American Council" as a counterpart here. Ashbee acknowledged the Trustees of Reservations, the Metropolitan Parks Commission, and especially American Scenic as the only American organizations "working in any large way on similar lines to ours." In fourteen states throughout the East and Midwest, Ashbee found most preservation efforts dominated by patriotic societies still pursuing the old ideal of historic monuments, and he thought that the "narrowness" of their pursuits meant that "with one or two noteworthy exceptions, their energies are often at present frittered away in doing comparatively trifling things."[79]

Ashbee urged greater ambition. The unity of scenic and historic preservation, embodied in American Scenic and his own National Trust, expanded in Ashbee's lectures to a whole family of reform movements, including park and civic-improvement groups, settlement houses, and good-government organizations.[80] Most of Ashbee's turn-of-the-century audience applauded his expansive vision of preservation. City Beautiful advocates, and the Bostonians who worked to save the Common, the Bulfinch statehouse, and Park Street Church, were concerned not only about landmarks but about their context, about the whole urban environment. Their concern led beyond preservation to regulation of private development.

CHAPTER 7

❧✱❧

The Sacred Sky Line

Boston State-House is the hub of the solar system.

— OLIVER WENDELL HOLMES SR.

How should private development contribute to the permanent city? Charles R. Ashbee's first item on the agenda for an "American Council" of preservationists was to "help the architects in their fight . . . for restriction in the height of building."[1] Ashbee spoke from his own transatlantic involvement in an American effort to do just that: a drive to secure views of the Bulfinch statehouse by restricting the heights of buildings around it on Beacon Hill.

Why such concern about tall buildings? Office buildings around the Athenaeum cut off its light and seemed to increase the danger of fire.[2] Even more fundamental to City Beautiful sensibilities, Ashbee thought tall buildings threatened what little orderliness had been accomplished in American cities. The Court of Honor of the 1893 Chicago Columbian Exposition, to which City Beautiful advocates pointed as an example of the visual harmony that was possible in urban development, took its harmony in part from a uniform cornice line imposed on buildings there. In Boston, tall buildings could destroy the setting of the statehouse, increase the pressure to replace historic buildings, and mar the ensemble of South End avenues and the Back Bay district. Neither deed restrictions nor private preservation efforts held any answer to this threat, so people concerned about these places began looking to public actions, in particular to laws restricting building heights. Massachusetts passed the country's first such law in 1891, limiting new buildings in all the state's cities to 125 feet, or about eleven stories.[3] Boston enacted further restrictions that became precedents for modern American land-use and urban-design regulation through zoning.

125 Ft.

The Police Power

Building-height regulation in Boston, and thus the United States, grew indirectly out of the preservation controversy at the Bulfinch statehouse. When the state was acquiring the reservoir lot for the annex, the city's negotiator was William H. Whitmore, who had fought for and carried out the Old State House restoration; Whitmore suggested in 1887 that the state ought to restrict heights on Beacon Hill to keep new buildings from "dwarfing the [Bulfinch] state house."[4] At this time no American city had yet regulated building heights; only a few cities on the European continent had done so, mostly within recent years. Only one small German city, three years earlier, had limited heights within a particular district as Whitmore was proposing.[5] The editors of the *American Architect* reported Whitmore's "amusing suggestion" with a vigorous defense of private property rights: "We doubt if even the beauty of the Massachusetts State House is worth preserving at the expense of the rights of citizens. . . . Its dignity cannot be enhanced by assaults upon the property of its neighbors, or by compulsory humiliation inflicted upon estates near by."[6]

To the limited extent that governments tried to regulate private development, they could rely on two branches of sovereign powers. Eminent domain is the state's power to take private property for public purposes, in return paying a fair price for it. The police power is the state's right to control individual behavior in the interest of public health, safety, and welfare. In addition to these specifically governmental powers, municipalities also acted through their own property rights, disposing of public assets in the interest of steering urban growth, as in Boston's South End and Back Bay.

Eminent domain was ordinarily used—by a unit of government or by a corporation to which the power was delegated—for public works that promoted urban growth. But it did not inherently favor change. Parklands were acquired in the pursuit of landscape permanence. The Old South Association had used eminent domain, and the Park Street committee proposed using it, for preservation. The definition of "public purposes" kept expanding. By taking not land but merely easements over its use, eminent domain could even become a tool of public control over private development.

The police power would eventually evolve into the basis for most public control over land use and development. This seemingly unbounded power was initially conceived as a conservative protection of private rights from behavior that might disturb their enjoyment. All property is held subject to the requirement that it not be used to annoy or harm any other's property; the police power gives the state a role in defining these interests. It could

166

and did become a medium for activist expansion of government powers, but it still had to be balanced against private rights, and courts in the nineteenth century were inclined to give the benefit of the doubt to private property rather than public regulation. Massachusetts led in the police power's evolution because its courts deferred to the legislature as the proper judge of the need for regulation.[7] Given the need, the courts examined the appropriateness of the means. One test of the validity of police-power exercises was that they should affect equally all whose circumstances were equal; they modified the definition of all property rather than taking some of it. Where the common good imposed a burden that fell unequally on different property owners, the solution was to compensate them under eminent domain.

The most readily accepted regulations involved safety. North American towns from the earliest settlement regulated buildings to control the danger of fire, and this category came to include structural codes as well. The police power also encompassed the notion of "public nuisances," activities that could be controlled because they inherently impinged on the rights of other property owners. Municipalities long regulated the operation and location of slaughterhouses, piggeries, and stables, and in the nineteenth century they added to the list various noxious industrial processes. Housing laws were a newer branch of the police power. These regulations grew out of a new empirical understanding of sanitation and public health, starting for Massachusetts with the Tenement House Act of 1868. The term *police power* itself dates from this period of expanding regulation.[8] Each of these applications of the doctrine helped avoid the worst problems of the increasingly complex processes of urban development, making them more efficient and thus generally fostering growth. However, once the government's control over private development was established, it could be applied to curb change as easily as to encourage it.

William H. Whitmore had the police power in mind when he proposed height limits on Beacon Hill. His suggestion bore no fruit at the time but resurfaced as a more traditional police-power question, to address problems of congestion, shadows, and especially fire safety, which Bostonians took very seriously. On Thanksgiving Day, 1887, alarm box 52 once again brought news of a major fire, which destroyed the Ames Building, a modern and supposedly fire-resistant warehouse. A new Ames Building, an office block on another site, rose to 190 feet in 1889, and the city council asked the legislature for a citywide building-height limit. The first building-height restriction in the United States made its way into law as a safety measure, with no protests about property rights. "The style came to us from the new prairie cities of the West, as an imported novelty devised by speculative and enterprising people; who being without traditions, are given to the wildest experiments," wrote the editors of the *Evening Transcript*. "We are a parent colony, and are looked to to furnish a conservative example."[9]

The citywide height limit embodied no preservationist intent, but if anything the opposite: some of its advocates hoped that prohibiting skyscrapers would help spread modern fireproof construction over a larger area, eliminating old "firetraps." But in restricting building heights, Boston had created a versatile and powerful new tool, which soon looked handy for other purposes. Its recent use downtown made it naturally come to the minds of proponents of environmental permanence—eventually around the Bulfinch statehouse where it started, but first in the Back Bay.

Haddon Hall

Developer W. H. H. Newman brought the issue of height restrictions from downtown to a more sensitive location in 1895 with construction of Haddon Hall at the corner of Commonwealth Avenue and Berkeley Street, a block from the Brattle Church tower.[10] Haddon Hall was an apartment house whose nine generous stories brought it up to the 125-foot limit, but this height looked bigger among Back Bay row houses than it had downtown. Thirty-five years of public development and regulation of private construction had finally produced the large-scale Beaux Arts cityscape it was intended to, and Haddon Hall did not fit in, especially if it was to be the first example of a new pattern of development. Bostonians were disturbed at the prospect of seeing this urban ensemble lost so quickly, after waiting so long to see it completed.

The residents of one block banded together to buy a lot at the Public Garden entrance to Commonwealth Avenue, where another tall apartment house was threatened, but this answer could not work everywhere.[11] Nor did private regulation have any tools for this problem. Back Bay deed restrictions specified a minimum height—three stories—aimed at preventing temporary structures and helping to achieve the even cornice line so important to the Beaux Arts aesthetic. When the restrictions were written in 1857, there was no apparent need to specify a maximum. The Hotel Pelham was built that year on Boylston at the corner of Tremont Street, probably the nation's first "French flats" or apartment house, and at seven stories it was a tall building, but the commissioners evidently did not foresee such structures spreading to the new land. Starting in the 1870s, they did indeed spread. As Douglass Shand Tucci writes in his architectural history of Boston,

the great height of most early apartment houses (which derived, of course, from the profit motive as well as from the increasing demand for suites) was a prob-

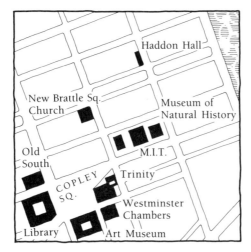

MAP 13

lem more easily solved on the inside than the outside, where such buildings seriously marred the established scale of town house streetscapes. . . . Ironically, if only the French flat fashion had caught on in Boston twenty years earlier, Commonwealth Avenue might have been a Parisian boulevard indeed; but by the time apartments were fashionable the low four-story town house had established a scale unsuitable to blocks of flats.[12]

Before Haddon Hall, the unsuitability of their scale was never quite so apparent. The most common apartment-house heights were six or seven stories; most of them occupied two or more house lots, and these squat masses were architecturally treated not unlike very big row houses or groups of row houses. Haddon Hall was a bit taller and quite a bit narrower than most, so that its proportions accentuated the vertical, and architect J. Pickering Putnam designed its facade to emphasize identical floors stacked one atop another, starkly different from the houses around it.[13]

Haddon Hall's neighbors mobilized to prevent any more such "monstrosities" from invading the district. It is tempting to look for social rather than visual causes for such visceral rhetoric, but it is difficult to support such an interpretation. The luxurious nineteenth-century apartment, according to Tucci, "early achieved social parity with the town house, to which it was comparable and in some respects superior." Apartments allowed successions of reception rooms on one floor, vital for the era's elaborate entertaining and impossible in a row house.[14]

The height-restriction campaign was carried out under the auspices of the Twentieth Century Club, a two-year-old organization that spanned the

FIGURE 7.1   *Haddon Hall, 1895, J. Pickering Putnam, architect. For the same site ten years earlier, see figure 6.7.*

whole range of progressive causes, and that later served as base for the Committee for the Preservation of Park Street Church.[15] In an effort led by George B. Upham, whose efforts to protect the Common had made him "the father of the subway," club members submitted to the 1896 legislature a bill to lower the height limit to 80 feet outside of a "high building district," where it would remain 125 feet. Building heights would be reduced in Beacon Hill, the Back Bay, and the rest of the city except downtown and the adjacent waterfront. Property owners would receive no compensation; like the original 125-foot limit, this new restriction was to be imposed under the police power.[16]

The rationale for the original height limit placed it squarely within the police power. It was a fire-safety measure, it reduced shading and congestion of the streets, and it applied equally to any building on any street in any city in Massachusetts. The police power could make spatial distinctions within a city, for example the fire limits within which wooden buildings were prohibited. Was it equally reasonable to reduce allowable building heights in the Back Bay while continuing to permit 125-foot buildings downtown? The editors of the *American Architect* thought so; unlike the Beacon Hill proposal a decade earlier, they thought, citywide districting distinguished between apartment houses and office buildings for valid reasons of public health:

Contagious diseases do not occur in office-buildings; they are vacated and aired during sixteen hours out of every twenty-four, and they are usually of solid, non-absorbent materials, scantily furnished, and well cared for. With apartment-houses the case is entirely different. . . . Commonly, the perfume from the cigar of the lodger in the sixth story, passing up through the pipe-sleeves in the floors, mingles with that of the cigarette of the occupant of the seventh story, while both together ascend freely to the eighth; and so on; the upper stories accumulating a combination of nearly all the different flavors of the house. Where the aroma of tobacco and coffee can pass, the infection of diphtheria and scarlet-fever can pass also.[17]

The real estate community in general supported the existing height restriction for its stabilizing effect on downtown land values and rents, but it was divided about this new proposal. Most real estate people did not object in principle to some further protection for residential areas; they did find fault with the particulars of Upham's plan. The Boston Real Estate Exchange, representing the largest and most established owners and brokers of both downtown and residential property, met to discuss the bill the day after the House passed it. Alexander S. Porter, who had recently stepped down as president of the exchange, thought the bill's new limits on tall buildings "would go a great deal further than was desired or necessary, and would prevent their erection along the waterfronts of South and East Boston and Charlestown, where there was a legitimate demand for high mercantile structures. The Back Bay was the portion of the city it was desired to preserve as it is." To this the exchange members had no objection, and they decided to promote an alternative bill to protect the Back Bay.[18]

Senator Charles F. Sprague of Boston, a young lawyer active in efforts to protect the Common, had introduced his own more modest and specific response to Haddon Hall. He treated it not as a citywide health or safety issue but as a local failure of deed restrictions. The Boston parks commissioners had been laying out new parkways with deed restrictions on their frontage lots limiting building heights to seventy feet. After seeing Haddon Hall, they asked for the power to impose such restrictions on existing parks and parkways such as Commonwealth Avenue. Sprague's bill allowed local parks commissions to establish building lines on lots facing parks or parkways and provided that where they did, "the extreme height to which buildings may be erected . . . shall be seventy feet, or such other height as the city council of a city or the inhabitants of a town may from time to time determine."[19] This measure relied on eminent domain; owners of height-restricted property would be eligible for compensation.

Both Sprague's eminent-domain bill and Upham's police-power bill made their way to a final vote in the Senate on the same day, April 21, 1896. The Senate passed the parks and parkways bill but at Sprague's motion tabled the districting bill; Upham and the Real Estate Exchange were now working together on an improved version. Sprague introduced it for them two weeks later, not as an amendment but as a new bill, so that the earlier version could still be enacted if the modifications were to fail. The Senate suspended its filing deadline and quickly passed the bill, but on May 14 the House rules committee refused to waive the deadline and thus killed it. The next day the secretary of the exchange—Frederic H. Viaux, a Realtor who had once sued for a commission on the preservation of Old South meetinghouse— wrote Sprague that his parks and parkways act made further action unnecessary and asked that Upham's bill be "quietly dropped."[20] Sprague, not yet aware of the House action and believing that the communication came from the exchange and Upham working together, did as requested. Upham said he was "left under the impression that I had been 'buncoed' by the Real Estate Exchange." Through this idiosyncratic process Massachusetts chose to pursue height districting of cities through eminent domain rather than the police power.[21]

The parks commission promptly imposed a seventy-foot limit on Commonwealth Avenue. This was the only place the commissioners applied the act; the city's use of this potentially systematic tool was still reactive. No one sought damages for these height restrictions.[22] Back Bay owners generally agreed that this was a reasonable limitation that unfortunately had been omitted from their deed restrictions, but their unanimity may have had a more prosaic explanation. Haddon Hall opened in the midst of a depression and at first paid no dividends, and owners would have had a hard time demonstrating damages from losing the right to duplicate an unprofitable building.[23] They may also have been confused. There was no precedent for taking air rights through eminent domain, but plenty of precedent for deed restrictions. Restrictions on Commonwealth Avenue originated with the state, and it would have been easy for owners to think of the new limit as a welcome addition to their deed covenants, without inquiring too closely how such an addition was possible.

Classifying this act as a parks measure was no mere rhetoric but a reflection of how Bostonians saw the issue. Haddon Hall's offensiveness came at least partly from Commonwealth Avenue's sanctity as a link in the "emerald necklace." The city had about completed the park system and was beginning to create its even more ambitious metropolitan parks. The emergence of City Beautiful aesthetics put a higher value than ever on harmonious development to make parks part of a larger urban ensemble. These sensibilities would lead to other measures to protect parks, and they would also soon produce Boston's biggest building-height controversy.

Westminster Chambers

When Trinity Church, the new Old South, and the Second Church relocated to Copley Square and the new Museum of Fine Arts located there, all in the 1870s, the square began to emerge as Boston's new institutional focus, an early, spontaneously originated prototype for the civic centers that the City Beautiful movement later advocated for other cities. Within a block or so were the Massachusetts Institute of Technology, Harvard Medical School, and the Museum of Natural History. Copley Square began as a grouping of separate buildings each individually designed to endure. These buildings, reflecting the period in which they were made, exhibited the greatest variety and exuberance of styles rather than the City Beautiful's ideal of unity, but C. F. McKim unified the composition with his Boston Public Library. The library, as ambitious in its programs as in its architecture, consolidated Copley Square as the cultural heart of the city in a way no other institution could have done. "Copley Square is at present, and is always likely to remain the intellectual and artistic centre of Boston, so far as this can be topographically expressed," said the *American Architect* in 1893.[24] Bostonians became newly and keenly aware of this place as an emblem of their city at the same time that the City Beautiful was giving them a new standard for evaluating such places, a standard that judged whole ensembles of buildings as architectural compositions. The library spatially redefined Copley Square's composition with a new emphasis on discipline and horizontal lines.

With the exception of the Museum of Fine Arts, each of the institutions facing the square felt that it had been forced out of downtown during the past generation, and was thus deeply sensitive to issues of neighborhood change. They intended to make their new locations permanent, to fight change rather than submit to it this time, an attitude evidenced not only in the enormous investments they made in their buildings but also in the activist posture they took toward protecting their new setting. The Old South Church, for example, bought several adjacent lots and resold them with deed restrictions limiting building height to four stories.[25]

This sensitivity was soon challenged by Westminster Chambers, Boston's next tall apartment building, which began construction in August 1897 at the southeast corner of Copley Square. Restriction of heights on Commonwealth Avenue the previous year meant that any new tall apartment buildings would have to be located elsewhere, and Copley Square, long an apartment district, was perhaps the next most desirable address. Westminster Chambers was planned as a ten-story building to rise 120 feet directly across the street from Trinity Church and the Museum of Fine Arts. Like Haddon Hall, Westminster Chambers did not fit; one critic invoked the square's symbolism of art, religion, and education to condemn this addition "representing Wealth, and looking down upon all the others."[26] The challenge was addressed more quickly here than on Commonwealth Avenue, thanks to momentum from that victory together with Copley Square's visual and symbolic prominence. The existing organizational framework of its institutions made for a rapid response, the first height-restriction effort to be directed at a building while it was still under construction, giving the Westminster Chambers fight a bitterness reminiscent of the Old South. Westminster Chambers took on lasting significance as the first case to bring height restrictions before a state supreme court, and ultimately to the U.S. Supreme Court. The case confirmed the precedent of restricting building heights through eminent domain but also established that such restrictions could involve real, substantial damages.

Public outcry against Westminster Chambers arose as soon as people learned how tall it was to be. An ad hoc committee of opponents organized in mid-October, headed by Frederick O. Prince, president of the library trustees and former mayor. Just as height restrictions on Commonwealth Avenue were meant to protect the city's investment in parks, on Copley Square these people sought to protect an enormous public and quasi-public investment both in cultural facilities and in urban design. The Boston Society of Architects offered the opinion that eighty feet was the tallest buildings could rise before they would destroy the square's proportions. As the citizens' committee asked, "Shall all that has been done to make [Boston's] chief square beautiful go for nothing?" [27]

Could Copley Square be protected through the existing Parks and Parkways Act? The act's applicability was at best debatable, because the square had not been formally dedicated as a park, and in any case the parks commissioners had not designated a building line there. However, the building-line mechanism was not well understood; many people thought the act by itself had restricted heights around all parks, and even the parks commissioners seemed confused as to whether they had established lines applying only to Commonwealth Avenue or to parks throughout the city. The city council and parks commission could have cleared up all these questions by taking new action to invoke the act, but this course was unattractive for several reasons. City officials knew that interfering with a building after its construction had begun would expose the city to liability for heavy damages; the project's opponents, on the other hand, believed that the restrictions were already in effect and did not want to initiate any action that would call them into question. This combination of fiscal constraints and legal ambiguities led the citizens' committee to seek fresh legislation. Only after new Copley Square height restrictions were before the legislature did the parks commissioners, on January 29, 1898, warn Westminster Chambers' owners that their property was subject to a seventy-foot limit.[28] Two months later the city filed suit to enforce this limit, but as the city law office quickly accepted a verbal assurance that the developers would not build above seventy feet before the legislature took final action, the suit seems to have aimed less at limiting the building's height than at limiting the city's potential liability.

The Westminster syndicate gave an early indication of just how much this liability might be when, as construction began, they offered to reduce the project's height by two or three stories for the price of $75,000 per floor.[29] This proposal, which opponents ridiculed as a "purchase of imaginary lines in the sky," may have been the first attempt to set a value on air rights established through public regulation, but it was taken at the time as mere impertinence.[30] Confusion over the Parks and Parkways Act led to an impression that the Westminster syndicate was flouting the law, and the syndicate's own actions contributed to the atmosphere of confrontation. Westminster Chambers' walls would block light from MIT's engineering studios next door; the developers offered to face that side of their building with light-reflecting bricks, but only in return for concessions from the institute. Henry B. Williams, who headed the syndicate, was Boston's third largest landowner, and some of his opponents remembered him in a similarly provocative role fifteen years earlier. On one of his three hotels, the Kensington, he built projecting windows in violation of Back Bay deed restrictions and then twice fought all the way to the state supreme court before he was finally forced to remove them.[31] The Westminster syndicate in Copley Square looked to many Bostonians like Mammon-worshiping barbarians in the civic temple; debate started out polarized and stayed that way.

When legislators convened in January, the Westminster's opponents presented nearly three thousand signatures from all over Massachusetts asking them to prevent what one of their lawyers called "this new Haddon Hall." By then the building's foundations were in the ground and its steel was beginning to rise. The Boston Public Library led the effort, represented by Col. J. H. Benton Jr., a library trustee whom legislators more often saw as a railroad corporation lawyer. Benton was assisted by Samuel J. Elder, representing MIT and the Museum of Fine Arts. The petition's signers owned an aggregate of $100 million worth of property, according to Benton; thus, as Elder pointed out, "no body of men in this community has more personal interest to safeguard the rights of property than have these petitioners."[32]

Yet these solid citizens asked for restrictions under the police power, without compensation, and among the petitioners was Charles F. Sprague, who had been responsible for sending Boston's height restrictions off in the direction of eminent domain. Their bill would impose an eighty-foot height limit on all property within five hundred feet of Copley Square.[33] The bill's opponents mostly raised questions of fairness. "Many owners of the property threatened by this measure are in the fullest sympathy with the spirit of preserving and adding to the beauty of Copley Square," wrote D. Webster King, who had considered building his own tall apartment house on the north side of the square, "but feel that they should not be immolated on the altars of sentiment or aesthetic beauty on account of their ownership of estates within five hundred feet of that square."[34] A group of these owners protested the bill but said they would have no objection if its eighty-foot limit were applied to the whole city. The Westminster Chambers owners engaged as their representative former state attorney general Albert E. Pillsbury, who argued that if the property were to be restricted at all, it would have to be under eminent domain with provision for compensation. The petitioners agreed to the insertion of a compensation clause, not to protect property rights on the restricted lots but to protect the act itself from being voided if found unconstitutional. Benton argued for a hybrid act that would provide for compensation only if it were judged invalid as an exercise of the police power: "Leave this question of the right to damages, where it belongs, with the Courts."[35]

The legislature disagreed and on May 23 gave final passage to Copley

Square height restrictions that unambiguously offered compensation both for the restrictions in the abstract and for changes to the one building in the area "the construction whereof was begun but not completed." The act applied only to buildings fronting on the square, setting limits of ninety feet on its south and west sides, including Westminster Chambers, and one hundred feet on the north side. At the developers' request, the act specifically exempted Copley Square from the Parks and Parkways Act and its seventy-foot restriction.[36] This was a more or less necessary corollary of the new limits, but it meant that the earlier act's applicability would never be decided, and it allowed the Westminster's opponents to go on believing that the building had been illegal from its inception. The new act allowed above the limits "such steeples, towers, domes, sculptured ornaments and chimneys as the board of park commissioners of said city may approve."[37] Although the restrictions were imposed by the state, damages were to be paid by the city of Boston.

On the day the act passed, seven stories of Westminster Chambers' steel framework stood completed, with three more stories sitting on the ground awaiting assembly. The developers had their architect prepare drawings of various alternatives for the building's completion—including a nine-story version which could not possibly have complied with the limit—and met with Mayor Josiah Quincy and city officials to consider their options. It was possible to build an eighth story and roof within ninety feet, but not the eighth story and roof that had already been fabricated, nor would the lower building have room for the elaborate terra-cotta frieze and cornice that had been produced to cap it. This was, in effect, the city's problem, as the act made it responsible for "the actual cost or expense of any re-arrangement of the design or construction" of the building. The mayor resented this legislative raid on municipal coffers and later challenged its constitutionality, but meanwhile he sought to minimize the "re-arrangements" for which the city might have to pay. The city's lawyers believed they had considerable latitude in interpreting the act, since enforcement of Boston's building laws had recently been put in the hands of the city rather than the state.[38] They agreed to a compromise: the building's eight stories would be built up to the ninety-foot limit, where its frieze and cornice would begin, with the roof behind them, rising to ninety-six feet under a permit from the parks commission as "sculptured ornaments." The parks commissioners at first declined to follow this script, instead sending the developers' plans back with a sketch suggesting how the building might be finished within the limit, at seven stories rather than eight. The developers, relying on their arrangement with the city, continued construction.

If all concerned were seeking a reasonable compromise, there was probably no better one available. But few people other than the mayor were interested in compromise. Many of Copley Square's defenders were disturbed even by the prospect of a ninety-foot building there; the first witness at the hearings had suggested a limit of forty-five feet.[39] The syndicate had tried to get the bill's limit amended to ninety-six feet, and the legislature refused. The city thus appeared to be conniving with the developers in a clear violation of the law, an impression that deepened in the coming months. Though Boston's municipal government during this period was a model of probity compared with the corruption in many other big cities, the growth of machine politics and patronage led people to interpret its actions in the worst light and led the legislature in Massachusetts as elsewhere to circumscribe municipal prerogatives at every turn, a pattern that the Copley Square height restrictions clearly fit. As soon as the developers' intentions were rumored, the art museum's trustees pressed Massachusetts attorney general Hosea M. Knowlton to sue. The city forestalled this action by filing its own suit and then let prosecution lapse while the contractors rushed to complete the building. The attorney general, concluding that enforcement by the city was no enforcement at all, authorized the museum to bring suit in his name. The parks commissioners, under new pressure from the city administration, retroactively approved the frieze and cornice on October 31, 1898. A year later, Massachusetts Supreme Judicial Court justice Marcus P. Knowlton—only a distant relation to the attorney general[40]—handed down the decision in *Attorney General v. Williams*: Westminster Chambers was six feet too tall.

The most important result of this decision was to establish the constitutionality of height restrictions. "The right to make such regulations is too well established to be questioned," claimed Justice Knowlton.[41] In fact, this was the first time any state supreme court had considered the question. The right was "established" only by eight years of unchallenged operation in Boston, and by more recent regulations in Chicago (1893) and Washington, D.C. (1894), neither of them tested yet in the courts. Precedents cited in the decision all involved more limited powers, concerning particular types of building or types of construction.

The Westminster case itself now moved back to the legislature, where the syndicate recast it as a campaign for relief of the city and "preservation" of the building's terra-cotta top. "Lawful or unlawful," wrote two of the partners, "it is not in the public interest to pull down the frieze and cornice, which is the only effect of this suit, and leave the building, as it will then be left, an object of public reproach and an injury to every building in Copley square."[42] The partners repeatedly stated their intention not to mend the appearance of the building in any way if they were forced to remove the terra-cotta work. "Do you suppose," asked Pillsbury, that the owners "will spend

FIGURE 7.2 *Westminster Chambers, 1899. On the left is Trinity Church; on the right, the Museum of Fine Arts. Society for the Preservation of New England Antiquities*

another $50,000, in addition to all they have lost, to put back the ornaments upon that building, to please the very people who have pulled them off? Never. It is not in human nature to do it. If these fanatics pull off the top of the building, they shall take the responsibility and the consequences."[43]

The legislators of 1900 at first rejected the developers' appeal but reversed their vote a day later, a conversion that the *Boston Herald* insinuated was a product of outright bribery. Governor W. Murray Crane vetoed the act. "In my opinion the vital point involved is not the appearance of the building," he said, "but it is rather whether the law may be violated only to be excused or condoned."[44] The Westminster owners returned to the legislature in 1901, 1902, and 1903, and two successive mayors of Boston and a large portion of the city's real estate community argued on their behalf that the case had become silly and vindictive. The "Copley Square Protective Committee" opposed them each year, invoking Crane's veto by arguing that Westminster Chambers was "not a question of Aesthetics, but of Law and Order."[45] Williams's Hotel Kensington, according to attorney Edmund A. Whitman, "was a monument to Massachusetts law, and the Westminster Chambers will be another."[46] Whatever legislators thought of the merits of the case, it was hard for them to find any political benefits in what their constituents would see as the rescue of a rogue real estate syndicate and its accessory before the fact, the Boston city government.

It was mainly the city that needed relief. Under the act the city would pay the cost of changing from a ten- to an eight-story building during construction; it would pay the additional costs that would have been saved if the building had been designed from the beginning to be eight stories tall. It would pay the developers for the two floors' worth of rent they lost, and on top of all this it would pay the enormous cost of lowering the roof of an occupied residential building. "If the city authorities have blundered in their interpretation of the law," said Williams, "why should they not be the sufferers?" Even before the decision the syndicate had filed suit for damages, but the municipal administration claimed that the act was unconstitutional and the city therefore exempt from liability. The prospect of being caught without anyone responsible for compensation must have been an important motivation in the owners' continuing search for legislative relief. Williams returned to the state supreme court arguing that they should not be made to take any action until some source of compensation was guaranteed. In March 1901 the court rebuffed him and ordered the building cut down to ninety feet. This was the decision he appealed to the U.S. Supreme Court, which in February 1903 upheld it and sent it back for the Massachusetts courts to work out the details of compliance and compensation.[47]

An owner of property on the north side of the square, Mollie R. Cole, had sued for compensation even before Williams did. The Superior Court's opinion in *Cole v. City* set a short-lived precedent strongly favorable to this use of eminent domain. A jury decided that Cole was not entitled to any compensation; the height restriction if anything increased the value of her midblock lot by preventing tall buildings overshadowing it. This precedent was reduced in scope, however, before the Westminster Chambers damages finally came to trial; corner lots were less subject to overshadowing, and their owners won compensation, including $17,000—more than the original price of the land—for D. Webster King, who was not immolated on the altar of aesthetics after all.[48]

After the initial state supreme court decision in *Attorney General v. Williams,* the Museum of Fine Arts withdrew from the case, because its trustees had decided to abandon Copley Square. This was Westminster Chambers' most far-reaching effect on its neighborhood. Although, in the trustees' words, they had "regarded the location on Copley Square as an ideal one and likely to remain the permanent home of the Museum," within months of Westminster Chambers' completion, and even as they were prosecuting its owners, they began to consider relocating. The museum was the only one of the square's institutions that had not moved before and apparently had not developed a corporate instinct to stand its ground. But it acted with a view to prospective permanence, buying the following year twelve acres on the Fenway that the museum's trustees found "sufficient for its needs for centuries to come."[49]

The museum's relocation was to be financed by selling its Copley Square property. Before the trustees announced their intention of leaving, they secured from the city the release of a restriction on the original grant of the property that limited its use to "promotion of the Fine Arts." When city council members learned of the museum's plans, they made an abortive attempt to rescind their release.[50] Though the museum remained for several years, Copley Square's magic as a civic center was finished. The trustees signed an agreement of sale with a group of real estate developers in time for Westminster Chambers' final appeal to the legislature in 1903. That year the Westminster owners put their relief petition in the form of a bill to raise the height limit to a uniform one hundred feet all around the square, arguing that the museum's departure would remove the logic for lower heights on its south side. Business and real estate people predicted that Copley Square would become a new downtown and therefore needed tall business buildings; the museum's purchasers agreed.[51] The museum's departure, however, worked in another way against relaxing the restriction. The trustees had allowed a three-year statutory limit to lapse without seeking compensation for the height restriction on their own property and had sold it subject to the ninety-foot limit. An increase in that limit would be a valuable gift from the legislature, and it seemed inappropriate to bestow such a gift upon a development syndicate instead of the museum, especially if the developers had cynically anticipated the increase all along.

The legislature let the restrictions stand, and in August 1903, contractors began the work of lowering the roof of Westminster Chambers. Charles Zueblin hailed this as a triumph of City Beautiful discipline. As the owners had warned all along, they made no effort to finish the truncated building. The city of Boston eventually paid them almost $350,000 in damages.[52] Ironically, the site is now occupied by the John Hancock Tower (1975), the tallest building in Boston, exactly seven hundred feet taller than the predecessor that the city paid so much to shorten.

In the Back Bay, publicly imposed height restrictions were used in a relatively new neighborhood to supplement deed restrictions in stabilizing the physical environment. While the Copley Square restrictions were new, before their drawbacks became apparent, the technique spread to yet another area experiencing a similar invasion of out-of-scale buildings. Preservationists took a legal tool that was handy thanks to the efforts in the Back Bay and brought it to Beacon Hill, where it had first been discussed. On Beacon Hill it was an extension not of deed restrictions but of a preservation effort.

Beacon Hill

By the beginning of 1899 the Bulfinch statehouse had been saved, its restoration completed under the direction of the committee appointed by Governor Roger Wolcott. The widespread interest in the building now took on a momentum of its own, traveling along a channel already marked by the Back Bay building-height controversies. Governor Wolcott in his 1899 address to the legislature called for Beacon Hill height restrictions to give the statehouse similar "protection."[53] Height restrictions, thus far enacted to preserve the visual character of a neighborhood and to make permanent the settings of some comparatively new buildings in it, were now invoked as a corollary of preserving one historic structure. The logic of using them there sheds light on why the building was valued and preserved: as an icon important not merely for itself but in its visual relationship with the rest of the city.

The icon was not so much the whole statehouse as its dome. Oliver Wendell Holmes Sr. described its place in a Boston cosmology, and by a synecdochic representation of the whole by a part, the city became known as "The Hub." "As the crowning and most conspicuous edifice of this city," wrote the 1867 statehouse commissioners,

its dome has always been the most noticeable feature of Boston in any distant view of this metropolis. Its happy adaptation to the position which it occupies, and its highly impressive outline, in such just and harmonious proportion to the mass of roofs around it, have made it through many years the familiar and recognized land-mark of the city. Its overshadowing presence has always conferred an unmistakable character upon Boston and constituted a marked and peculiarly striking feature, towards which the eye of every son of Massachusetts, in approaching her capitol, turns always, with instant recognition.[54]

Unfortunately for the harmonious proportion of distant views, neither the dome, the statehouse, nor the hill on which it stood was especially tall. Engravings usually exaggerated the dome's size, but an examination of contemporary photographs shows that its "instant recognition" had more to do with familiarity than with visual dominance. "With the great extension of

FIGURE 7.3 *Removing the cornice from Westminster Chambers (detail), 1903.*
Society for the Preservation of New England Antiquities

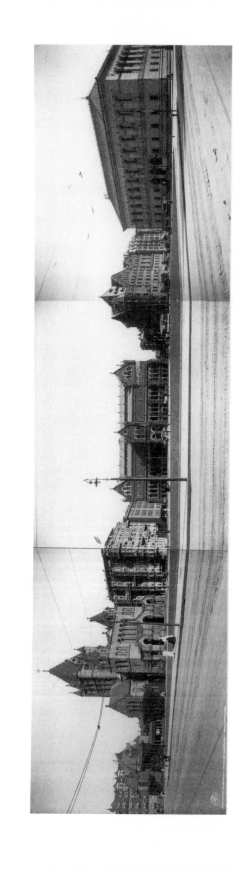

the city, however, within the past few years," the commissioners pointed out in 1867, "and the erection of other and loftier structures in its neighborhood, the dome now hardly maintains its relative importance as to height and mass, in comparison with the rest of the city, which it possessed at the time of its erection."[55]

Their answer was a taller dome: 268 feet tall, in Bryant and Estey's design for a new building, compared with Bulfinch's 120 feet. If the Bulfinch building were to be kept instead, they would at least raise the existing dome by inserting a colonnade under it, and they believed this so "indispensable" that they included it even in their Plan No. 1, the budget alternative that addressed only "the most pressing wants" of the building.[56] When the legislature took a more parsimonious view, it sought to achieve the same visual prominence instead by painting the dome gold, and then in 1874 by covering it with gold leaf.[57]

By the 1880s, growing preservationist sentiment suggested that the problem of the relationship between the dome and its surroundings should be treated not by changing the dome but by controlling change in the surroundings. The "most imminent danger" to the statehouse, wrote the *Evening Transcript* editors in 1886, was

being dwarfed by high adjacent buildings on either side on Beacon Street. Already the great hotel on the corner of Joy street hides the State House dome from the Back Bay section, and should elevated structures also be erected on the corner of Hancock avenue and upon the lot bordered by Mt. Vernon, Beacon and Bowdoin streets, . . . the grand effect which the Capitol now possesses would be entirely nullified, and the historical landmark would have lost its chief claim for preservation.[58]

In this pre-height-restriction year, the *Evening Transcript* endorsed a proposal that the state buy up these critical blocks, to build a low government office building on the downtown side and simply to hold the buildings on the other side so that "the land could not be built upon in a manner to injure the appearance or outlook of the State House." Indeed, the legislative committee that first recommended expanding the building contemplated purchasing land "either for use or protective control." Governor Ames's plan for the capitol, announced in January 1887, included acquisition of all the property facing the statehouse grounds east and west, "to protect the State House from the danger of injury to its present outlook and appearance by the erection of lofty structures."[59]

FIGURE 7.4 *Copley Square panorama—after. Photographed by Henry Peabody. Society for the Preservation of New England Antiquities*

FIGURE 7.5 (TOP) *Statehouse dome as icon, 1854. Society for the Preservation of New England Antiquities*

FIGURE 7.6 (BOTTOM) *The statehouse dome in the skyline, c. 1874. Society for the Preservation of New England Antiquities*

Shortly thereafter, former city council president William H. Whitmore made his suggestion that the state might accomplish this same end by a law restricting building heights. The *Boston Journal* endorsed the recommendation because its editors feared that this purpose would otherwise result in overly ambitious schemes of land acquisition.[60] Such land acquisition might be fiscally alarming, but it also troubled preservationists such as Whitmore because it could be the first step in solving the height problem with a new, bigger statehouse. Thus four years before height restrictions were enacted anywhere in the country, and eight months before the Thanksgiving Day fire brought attention to them for reasons of public safety, they had already entered public discourse with a preservationist rationale. During the decade between this proposal and Governor Wolcott's 1899 speech, the Bulfinch statehouse had been saved without the use of building-height restrictions, and Boston had adopted them in other places, by various means, for various ends.

The issue arose again in 1899 because of two new tall buildings under construction on Beacon Street, the Hotel Bellevue and the Women's Club. The governor's call for height restrictions that year followed logically from the decision to preserve and restore the statehouse. The state's efforts to make permanent the Bulfinch capitol would be incomplete, even pointless, if they did not also secure the view of its dome upon the hill. As on Commonwealth Avenue and Copley Square, height restrictions would protect a public investment and a civic icon. The fight to save the statehouse from decay and from the legislature now became a fight to save it from its changing neighborhood, and the same people fought both. They included Governor Roger Wolcott, former state senator Alfred Seelye Roe, and the many chapters of the Daughters of the American Revolution that helped make the earlier campaign a statewide one and started this one off the same way with a massive petition drive.[61]

George B. Upham, who had tried for the previous three years to get the legislature to lower heights in residential districts, represented the petitioners for Beacon Hill height restrictions. The old solution to the problem of tall buildings around the statehouse was to buy the neighboring property, but now there appeared to be several less expensive alternatives. Upham still argued, as Benton had at Copley Square, that a height district could be imposed at no cost under the police power. Even under eminent domain it seemed possible that a restriction might cost little or nothing; the Westminster damages were still years in the future, and only Mollie Cole's ultimately fruitless pursuit of compensation had come before a court. Upham's bill provided for compensation but did not use ordinary eminent-domain language and evidently was intended like Benton's Copley Square bill to provide pay-

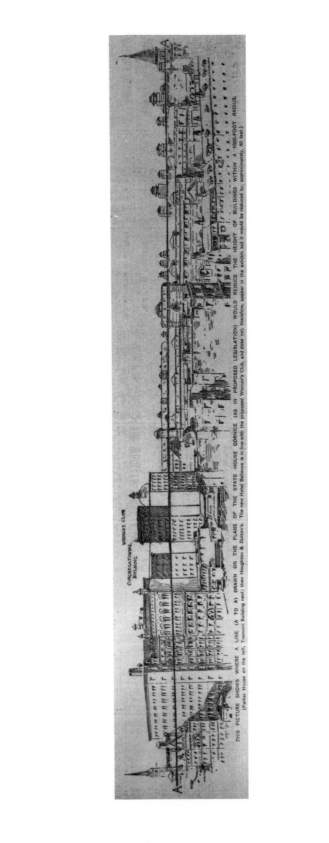

CONGREGATIONAL BUILDING

WOMAN'S CLUB

THIS PICTURE SHOWS WHERE A LINE (A TO A) DRAWN ON THE PLANE OF THE STATE HOUSE CORNICE (AS IN PROPOSED LEGISLATION) WOULD REDUCE THE HEIGHT OF BUILDINGS WITHIN A 100-FOOT RADIUS. (Parker House on the left, Tremont Building next; then Houghton & Dutton's. The new Hotel Bellevue is in line with the proposed Woman's Club, and does not, therefore, appear in the exhibit, but it would be reduced by approximately, 40 feet.)

ment only if it were thrown out as an exercise of the police power. Future U.S. Supreme Court justice Louis Brandeis, among others, assured legislators that no compensation would be necessary.[62]

Though the bill's legal rationale was murky, its design intent was clear. All buildings within a thousand feet of the statehouse would be limited to the height of "the main cornice of the Bulfinch front of the state house."[63] This language made explicit the bill's aesthetic purpose of maintaining the dome's visibility; its proponents made no attempt to cloak it in traditional police-power concerns of health and safety. At the same time, the bill avoided the arbitrary boundaries that had thus far worked against height districting under the police power. A thousand feet from the statehouse in almost every direction, the ground falls away to more than 125 feet beneath the cornice, so buildings there could be built to the existing limit, which simply would no longer follow the topography up Beacon Hill. Buildings would conform to an absolute height limit rather than one relative to the ground; no tall building could look down on its neighbors across a legislated line. This new flat ceiling as first written would have reduced allowable heights on several valuable downtown blocks, but Upham quickly retreated from this direction.

Many members of the Women's Club petitioned for the restriction, but the Women's Club House corporation retained former attorney general Pillsbury, Westminster Chambers' lawyer, to oppose the bill. Pillsbury argued that the bill's aesthetic purpose made it unconstitutional whether or not it claimed to be an exercise of the police power. "Powers of eminent domain can be extended only to public uses," he said. "To prevent interference with a view of the State House is not a public use."[64]

The Hotel Bellevue syndicate opposed the bill through its trustee, William Minot, a lawyer who controlled more Boston real estate than any other individual. Minot was a staunch supporter of height restrictions in general. As a member of Boston's building-code commission in 1892, he was responsible for making the limit more stringent on narrow streets, and more recently his support had been influential in passing the Copley Square restrictions. Now he explained why he thought the Beacon Hill proposal was a bad idea.

Copley Square, said Minot, was "unique. . . . It has been mistaken for a precedent, and as a precedent it is certainly dangerous." He drew a distinction between the design intent of the Copley Square restrictions and those proposed for Beacon Hill. The goal at Copley Square "was to preserve the whole of it, to be seen upon the spot"; regulation of private buildings was essential because they were part of the composition. On Beacon Hill no such

FIGURE 7.7 *The statehouse cornice height mapped onto nearby buildings,* Boston *Herald, March 16, 1899. Boston Public Library*

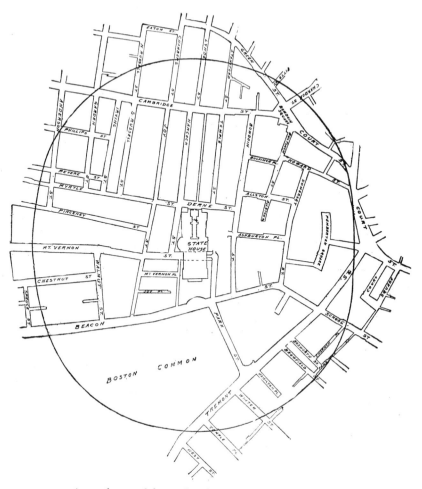

FIGURE 7.8   *A one-thousand-foot radius from the statehouse,* Boston Herald, *March 16, 1899. Boston Public Library*

composition existed; the whole was being made subordinate to one part of one building, for the aesthetically ill-defined aim of maintaining its visibility from all directions, some of which in fact had good views and some of which were already obstructed. This difference in design intent could be expressed as a public-policy question in quantitative terms: at Copley Square the property benefited was worth ten times as much as the property restricted; on Beacon Hill the ratio was reversed.[65]

William Minot was sympathetic with the goal of protecting and enhancing the Bulfinch statehouse, but he felt that the bill's sponsors were using it as an "excuse." "These petitioners," he said, "as represented by Mr. Upham, are not interested in the preservation of the statehouse; they are only interested in the restriction of the height of buildings." Ironically, Minot advocated Upham's original, now abandoned approach, a general lowering of the height limit in all the city's residential areas; he even thought, harking to the private medium of deed restrictions, that "in large sections of the city it might be accomplished by obtaining the actual consent of every owner."[66]

Minot saw confusion or irresponsibility in discussing air rights. "There seems to be a vague sort of feeling," he said, that "taking away the right to build to the height allowed by law is not really sequestration of property, but simply the enforcement of a rule which will not entitle the owners to damages." "What is to be taken does not seem like a real thing," he said, offering a not entirely parallel example to explain it: "The hotel Tudor, on the corner of Beacon and Joy [Streets], is an eyesore, which has caused universal complaint. It obscures a view of the statehouse. If it were proposed to remove the upper stories of the hotel Tudor for the purpose of giving a view of the dome, you would not do it. You would be destroying actual property for a purely aesthetic purpose, and you would think it wasteful."[67]

The Committee on Cities sent the bill to the legislature with a negative recommendation. Rather than letting the project die, Representative William Schofield of Malden substituted on the House floor a more limited restriction that applied only to the two blocks immediately west of the statehouse. Unlike the original proposal with its cornice-line datum, the new version specified a seventy-foot height measured at each property. Schofield intimated that no compensation would be required because the affected owners were "practically all in favor" of the limit.[68] The two blocks did not include either of the buildings under construction that had raised the issue, so the state in any case spared itself the ordeal to which it had subjected the city at Westminster Chambers.[69]

A competing idea of public action to "protect" the statehouse was to clear buildings and extend the park around it. Compared with demolition schemes, building-height restrictions were unsatisfyingly passive; they did not appeal to the legislature's men of action. Limiting building height would at best keep Beacon Hill as it was. Clearing, these people believed, would improve it; they were still looking for material progress. They also realized that height restrictions would offer little for them to show their constituents what the state had spent money on. Minot, ignoring his own lecture about the reality of air rights, recommended that the legislature protect the statehouse by taking abutting land outright, so that the state "will obtain an actual asset for its money." The statehouse's longtime friends thought this idea at best misguided. Clearing a park without imposing height restrictions, said statehouse preservation committee member William W. Vaughan—who was also

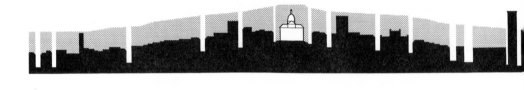

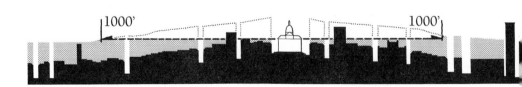

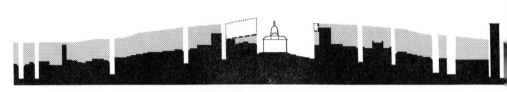

FIGURE 7.9   Top panel: *Beacon Hill in 1899; vertical dimension exaggerated 2:1. A block from the statehouse dome, to the left, is the Hotel Tudor. A block to the right the Hotel Bellevue is under construction. At far right is the 190-foot Ames Building, tallest in Boston; shading shows the heights allowable under the 125-foot limit it inspired.* Center: *George B. Upham's proposal, limiting buildings within one thousand feet of the Bulfinch statehouse to the height of its main cornice. Topography makes the limit most stringent nearest the statehouse.* Bottom: *The Beacon Hill height restrictions as adopted. Adjacent to the statehouse, on the left, is the seventy-foot limit of 1899. To the right, across the new park, is the one-hundred-foot limit of 1901, applying only to the front of each lot. Distant views of the dome remain in jeopardy.* Drawing by author

busy fighting Westminster Chambers—would be an invitation for construction of tall apartment buildings around it.[70] A pragmatic reason for taking land around the statehouse was the commonwealth's need for more office space; proponents argued that the land should be acquired before it came to be occupied by expensive new structures. Schofield's height-restriction bill prevented expensive new buildings that could complicate future statehouse expansion while deferring the cost of acquiring property until such time, if ever, as the state was ready to use it. It created a land bank with the land remaining in private hands.

The legislature in 1899 adopted Schofield's bill as a compromise response to demands for a statehouse park and for Beacon Hill height limits. Because his restrictions applied only to one side of the statehouse, they left unsatisfied not only the reformers like Upham with ambitions for protecting large areas of the city but even those preservationists concerned only about buildings directly fronting the statehouse. They continued pressing their case and were rewarded in 1901 with an extension of the height restriction, in an even more narrowly drawn area. As part of the final scheme for laying out the park east of the statehouse—the blocks that had been bought early in the 1890s—the legislature imposed a one-hundred-foot height limit on the blocks fronting this park. The restriction did not apply to the whole of the property, however, but only to the front forty-two feet of each lot. Thus this act sought to preserve not distant views of the dome but the appearance of the statehouse and its park as seen on the spot.[71]

*T*hough the Beacon Hill restrictions as enacted were much less ambitious than Upham had proposed, they once again expanded the portion of the city that was taken as permanently settled. Copley Square was, as William Minot said, a special case; so were parks and parkways, and so was Beacon Hill. Much of Boston was special, and Bostonians were willing to use public powers to keep it that way.

PART III

CONTROL

CHAPTER 8

❧❦❧

The Limits of Permanence

Just as the literary class in China ruinously opposes change of any kind,
so there is with us a comparatively small, but influential, body of refined
persons . . . who most unfortunately, though unintentionally, assist in
the triumphs of ugliness by blindly opposing all attempts to adapt
land and landscape to changed or new requirements.

— CHARLES ELIOT

By the turn of the century, Americans had succeeded in many of their efforts
to freeze environmental change. The post–Civil War generation set aside
parks, historic landmarks, and neighborhoods legally protected forever. But
intentions of permanence had to be reaffirmed by continuing care. The next
generation of Bostonians did keep nearly everything that had been saved for
them, though looking after buildings, landscapes, and neighborhoods required a great deal of effort and sometimes required further choices about
issues that had once seemed settled.

Managing the Permanent Landscape

Preservation was often thought of as a discrete act, like plucking a drowning
swimmer from the water, but in practice it was an ongoing activity. The Old
South Church, like the Common, like anything saved, needed to be maintained.[1] Each needed to be defended from new threats, over and over again.
The price of permanence was eternal vigilance. The keepers of landscapes
discovered faster and more thoroughly than others how constant their care
would have to be. As any farmer or gardener knows, human landscapes do
not maintain themselves.

At Mount Auburn Cemetery, trustees before the Civil War turned their attention from laying out the grounds to setting up the financial mechanisms
for permanent maintenance. In the 1870s they began selling plots endowed
for "perpetual care," and by the turn of the century perpetual care had be-

197

come the norm for American cemeteries, shifting emphasis from the landscape's form to practical arrangements for its permanence.[2]

From the very beginning the new landscape of parks brought new issues of management. Parks commissioners, wrote Frederick Law Olmsted, had two duties: "first, that of forming parks; second, that of keeping them. . . . The second is the graver responsibility." Keeping parks required not only physical but social maintenance. Olmsted said that his most important role in creating Central Park was organizing a police force of "park keepers" who instructed New Yorkers in the appropriate use of their new pleasure ground. "Public reservations are worse than useless," Charles Eliot wrote later, "if they are not as carefully controlled as they are wisely developed."[3] Even wilderness required protection from poachers and squatters. For the national parks, protection was initially provided by the U.S. Army.

In Boston, Olmsted designed Franklin and Jamaica Parks to make only modest changes in the existing landscape, yet some Bostonians found even those limited alterations a betrayal of the parks' underlying preservationist purpose. Many of the changes stabilized ground and vegetation to make permanence workable. In 1894 Eliot responded to a complaint about preparatory work in the new metropolitan parks: "Experience has shown the impracticality of leaving such public reservations as that at Waverley in their original condition, after the public begins to resort to them in any considerable numbers. . . . To preserve the attractiveness of much frequented places, some of the lesser elements of attractiveness must be sacrificed." Parkland acquisition often left sites idle for years, reinforcing the misperception that parks were meant to freeze change. In 1896 an exasperated Eliot wished for "a little less selfish contentment in the doomed landscape of the present."[4]

Olmsted complained of well-intentioned preservationists who sacrificed the forest for the trees. Felling any tree in a park, he said, was treated as "a startling public outrage." But his designs were meant to mature over decades, a human-guided natural succession that included tree cutting, and if human guidance lapsed, the design failed. In Central Park, for example, he planted "nurse trees" whose shade protected young hemlocks as they grew; his successors, cowed by public opinion, left them until they strangled the hemlocks, and then the short-lived nurses themselves began dying. In a well-managed landscape, as *Garden and Forest* paraphrased Olmsted, "the axe should never be allowed to rest."[5] Continuing management was necessary for permanence, yet any continuing intervention could look like unwanted change.

The demands of maintenance drew energy away from new preservation efforts. "The majority of people who saved old houses," writes Charles Hosmer, "did not understand that the word 'preservation' really meant mainte-

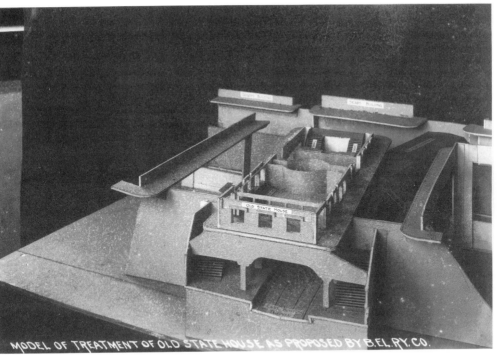

FIGURE 8.1   *Boston Transit Commission model of proposed station entrance through Old State House, 1905. Society for the Preservation of New England Antiquities*

nance of these structures throughout the years that followed." In 1915, after twenty-five years' experience with landscape maintenance, the Trustees of Reservations refused to accept a forest bequest because its endowment was inadequate to fight the gypsy moths that had infested it.[6] Similar concerns kept them from accepting any historic buildings for decades. By 1899 they had already declined some, they explained, because "this corporation has no fund with which to defray the expenses of care and maintenance which their acceptance would bring with it. This is especially true of the old and historic houses of this Commonwealth, which are generally of wood, and, if still in their original form, are often in a precarious condition of repair. . . . This corporation is a voluntary association, and can hardly be expected to find among its members any one who is willing and able to give the attention to details which such property demands."[7] The trustees sought local assistance in managing their scattered properties and eventually transferred their first reservation to the Metropolitan Park Commission. In the Adirondacks, where New York State was slowly buying land within the "Blue Line" of park boundaries, the American Scenic and Historic Preservation Society tried to

199

separate landscape management from acquisition by advocating public controls on private forests.[8]

More alarming than maintenance, but almost as regular, was the need to defend preserved landmarks and landscapes from new threats. Years after the Old South and the Old State House were saved, transit construction seemed to threaten them again, just as it threatened neighborhoods farther from the center. A subway station next to the Old South was negotiated to preservationists' satisfaction, and another one inserted underneath the Old State House. When the commission in 1905 proposed expanding the station to part of the building's first floor, patriotic societies across Massachusetts mobilized and fought off this new indignity. The first Harrison Gray Otis House, saved by preservationists in 1916 (see chapter 9), was threatened by street widening in the 1920s.[9]

Yellowstone had to be defended, and the meaning of the national parks sorted out, when a railroad across it was proposed in 1886. Railroads, Congress decided, did not belong in parks. Niagara Falls had to be defended not only from inappropriate development around it but from hydroelectric diversions that threatened to dry up the falls itself. Continuing defense of Niagara became one of the institutional missions of American Scenic. After the turn of the century, San Franciscans proposed a reservoir flooding Yosemite's Hetch Hetchy Valley, and wilderness advocates mounted a national campaign against this encroachment on a landscape they thought had been saved for all time. But the 1906 earthquake and fire left Americans sympathetic with San Francisco's water needs, and urban park-building experience made a new lake, unlike a railroad, seem perhaps acceptable. Congress in 1913 voted to allow the Hetch Hetchy dam. The fight nevertheless left the conservation movement better organized, and two years later it succeeded in setting up a National Park Service to better guard the parks.[10]

Urban parks shared Boston Common's experience as large chunks of land where land was in great demand. Central Park by the early twentieth century had been defended from streetcars, an opera, a cathedral, a cemetery, a fire station, an industrial exhibition hall, historical society and parks department headquarters, and a World's Fair.[11] Proponents argued that these were appropriate uses for New York's premier public ground; indeed, pride of place was sometimes their main argument for the site.

Central Park was also defended from ball fields, sandboxes, swimming pools, a stadium, and a zoo—all familiar park uses today, some of them now in Central Park. The growth of active sports was a new phase of the parks movement, unrelated to any preservationist aims. In Boston, Olmsted had learned from his New York experience and made room for organized sports, formal gardens, an amphitheater, and a small zoo, all outside Franklin Park's main expanse of "country park." The parks commissioners during the 1880s managed the space as Olmsted intended, banning or limiting sports and organized gatherings in favor of restful contemplation of the rural landscape. But sports crept in anyway, in the form of lawn tennis and bicycling, and the seemingly innocuous addition of golf on the sheep meadows. Historian Alexander von Hoffmann quotes a local newspaper that in 1909 "complained that Franklin Park was 'aesthetic' and not 'practically useful' as a play area." Golf gradually took over the otherwise empty-looking country park; in the next few years the commissioners added a greatly expanded zoo, and later a sports stadium.[12]

Turn-of-the-century Americans learned that permanence was not simple. What they had accomplished was to exert control over parts of the environment, and permanence would depend on their clarity and consistency in exercising that control. Permanence requires continuing effort in management, but if people's goals and values have changed, they may fail to manage, or may manage a place for different ends. Preservationists and parks advocates learned this lesson first, but it turned out to apply equally well to the rest of the urban environment.

Too Much Permanence?

Neighborhood protection through deed restrictions was in practice like preservation, not a single act but a process of continuing management. By the early twentieth century, restrictions had become ever more elaborate and were being applied to an increasing portion of subdivisions, until most urban development in the United States took place under this system of private land-use planning, which aimed to secure a degree of stability in the newly made urban environment. Developers, learning from the experience of administering restrictions, became more sophisticated in drafting them so that they could continue to function over long periods of time.

They did this in part through standardization. The Olmsted firm offered its clients a printed form of restrictions, which local lawyers could adapt. The restriction brochures that developers distributed as a marketing tool served also as prototypes from which others copied, and helped spread details of practice beyond local communities of real estate operators.[13]

Enforceability was aided by more careful legal draftsmanship. Language became increasingly specific, so that restrictions with the same substantive intentions were expressed in ever more precise terms. The first Back Bay deeds allowed "steps, windows, porticos, and other usual projections" beyond the building line, but after six years of practice the commissioners drafted a new form of deed that replaced those 7 words with 164 words of detailed specifications, which the commissioners insisted were identical in meaning.[14] In other deeds, elaborate new language defined single-family use.[15] These simple measures recognized that restrictions might in fact be invoked after a long period of time, when intentions would otherwise be difficult to ascertain.

One of the most important of intentions was the question of who could enforce restrictions. At first, enforcement clauses aimed at ensuring that the restrictions would be interpreted as equitable easements, not mere personal agreements with the subdivider. Later, J. C. Nichols expanded the scope of deed restrictions to something akin to public zoning, by writing into his deeds enforceability even by people outside his subdivisions, in return for reciprocal rights in surrounding developments.[16]

Real long-term enforceability could best be accomplished through self-perpetuating groups for administering restrictions. Since the early nineteenth century, neighborhood associations had been set up for the limited purpose of maintaining common spaces of urban subdivisions such as Louisburg Square and Pemberton Square on Beacon Hill, Gramercy Park in New York, and the private streets of St. Louis. After the turn of the century, large-scale developers set up community organizations that were also charged with approving construction and alterations within the development. In its fully articulated form this method involved a homeowners' association to levy fees, arrange maintenance and services, and enforce restrictions, and a separate architectural board of review or "art jury"—sometimes paid professionals—to examine the designs of proposed improvements. As an enforcement agency the homeowners' association embodied the permanence and community self-interest of neighbors. In such developments deed covenants also took on the new role of subjecting owners to the private assessments that ensured resources for enforcement and reinforced the institutional permanence of these private quasi-governments.[17]

The evolution of deed restrictions was not, however, a triumphant march toward ever greater permanence. Listing actual deed restrictions arranged by the date they were imposed, for example, does not appear to show any trend toward longer specified durations.[18] This is inconclusive, however, for several reasons. First, restrictions were applied to an increasing percentage of new subdivisions, so comparisons from one period to another can end up comparing different classes of development. Second, courts in many jurisdictions outside Massachusetts refused to honor permanent covenants, and developers everywhere responded by switching from perpetual durations to finite ones. Other kinds of evidence point to a growing embrace of long-term if not permanent environmental stability: both the increasing use of restrictions and the increasing care taken to ensure that these restrictions remained unambiguously enforceable after many years.

What is clear in this evolution is that a steadily growing amount of attention was paid to issues of duration and permanence, and that this attention was directed toward devising practical mechanisms for controlling environmental change. When participants in this process looked around at what they had accomplished, however, many had second thoughts about the practicality of environmental permanence.

How could property owners tell which restrictions were permanent? *Parker v. Nightingale* (see chapter 3) appeared to breathe eternal life into many old restrictions, most of which were probably never intended to be perpetual. Their authors were no longer available to clear up their intentions, and courts had a way of consulting their own preferences instead. On these unpredictable results could depend most of the value of a piece of property. For example, three lots on Beacon Hill's Mount Vernon Street had been conveyed between 1806 and 1808 with the provision that stables then standing on them should "never" be raised above their height of thirteen feet. Did the word *never* create a permanent restriction limiting any future buildings on this land to the same height? It took two separate suits before the Supreme Judicial Court in 1874 and 1875 to establish that buildings there would indeed be limited to a single story forever.[19]

Once restrictions were in force, how could they be ended? First, they could be ended by their own internal mechanisms, the simplest of which was a finite duration. Restrictions without expiration dates might specify some procedure for modifying or abrogating them, usually a majority vote of lot owners. Few early deeds contained any such internal mechanisms. Second, restrictions could be voluntarily terminated either by unanimous agreement among the owners or by reassembling all the affected lots into a single ownership. It was the existence of these mechanisms, external to the provisions of the deed itself and available at any time, that kept permanent restrictions from violating the rule against perpetuities. Finally, restrictions could be terminated by the courts. If the restriction was properly drawn and ran with the land—if, in other words, it was in force to begin with—a court might set it aside for one of two reasons. Either a failure to enforce the restrictions or a change in the neighborhood on which they operated could in the judgment of a court render their enforcement inequitable.[20] Permanent restrictions without internal provisions for modification were durable indeed; they could be altered only by a court or by unanimous action among all the owners in a subdivision.

At the same time that real estate dealers were learning to sell permanence, the increasing patchwork of permanent conditions and restrictions led to a growing unease among the real estate conveyancers and lawyers who dealt with them professionally. In 1886 a group of them petitioned the Massachusetts legislature to reform this system of land regulation, complaining that "many real estate titles especially in Boston and vicinity are incumbered with burdensome and vexatious conditions and restrictions, in some cases exposing valuable estates to the risk of forfeiture, on grounds comparatively insignificant; that those incumbrances frequently prevent the improvement of such real estate and subject the persons holding such estates to great trouble, annoyance and expense and that no adequate legal remedies exist for these evils." The petitioners asked for "laws to limit and regulate the power of imposing such conditions and restrictions . . . and to define the remedies & rights of all persons interested" in them.[21]

The professional drafters and examiners of deeds were mainly concerned about conditions, with their potentially drastic consequences for land titles, but they also included restrictions in their petition, and these people if anyone understood the distinction. The petition was accompanied by a bill that focused on conditions; after a specified deadline most of them would be treated as restrictions, and they could henceforth be created only by strictly defined language. A final section dealt with restrictions and their duration: "No restriction on the mode of use of real estate . . . shall be hereafter created to be in force for more than twenty years from the date of the deed . . . unless the time during which such restrictions shall be in force is expressly set forth."[22] The judiciary committee recommended against the bill and in 1887 revived only the part limiting the duration of restrictions. The committee increased the default term to thirty years, and the legislature enacted it. From then on, new restrictions with expiration dates could run as long as anyone liked, but if they were "unlimited as to time," they would "be construed" as lasting thirty years.[23] In Massachusetts, restrictions on land use could no longer be permanent.

It was not clear in practice exactly what was to be limited to thirty years. Did "use of real estate" refer only to, for example, a limitation to single-family dwellings, or was it to be understood in a broader sense as including location of buildings, their height—in effect the whole substantive content of restrictions? Developers already distinguished between dimensional and use restrictions, sometimes with differing durations. All the city's South End deeds limited buildings to residential use for twenty years and also imposed dimensional and construction requirements that were not limited in duration. Justice William C. Loring in 1910 speculated that the dimensional requirements themselves might have been intended to control uses after twenty years, in effect limiting uses to those compatible with a residential neighborhood: "Whatever may have been the scheme which was to exist after the twenty year period as to the use to be made of the buildings had expired, I do not see why that scheme cannot be maintained."[24] A restriction on the height of houses written after the 1887 act was deemed perpetual in an 1897 decision, supporting the idea that the limit on duration applied only to restrictions on land use.[25]

The act caused another kind of confusion by specifying a default term which was misunderstood as a maximum by some people, apparently including Associate Justice Marcus P. Knowlton of the Supreme Judicial Court, who in a 1903 decision about an early-nineteenth-century deed mentioned that restrictions created since the 1887 act "cannot remain in force longer than thirty years."[26] Given these confusions, subdividers might have felt discouraged from writing restrictions for very long terms. Nevertheless, some did impose them for finite terms considerably longer than thirty years, and they were ultimately upheld.[27] Others continued writing restrictions on use "forever," which though unenforceable offered their customers the illusion of permanence.[28]

Since the 1887 act allowed finite terms no matter how long, its real target was unintentional permanence. No longer would property owners and courts have to wonder whether a subdivider's omission of an expiration date was a product of deliberation or of sloppiness. The act applied only to new restrictions, however, and thus did not address the early-nineteenth-century deeds that most often presented these questions. Two years later a companion act addressed conditions and restrictions already on the books. It simply allowed property owners to ask the Supreme Judicial Court to rule on the validity of covenants more than thirty years old.[29] Wary of unconstitutional interference with private contracts, the legislators offered the court none of the substantive guidelines rejected in the 1886 bill. It was a purely procedural reform that reduced the contentiousness of private land-use regulation by allowing doubts about restrictions to be resolved before rather than after they were violated. By addressing the dubious language of old deeds, the legislature implicitly acknowledged changing standards of permanence, in effect admitting that the Hayward deeds, and others like them, did not necessarily mean what Justice Bigelow had said they meant. Even more important, it would provide a less adversarial way of determining where intentions had been fatally undermined by neighborhood change.

The leading case on neighborhood change, for Massachusetts and for the nation, was *Jackson v. Stevenson*, decided in 1892. In an 1853 residential subdivision at Boston's Park Square, the city imposed restrictions that, among other things, defined rear yards to remain free of buildings. Nearly forty years later, as the area was being absorbed into the expanding downtown,

FIGURE 8.2 *Park Square, c. 1870. Society for the Preservation of New England Antiquities*

one owner sought to enforce the restriction to keep another from expanding his store. "It is evident that the purpose of the restrictions as a whole was to make the locality a suitable one for residences," said the court,

and that, owing to the general growth of the city, and the present use of the whole neighborhood for business, this purpose can no longer be accomplished. If all the restrictions imposed in the deeds should be rigidly enforced, it would not restore to the locality its residential character, but would merely lessen the value of every lot for business purposes. It would be oppressive and inequitable to give effect to the restrictions; and since the changed condition of the locality has resulted from other causes than their breach, to enforce them in this instance could have no other effect than to harass and injure the defendant, without effecting the purpose for which the restrictions were originally made.[30]

This passage established a two-part test to determine whether restrictions remained valid in a changing neighborhood. Had the change been caused by violations of the restriction? Would enforcing the restriction restore the district to its intended character? Park Square failed both tests, so the court declined to enforce the restriction there and instead called for the lesser remedy of monetary damages.

A string of decisions expanded the *Jackson v. Stevenson* principles into a judicial doctrine of neighborhood change, defining the extent of changes, both geographical and substantive, that would render restrictions invalid. The mere existence of the doctrine undermined the pursuit of permanence. The discretion exercised by courts made deed restrictions seem unreliable as a long-term tool for controlling land use and built form. "We all know what these private restrictions, as a rule, are worth," said city planning expert Lawrence Veiller in 1916. " 'There ain't no such animal' " as a long-term restriction, he said, "because we all know that 25, 50, or 75 years after the development has been made, conditions change and the courts step in, and the man who placed the restrictions being dead, the courts as a rule say, 'We will not maintain these restrictions any longer.' "[31]

Many developers still continued selling permanence, and so in this more skeptical judicial climate they had to modify their products. One response was restrictions of finite duration with simple procedures for renewal. In a further innovation, developers offered de facto permanence by making the restrictions self-renewing, shifting the burden of action from those who would like to continue them to those who wanted to change them. Helen Monchow thought that by 1929 this had become the most common form of restriction.[32] J. C. Nichols claimed to have used it first in Kansas City:

The restrictions automatically extend themselves unless the owners of a majority of the front feet execute and record a change or abandonment of the restrictions five years before the respective expiration dates. . . . In the Country Club District the presumption in favor of the established character of the development for home purposes has prevailed. . . . With the greater protection to property through such automatic extension of restrictions, . . . the original restriction period need not be so long. Perhaps 25- to 30-year periods are long enough to give reasonable assurance and yet short enough to permit readjustment of restrictions to changing modes of life.[33]

"Changing modes of life" challenged the mechanisms of environmental permanence at least as much as did changing neighborhoods. Norms as well as neighborhoods evolved over time and could leave restrictions behind. The deeper intent of restrictions—maintaining a certain neighborhood character—often could not be reduced to permanent objective rules, and attempts to do so could skew a neighborhood's development in unwelcome ways. Restrictions had to be interpreted flexibly to follow their intent rather than their letter when tastes changed, or when whole unanticipated categories of land use arose, like elevator apartments in the Back Bay, or like garages. "If we had made a restriction a few years ago against garages or outbuildings, we would be up against it to-day," said Nichols in 1916. "It may be that in ten or fifteen years we might want housing for aeroplanes." The Massachusetts Supreme Judicial Court grappled with garages in a suit filed in 1907 in the Back Bay extension, where restrictions written in 1890 prohibited stables but allowed other "usual outbuildings." Well, said the court after four years, a garage is not a stable, but then again it certainly was not in 1890 a usual outbuilding, either.[34] To property owners who needed to know what they could build, such deliberation was alarmingly academic and time-consuming.

By inserting internal provisions for modifying restrictions, developers acknowledged their potential obsolescence and aimed for longevity through flexibility. These provisions put the power of amendment into the hands of owners in an attempt to keep it out of the hands of courts. One aim of this flexibility was to create a judicial presumption of validity whenever restrictions had *not* been altered. The restrictions in Palos Verdes, begun outside Los Angeles in the 1920s to the plans of Frederick Law Olmsted Jr. and Charles H. Cheney, included a complex system of different approval requirements for modifications, depending on the area they would affect and on whether the provision was deemed "basic."[35]

Discretion in administering restrictions could offer even more flexibility than the process of amending them. Developers learned to value such flexibility when inflation during World War I rendered obsolete the house-cost figures in deeds. Revising these figures was difficult, but even if it were possible such revisions would present marketing problems. "People still think they can build a house for six thousand," said Columbus subdivider King Thompson, "but we know they can't, and we know it will cost them eight or ten." E. H. Bouton, developer of Baltimore's Roland Park, argued against restricting house costs at all. "If we have a restriction on approval of plans, I think it is wholly unnecessary."[36]

Delegating review to a homeowners' association handled both unanticipated change in circumstances and evolving neighborhood standards. "The theory," wrote J. C. Nichols, "is that these directors have a vital interest in the continuance of the established character of the development, they are elected by vote of their neighbors and thus represent the lotowners and afford a sound medium for perpetuating the ideals and standards of the development."[37] Monchow in 1929 found that requiring review of all building plans, rather than mere conformity to preset objective standards, was "comparatively new and . . . its use is increasing."[38] Attorney Charles S. Ascher in 1932 wrote "Reflections on the Art of Administering Deed Restrictions," defining his art as "the free rendering of the black and white of legal documents in the pastel shades of human conduct and desire." Whatever mechanism mediated between legal documents and human conduct, it was to "perform the vital function of making the plan serve the people for whom it was intended but who could not be consulted in its preparation, instead of making the residents slaves to the preconceived plan."[39]

When developers applied this new philosophy of flexibility, they sometimes retained more control for themselves than they allowed to their customers. For example, Frederick Law Olmsted Jr. advised Baltimore's Roland Park Company to plat "sketchily and only as needed" for the sake of flexibility, and the company's deeds retained the right to modify restrictions on land it still held.[40] This was a partial return to the original system that preceded equitable easements, and it could work only when, as in Roland Park, the developer's integrity was above question and the flexibility was clearly being used only for adjusting designs within their original intentions. Monchow found such provisions common, usually tempered by definite limits on the developer's prerogatives, or requirements for consent, to avoid producing "a feeling of insecurity" on the part of residents, the very feeling that restrictions existed to alleviate.[41]

Developers retained even more control when they kept enforcement powers for themselves rather than for neighbors. By the 1890s, Boston's Riverbank Improvement Company in its Beacon Street subdivisions included restrictions limiting owners' enforcement rights to their own block, while the company could enforce them throughout the district. A more extreme version appeared a few years later in Newton Center, written by a subdivision syndicate that included one judge from the Superior Court and one from the Supreme Judicial Court. The latter tribunal later wrote with glee of these part-time developers who "all had a wholesome fear of equitable restrictions, and a desire to profit by them." These legal savants broke all the rules for creating equitable easements, varying both the substance and the duration of their restrictions from one lot to the next. Clearly this was deliberate, said the court; they "intended to retain a power in themselves to change their system of development; and, while restricting the several lots as they were granted, they intended to avoid granting power to the purchasers" to insist upon uniform restrictions. Some developers used a similar approach when faced with fluctuating building costs, inserting one minimum in deeds and another, higher one in sales contracts where they alone could enforce it, and thus could waive it if prices came back down.[42]

All of these issues faced developers and their customers in new subdivisions, where restrictions worked best. Elsewhere, homeowners found their limitations even more serious. In older residential plats, restrictions often had become obsolete, or had lain inactive long enough to be of uncertain validity. The expiration of time-limited covenants brought residents an unwelcome awareness of their neighborhoods' new vulnerability; a transition period of changes in ownership and occupancy often began in advance of the expiration date. Since land in an established neighborhood often increased in value when its restrictions expired, even resident owners might have an incentive to celebrate their passing. Where owners favored continuing the restricted status quo, they could accomplish little unless they acted in unison. If a restriction against, for example, apartment houses did not apply to every lot on a block, it merely conferred a monopoly on the owners of unrestricted lots. This was an incentive for owners to hold out from renewing restrictions, and in areas originally subdivided without them, the need for unanimity made them nearly impossible to initiate afterward.[43]

The intentions that determined environmental permanence were not those of the generation that wrote restrictions but those of the generation that enforced or failed to enforce them. Courts inevitably had a great deal of discretion, affording a flexibility that could defeat environmental permanence but was necessary for truly achieving it. For deed restrictions to be effective over a long period, they had to be taken literally when they said "no" and literally when they said "forever," yet their interpretation had to be supple enough to meet new problems as they arose. Flexibility could be built in by creating permanent associations to administer restrictions, but such groups brought their own social and administrative issues for residents and for big developers, or "community builders," who might have to deal with them for years. Like park landscapes, the legal landscape of neighborhood change had to be managed.

Control

The most important effect of deed restrictions was to challenge real estate orthodoxy, undermining the culture of change. Neighborhoods could indeed remain stable, and speculation on continual land-use conversion was not the only way to make money in real estate. "Through the use of private deed restrictions," says real estate historian Marc Weiss, "residential subdividers had already market-tested the value of land-use regulations and found them to be most desirable."[44] Deed restrictions also showed through their lack of flexibility that private controls by themselves were not enough. The presence of unrestricted land and the emergence of unanticipated issues eventually led homeowners and the real estate industry alike to embrace other more flexible mechanisms, public regulations that would act like restrictions while overcoming their limitations. This growing appreciation for flexibility was a new phase in the reaction against the culture of change.

One early form of public land-use regulations, similar to deed restrictions in the way they worked, were "frontage consent ordinances." This technique was developed furthest in Chicago. By 1893, ordinances there prohibited locating on residential streets any commercial stables, saloons, gas houses, varnish works, or carousels without approval of the owners of a majority of the block's frontage. In Massachusetts an 1881 law allowed a veto of saloon permits by owners of adjacent property. Similar methods were used in many American cities, usually to regulate subjects that were already discretionary under the law, such as liquor licenses or transit franchises. Frontage consents were an evolutionary link between deed restrictions and modern zoning.[45]

Zoning

Another link was regulations like Boston's early height districts, imposed through eminent domain. Their "takings" were not pieces of land but some part of the land's development rights, easements like private restrictions but enforceable by the government. The first such Massachusetts measure was an 1893 act enabling cities and towns to establish building lines—minimum front yards—along public streets. The act drew from the familiar language of deed restrictions which had long accomplished the same end. Laying out the lines would follow the same procedures as taking the streets themselves. The bill was proposed by Boston's Board of Street Commissioners, and at the request of a Brookline representative the mechanism was made available throughout the state.[46]

The building-line act originated as an answer to expiring restrictions, in effect correcting their omission of a renewal clause. "The restrictions are running out" on Columbus Avenue, complained residents there, and the avenue "fast becoming a business street."[47] Columbus Avenue "is a very fine avenue, most of the estates are under certain restrictions as to the building line," explained South End alderman Charles W. Hallstram, "but there are three or four lots there on which there are no restrictions and the parties are beginning to build out, thereby annoying the abutters and disfiguring the avenue." If the offending construction continues, he said, "it will cost the City of Boston a great deal more money than it will at present to abate these nuisances."[48] One way or another, Hallstram assumed, the failure of deed restrictions was a subject for municipal attention.

By the end of 1895 the Boston street commissioners had received only

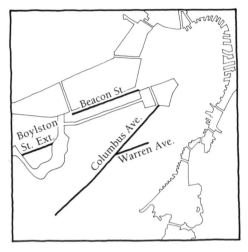

MAP 14

three petitions for building lines, all reacting to threats of change in established neighborhoods. The first was from Alderman Hallstram's constituents on Columbus Avenue. On nearby Warren Street, residents hoped to block "a new building that is about to be erected on a lot of land where the restrictions have recently expired." Both Columbus Avenue and Warren Street residents tried to use the new procedure to ward off commercial encroachment, but in both cases the owners of unrestricted land sought substantial compensation, and the commissioners therefore declined to act.[49] The first petition they approved was to confirm the existing building line on aristocratic Beacon Street, where public hearings showed no opposition and thus no need for compensation.[50] Brookline eventually refused to use the act on existing streets except where property owners posted bonds to indemnify the town.[51] By using eminent domain as the basis for building regulations, the legislature recognized development expectations as property rights. In established neighborhoods these new powers were of little value without new funds, which probably explains why so few neighborhoods sought to use them.

In newly developing areas, public building lines could be used in a different way, giving municipal sanction to private restrictions. This neatly avoided damage awards while providing enforcement mechanisms less cumbersome than lawsuits. An 1894 act recognized this potential usefulness by requiring public building lines in yet-undeveloped parts of the Back Bay; Boylston Street's extension was immediately laid out this way. Brookline later adopted building lines on all new streets.[52] The building-line act set a legal and conceptual precedent for public intervention to address neighbor-

212

hood land-use issues, but it did not immediately change the ordinary way of doing business.

Another category of public actions addressed deed restrictions' deficiencies not through eminent domain but through the police power. These public-health, housing, and nuisance controls flowered in Massachusetts by 1870, and they covered some of the same subjects as deed restrictions, such as the location of stables.[53] When garages replaced stables and courts struggled to adapt old private restrictions, the Massachusetts legislature in 1913 created a second method of control by empowering Boston's Board of Street Commissioners to regulate garage locations. After a public hearing on each application, the commissioners were to weigh the "requirements of public convenience" against the "general character of the neighborhood."[54] This procedure was analogous to a special exception under modern zoning. Unlike most deed restrictions, this control was flexible. The commissioners could weigh the facts of each case and avoided fixed rules for a rapidly evolving land use.

Many regulatory issues emerged where private rights met public interests around parks and parkways. Enormous public investment had produced the parks, and ideally, adjacent landowners would feel a responsibility to contribute their part to the ensemble. Bostonians would not tolerate seeing this investment undone by selfish and inappropriate private development that took its value from the parks while ruining their appearance. Along new parkways, the parks commissioners established elaborate restrictions, addressing everything from where laundry could be dried to the costs and heights of different kinds of buildings.[55] The 1896 Parks and Parkways Act allowing retroactive establishment of building lines and height limits was thus from the commissioners' perspective not radical but remedial legislation, rectifying inconsistencies in their early deeds.

Even the parks commissioners' detailed restrictions neglected the most parasitic of private developments, billboards, which William Wilson has called "the bane of the City Beautiful." Bostonians made billboard control a national campaign, through the American Park and Outdoor Art Association, led by Warren H. Manning of the Olmsted firm. The Boston parks commissioners for several years after 1896 sought to expand their powers over adjacent lands to include signs. The legislature asked Massachusetts attorney general Herbert Parker whether such rules would entitle owners to compensation. Parker replied with an early endorsement of aesthetic regulation under the police power. "Noises and odors have always been treated as nuisances," he wrote. "There is no legal reason why an offence to the eyes should have a different standing from an offence to the other organs." Nor did he see any problem with singling out particular locales for stricter regulation. If the

213

city could spend millions of dollars creating parks, then the public welfare could require special controls "to preserve the effect for which the public money was spent."[56] In 1903 the commissioners finally received the power to make rules relating to "the displaying of advertisements, and to the height and character of fences," but Parker's confidence was premature. The Massachusetts Supreme Judicial Court overturned the law in 1905, making this just an opening skirmish in a decades-long national fight to control billboards.[57] Parks, originally conceived as a way of making certain pleasing kinds of landscape permanently available to city dwellers, now required a whole range of new public powers to ensure the permanence of their own environments.

During the 1890s, Bostonians figured out that governments could control change in the urban environment in ways that private actions could not, responding to new problems without having to anticipate every possibility in advance. Citizen activists and their allies in the legislature found or created new powers that allowed government intervention where the city's physical stability was threatened. These public powers of enormous potential were used at first in the same ad hoc ways that had been appropriate for more limited private responses, so by the end of the decade they were still more important in the abstract than for anything they had yet accomplished. Public action in the Back Bay succeeded in its specific aim of preventing more Haddon Halls on Commonwealth Avenue. It even succeeded reasonably well in the larger aims of protecting the overall Back Bay streetscape, though it consisted only of height restrictions on one street and building-setback lines on two. Its real success may have occurred by reinforcing residents' sense of control over their neighborhood. Back Bay residents expressed that sense of control emphatically on Copley Square, where they initiated public action that succeeded in its specific and extraordinary aim of determining, against a property owner's will, exactly how high his building could stand. Public action was not so successful in its larger goal of ensuring the permanence of Copley Square's architectural composition or its symbolic place in the structure of the city.

Developers had learned, as had landscape preservationists before them, that the environment cannot be frozen in a fixed state but grows and changes and needs to be managed continually. Two generations of long-term restrictions had imposed an unwelcome degree of inflexibility on some places, and Americans began to conclude that their ideal was perhaps not permanence after all but rather the ability to control environmental change. In resisting change, they made tools that could be used to shape it.

CHAPTER 9

Institutionalized Preservation

> *I am . . . the most conservative restorer of the entire lot and a building*
> *is in the safest hands when I have charge of it.*
> — WILLIAM SUMNER APPLETON

Preservation required continuing effort and repeated defenses, but throughout the nineteenth century, preservation campaigns were spontaneous
efforts. After the turn of the century, preservation matured from a string
of ad hoc actions to an institutionalized movement. In the process both its
aims and its methods were fundamentally transformed.

When the *American Architect* in 1886 first reported on threats to the Bulfinch statehouse, its editors assumed that Boston already had institutions to
look after preservation. "We trust," they said, "that the Massachusetts Historical Society, the Bostonian Society, and the Boston Society of Architects
will" defend the building.[1] The unprecedented role ultimately taken by the
architects' society in that campaign was all the more remarkable because the
other two groups, though well represented by individual activists, did not
consider the issue an appropriate one for institutional action.

The Massachusetts Historical Society, like its counterparts in other states,
saw itself as a scholarly clearinghouse, a library, and above all a unique re-
pository for manuscripts. Though the society asked the legislature to protect
ancient burial grounds, it ordinarily remained aloof from politics, even the
politics of preservation. Concerned mainly with protecting its collections,
the society had little direct use for historic structures; it had shied away from
the Old South Church, and in 1898 it moved altogether out of the center of
Boston, to a new fireproof headquarters on the Fenway.[2]

The Bostonian Society was chartered in 1881 "for the purpose of promoting the study of the history of Boston, and for the preservation of its
antiquities." Its predecessor, the Boston Antiquarian Club, initially set a
preservationist course when it led the fight to save the Old State House; it
incorporated specifically to create a legally responsible custodian and occu-

pant for the building. After this, however, it relaxed into a less activist role, defining the "antiquities" it would save mainly as documents, views, and historic bric-a-brac, and its members returned to the old antiquarian habit of lamenting the passing of landmarks as they fell and reminiscing about them afterward.[3] The Bostonian Society limited its intervention to placing historical tablets. The afternoon before the Committee for the Preservation of Park Street Church was organized, Bostonian Society president Curtis Guild called attention to the issue, not with a plea for preservation or any mention of the next day's meeting, but with a call for more plaques.[4]

A growing number of organizations shared this territory on the periphery of preservation. Increasing preoccupation with pedigree led to the multiplication of patriotic and genealogical societies. The national Daughters of the American Revolution was organized in 1890, with preservation as part of its agenda; its Massachusetts chapters quickly found an outlet in the Bulfinch statehouse campaign.[5]

Elsewhere in New England, local historical societies and other groups, spurred by the 1876 Centennial and the Old South success, set out to save old buildings in their towns. Most of these were selected for their associations with illustrious ancestors or the Revolution. Lexington, Massachusetts, eventually preserved a collection of buildings connected with the battle there; the town conceived the project as part of its park system. In Ipswich the historical society in 1898 bought as its headquarters the seventeenth-century Whipple House, not for any historic occupant or events there, but as an artifact inherently interesting on account of its age, "a link that binds us to the remote Past" and its "manner of living," said the society's president.[6] Such concern with material culture—the tangible "manner of living" of the remote past or other times—was a new motive for preservation, eventually embodied in the Society for the Preservation of New England Antiquities.

The Paul Revere House

Preservation of material culture came to Boston proper in 1905 in a movement to save Paul Revere's house. Revere's conspicuous place in the revolutionary pantheon gave the house conventional historical value, but it was also the oldest remaining structure in the city, dating from sometime between 1676 and 1681. It stood on North Square, fashionable in Revere's day but in 1905 at the heart of the immigrant North End. Tall brick buildings loomed over it, and the house had been raised one story and subdivided into a grocery store, tenements, and a cigar factory. Generations of antiquarians and tourists made the pilgrimage through a district they found alien and threatening, where they endured, said one, "the vile odors of garlic and

216

NORTH
END

Revere
House

Old State House

Bulfinch
State House

Old South

Park Street Church

MAP 15

onions" to gaze at the greatly altered structure sporting a commemorative plaque and a "variety of signs with Italian names," which the *Boston Globe* found "strangely out of harmony with the memories of its earlier history."[7]

The house was surely destined for eventual replacement by a larger tenement building, although it is not clear that this threat was ever imminent. It was effectively saved at the end of 1902, when it was bought for $12,000 by a Revere descendant: John Phillips Reynolds Jr., the real estate developer then trying to tear down Park Street Church. In April 1905 he and several other prominent men organized the Paul Revere Memorial Association, to raise money to cover his purchase, restore the house, and open it "for some historical, educational, or patriotic purpose." Without publicizing Reynolds's ownership, their solicitations warned that the structure "is in danger of destruction, and prompt steps are necessary in order to preserve it."[8] By the early part of 1907 they had raised enough to take title and begin restoring the building.

The Revere House restoration was unlike any other Boston had seen. The Old South Church, Faneuil Hall, and the two statehouses were major public buildings, their exteriors and at least potentially their interiors a part of most Bostonians' experience. Their design and their construction were familiar, and their alterations were comparatively well documented, so appropriate treatments for them were matters of widespread amateur debate. The Revere House, on the other hand, was outside the daily ambit of its preservers and had undergone radical and unrecorded changes. As it was agreed in principle that the building, contrary to Ruskinian precepts, ought

217

FIGURE 9.1 *Paul Revere House, 1895. "Neighborhood youngsters," notes archivist Philip Bergen, "greet the photographer with a timeless gesture." Bergen,* Old Boston in Early Photographs, 1850–1918 *(New York, 1990), 25. Courtesy Bostonian Society, Old State House*

to be returned "to its original condition," its treatment became not a subject for public discussion but instead a matter for expert investigation, an essentially private question. It was not architecture but archaeology. The work was undertaken by restoration architect Joseph Everett Chandler, whose interest was mainly in the original seventeenth-century construction, rather than the period of Revere's residency a century later, with the result that, as Walter Muir Whitehill wrote, "Paul Revere, were he to return to North Square, would not recognize it as the house in which he long lived." To satisfy the project's patriotic sponsors, the second-floor interior was restored to an approximation of its appearance in Revere's day.[9]

The Society for the Preservation of New England Antiquities

The Paul Revere Memorial Association's greatest contribution to preservation, as it turned out, was helping awaken to his life's work the association's secretary, William Sumner Appleton Jr., who would found the Society for

FIGURE 9.2 *Paul Revere House after 1907 restoration. Courtesy Bostonian Society, Old State House*

the Preservation of New England Antiquities. Appleton was not America's first full-time preservationist—that was surely Ann Pamela Cunningham, of the Mount Vernon Ladies' Association—but he became the first professional preservationist. He brought to the field systematic methods and a standing institution independent of any particular cause.

In 1905 William Sumner Appleton Jr. was a thirty-one-year-old Brahmin without portfolio, trying to figure out what to do with his life.[10] Sumner—so called to distinguish him from his father—grew up at 39 Beacon Street, a mansion built for his grandfather in 1816, facing the Common two blocks from the statehouse. In 1886, when he was twelve, as apartment houses rose nearby and legislators debated tearing down the statehouse, his father sold the Beacon Hill house and moved the family to the comparative stability of the Back Bay. If Appleton's background gave him this small taste of urban change, it also gave him a more than average introduction to Boston's search for permanence. His father joined in founding the Bostonian Society and the American Historical Association and, as an officer of the Massachusetts Historical Society, petitioned to protect ancient burial grounds. Sumner's uncle Nathan Appleton spoke for preserving the Old South Church. His

FIGURE 9.3 *William Sumner Appleton Jr., c. 1917. Society for the Preservation of New England Antiquities*

older cousin and good friend Alice Longfellow (the poet's daughter) served the Mount Vernon Ladies' Association as vice regent for Massachusetts. One of his uncles nearly bought the Hancock House, and did in fact salvage its staircase for his country house. Appleton must have been conscious even as a child of the building's site down the street from 39 Beacon.[11]

Appleton studied at Harvard with Charles Eliot Norton, the Ruskin disciple who had recently written his article bemoaning the lack of old houses in America. After he graduated, he set up in business as a real estate broker for three years until this career was cut short by what he described as a "nervous breakdown."[12] Appleton's father died in 1903, leaving his inheritance in a trust that would provide a comfortable income for life without allowing him to touch the principal. Appleton tried managing the family farm. He toyed with becoming a mining engineer in the West. He lived at his club and catalogued his father's coin collection.

Appleton came to the Revere House effort through the Massachusetts Sons of the Revolution. His considerable work for the Memorial Association—as its secretary, he took on most of its organizational chores, and one newspaper credited him as the "architect" of the campaign[13]—seems to have been motivated by the house's patriotic associations. He bought a camera and began touring and photographing the towns of eastern Massachusetts, paying special attention to their oldest structures. He became active in the Bostonian Society. When the transit commissioners in 1905 proposed expanding the subway station in the Old State House, the society's directors at first acquiesced; it was Appleton who organized protests from around the state, proposed alternative solutions, and led a committee that lobbied the governor and the mayor until they relented. On a tour of Europe in 1909, he took note of preservation and restoration efforts.

When Appleton returned, he pursued this interest by attempting, as state vice president of the Sons of the Revolution, to intercede in the impending alteration of Lexington's Jonathan Harrington House, the owner of which found it ill suited for modern living. Harrington, shot in the battle on April 19, 1775, made it back across the Common to die at his wife's feet on his own doorstep. "This story had always made a strong appeal to me," Appleton recalled later, "and it seemed as though a house having such associations should be safeguarded against all alterations." While Appleton's interest, like earlier preservation efforts, stemmed from patriotic associations, the threat that motivated him here as at the Old State House was an architectural one—not demolition but renovation. He was frustrated to find himself powerless to protect the house in any way. "From that moment on my life's work seemed to be cut out for me."[14] He was "ripe" for such a discovery, says a recent biographer: "Sumner Appleton was thirty-six years old, midway in life. He had felt like a failure. He had no occupation, no wife, no child. What he did have was a trust fund which freed his energies. He had some real estate experience, a little formal coursework in architecture, in public speaking, in publication. He had been in society on the hill which spread out to include Harvard—his acquaintance stretched through a vast and well-placed family into an erudite, if occasionally precious, world." [15]

Appleton put all this background to work as he set out on his new mission. He prepared a charter for a "Society for the Preservation of New England Antiquities" (SPNEA) and "fixed it up" with connections in the legislature to exempt from taxes the society's as-yet-hypothetical properties.* He enlisted Charles Knowles Bolton, the Athenaeum's librarian, as president and chose for himself the position of "corresponding secretary." He rounded up a board of directors chosen, according to Charles Hosmer, "more for the connections of its members than for their antiquarian knowledge," and in April 1910 they held the new society's first meeting. [16] In May, Appleton publicly launched the group's membership-building phase by publishing the first issue of its *Bulletin*.

The first *Bulletin* was a manifesto, a well-thought-out preservation program of unprecedented ambition. Its cover featured a photograph of the John Hancock House. "Built 1737 by Thomas Hancock. Destroyed 1863," said the terse caption. "The fate of this house has become a classic in the annals of vandalism." The next two pages presented more encouraging illustrations: four houses preserved in towns around Boston, including the Whipple House in Ipswich. "Our New England antiquities are fast disappearing," began the text, "because no society has made their preservation its exclusive object. That is the reason for the formation of this Society." Appleton reflected on ad hoc efforts such as his own Paul Revere House campaign. "This is splendid as far as it goes, but since the mechanism is elaborate it is seldom used, and it is wasteful because without much more elaboration it can be used to cover the whole field." [17]

The whole field, to Appleton, meant all six New England states. Nowhere in the United States had preservationists attempted such a regional organization. The closest prototype was the Association for the Preservation of Virginia Antiquities, which Appleton had joined in 1907 and on which he modeled the society's name, but he was not interested in copying APVA's decentralized structure of local chapters. Even more than the Bostonian Society, the APVA valued commemoration over preservation. For the 1907 Jamestown Tercentenary it approved a fanciful reconstruction of the settle-

---

*Appleton himself admitted that he had coined an unfortunate mouthful, and his successors are not offended if it is pronounced "spih-NEE-uh."

BULLETIN OF
THE SOCIETY FOR THE PRESERVATION OF
NEW ENGLAND ANTIQUITIES

VOLUME I   BOSTON, MAY, 1910   NUMBER 1

THE HOME OF JOHN HANCOCK, BEACON STREET, BOSTON

Built 1737 by Thomas Hancock. Destroyed 1863. The fate of this house
has become a classic in the annals of vandalism. Governor Hancock is
said to have intended to bequeath his home to the Commonwealth, but
he died without giving effect to this intention by will. In 1859 a strong
effort was made to have the Commonwealth purchase the house at a low
valuation. This effort failed, and later the heirs offered the house with
some of its contents to the city as a free gift, the house to be moved to
another site. This plan also failed, and in 1863 the house was destroyed.

FIGURE 9.4 Society for the Preservation of New England Antiquities Bulletin
cover, vol. 1, no. 1. Society for the Preservation of New England Antiquities

ment's church, built of bricks taken from two genuine colonial buildings that were demolished expressly for the purpose.[18] The Trustees of Reservations and the American Scenic and Historic Preservation Society were geographically ambitious, but both put their energies into landscapes, which did not concern Appleton. Charles Eliot had conceived the Trustees of Reservations as a model for public action, and after the metropolitan parks were begun and Eliot died, the trustees slipped into decades of dormancy without saving any buildings. American Scenic among its many efforts did save buildings in New York State, but it acted mainly through the slow and uncertain process of lobbying the legislature.[19] What Appleton had in mind was a sort of institutional deus ex machina: "The situation requires aggressive action by a large and strong society, which shall cover the whole field and act instantly wherever needed to lead in the preservation of noteworthy buildings and historic sites. That is exactly what this Society has been formed to do."[20]

He went on to enumerate the sorts of "noteworthy buildings and historic sites" he had in mind: "blockhouses and garrison houses, of which but few are left; the oldest settlers' houses"; "Georgian" houses and "town houses"; battlefields and taverns. "We may also include Indian names, old trails, roadside watering places and other objects of note." Conspicuously absent from the list were public buildings of any sort, even churches. Nowhere did Appleton mention Faneuil Hall, either statehouse, or the Old South, which Eliot had invoked as an inspiration for the Trustees of Reservations. The only Boston antiquities he discussed were the Hancock and Revere Houses and the Old Feather Store, three buildings of domestic scale. The society's program embraced only such modest structures. "It is proposed to preserve the most interesting of these buildings by obtaining control of them through gift, purchase, or otherwise, and then to restore them, and finally to let them to tenants under wise restrictions."[21]

At the end of a year the society had more than three hundred members in twenty states, with local officers in all six New England states and a treasury of more than $3,000—but as yet no antiquities. Three months later SPNEA bought the 1670 Ilsley House in Newbury, Massachusetts, which "put the Society immediately in the long hoped for position of having actually done something," a position that Appleton knew was necessary for sustaining interest and continuing to build membership. By the end of the society's second year, it owned two houses and was undertaking a fund drive through which it would soon buy a third.[22]

SPNEA had already established the patterns of operation it would follow, with only tactical adjustments, for decades to come. Appleton discussed them in his second annual report as he reviewed the year's ten "completed transactions." In addition to the two houses purchased—one as a rental in-

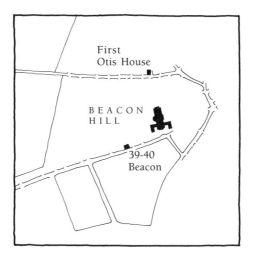

First
Otis House

B E A C O N
H I L L

39-40
Beacon

MAP 16

vestment and the other subject to a life occupancy which substantially reduced its price—he listed one house promised to the society as a gift, two for
which other groups were found as agents of preservation, three that made
their way into sympathetic private ownership, and one that was dismantled
for later reerection. In only one case had the society's efforts utterly failed.
"What it seems to show is this: the mere existence of this Society is a safeguard for all our finest old houses. When one such is in danger of destruction
the possibility of our intervening seems to occur more and more frequently
to those whom ties of residence or family bind to the old building." [23]

The society would never be able to acquire all the properties that came
to its attention each year, and Appleton tried to maximize its effectiveness
by husbanding resources of both money and energy. He sought local groups
to undertake preservation campaigns, organizing new ones where necessary, in order to leave SPNEA as a purchaser of last resort. Even then, the
society used its funds only as a catalyst for raising money from townspeople
or descendants of a building's occupants. It would soon begin making small
grants-in-aid to other groups' preservation efforts and increasingly assisted
them not with money but by lending SPNEA's regional fundraising abilities.

SPNEA's third acquisition was the 1657 Cooper-Austin House in Cambridge, but otherwise the society was not especially active in Boston's immediate area for several years. For both the Shirley-Eustis Mansion in Roxbury and the Cary House in Chelsea, it spawned separate societies that
undertook fundraising on their own. Appleton's main Boston venture was
his search for a headquarters; the society was housed first in a shared rented

225

office and then in two rooms of the New England Historic Genealogical Society. In 1913 he tried to find a donor to present SPNEA with the Parker-Inches-Emery House at 40 Beacon Street, the twin of his boyhood home. The house instead became the headquarters of the Women's City Club; Appleton grudgingly approved and continued his search for "a suitable building somewhere on Beacon Hill."[24] In 1916 he found it, just off the hill on Cambridge Street, where the society with the assistance of fifteen wealthy donors bought Bulfinch's first Harrison Gray Otis House of 1795. With this single purchase half the organization's assets were suddenly in Boston real estate.

The Otis House was SPNEA's fifth acquisition. Ten years after it was founded, and despite the war and recession, the society owned seven properties in three states, and when Appleton died in 1947 it owned fifty-one.[25]

Theory

William Sumner Appleton saved a lot of buildings—probably more than anyone else in the country before John D. Rockefeller Jr. in the late 1920s set out to restore Virginia's colonial capital of Williamsburg—and in the process reshaped both the practice and the theory of preservation. Appleton developed methods that became a model for much of what preservationists did during the next fifty years (about which more below). Even more fundamental, however, was his contribution to the philosophy of preservation. Appleton made systematic an activity that had been entirely ad hoc, and his system helped steer the movement in a new direction.

Preservation is inherently reactive. It seeks to protect buildings and sites from a variety of human and natural threats, and so its tactics must respond to the nature and timing of those threats. Throughout the nineteenth century not only the tactics but the objects of preservation were decided by reaction, whether to a threat, as at the Old South, or an opportunity, as in Reynolds's purchase of the Paul Revere House. The objects fit for preservation were simply those buildings or places that aroused movements in their defense. The list was compiled empirically: Park Street Church was worth fighting for; but if St. Paul's congregation had decided to sell, would Bostonians have fought for that one instead? Would they have fought for both?

SPNEA like earlier ad hoc efforts necessarily responded to immediate threats, but from the beginning it did so within an intellectual framework postulating a comprehensive and consistent standard of value. Appleton meant to substitute system for sentiment. Architect Thomas A. Fox offered an early glimpse of this idea at the 1896 Bulfinch statehouse hearings: "I do not think that the laity in the United States quite understand what constitutes a historical monument. The phrase 'historical monument' means a building which is a creditable piece of architecture, which represents [a] certain period of architecture, and which has been made valuable by historical associations."[26] Appleton's system was more flexible; a building might be worthy of preservation for history, architecture, or even age alone. Appleton viewed the built environment as an expression of material culture and assigned value mainly according to an art-historical or archaeological approach. He saw buildings not as unique landmarks but as exemplars of types. Each could be ranked relative to others of the same kind according to its adherence to type, or the significance of its departures, and the result further calibrated according to the importance of the type itself and the rarity of surviving examples.[27] He valued buildings that could be read as "documents," displaying either a cross-section of material culture at a particular time or a longitudinal view of its evolution through time. He did not ignore historical significance—the loci of events unrelated to the evolution of material culture—but in his descriptions of buildings these associational values usually supplemented their inherent value as artifacts.

A systematic approach to value in the environment meant that objects worthy of preservation could be identified before they were threatened. Appleton's first *Bulletin* began such a process with its list of building types. He soon referred to at least a hypothetical list of particular buildings: "There are in New England several score of houses of supreme interest historically, architecturally, or both, the future of which is wholly problematic." These systematic priorities were meant to govern preservation activity; he closed an article on one building saved in Salem with a list of other candidates that he called "the minimum at which Salem should aim." SPNEA's first purchase, ironically, would not have been on Appleton's inventory if he had actually compiled one. He had inspected the house and reported that it "lacked sufficient historic association and architectural merit to justify the Trustees in making a purchase," but an offer of substantial financial assistance, together with the trustees' impatience to "make a beginning with some house" led the ever-pragmatic Appleton to relax his standards.[28] Even such compromises he soon reduced to a system: "It must be our policy to pick out the very best houses of each type as the ones for the preservation of which we are to work. Various factors will appear to modify this rule slightly. The very best may be in no danger today, whereas the second best may be doomed unless instantly protected; or perhaps the third best may be offered on such exceptionally good terms as to make it wise to postpone the others for the moment. Such circumstances will not alter the rule; they will be merely the exceptions to prove it." He was often delivering the bittersweet verdict that "these are so good that they warrant local effort to save them, but they are not of sufficient importance to interest our Society."[29]

Preservationists before then had not addressed the abstract question of defining everything in the environment worth saving. Extrapolating from the variety of their efforts—for the Park Street Church and Brattle Church tower, the trees and malls of the Common, the Athenaeum and all the graveyards—by implication they would have selected much more of it than Appleton, and done so without such internal consistency. This variegated list would have included more failures than Appleton was willing to accept. He rejected such an ad hoc approach because it was "wasteful," not only of organizational effort but of buildings themselves; the movement's fragmented efforts saved too little of what was most worthwhile. He was impatient with local historical societies, spending their efforts on whichever house happened to be threatened at the moment and then, overwhelmed, neglecting more valuable structures.[30]

The logical extension of systematic preservation was an actual inventory of worthwhile buildings. Architectural historians within the national American Institute of Architects during the teens and twenties pushed for such inventories, preferably in conjunction with a program of graphic recording. In 1914, SPNEA began cooperating with the Boston Society of Architects in listing houses to be measured and drawn by volunteers. Appleton was ambivalent, however, about making public the inventory he carried in his head, since he conceived it mainly as a list of potential acquisitions and found that divulging his priorities could make negotiations difficult. When the national inventory was finally begun in the 1930s as the Historic American Buildings Survey, Appleton was able, quickly though reluctantly, to provide lists of eligible structures throughout New England.[31]

Appleton's systematic standards steered preservation effort away from some directions but significantly broadened it in others. Turning from heroic and patriotic traditions to the study of material culture embraced a more inclusive view of history. While Appleton's aristocratic background sometimes made him an elitist in dealings with his contemporaries, he was staunchly egalitarian toward generations that were safely dead. Raising funds for a seventeenth-century house in Saugus he believed had housed some of Cromwell's Scottish prisoners of war, he urged that "it should become a memorial to the humble beginnings of many Scotchmen." Perhaps not surprisingly, this chord did not prove resonant.[32]

Preservationists' purview was also broadened by the shift from a visual to an archaeological orientation. This produced strange results in the case of Boston's 1679 Province House, the colonial governors' residence, gutted in a nineteenth-century fire and its ruins converted into a minstrel hall. Preservationists had long counted the Province House as one of Boston's losses. But Appleton the archaeologist took a new interest in its fragmentary remains.

228

FIGURE 9.5 *Remains of the Province House, 1922, with Old South steeple in the background. Society for the Preservation of New England Antiquities*

"To many it may come as a complete surprise to know that any part of the old Province House, used by the Provincial Governors of Massachusetts, is still in existence. What is left in place is the entire front or southeast wall minus the porch and steps; practically the entire northeast end wall with its enormous stepped and arched exterior chimney; and a portion, perhaps as much as half, of the southwest wall."[33] When the site was to be cleared for an office building in the 1920s, he tried to have the chimney incorporated

FIGURE 9.6 *Remains of the Province House, 1922. Society for the Preservation of New England Antiquities*

into one of the new building's walls but had to settle for photographing the remains during demolition.[34]

Appleton's inclusive vision indirectly refocused preservationist attention on periods even earlier than the heroic 1770s.[35] While he probably hoped to save every seventeenth-century house in New England, Appleton knew that there were too many eighteenth-century structures for a "colonial" date automatically to guarantee preservation. He referred to one 1774 house as "not very old" and to the 1755 extension of another as "containing absolutely nothing of interest." But he also helped move forward the chronological threshold of buildings that could be considered eligible for preservation. The society's second acquisition was a house built in 1809, and he found it "gratifying" when a local historical society for the first time preserved a house in the comparatively recent Greek Revival style. In 1920 he examined an 1854 building near Boston that he thought "would make an ideal period house for the display of mid-Victorian black walnut," but he regretted that "the present is probably fifty years too early for anything of the kind."[36]

System in setting priorities for buildings naturally extended to system in setting value on different parts of each building's fabric; and it was here that Appleton's archaeological approach showed most clearly. When he was criticized for restoring to the Otis House a porch that, though accurate, looked too small even to him, he responded, "It would have been very easy to have designed a larger and more imposing porch which would have given the house more distinction, but, after all, what is the object of a restoration? . . . To ignore the evidence and make what may be more beautiful . . . [would be] telling an archaeological falsehood."[37]

Except where recent alterations were entirely inappropriate, he felt that buildings should display the visible record of change over time. He cautioned the Lexington Historical Society against bringing its Buckman Tavern back to a static historical moment: "The 19th of April, 1775 is the tavern's historic day but a great part of the interior finish is more recent, and the house is emphatically one to be preserved about as found, in order to show the evolution of various periods and styles." He promoted "the Society's thoroughly conservative rule that what is left today can be changed tomorrow, whereas what is removed today can perhaps never be put back." In this, SPNEA followed the "anti-scrape" gospel of England's Society for the Protection of Ancient Buildings. "The spirit of the work of the two societies is almost identical," said Appleton. As James M. Lindgren has shown, SPNEA and its architects did in fact scrape, where aesthetic or ideological preferences favored earlier periods, but Appleton may indeed have been the most conservative restorer in the United States at the time, and his long and reflective stewardship helped frame these issues for others. His conservatism extended beyond materials themselves to the information embodied in buildings; to the extent possible, he made his interventions evident and therefore reversible, and he experimented with methods of marking replacement parts, without which restored buildings would lose "any documentary value."[38]

Systematic preservation as practiced by SPNEA reversed preservationists' earlier trend toward increasingly general concern with the city. Such a reversal was inherent in any consistent approach to assigning value in the environment, because it replaced subjective reactions that came from experiencing the city as a topographic whole. But Appleton's particular approach refocused attention even more sharply.

Appleton saw buildings not as parts of the environment but as objects complete in themselves; his view of material culture did not encompass the city as an artifact. When he thought about any scale other than that of buildings, it was usually the smaller scale of furnishings and structural components, not the larger scale of sites and relationships among buildings. Sites were background; he sought additional land around many SPNEA properties so that each could exist as an island apart from the town around it. Critic Robert Campbell calls Appleton's approach "the architectural embodiment of an elitist withdrawal from a pluralist city." [39] The scale of Appleton's concerns became further evident in his attitudes toward moving buildings. While he urged preservation *in situ* whenever possible, he did not argue like Joseph Chandler that every old building "is connected with the history of the neighborhood and should remain where it is," nor was he concerned with the archaeological value of the site. He simply wanted to avoid the damage done to buildings in transit, especially the destruction of original chimney cores. The seventeenth-century Becket House in Salem, located "near coal wharves and tenement houses," had already lost its chimney, so he felt that "its removal to a more suitable neighborhood is unquestionably a gain for all concerned." [40] Similarly, he did not see graveyards as parts of the urban landscape, nor did he view them sentimentally: he described ancestral remains as "a thin layer of slime" with "a few metal buttons." With his concern for material culture, it was the gravestones that were of "permanent value," which he thought could best be protected by moving them into museums. [41]

SPNEA's regionwide scope further undermined any concern with the urban environment. If Appleton had been inclined to preserve larger pieces of the city, this geographical range would have been impossible. Acquiring buildings one by one was relatively simple compared with the expense of acquiring groups of buildings or the complexity of dealing with planning issues. Appleton judged buildings in Boston by the same standards as those in towns throughout New England: intrinsic archaeological interest, independent of their contribution to the townscape.

Only Beacon Hill was an exception, where Appleton's own subjective attachments were reinforced by finding enough buildings of value to begin viewing them as an ensemble. In his campaign for the Parker-Inches-Emery House, he argued that "the integrity of this house is absolutely essential to the preservation of the stately old-time appearance of Beacon Street as we know it. The best portion of the street is from No. 39 [his boyhood home] to No. 45." Even so, he listed the building's interior as the most important reason for saving it. Also on Beacon Hill, Appleton took uncharacteristic interest in a major public building and made a rare attempt to influence public action in the 1914–17 expansion of the Bulfinch statehouse. The legislature, overruling its architects, specified white marble cladding for the wings, and preservationists worried that this would lead to placing the same material on the Bulfinch front itself. SPNEA withdrew from this fight, and Appleton said that "when a direct attack is made on the old work of Bulfinch there will be ample time to rally to its support";[42] Bulfinch's bricks ended up painted to match the marble. Appleton's interest was in artifactual integrity, not environmental aesthetics.

Appleton's interests mattered because his comprehensive organization prevented the emergence of competing institutions. The chairman of the American Institute of Architects' preservation committee, surveying architects' preservation efforts nationwide in 1915, noted that in New England no AIA chapters had mobilized for preservation. "It is claimed," he said, "that the necessity is met by the existence of the Society for the Preservation of New England Antiquities."[43]

Unlike the architects, Appleton was willing to give up on most of the city. In a recent study of SPNEA, James M. Lindgren attributes this to his reluctance to offend the business interests he hoped would support the society.[44] From Appleton's perspective, with private purchases or gifts as his only tools for preservation, he was simply facing reality. After the Province House was gone he wrote:

It may well be asked how the destruction of such a house could be tolerated and why was its preservation not taken in hand and carried through to success. . . . There is no question but that the saving of what was left would have been undertaken except for the prohibitive cost involved. The house stood on some of the most valuable land in Boston, the entire lot, including much that could have been dispensed with, being assessed for $1,800,000 and worth considerably more. The building was doomed from the moment the contract for the new building was signed.[45]

But the Province House stood across the street from the Old South Church, and Appleton could have chosen that instead of the Hancock House as his urban object lesson. His abandonment of antiquities in the city must be seen at least in part as his own choice.

This choice reflects a cultural cleavage in early-twentieth-century America, a potential rift in preservationist ranks, brought about by growing numbers of "medievalists," who valued the most primitive rather than the most accomplished architecture. They found medieval virtue in the simple structures of the early colonial period; they equated with Renaissance artificiality the later Georgian and Federal classical buildings that most urban preservationists valued. Medievalists were one group of what historian T. J. Jackson Lears calls "antimodernists." Through the Arts and Crafts Movement, Gothic Revival architecture, and preservation of folk culture and vernacular building, they reversed the earlier dictum and now declared that what was new was corrupt.[46]

Appleton's sympathies lay with the medievalists. Preservationists of the older urbanist tradition thought the society concentrated too much of its resources on what one called "'those little wooden houses' in the country." Even SPNEA's second acquisition, the 1809 Fowler House, shared the severe simplicity of earlier buildings, and Appleton acknowledged opposition from members who were "disappointed that it is not ornate." Appleton was most interested in structures like Salem's Old Bakery, which he described as "almost brutal in its simplicity. . . . The whole work is essentially medieval, and the decorative motives are of Gothic extraction." As he elaborated on the theme in private correspondence regarding another building, "To my mind the 17th century is the more strictly New England type, or I might say Anglo-Saxon type. The other [Georgian] is after all but an importation from the Latin countries, bringing with it the flavor of Greek and Roman civilization, with which our ancestral lines are not particularly connected."[47]

The earliest preservationists responded primarily to threats of physical change, but by the early twentieth century, social change seemed more overwhelming. Just as deed restrictions, first developed to shape physical form, were increasingly put to use solidifying social geography, so preservation increasingly became part of a matrix of class and ethnic definition. The audience for patriotic education shifted from "us" to "them." The first guardians of the Old South and the Old State House expected these monuments to convey shared values to their own progeny. By the early twentieth century the second editor of SPNEA's *Bulletin*, George F. Dow, would describe one of preservation's missions as "informing foreigners and less enlightened natives as to American traditions and values." The earliest preservation controversies were largely among upper-class Anglo-Saxons. By the twentieth century, conflicts often pitted Brahmins against other groups. As the Irish and newer immigrants became economically and politically ascendant, white Anglo-Saxon Protestants awakened to a group identity of which they had not been so acutely aware, and they asserted it through the formation of genealogical and patriotic societies. SPNEA was part of this organizational constellation and at one point stretched its definition of antiquities to take up the issue of "persons changing their family names . . . for the purpose of assuming an old New England name of long and good standing."[48] After Brahmins lost power in Boston to an Irish-dominated political machine, they gradually disengaged from the political life of the city. Many turned their minds instead to more satisfactory bygone days, and to the still comfortably Anglo-Saxon countryside, their residences and preservation attention following. Thus while SPNEA's direction came from Appleton, its popularity and success—and the fact that no competing organization emerged to complement its deficiencies—resulted from a constituency concentrating on its own ancestral rather than public past.

This new concern with a smaller scale of building changed the nature of preservation conflicts: instead of confronting governments or quasi-public institutions, preservationists found themselves dealing with individual property owners; in the oldest, often run-down parts of Boston and smaller towns, those individuals were increasingly likely to be Italians, Jews, Poles, or other eastern Europeans. William Sumner Appleton often faced "the difficulties involved in trying to do business with a foreigner, whom fortune had made for the moment the custodian of a really interesting New England antiquity," and he was by both background and inclination unprepared for the task. At the Saugus House he told a correspondent, "Our neighbors are callabrian Italians who are not famous for their good behavior."[49] Appleton's approach to managing properties in ethnic neighborhoods, says Lindgren, "bordered upon a siege mentality," but he had to deal with real vandalism and saw one seventeenth-century house purchased by a family association only to be destroyed by arson.[50] Whatever his attitudes, his actions can be explained by sincere concern for the physical protection of SPNEA's properties. Other preservationists worried about less tangible threats. Mary Desha, one of the founders of the national Daughters of the American Revolution, called upon that organization in 1898 to keep historic buildings from "passing into the hands of improper people."[51]

The link between preservation and nativism should not be overdrawn. A resurgent xenophobia was part of America's cultural mainstream at the turn of the century; it did not produce the preservation movement but merely tugged at it with its current. Indeed, when SPNEA is considered in the context of other traditionalist groups, its significance is that it so steadfastly concentrated on buildings and objects, making little concession to patriotic cant. Curtis Guild Jr., lieutenant governor of Massachusetts and president of the Paul Revere Memorial Association, tempered nativist excess by reminding donors that "Paul Revere, like the children who now play around his venerable home, was himself the son of an immigrant." The house could help teach those children American ways, but it could teach nativists too, "as a reminder to the Commonwealth of the services rendered by new citizens and by their children." Appleton could work with non-WASP institutions—the First African Methodist Episcopal Church in Boston, the Cercle

Social Franco-American in Rhode Island—when that would help preserve a building.[52]

Most important, broadening the preservation movement to include the ordinary life of earlier generations eventually worked against nativism. Even if it was conceived by some adherents as an affirmation of Anglo-Saxon precedence, it defined a powerfully inclusive subject matter which, as preservationists' chronological frontier moved forward through the nineteenth century, would embrace the very groups it had earlier excluded and allow later preservationists to take an interest in workaday parts of the environment their predecessors sought to escape.

As the field of preservation grew more active in the teens and twenties, it became ripe for organizing ideas, and Appleton's had particular force because of his unique national position. Not only did he run the largest, most ambitious, and most rigorous preservation organization of the time, but his *Bulletin* was the only American periodical devoted exclusively to the subject. An indefatigable correspondent, he advised countless individuals and groups all over the country, making SPNEA a national clearinghouse for preservation information and helping to provide a philosophical frame of reference for activists who were often otherwise isolated from one another. They sought his advice because SPNEA's methods worked.

Practice

Appleton's contributions to preservation's methods, like those to its philosophy, were to make them systematic, effectively professionalizing the field. Appleton himself remained literally an amateur, never drawing a salary, but this paradoxically contributed to his professionalization. Appleton's trust fund figured decisively in SPNEA's tactical success, serving as a de facto endowment. It gave him the luxury and the responsibility of planning for the long term, thinking through not only his philosophy of preservation but also how he should go about it, knowing that his full-time status was secure.

Systematic priorities brought increased reliance on experts able to evaluate them. SPNEA was aided by, and itself assisted, the emergence of restoration architecture as a distinct profession, following principles that had more to do with archaeology than with design. The society was a continuing source of commissions for established practitioners such as Joseph E. Chandler of Boston and Norman M. Isham of Providence, as well as for newer entrants to the field. Even more important, it served as a sort of continuing, informal professional seminar. "Practically every architectural scholar in New England," says Charles Hosmer, "toured with Appleton at some time."[53] He insisted on a rigorous regimen of investigation and recording in the restoration process, laying the basis of a cumulative body of professional knowledge. He made SPNEA an essential institution for the profession, acting as depository for a massive archive of the documentation necessary to support comparative study.

Appleton also elaborated the preservation movement's techniques of private intervention. He honed adaptive use as a preservation tool, in his program to restore buildings and then "let them to tenants under wise restrictions." The idea that restored buildings could continue in the life of their community was a powerful one, though Appleton meant it more as an expedient to husband SPNEA's funds not for house museums but for saving more buildings. He was innovative in his means of getting control of properties, seeking gifts and bequests, buying houses subject to life occupancy, and financing restorations in return for reversion of property on the owners' deaths. He originated the now familiar "revolving fund," in effect an organized approach to crisis response. The Helen F. Kimball Emergency Fund was established in 1912, $1,500 on hand that could be used quickly without approval by the trustees but had to be paid back in full before the fund could be tapped again. This allowed Appleton to raise money for the particular building he was saving as well as for the fund itself as a tool for meeting the next crisis.[54]

Appleton's most significant contribution to preservation technique was to recognize preservation as an ongoing rather than a finite action, an issue not of permanence but of control. A choice of phrase is revealing: when a Federal mansion in Providence was bought by an individual intent on saving it, Appleton wrote, "We may well hope that preservation of this splendid example of New England town architecture may be continued." Continuing preservation required financial endurance. Appleton noted that "the financial weakness of the holding organization" for the Shirley-Eustis Mansion "had for a long time endangered the permanence" of the preservation effort. The 1773 West Roxbury meetinghouse, "saved" by an ad hoc committee including Edward Everett Hale, was destroyed in 1913 after SPNEA refused to accept it with a mortgage. Appleton was even prepared to decline properties offered to the society unmortgaged but without endowments. "The safety of some houses might be jeopardized by this policy, but the security of the Society as a whole would be much increased."[55]

The security of the society was central to Appleton's vision of preservation. He was deeply skeptical of any scheme other than ownership by some institutional guardian, preferably SPNEA. He was almost insulting in his dismissal of preservation by individuals, no matter who: "The two president's [sic] houses in Quincy, although now occupied respectively by the Quincy Historical Society and the Adams Chapter, D.R., cannot with certainty be counted among buildings permanently preserved, since they are still in the hands of the Adams family, and the most casual knowledge of the fate of old buildings shows the uncertainty of such private tenure." It was "essential" that historic buildings "be placed in the hands of permanent corporations."[56]

William Sumner Appleton transformed the preservation movement into one that was better organized and more effective but with more restricted aims than before. He institutionalized preservation by creating "an enormous operation," says Charles Hosmer, "that maintained many important buildings in a form of historical cold storage. The number of houses lost in New England was remarkably small between 1910 and 1947."[57] He honed a single existing tool for preservation: ownership by a private group, usually through purchase. It was the most thorough solution where it could be used, but it could not be used often. Appleton did not see any need to transcend the limitations of this system, and he did not pick up any of the tools for public intervention that others had been forging.

Preservation as Public Policy

No government body anywhere in the country took on preservation in any systematic way comparable to SPNEA's private program. Cities, states, and the federal government preserved some buildings that they already owned. In rare instances they bought buildings or sites specifically to preserve them, starting with New York State's purchase of the Hasbrouck House in 1850. Half a century later this governmental role still remained embryonic; it did not come to Massachusetts until 1913, when the Lexington town meeting voted to help purchase the Buckman Tavern.[58] In each case public action resulted from the same sort of expediency that led Bostonians to ask city and state help in saving the Hancock House, the Old South, and Park Street Church. Governments provided funds or served as permanent custodians; they were seldom called upon to do anything that private groups could not in theory undertake. And in Massachusetts, landmarks that started out as private property either were saved by private action or were lost. The state government pioneered in landscape preservation, but public policy toward landmark structures was incoherent and ineffective.

One reason well-to-do Bostonians did not look to government for preservation was their distrust of the ascendant immigrant political leadership. They saw their suspicions amply confirmed by the city's treatment of its environmental heritage. At the apex of Brahmin demonology was James Michael Curley, mayor from 1914 to 1917, and then off and on again until 1949; he and his lieutenants, wrote SPNEA president Charles Knowles Bolton in his journal, were "surely ridiculous rulers of a million people anywhere but in a democracy run mad." Curley returned the compliment by proposing to sell the Public Garden to finance neighborhood parks, using the environment to tweak his Brahmin opponents. He expanded a confrontational brand of urban politics begun in 1905 by Boston's second Irish mayor, John "Honey Fitz" Fitzgerald, who proposed selling building lots blocking water views from aristocratic Beacon Street.[59] Curley appointed as building commissioner Patrick O'Hearn, a tenement builder who threatened to tear down the colonial Shirley-Eustis Mansion for building-code violations. Preservationists appealed to the legislature, which specifically exempted it from the city's code.[60] When Henry Statler hesitated to build a hotel in Boston in 1923, Curley helped lure him by raising the city's height limit from 125 to 155 feet and announced that if this was not tall enough he would try 200 feet. Later he attempted to remove the special height restrictions on Commonwealth Avenue.[61] Aristocratic Bostonians could not feel comfortable putting environmental stability in the hands of government while the government was in hands like Curley's.

William Sumner Appleton epitomized this Brahmin ambivalence. Government action for preservation was difficult to accomplish, he wrote in 1918,

and for some reasons not to be desired. That part of the public capable of appreciating a handsome building for the sake of its artistic merit, is small indeed, and the chance of obtaining support from the public treasury is too negligible to notice, except in the case of public buildings of historic interest, like Faneuil Hall in Boston, and Independence Hall, Philadelphia. On the other hand, even if this were not the case, our political system, with its almost total lack of responsibility, as well as its widespread tendency to the spoils system, makes public action extremely dangerous.[62]

On the whole, Appleton tried to avoid government and politics. When he wanted some government action, he "fixed it up" quietly if he could. He did not organize SPNEA for the sort of lobbying he had used against the subway at the Old State House. He addressed his fundraising to the wealthy, not mass campaigns like Mount Vernon and the Old South that built political along with financial support. But Appleton was too much a pragmatist not to look longingly at the tremendous resources of governments.

A logical first step in tapping government resources was safeguarding historic properties that were already publicly owned. The federal government had begun protecting prehistoric sites under the Antiquities Act of 1906, which historian Ronald F. Lee called "the first national historic preservation policy for the United States." Appleton was interested in Maine's frontier fortifications, abandoned and decaying but still in War Department ownership, and in 1912 he wrote Smithsonian Institution secretary Charles D. Walcott to ask whether the Antiquities Act could be used to preserve them. In law, the answer was yes: the act allowed the president to designate as "national monuments" any "historic landmarks, historic and prehistoric structures, and other objects of historic or scientific interest" located on any federal lands. Despite its inclusive language, the act had been conceived and until then used only for sites of archaeological or geological interest, all of them in the West.[63] Walcott gave Appleton a taste of his own medicine when he suggested that Maine's blockhouses possessed "a local rather than a National interest or importance." Appleton tried to invoke a national scope by pointing out that "there must be many more such properties scattered all over the country," but the prospect of endless, piecemeal involvement with local preservation concerns may not have been the best way to woo Washington officials. Appleton eventually found private methods to save the blockhouses. The Antiquities Act was not used for any historic—as opposed to prehistoric—landmark until 1924, and then it was applied with a view to supreme national significance, though not necessarily great antiquity; among the first of these historic landmarks was the Statue of Liberty.[64] The kind of small-scale preservation of surplus properties that Appleton had in mind was not begun by the federal government until 1944.[65]

Without government assistance, preservation's basic limitation was a lack of available resources. Private subscription and purchase accomplished more in eastern Massachusetts than anywhere else in the country, yet it was clearly inadequate in urban areas. The Park Street preservation committee, despite its effectiveness at soliciting pledges, had to turn to the legislature if it was to save the building by purchase. William Sumner Appleton was unwilling to seek government involvement, so his goals in city centers had to be very modest. John D. Rockefeller Jr. at Williamsburg and Henry Ford at Greenfield Village, Michigan, each spent over $25 million on preservation, and Appleton tried unsuccessfully to interest one of them or their financial peers in endowing preservation elsewhere.[66] Without a fund of such magnitude, private preservation would inevitably remain fragmentary.

Preservation by purchase operated through the market, so it did not fundamentally challenge real estate interests. It exempted a few places from developers' rules, but it did not change the rules. Many developers could see the appeal of the buildings they were destroying, and they saw no contradiction in participating in the preservation movement at the same time. John Phillips Reynolds Jr. was buying the Paul Revere House even as he tried to tear down Park Street Church. Similarly, Alexander S. Porter, a president of the Boston Real Estate Exchange, offered the Old South for sale and redevelopment and put together the syndicate that would have razed St.

Develpers (handwritten annotation)

Paul's Church, yet he took a sympathetic interest even in the buildings he tore down, lecturing on them and amassing an important collection of antiquarian photographs.[67] Porter led in organizing the Committee to Preserve Park Street Church and joined SPNEA shortly after it was founded. He evidently felt that tearing down St. Paul's would have been a reasonable way to make a profit, and preserving Park Street Church across the street a reasonable way to spend it; market-based preservation allowed individuals to make their own decisions where to draw the line against change. Other developers were happy to cooperate with SPNEA in recording structures or offering them to be moved, secure in the knowledge that their fundamental right to clear sites went unquestioned.[68]

Preservationists from the earliest days of the movement had argued that historic buildings were an economic benefit to their communities, and by the early twentieth century the argument was well accepted by businesspeople. The Providence Board of Trade published a laudatory article on SPNEA in May 1914 and later that year noted that "Boston, by playing up its historic attractions for several generations, has vastly profited in a commercial way." The Boston Chamber of Commerce agreed: "Preservation . . . pays as an investment."[69]

An audience this diverse helped institutionalize preservation in another sense; it came to be assumed in decision-making about the built environment, although not always in the methodical way Appleton advocated. George G. Crocker headed the Boston Transit Commission, potentially among the city's most powerful engines of environmental change, but he ran it according to his own preservationist views that earlier made him defend the Common and the Old South. Now he sat on the Old South Association Board of Managers, and even Appleton thought that the transit commission plan "amply safeguards the Old South Meeting House." Crocker felt he was doing the same at the Old State House, where he wanted to use existing doorways as a subway entrance, making no changes to the building's exterior except to add historical plaques. He argued that Appleton's alternative of new station kiosks would ruin views of the building. Appleton admitted that if the station really needed more of the Old State House, "it would be hard to devise a less objectionable plan." He fought it in part because he feared that the station would prove inadequate and then Crocker's plan would be replaced by a worse one. The whole battleground had shifted toward preservation: this time no one suggested tearing the building down.[70] A similar example is the Custom House Tower, proposed by architect Robert S. Peabody in 1909 and constructed from 1911 to 1915. Critics found much about its design impractical and expensive, but few questioned the extraordinary

FIGURE 9.7 *Custom House Tower under construction. Courtesy Boston Public Library, Print Department*

basic premise of preserving Ammi Young's 1837 Greek Revival custom house by putting all the new offices in a slender tower perched atop it, rather than clearing the site.[71]

The strongest use of government powers would be to force preservation over the will of private owners, as historic districts and landmark laws can do today under the police power. Preservationists first explored the power of eminent domain as an ad hoc response through frustration with intransigent owners: the Massachusetts legislature granted eminent-domain powers to the Old South Association, and the Virginia legislature to the APVA in its campaign to preserve the Jamestown settlement site. When a streetcar company proposed a tourist line through the Gettysburg battlefield, Congress in 1894 authorized taking the trolley route as part of a National Military Park, and two years later the U.S. Supreme Court upheld the taking as serving a valid public purpose.[72] Preservationists in 1912 suggested that the federal government use condemnation to gain possession of Thomas Jefferson's Virginia home, Monticello, but William Sumner Appleton protested: "I am a strong believer in buying Jefferson's home for preservation, but as luck will have it I am also an ardent Jeffersonian in my principles, and can't help feeling that Jefferson would turn in his grave at the mere suggestion that the Federal Government should buy his home by right of eminent domain."[73]

Despite his mistrust of government, Appleton was serious enough about preservation that five years later he too explored this tool. He began to consider eminent domain as an extension of the cultural-patrimony laws by which European nations guarded their tangible heritage against plunder by wealthy foreigners, often Americans. Great Britain, for example, passed its first compulsory preservation act (relying on eminent domain) in 1913, after Americans began dismantling Tattershall Castle.[74] Similarly, museums and collectors in New York and other cities were stripping the interiors of early houses in New England and the South, leading Appleton to consider seeking some sort of cultural-patrimony legislation. He saw the removal of building parts as, in effect, raids by foreigners. This regional parochialism, together with disgust for the owners—often lower-class, sometimes immigrant—who allowed their buildings to be broken up, blunted Appleton's usual conservative regard for property rights and his distaste for government action.

Appleton appeared to succeed spectacularly by incorporating eminent domain into the first preservation amendment to a state constitution: "The preservation and maintenance of ancient landmarks and other property of historical or antiquarian interest is a public use, and the commonwealth and the cities and towns therein may, upon payment of just compensation, take such property or any interest therein under such regulations as the general court may prescribe."[75] Years later Appleton laid modesty aside as he reminisced about the amendment:

I thought it up as I was crossing the Common one day as the last Constitutional Convention was in session here and finding the judiciary committee was in session, appeared before it and presented my proposed amendment. They asked what organizations and individuals would appear in addition. I said none; it was my own idea and I was appearing alone. There was nobody in the room but the committee and myself and they seemed very much amused. However, on talking the matter over in committee it seemed to them a good proposition and they commended it to the Convention. There it would have failed excepting that a member from Lexington spoke so strongly in its favor that it went through.[76]

It became amendment 51 to the Massachusetts constitution when voters approved it on November 5, 1918, by more than 2 to 1 statewide and more than 4 to 1 in Boston. "I am surprised that you can reach so many people," wrote one convention delegate to Appleton.[77]

This great preservationist victory turned out hollow because of the same political naivete that had so amused the convention delegates. Appleton petitioned the next legislature for the enabling "regulations" needed to make the amendment operational, but he did not even bother testifying for them. "If the people wanted the amendment," he wrote plaintively to the judiciary committee chairman as his bill died there, "it seems to me that they are entitled to some act giving the amendment force." After sporadic attempts to revive it, he did not return to the issue again until the mid-1930s. Such abstract measures were not important to him; he could not point to a single specific building they would save.[78] In the SPNEA *Bulletin* he gave only a short notice to the amendment, and no mention at all of the attempt to secure follow-up legislation. Significantly, given Appleton's regional mind-set, he made no suggestion that New England's other five states ought to follow the example.

William Sumner Appleton led Boston's third generation of preservationists. The movement had evolved from an historical to a visual to an archaeological sensibility. First, it saved monuments such as the Old South and the Old State House, sanctified by their associations with historic events and valuable to the present for their ability to evoke them. Second, it saved landmarks such as the Common and the Bulfinch statehouse, important for their visual role in the urban landscape. Finally, it saved artifacts such as SPNEA's old houses, structures significant for what they revealed about the material culture of the past, which in turn could reinvigorate the culture of the present. These sensibilities did not necessarily supplant but added to one another, each contributing a new way of looking at what earlier efforts had accomplished and redefining what still needed to be done. The shift of preservationist attention from the public environment to private, domestic environments was in part a mark of success; the most important public landmarks were secured, and preservation had indeed become enough of an assumption that planners would exercise at least some regard for landmarks. The fourth generation of the movement would again turn toward the city, but not through Appleton.

CHAPTER 10

❧❧❧

Public Control

The [Beacon Hill height] statute was passed . . . to save the dignity and beauty of the city at its culminating point, for the pride of every Bostonian and for the pleasure of every member of the State. . . . Such a law is no less valid when passed to satisfy the love of beauty than when passed to appease the fear of fire.
—OLIVER WENDELL HOLMES JR.

In the early twentieth century, ad hoc efforts for environmental permanence grew less prevalent, replaced by institutionalized means of environmental control. These methods started out private—deed restrictions, preservation organizations—but as the limitations of private action became apparent, Bostonians turned to public controls. At first, public action was piecemeal: a building line here, a height limit there, now a permit for garages. But the comprehensiveness of urban change led to a demand for equally comprehensive controls.

Bostonians discovered limitations in stabilizing the physical city through the private market and private institutions, leading them to explore public powers. Saving whole urban compositions such as the statehouse, the Common, and the churches and houses around them brought preservationists' attention to a scale at which purchase was almost irrelevant; neither Rockefeller nor the commonwealth of Massachusetts could buy Boston. Maintaining urban design by paying for air rights raised the same problems. Solving those problems created a much more versatile and potentially universal system for regulating development, which was then shaped into modern zoning.

"Fixing a Constitutional Limit"

When Haddon Hall in 1896 spurred consideration of regulating building heights in specific locales, the Massachusetts legislature conservatively chose to act under eminent domain rather than the police power. The state respected vested rights in property by paying for them. But were 125-foot-tall buildings, the statewide limit enacted in 1891, a right or merely a maximum? Members of the Boston Real Estate Exchange and the Twentieth Century Club believed in 1896 that the limit might be further reduced according to local conditions. George B. Upham and others, including Louis Brandeis, continued advocating the police power as a basis for regulatory distinctions between different parts of the city. In 1899, when it became clear that the legislature was unwilling to divide the city into districts, they tried imaginative variations such as the Beacon Hill ceiling projected from the statehouse cornice. Upham submitted another bill the same year applying an eighty-foot height limit only to apartment buildings and hotels and providing that the mayor could issue exemptions "if satisfied that the location designated is fairly within a business district as distinguished from a residential district." [1] Either of these, if enacted and sustained by the courts, would open the door for citywide height districting without compensation. [2] If Upham and Brandeis were correct, the city and state were paying for rights that did not exist.

The police power appealed to fiscal conservatism, as opposed to the ideological conservatism of eminent domain. Legislators acknowledged this conflict by writing height restrictions that were increasingly ambiguous about what compensation they offered. The Commonwealth Avenue and Copley Square acts in 1896 and 1898 were unambiguous: it was the city of Boston that would have to pay, and since it was citizens of Boston who wanted the restrictions, that seemed fair to legislators who were mostly from elsewhere. But on Beacon Hill the state would have to pay, and legislators began to see the appeal of the police power. In drafting the 1899 Beacon Hill restrictions they were noncommittal about compensation; the state would pay only "if and in so far as this act . . . may deprive any person of rights existing under the constitution." [3] Since the courts would ultimately decide whether or not police-power districting was valid, why not leave the whole sticky issue to them?

Massachusetts chief justice Oliver Wendell Holmes Jr., however, would not allow the court to be drawn into "the difficulty of fixing a constitutional limit by feet and inches." He upheld the Beacon Hill restrictions in *Parker v. Commonwealth,* on March 1, 1901, but rejected any interpretation of the act's language as "importing an exercise of the police power so far as the Legislature constitutionally could go, and as saving a remedy for all damages beyond that limit." The act, he said, "treats the limits of the police power as if they were a matter which might be left to this court to fix in the first place without any preliminary exercise of legislative judgement." But the police power by its nature balanced individuals' rights against their responsibilities to others, a balance that Holmes insisted was to be politically decided, not judicially discovered. "While we can gather that the Legislature was willing to take anything without paying for it that this court should say that it could," wrote Holmes, it nowhere made the explicit judgment of public necessity that would support an exercise of the police power, and the restriction was therefore a taking.[4] Until the legislature could decide for itself where lower height districts were reasonable without compensation, it would have to go on paying for them.

In the evolution of American land-use law, Boston's exploration of eminent domain turned out to be a dead end, but it may have been a necessary experiment. Different treatments for different places within the city appeared problematic under the police power. Eminent-domain restrictions allowed site-specific limits without having to resolve for the moment the difficult ideological questions of private property rights. This exploration was a success; it showed that height districting was not the "special case" that William Minot had thought at Copley Square but a technique of potentially widespread usefulness in controlling environmental change. At the same time, Boston's experience showed that relying on eminent domain would make the tool too unwieldy to realize that potential.[5] Early impressions on Commonwealth Avenue, where no owners asked for compensation, and on Copley Square, where Mollie Cole asked but did not receive it, were giving way to a more sobering understanding that damage awards would be widespread and substantial. The Westminster Chambers case was making its way through the courts. Damage awards elsewhere on Copley Square, together with Holmes's decision on Beacon Hill, destroyed any hope that compensation would be limited to this extreme case of cutting down a completed building. The right to build tall had a value, and taking that right was proving expensive.

A combination of events pushed Boston toward ending its experiment with eminent domain while pulling it toward police-power regulations. The push began on December 31, 1902, when hearings opened to set the compensation for height restrictions on Beacon Hill. Substantially all the affected owners asked for damages, starting with Robert Treat Paine, one of the original petitioners for the restriction. Though he and his neighbors favored the restrictions, there was no pretense on Beacon Hill that their sacrifices were solely for their own mutual benefit. For almost twenty years various statehouse plans had contemplated taking their property. Now the state was taking part of it, and Paine's attorney suggested that the legislature acted "with a view of so depreciating the value of that section" that it could later pick up the land at bargain rates.[6] The owners asked an average of $100,000 each, an astronomical total of $5–6 million, which would dwarf the cost of Copley Square's restrictions.[7]

The pull toward the police power came from the courts. In the *Attorney General v. Williams* decision upholding Copley Square's height districts in 1899, Associate Justice Marcus Knowlton of the Massachusetts Supreme Judicial Court wrote that "it would be hard to say that this statute might not have been passed in the exercise of the police power." Oliver Wendell Holmes Jr.'s 1901 *Parker v. Commonwealth* decision, in which Knowlton joined, gave legislators a further invitation; while the geographical specificity of the Beacon Hill restrictions "would present grave difficulties" under the police power, he discussed other circumstances in which such regulations would be allowable. On February 23, 1903, as the state was still evaluating the cost of those restrictions, the U.S. Supreme Court affirmed *Attorney General v. Williams,* the first time building-height restrictions anywhere had come before the high court. The opinion was not a ringing endorsement of Knowlton's every word: "We have not . . . stopped to comment on the suggestion made by the Supreme Court of the State," wrote Justice David J. Brewer, "that this statute might be sustained as an exercise of the police power, or . . . that it could be enforced without any provision for compensation."[8] But Brewer confined the opinion to narrow issues without examining Knowlton's sweeping affirmation of height restrictions in general, implying that states would be allowed discretion in settling these questions themselves. A few weeks earlier Marcus Knowlton had become chief justice of the Massachusetts high court, so discretion there would likely be exercised in favor of the police power.

That summer, Westminster Chambers' roof came down, slowly and expensively, clearly not a good model for future regulation. At least five new structures had risen above one hundred feet in the Back Bay since Haddon Hall, maintaining a certain urgency about the issue of tall buildings. After the Supreme Court affirmed *Attorney General v. Williams,* a new height-districting bill was submitted to the 1904 legislature, this time with city support. Instead of letting the legislature argue over the boundaries, as Upham had done, this bill created a three-member commission to carry out the delicate task of drawing them. The commissioners would delineate district A, "those parts of the city in which all or the greater part of the buildings" were then "used for business or commercial purposes," where buildings could still be built to 125 feet, and district B, all the city's residential quarters, where allowable height would be reduced to 80 feet.[9]

The bill said that the boundaries "shall be determined for ten years," a period that the Committee on Cities increased to fifteen years.[10] Assigning a duration to the boundaries, rather than to the restriction itself, implied that the eighty-foot limit would continue indefinitely, with only its geographical extent revised after fifteen years. The act, however, made no provision for

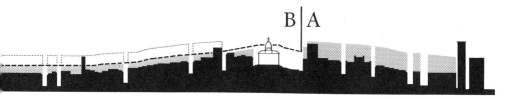

FIGURE 10.1 *The height districts as they applied to Beacon Hill; vertical dimension exaggerated 2:1. The eighty-foot limit of the B district protected views of the state-house dome from all sides on which that was economically feasible. It also prevented further development of tall apartment buildings throughout the residential parts of Beacon Hill. Drawing by author*

what was to happen then. As with deed restrictions by this time, the initial development of a tool for ensuring permanence was followed by a realization that the tool was more versatile if used not to freeze change but to exert control over it. Consensus on a permanent shape for the city was difficult to achieve; it was easier for people to agree on short-term controls, so that change would proceed along predictable lines.

The legislature passed the act, and Mayor Patrick A. Collins promptly appointed a commission of three real estate experts to draw the boundaries, including former mayor Nathan Matthews, whose administration submitted the original 125-foot bill in 1891, and who had advocated further height restrictions ever since.[11]

The boundary they drew did not look at all like the convoluted figures of modern zoning maps but was instead a single line across the peninsula, for most of its length following within two blocks of Upham's original 1896 proposal. The commissioners drew the line cautiously, looking to the act's plain distinction between commercial and residential uses. Beacon Hill was residential, so its old houses would not be replaced by tall buildings—an eighty-foot limit imposed for free surrounding the two blocks where the state was paying for a seventy-foot limit. But the commissioners did not make other preservationist adjustments; they did not attempt to lower heights on the downtown side of the statehouse, or on Park Street, where their line ran right past Park Street Church during its hour of need without offering it any protection. Regulation according to aesthetic criteria was of uncertain constitutionality, they said, so they ignored aesthetics. The act gave the commission no guidance as to how big were the "parts of the city" it should look at. All precedents for small districts provided compensation, while police-power districts such as fire limits involved some "considerable part of a city," so they avoided small districts. They left the whole residential area of the immigrant North End in the A district rather than make a protected island

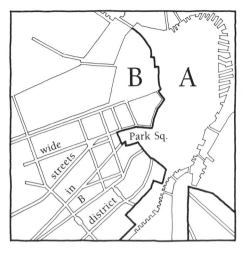

MAP 17

of it. They refused to extend the A district in fingers radiating from the city center along the major commercial thoroughfares, because "it seemed to us that the Legislature could not have intended that we should create districts out of single streets and thus permit the residential sections of the city to be covered like a gridiron by long lines of 125-foot buildings." The pressure for small districts came from Back Bay landowners. While the commissioners noted business incursions there, they found the Back Bay as a whole "distinctly residential in character according to the test prescribed by the act."[12]

The Back Bay was the place that made height restrictions important, and the place that made them difficult, for Upham in the 1890s, and for Matthews and his fellow commissioners in 1904. "When the best residence district is determined, the main growth of the city is quite certain to follow it," New York real estate expert Richard M. Hurd had written a year before in his *Principles of City Land Values,* "as note the movement of retail stores after the best residences . . . on Boylston Street in Boston." The axis of Boston's "best residence district" extended through the Back Bay to Brookline and then Newton; Boylston Street, almost entirely residential in the late 1880s, had become a commercial district advertised as "Boston's Fifth Avenue" ten years later. These were the years when civic and commercial uses fought for the soul of Copley Square, with the top six feet of Westminster Chambers their battlefield. By the time the commissioners were drawing their boundary line, the *Herald* found many businessmen who believed that "commercial Boston, in spreading outward, would naturally seek Copley Square for its new center." [13] Their ambitions were even higher for the former Park Square complex of the Providence Railroad, a large piece of land centrally located between Copley Square and downtown that could be developed without immediate damage to the existing Back Bay streetscape.

The commissioners felt no inclination to assist in the Back Bay's transformation; they believed that the act's purpose was "to prevent the erection of very high buildings in those parts of the city which, unlike the down-town section, are not yet condemned by the number of high buildings already erected to the perpetual toleration of this evil." When Back Bay investors loudly protested the inclusion of their commercial properties in the residential B district, the commissioners left most of them unsatisfied, jogging their boundary only slightly to put Park Square and the beginning of Boylston Street in the A district. [14] They also suggested, since the next legislature "will undoubtedly be asked to amend the Act of 1904," that it meet the protests by permitting buildings on wide streets in the B district to the intermediate height of one hundred feet. [15] The *Evening Transcript* endorsed this proposal, not because its editors liked tall buildings, but because they thought it would remove any need for future revision of the limits: "There is no reason why the rest of the city should not be protected for all time against sky-scrapers on the Back Bay and in other residential districts. If the character of those districts changes so that in time they become devoted to business uses, the limit of 100 feet will permit the erection of buildings which are high enough." The commissioners also urged that district boundaries "should be permanent": "If the limits adopted are satisfactory, we see no reason for holding out any definite expectation of a change. The Legislature has, and will continue to have without express reservation, the power to modify the law, but the existence of a statute expressly providing for modifications at stated periods can only have an unsettling effect on real estate values." [16]

The following year, as the commissioners predicted, scores of real estate owners petitioned the legislature to repeal the height-district act. Most of them owned property on Boylston Street and Huntington Avenue, two of the arteries that met at Copley Square, where owners had every reason to believe that high buildings would soon be profitable. The damages already paid under the several eminent-domain acts may have helped owners imagine the value of the air above their roofs. The legislature did not repeal the act. It passed the commission's recommendation that on wide streets owners should have the right to build to one hundred feet; it did not make the restrictions permanent. [17]

The height districts were meant as a preservation measure. Of fifteen backers cited in City Council debate, at least ten had worked to preserve the Old South, the Bulfinch statehouse, Park Street Church, the Paul Revere House, and the Common. Of the eighty-four petitioners for repeal the following year, only one had joined in any of those causes.[18]

When the eighty-foot B district survived the 1905 legislature, it was promptly challenged in court. Francis C. Welch, who owned a lot facing the Public Garden at the corner of Arlington and Marlborough Streets, applied to build a 120-foot building there, and when the city refused him a permit, he claimed that he had been unconstitutionally denied equal protection and deprived of his property without compensation. Marcus Knowlton, now chief justice, wrote the opinion of the state's high court affirming the limit,[19] and Welch appealed to the U.S. Supreme Court.

Justice Rufus W. Peckham delivered the Supreme Court's decision on May 17, 1909, upholding Knowlton's opinion so enthusiastically that it spurred development of police-power districting—what came to be called zoning—in this country. The validity of police-power measures is a matter of the fit between their ends and means, and the reasonableness with which they balance private rights with the public good, questions that turn on the facts of each case. "This court is not familiar with the actual facts," wrote Peckham,

fire

but it may be that in this limited commercial area the high buildings are generally of fireproof construction; that the fire engines are more numerous and much closer together than in the residential portion, and that an unlimited supply of salt water can be more readily introduced from the harbor into the pipes, and that few women or children are found there in the daytime and very few people sleep there at night. And there may in the residential part be more wooden buildings, the fire apparatus may be more widely scattered and so situated that it would be more difficult to obtain the necessary amount of water, as the residence quarters are more remote from the water front, and that many women and children spend the day in that section, and the opinion is not strained that an undiscovered fire at night might cause great loss of life in a very high apartment house in that district.[20]

Judging whether these things were true, and whether they merited discriminating between different parts of the city, required an understanding of local conditions that could be found in legislatures and state courts better than in Washington, Peckham said, so the high court would not interfere unless these local officials were "plainly wrong." Boston's distinction between districts, far from being wrong, was "reasonable, and is justified by the police power." Peckham concluded by allaying the commissioners' fear of permitting any taint of aesthetics in their criteria: "That in addition to these suffi-

police power

252

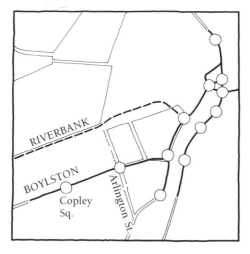

MAP 18

cient facts, considerations of an aesthetic nature also entered into the reasons for their passage, would not invalidate them."[21]

Revisions

While the courts were endorsing Boston's building limits, the facts on the ground were changing, and continued business expansion eventually unraveled the A/B line. A 1906 master plan by the Boston Transit Commission noted that streetcar traffic "has practically reached its limit" on Boylston Street, "in which direction the shopping district is extending," and recommended an immediate extension of the subway under Boylston Street to Copley Square or farther. The legislature instead selected an alternative route next to the river. Merchants were not happy being bypassed, and by 1911 they convinced the legislature to order construction of the Boylston Street line. One member of the transit commission, Horace G. Allen, dissented as he contemplated the uninterrupted run of four thousand feet from Copley Square to the existing downtown station at Tremont Street. "It is difficult to see what good such a subway can do business interests on Boylston street between Clarendon and Tremont streets."[22] Even before the line opened in 1914, merchants imagined thousands of passengers a day disappearing from in front of their doors, and they saw Allen's point. They agitated for an intermediate station at Arlington Street. The transit commissioners recommended stations fifteen hundred feet apart in the business district, and this, insisted property owners, was a business district.[23] They could point to the building-height district to prove it: their proposed station was just inside the A district's Park Square jog. "While it now appears an outpost," reported the *Evening Transcript,* "on the first revision of the boundaries there can be no question but what it will be far more central."[24] The Boston Elevated Railroad Company, which held the transit franchise, opposed the new station, and the legislature in 1914 narrowly rejected it.

Boylston's real estate owners would not take no for an answer. With neither streetcars nor a station, their properties were worth less, they reasoned, so they were entitled to a tax abatement. Mayor Curley, who cared not a whit about the residential sensibilities of the Back Bay, cared a great deal about the city's tax base and supported a renewed push for an Arlington Street station. At the same time, he asked the legislature for a new building-heights commission to redraw the B district boundary even before its fifteen-year life was up.[25] The two measures together complemented the city's recent extension of Arlington Street across the Providence Railroad lands to encourage expansion of the city's commercial center, a clear public policy in favor of changing urban form. Arlington station proponents played their legislative politics well, submitting their bill with twenty thousand signatures, mostly suburban commuters. The station bill and the district-revision bill passed together.[26]

The original height districts had not lasted through their fifteen-year term, and the act called for new ones to remain in effect for only ten years.[27] Unlike the 1904 act, it specified no standards for revising the lines, and so the new height-district hearings became not a factual investigation into Boston's geography but rather an unprecedented forum on permanence and change in urban form and the idea of a public policy deliberately addressing them.

Deed restrictions provided a powerful analogy for understanding controls on environmental change. The B district's specified duration reinforced the analogy and led people to express dismay at premature tampering with an arrangement that appeared settled.[28] Like deed restrictions, these publicly imposed regulations seemed to create vested interests in those who had built in reliance on them. W. W. Vaughan, a developer who had campaigned against Westminster Chambers, explained that

you have had ten years of building under that restriction, the owners at the time they built not knowing on the face of it that there were any signs of its being changed. You will remember that the present law was supposed to be established for fifteen years. . . .

Property owners thought it was to run on indefinitely. We recognized the fact, of course, that in fifty or even one hundred years the city would change, but we did not realize that within ten years' time a law might be passed so that it would all be thrown open again.[29]

Vaughan, like many of the commission's witnesses, thought that "these laws ought to be as nearly permanent as possible." This principle was urged even by people who opposed the restrictions, because they felt that the real estate industry demanded certainty. Isaac F. Woodbury, one of Westminster Chambers' developers, advocated eliminating all height distinctions in the city but agreed with his old adversary enough to oppose piecemeal adjustments to the boundaries, saying, "My idea would be to leave the matter as it is, but leave it there for good—or else, change the whole business." John J. Martin, former president of the Massachusetts Real Estate Exchange, explained that the "present uncertainty in regard to District 'B', with the chances of the lines of the District being changed from time to time, retards development."[30]

With no requirement that boundaries reflect existing land uses, some speakers projected land-use trends into the future and asked the commissioners to draw lines around their projections. "The whole of the Back Bay," said Frederick O. Woodruff, a downtown developer active in the Massachusetts Real Estate Exchange, "has got within a few decades to be all business; there will be no residences between Arlington street and Massachusetts avenue and the water. That is coming, and it is only a question of time." Architect and developer Clarence H. Blackall agreed: "Why, I believe that Commonwealth avenue is going to be the retail street of this city some day." The commissioners paid attention to these projections, when they thought them accurate, and took into account "the general and probable trend of business development" in setting the new boundaries.[31]

Witnesses' accounts of what would be were shaped by their feelings about what ought to be, and some speakers urged the commissioners to go beyond passively identifying trends to selecting among them. "I would like to see that Back Bay district opened up," said Charles A. Ufford, who had long worked for a new downtown around Park Square.[32] The height-district tool, invented and honed for preventing change, was now being examined as a means of steering development, encouraging particular changes that seemed desirable.

No matter how much developers hoped to promote change, they showed an almost universal acceptance of the idea that some places should be exempt from it. On the first day of testimony, Woodruff advocated eliminating the B district entirely, saying, "I tell you that in real estate this idea of regulating business is a great mistake." But when chairman Ralph Adams Cram asked if he would continue the restrictions around the statehouse, he

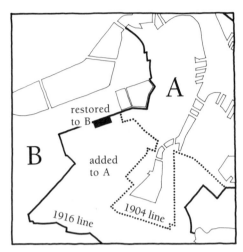

MAP 19   *Revised height districts, 1916*

answered, "Yes, I would except that. I didn't think of that."[33] Everyone who admitted exceptions named Beacon Hill as one of them, but developers, investors, and residents argued about the Back Bay, street by street. George F. Washburn, president of the Massachusetts Real Estate Exchange, reported a poll of its executive committee, which wanted the right to build tall "over every part of Boston" yet asked that the commission "protect Beacon Hill, where the sky line would be noticeable if there was an irregularity of heights along there in the buildings. And from Newbury Street to the water. That would leave Boylston street with the privilege of building to 125 feet except where it passes through Copley Square, which under the law of course would not be affected. . . . That reserves the residential section which is held rather sacred by Boston society."[34]

Even these people, whose counterparts fifty years earlier had been the prophets and engines of change, had thoroughly internalized the idea that public policy was to control environmental change, and that control would be exercised both to encourage certain desirable developments and also, at least in certain agreed-upon places, to prevent change.

The building-height commissioners announced their new boundaries November 2, 1916, more than doubling the area of the A district, bringing into it all of the South End and wide swaths of South Boston and the waterfront. The Back Bay proper remained in the B district, but they drew the boundary line down the middle of Boylston Street, allowing tall buildings around Park Square and in the vicinity of Copley Square, except where the 1898 limits applied. After the library trustees and Trinity Church complained, the commissioners lowered the maximum back to eighty feet in a small area around Copley Square.[35]

The Zone System

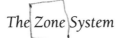

While Bostonians were adjusting the controls they had invented twelve years earlier, public regulation of change in the urban environment was evolving into its mature form elsewhere. That form was comprehensive zoning, more or less as it is still practiced today, and its advent was a direct result of Boston's development of height districting under the police power.[36]

Elsewhere in the country, districting followed a separate line of development regulating buildings' uses rather than their forms. As early as the 1880s, California courts upheld ordinances regulating the location of potentially offensive land uses, not as in Chicago through frontage consents, nor as in Boston through a permit process, but by dividing cities into districts under the police power.[37] The first of these ordinances regulated hand laundries, as a means of segregating the Chinese population, but the technique once upheld was applied to more legitimate land-use concerns such as livery stables, slaughterhouses, and saloons. In 1908, Los Angeles made an important conceptual refinement to this technique, going beyond regulation of specific proscribed uses to designate "residential districts" encompassing most of the city's area, within which nonresidential uses would be allowed only through a special "exception" process. Los Angeles' action came after the Massachusetts high court upheld Boston's residential height districts in *Welch v. Swasey* but before the U.S. Supreme Court heard the case.

Planning activists in eastern cities were beginning during this period to think about comprehensive systems of building regulation by district, which would bring together height, use, and lot-coverage rules. Housing reformers, for example, did not want tenement laws based on slum conditions to determine the form of outlying development. Such concerns were especially strong in New York City, which in 1898 annexed the vast and mostly undeveloped areas of Brooklyn, Queens, and Staten Island. If Manhattan standards were applied to suburban areas within these new boroughs, they would be essentially unregulated. These reformers discovered the German "zone system" of building regulation, in which concentric rings of each city were subject to different building-height and area standards permitting progressively less intense use of land with increasing distance from the city center.[38] One of the zone system's popularizers was Benjamin C. Marsh, executive secretary of New York's private Committee on Congestion of Population, who together with other members of the committee organized in 1909 the first National Conference on City Planning.

The conference opened in Washington four days after the U.S. Supreme Court upheld *Welch v. Swasey*. The first speaker was Henry Morganthau, a New York real estate operator and chairman of the Committee on Congestion of Population, who devoted much of his talk to the possibilities of building districts. He was apparently under the impression that Boston's "residence" and "business" districts were prescriptive rather than descriptive and announced that "it has been decided by the Supreme Court of the United States that it is within the police powers of a community to restrict the heights of buildings and confine the use of certain parts of a city to residences and of other parts to business purposes." Other speakers joined him in his call to bring the zone system to America.[39]

At the third national conference, held two years later in Philadelphia, a Committee on Legal and Administrative Methods presented the first pieces of a proposed uniform code of city planning. Andrew Wright Crawford, Philadelphia's assistant city solicitor, explained that the committee members omitted provisions for zoning of building uses because they could not yet find a consensus as to how it ought to work. "We do present an act, however," he went on, "looking to the districting of cities, so far as the height of buildings is concerned; an act that simply enables cities to follow the example of Boston."[40]

Ernst Freund, foremost expert on the police power and a German by birth, approved of this height-districting measure but thought it fortunate that the committee was not trying to import the whole German zone system because, he said, "there is a fundamental difference between American cities and German cities." He contrasted New York and Frankfurt, which in the past generation had grown by similar proportions:

In Frankfurt the business district is now exactly where it was; no neighborhood, no quarter of Frankfurt has changed its character—excepting of course the quarter that has been added to the city. New York, as you all know, has profoundly changed. Residence districts have first become business districts; and now they have become factory districts. . . . Therefore, the districting power in Germany means that it simply registers conditions that are more or less permanent; in this country, it would mean that the city would impose a character upon a neighborhood which that neighborhood, in the course of time, would throw off.

In the discussion following the sessions, conference participants rejected Freund's conclusion, arguing instead that "in a country of rapid changes in the use of property there was all the more need for control."[41]

Massachusetts was the first state to act in the spirit of this movement. The legislature in 1912 enabled a form of zoning for Massachusetts cities and towns other than Boston, through an amendment to the fire-code act that for forty years had allowed cities to delineate fire limits and regulate construction within them. The amendment added public health and morals to the permissible regulatory purposes, and building heights and uses to the permissible regulations, making them potentially as versatile as the German system. The suburb of Lexington tried to use the law to exclude all manufacturing from the town, but the Supreme Judicial Court ruled that this exceeded even the broad authority granted under the act. If any other municipalities took advantage of the 1912 statute, their actions were not publicized and did not find their way into the courts; Massachusetts provided neither the legal nor the practical precedent the zoning movement needed.[42] Several states and cities across the country passed versions of districting in 1913, including one that applied to New York State's smaller cities, but all of these involved use regulations alone.[43]

The movement's national precedent came, much more conspicuously and with greater deliberation, in New York City's formulation and adoption of a comprehensive zoning ordinance. New York's zoning resulted in part from an unusual quest for environmental stability, a crusade by the Fifth Avenue Association to fix in place once and for all the fashionable retail district. It had been migrating northward at the rate of twenty blocks each generation, advancing by displacing the homes of the wealthy and being chased from behind by the garment industry, which sought proximity to its retail customers. The association sought to thwart not commercialization but industrialization; the high-class shopping district had itself become a valued and threatened icon. The industry's looming loft buildings shaded sidewalks, and its immigrant workforce crowded them, both of which disrupted what one association representative called the "sensitive and delicate organism" of a luxury retail street. Merchants had already begun the next uptown march, to the forties and fifties, but many feared that this was only the beginning of another self-defeating cycle. Like the Back Bay's residents and Copley Square's institutional directors, they resolved to stand their ground and fight, and they found that Boston had provided them a weapon. The Fifth Avenue Association lobbied for a height district there restricting buildings to 125 feet, which merchants hoped would make further construction of manufacturing lofts uneconomical.[44]

New Yorkers had struggled for decades with the need to regulate buildings that rose much taller than those in Boston, creating development expectations that made impractical a citywide ceiling like Boston's original 125-foot limit. The Supreme Court's affirmation of height districts in *Welch v. Swasey* offered wide latitude in using the police power and made a more complicated set of regulations seem possible for New York's more complicated conditions. In 1913 the city set up a commission to consider regulating the "height, size, and arrangement" of buildings—their uses were not yet part of the formula—by dividing the city into "zones." These New York City commissioners took the unusual step of holding a public hearing in Boston, and on the steamboat that brought them back home they discussed what they had heard about that city's experience with height districts. As commission vice chairman Lawson Purdy recalled, they concluded that this was indeed "the answer" for New York. When they later decided that district regulations ought to encompass not only buildings' forms but also their functions, they laid the groundwork for the first American comprehensive zoning ordinance, which would dictate with great specificity the height, use, shape, and siting of buildings throughout the city.[45]

The commission endorsed the proposed Fifth Avenue height limits, further recommending that the area also be put off-limits to manufacturing uses, because "the preservation of that thoroughfare as a high-class shopping center is essential to the business prosperity of the entire city." As Seymour Toll points out in his history of New York's zoning, the Fifth Avenue Association was not quite the defender of tradition it made itself out to be: "The fact is that the drive to get law onto Fifth Avenue was really not a struggle to preserve a tradition at all. . . . The retailers and many of the landowners were only the latest of Johnnies-come-lately. The struggle was actually about getting some kind of public control under which an urban tradition—this one happened to be the elegant shopping boulevard—might now begin with some assurance that it could continue."[46]

After the commission presented its recommendations, debate in New York tipped decisively in favor of zoning because of a single extraordinary structure then under construction. This was the new Equitable Building, the largest office building in the world, filling an entire block of lower Broadway straight up from the sidewalk to the height of 496 feet. Commercial tenants nearby, most of them on the short leases then customary, fled its shadow after it was completed in 1915, and eventually the city had to reduce real estate assessments for four blocks northward. This was an eloquent demonstration of real estate's financial reliance on environmental stability, and a powerful concrete argument for public regulation to achieve it. On July 25, 1916, New York City enacted its zoning ordinance.[47]

Zoning spread rapidly to other cities throughout the United States. It was generally supported by the larger and more established developers, brokers, and investors in each place, who increasingly valued stability of investment over potential speculative gain.

Zoning could promote stability at two different scales. First, at the small scale of individual neighborhoods it protected individual lot owners from inharmonious structures or uses nearby. Zoning was the culmination of

260

the search for public controls to make up for the shortcomings of private deed restrictions, stabilizing neighborhoods by protecting them from encroachments. Duncan McDuffie, the largest developer in northern California, advocated a zoning ordinance for his hometown of Berkeley because it would "give property outside of restricted sections that protection now enjoyed by a few districts alone and will prevent deterioration and assist in stabilizing values." McDuffie used deed restrictions in his own subdivisions, and zoning could extend similar controls to adjacent land he did not own.[48] The commission drawing New York's zone boundaries was flooded with requests from homeowners who wanted their property included in the most restrictive district so that it would remain protected after deed covenants expired. George B. Ford, who headed the New York commission's staff, said that "about two thirds of the whole city has been set aside for all time for strictly residential use."[49]

Second, at the scale of the entire city, zoning might protect investment from decline due to unpredictable shifts in urban structure. It would accomplish this by freezing the character of districts, an imposition of will on the city that Freund felt could not work in America, but for which his audience yearned. This antispeculative function of zoning was in fact less evident in Boston, where conservative real estate trustees kept much of the business development to a small downtown area, than in places with a more entrepreneurial real estate tradition, such as New York and Los Angeles. The uptown march that once symbolized progress to New Yorkers, especially those with any interest in real estate, became a problem when people found themselves losing money on it. Los Angeles' downtown real estate community used zoning in an unsuccessful fight against the decentralization of business onto Wilshire Boulevard.[50]

The year after New York passed its zoning ordinance, a Massachusetts constitutional convention proposed one of the first state constitutional amendments for zoning. Many reformers assumed that such amendments would be necessary to resolve doubts about this expansion of the police power. In view of Massachusetts courts' friendliness to the police power, an amendment there was perhaps an excess of caution, but no court had yet affirmed the 1912 zoning statute, lawyers were skeptical that California precedents would carry much weight in the East, and the convention already in session was a one-time opportunity. Voters in 1918 passed the amendment by a nearly 2-to-1 margin statewide and by an even larger margin in Boston, in the same election that approved Appleton's preservation amendment.[51] The legislature took more interest in zoning than it did in Appleton's cause and in 1920 passed an enabling act.[52] During the next three and a half years a dozen Massachusetts cities and towns adopted zoning.[53]

261

Both Boston and Los Angeles, having pioneered early districting measures, were slow to adopt comprehensive zoning. Their residents felt less urgency than people in cities where development was still completely unregulated. The Boston City Planning Board had been asking for zoning since 1915 but did not begin to get it until 1922, when Mayor Curley appointed an advisory commission that was to help the board prepare the city's zoning, working with consultant Edward M. Bassett, the lawyer who wrote New York's ordinance. Boston's zoning passed the legislature and took effect on June 5, 1924.[54] 1924

Historic Districts

While some preservationists like William Sumner Appleton turned away from the city to the remoter past in New England's countryside, others found value in their urban neighborhoods. Unlike Appleton, these neighborhood preservationists could see the usefulness of government action. On Beacon Hill, height restrictions were helping to maintain the visual relationship of the newly restored statehouse to its surroundings. When preservationists turned their attention to whole neighborhoods—a nascent movement later called area preservation—then such controls might address inappropriate development throughout them.

Before the advent of height restrictions, the statehouse undermined the stability of its Beacon Hill neighborhood. Long uncertainty over the direction and extent of its expansion brought a feeling of tentativeness to the tenure of even those well-to-do neighbors who could not be economically dislodged by other land uses. By the 1880s the neighborhood was perceived as declining. Buildings there were "old and of but little value," said Governor Ames. The *Evening Transcript*'s editors thought that settling the uncertainty with a definite statehouse plan would ensure that "property all around must appreciate greatly, whether the hill shall continue a residential locality or shall be given up to professional and business purposes."[55] By the real estate orthodoxy of the time, even if Beacon Hill remained residential, it would improve only by building anew, or reconstructing existing houses so thoroughly as to amount to the same thing.

The turn of the century was Beacon Hill's low point, after a generation of decline when the neighborhood's frontier retreated before both the statehouse and the growing downtown, and the Back Bay rose as an equally fashionable and much larger district. Height restrictions around the statehouse in 1899 and 1902 came just as Beacon Hill residents began working to reverse that decline. Many statehouse neighbors seemed sincerely concerned about the dome's visibility, but they were also happy to have found a way of relieving pressures for replacement of existing old houses by large apartment and office buildings.

Beacon Hill maintained at all times a core of aristocratic residences and residents. Among them were generations of the Codman family, including real estate broker William Coombs Codman. Shortly after the turn of the century, Codman began buying, restoring, and reselling old houses on Beacon Hill. He induced many of his friends to move to the district, including architect Frank A. Bourne, who came from the Back Bay and began a prolific practice serving a growing influx of well-heeled Bostonians whose domestic ideal was a completely up-to-date interior within a quaint exterior on an historic street.[56]

This clientele was not necessarily disciplined by Appleton's principles of archaeological truth. Their "restorations" often brought a nineteenth-century building back to a colonial or even medieval past it had never seen. Yet their attraction to the area was clearly its antiquity; material progress was an ideal only indoors. On the exterior, they like Appleton were practicing preservation by purchase, and they were using his tool of adaptive use, but for their own purposes rather than in the service of a preservation organization. Their housing preferences brought this approach out of the realm of philanthropy and into the market, where it could accomplish more through the aggregated budgets of many people.

These neighborhood improvers expanded their activities beyond the traditional aristocratic south slope of Beacon Hill to its north slope and to the flats on the river side of Charles Street, areas that had been occupied by the servants and stables of the hill's elite, and by a long-established black neighborhood. The newcomers thought of themselves, in writer Margaret Deland's words, as "redeeming" the area "to something like its old desirability as a residence neighborhood."[57] In fact, however, its erstwhile desirability, like its colonial building details, was a modern invention; the area became more quaint and more fashionable in the twentieth century than it had ever been in the nineteenth.

The area's new and old residents achieved an uneasy alliance at the Charles Street meetinghouse, occupied by the First African Methodist Episcopal Church, where neighbors raised money for Frank Bourne to restore its 1807 exterior. In return the congregation agreed to give the Society for the Preservation of New England Antiquities an option of first refusal in case the building was ever sold, a safeguard that later became common practice in preservation grants but that seems to have been thought up specifically for this case. The more frequent relationship between new and old residents was simple succession, as in Deland's description of "a pair of tumbledown wooden tenements" occupied by "twelve families, who were speedily induced to seek other accommodations." These improvers were untroubled by such displacement, which for Deland seemed the whole point of the architectural exercise; it "brings a most desirable element into a part of the city which badly needs such associations." In 1922 the neighborhood institutionalized its reasserted identity by organizing the Beacon Hill Association, "to keep undesirable business and living conditions from affecting the hill district."[58]

Similar neighborhood restoration, in New York's Greenwich Village, in Providence's College Hill, in Charleston's Battery district, and in other American and European cities, challenged the real estate doctrine of inevitable decline and conversion. In 1915, Edward H. Clement, a former editor of the *Boston Evening Transcript* and one of the Park Street Church preservationists, described the process as it worked in New York: "After the boardinghouse period, that the swell mansions of other days pass through, when at last they are utterly run down and too drear and dirty even for lodging houses, the taste of the artist converts them into something so desirable that the tide of values in the whole neighborhood is often set running in the opposite direction to that in which it has been setting for a generation or two."[59] This was the urban counterpart of a similar contemporary tide change, the restoration of derelict farmhouses as automobiles began making them accessible. Even the businessmen of the Board of Trade in Providence recognized the rehabilitation of "old favorite residential quarters" as a new "phenomenon of modern city growth."[60]

Beacon Hill residents saw that their area-preservation efforts required reinforcement through government powers. Height restrictions kept apartment buildings from overwhelming the neighborhood. The street commissioners' regulation of building lines kept commercial uses on Beacon Street from becoming obtrusive. The same commission's review of commercial garage locations was of particular interest because Beacon Hill's boundaries were insecure where the "revived" neighborhood met its utilitarian surroundings.[61] A representative of the Beacon Hill Association appeared before the legislature to support Boston's zoning bill. Not only preservationists but planners too acknowledged the relationship between zoning and preservation. Zoning in many cities benefited outlying areas of suburban character while providing little or no protection to old residential areas near the city center, but Boston's zoning did protect close-in neighborhoods, and did so with an avowedly preservationist rationale. "A direct benefit of zoning," said the planning board in explaining the new zoning law, "which is perhaps of more value in Boston than in any other city in the United States, will be the protection and preservation of old historical buildings and sites," such as the "famous Beacon Hill district."[62]

Neighborhood preservers soon worked through zoning. Significant new development now required zone changes, and the Beacon Hill Association set up a "Zoning Defence Committee" to fight them, led by restoration architect Frank A. Bourne and Realtor William Coombs Codman. They went beyond defense, initiating zone changes reducing allowable density and, they hoped, preventing further apartment construction on the hill.[63] In the Back Bay, whose future was a less settled issue, development proposals also became zoning controversies. Beacon Hill activists joined Back Bay residents in these fights, both to protect the hill's views across the Public Garden and to help a neighborhood in the same position their own had been in a generation earlier. They lost significant battles in the Back Bay, such as a 1926 zone change allowing the Ritz-Carlton Hotel on Arlington Street. Zoning came to seem a threat from which they needed defense, as well as a means of defense from other threats.[64] Because it was a flexible control, it served not as an assurance of permanence but as a new battleground on which to fight for environmental stability.

If zoning was about environmental stability, could it be written to protect old buildings directly? Historic district zoning was a natural synthesis of all the branches of the search for environmental permanence, combining development controls, which had evolved into zoning, and preservation, which was evolving toward area restoration. This synthesis appeared first not in Boston or New York but in southern cities.

Even as Boston was adopting its conventional zoning in 1924, New Orleans was preparing an historic district preservation measure, although it was not enacted until after a state constitutional amendment in 1936.[65] Charleston, South Carolina, enacted the first American historic district zoning ordinance in 1931. Within the designated "Old and Historic Charleston" district, no exterior alterations could be carried out until a Board of Architectural Review granted a "certificate of appropriateness."[66]

Why did southern cities arrive first at this synthesis of preservation and zoning, when both movements had been active so much longer in Boston? Northerners' longer experience with zoning made them less likely to think it could encompass preservation. Northern planners and lawyers were nervous, especially before the U.S. Supreme Court in 1926 first upheld a zoning ordinance in *Euclid v. Ambler,* about dubious regulations that might bring down their constitutional house of cards. They thought of preservation as a special case of aesthetic control and cited *Welch v. Swasey* as authority that aesthetics alone would not support use of the police power. Southerners were not paralyzed by such legal niceties—Charleston mayor Thomas P. Stoney cheerfully acknowledged himself "incompetent to judge how a city should be zoned"—and their comparative inexperience left them free to improvise. Charleston still had no zoning in 1929, as its citizens were becoming concerned about business incursions into the city's historic Battery district. The preservation impulse preceded organized city planning there, and citizens expected that planning and zoning would answer it. Mayor Stoney created a temporary city planning and zoning commission charged with reviewing applications for commercial construction. When the commission refused permission for a proposed gas station in the old part of Charleston, the city was impelled to create a legal framework that would legitimize the action. For years afterward Charleston emphasized persuasion and compromise in order to keep its historic district out of court, apparently assuming that any test case was likely to overturn it.[67]

While experience with zoning made northerners less apt to think historic districts possible, experience with preservation made Bostonians less likely to think them necessary. Charles Hosmer attributes their origins in the South to the recognition that cities there could not afford to save whole urban landscapes piecemeal. But Boston had already done just that. It had saved its Common and Bulfinch statehouse, kept both from being overwhelmed by skyscrapers, and housed an elite large enough and moneyed enough that all of fashionable Beacon Hill could be restored and even expanded. Surrounded by such successes, Bostonians saw no need for radical measures, and the politics of a northern city made municipal control over matters of architectural taste seem more radical there than in the South. If preservation's means came more easily in Boston, preservation seemed more important as an end in southern cities. Not only did elites look more longingly to the past in the former Confederacy, but sleepy southern cities were more in need of the economic boost their historic ambiance could give them through tourism.[68]

When Charleston was first considering how to protect the Battery district in 1929, preservationist Samuel G. Stoney wrote to William Sumner Appleton for advice: "Has any attempt been made in New England communities to regulate such affairs through municipal government?"[69] "As I understand it you are not asking for any advice concerning the preservation of any particular house," replied the puzzled Appleton in a long letter that evidently meant to be helpful but nowhere touched upon Stoney's question. Why did public regulation so elude Appleton's understanding? He was blinded by a conservative aversion to the use of government powers, compounded by mistrust of the people who now made up the government, such as the legislators whose inaction left his constitutional amendment inoperative. Appleton was even more conservative about property rights than were the many property owners and investors who were embracing public regulation, because his conservatism was defined by principle while theirs stemmed from the more flexible calculus of self-interest. Appleton had no faith in any preservation technique except ownership by an organized society, preferably his own. He expressed skepticism about the idea of private restoration and resale, even though it had been working in Boston for a generation and in Charleston for at least a decade.[70]

Appleton also distanced preservation from planning through his art-historical definition of the field. He saw houses as antiques. This view uncoupled preservation from the parks movement, which had changed emphasis itself to focus on active recreation rather than saving landscapes for their intrinsic qualities. As professional preservationists gained the academic perspective to evaluate individual historic structures more or less objectively, they lost some of the resident amateur's ability to see them subjectively together, "tout ensemble," as New Orleans preservationists put it.[71] Appleton's consistency and comprehensiveness were essential in developing the systematic preservationism that would make historic districts permissible under the police power, but the motivation for attempting them was the earlier subjective appreciation that had saved so much of the center of Boston.

A few Bostonians did make the arguments that would later form the basis for landmark regulation. They had argued that Park Street Church, and the Old South before it, belonged to the public. Their proprietors were in preservationist eyes trustees, just as the city of Boston was in holding the Common for the people. Similarly, owners of property on Commonwealth Avenue, in Copley Square, and around the Bulfinch statehouse had responsibilities toward the urban ensemble from which their land took much of its value. Such views did not seem radical when they were first urged in the 1880s and 1890s; their most forceful proponents included a city council president, a mayor, a state attorney general, a justice of the state supreme court, and some of the city's biggest property owners. By the end of World War I, these ideas were in the mainstream of discussion about city planning, but Appleton was leading preservation away from this part of its past. The philosophy and personnel of the preservation movement had undergone a shift that kept it from coalescing during this period around any consensus for public action, even as action was becoming possible.

Preservationism grew increasingly irrelevant to most of Boston's urban landscape. As the old aristocracy became less effective in civic affairs, it also became less interested in the public environment, retreating to still Anglo-Saxon suburbs or to constricted orbits within the city. Preservationists continued defending the landmarks they had already saved, but they took few new initiatives. Boston eventually became the first northern city to enact historic district zoning, for Beacon Hill, but did not do so until 1955, two decades after Charleston and New Orleans pioneered it and after a number of other southern cities had followed their example.[72]

Conclusion

By the 1920s, environmental change had come under control to a degree nearly unimaginable in America fifty years before. The search for permanence produced a rapidly expanding set of tools for public control of change, powerful tools that reformed the way urban development worked. Their very power left them to be explored, shaped, and expanded by people who, unlike Boston's Brahmins, were still willing to climb into the public arena. Some were reformers motivated by altruism; more were motivated by self-interest; few were primarily concerned with environmental permanence.

A variety of efforts grew out of a widespread and largely undifferentiated rejection of the culture of change in the urban environment. As Americans searched for an alternative environmental culture, specific issues elicited specific responses. To build for permanency in new parts of the city, they invented the private planning mechanism of deed restrictions. For valued places that seemed permanent but in fact had no guarantees of survival, they formulated a range of tactics for building and landscape preservation. As they gained experience with these techniques, their shortcomings led people increasingly to explore public controls on environmental change. At first a bewildering variety of them, often quite specific, resolved particular problems in particular places. Eventually they came together as zoning, a single, systematic form of regulation asserting public control over most significant physical change in the city.

Zoning absorbed the rudimentary public height and use regulations that had preceded it, and also much of the tradition of private planning through deed restrictions that lay behind early public controls. As we have seen, many simple land-use controls were applied with complex ends in mind, such as the attempts to use front-yard setbacks to thwart conversion of residential avenues to shopping streets. Comprehensive zoning addressed such issues more directly and better matched their complexity. Zoning itself grew more complicated as planners' understanding grew more sophisticated, and as expectations rose about what it could accomplish. Developers continued using deed restrictions for many purposes, but their main original aims were answered by zoning, and at least a few observers thought at first that zoning would render such restrictions entirely obsolete.

City planning also absorbed much of the broad and eclectic preservation movement that C. R. Ashbee had found on his visit to America at the turn of the century, the ad hoc campaigns by which Bostonians had defended increasingly large pieces of the city center, until they treated whole districts as historic fabric and took steps to keep it in place. William Sumner Appleton was not concerned with such large-scale environments but with a scattered set of ancient houses, and he institutionalized a purist preservationism that helped drive people with broader and more heterogeneous interests elsewhere. At the same time, the city planning movement, also newly organizing, was expanding from its engineering and landscape architecture origins to encompass all aspects of the urban environment.

If zoning was the culmination of these various campaigns, then historic district regulation was an integral part of it. Charleston's naive view of zoning was a natural view; it was fundamentally about controlling change, and historic districts were the places where such control was most essential. Northern preservationism, by turning away from the city, was growing away from its roots. Similarly, planners turned their backs on anything that smacked of aesthetics, including overt preservationism; they too were turning away from their field's ancestry. The nationwide spread of historic district zoning starting in the 1950s was less an innovation than a belated family reunion.

In two generations Americans in their cities had moved from celebration of change, first toward an ideal of permanence, and then to a reality of controlled change. In the process of subjecting environmental change to conscious communal will, the ideal of permanence that had motivated people at first lost much of its appeal and was replaced by the more modest and pragmatic ideal of stability. Permanence had been attractive because it was the opposite of change; once change began to seem controllable, it ceased to be so frightening.

By the teens, the permanence of Boston's urban form seemed alarming rather than reassuring. When Bostonians first set out to pursue this goal in the 1870s and 1880s, the same environmental changes that made people yearn for stability also provided evidence of the city's vitality—the enormous Back Bay land-making, the annexations that multiplied the city's area. A generation or so later, however, Bostonians could read many signs giving opposite indications. They were acutely aware of their cramped little business district; they lacked a modern skyline because of their own building-height restrictions; traffic kept worsening around the sacrosanct Common, where almost every street-improvement scheme in fifty years had come to nothing; and though the metropolitan area was still growing apace, it did so in suburban towns that the city was utterly unable to annex. Boston's stability began to look like stagnation, and this made change, if properly channeled, more attractive than permanence.

City planners after the City Beautiful concerned themselves with controlling rather than preventing change. Modernist architects promulgated a new incarnation of the idea that old is corrupt. Even most preservationists agreed, when the "old" in question was the late Victorian excess that surrounded them and had erased so much of what they revered, and so these preservationists could accept change as long as it respected the few islands they valued.

Within their own sphere too, preservationists had moved beyond the simple notion of permanence. Appleton indeed wanted his houses to last forever, but he understood that permanence was not a status to which a building could simply be elevated; it was a result that had to be accomplished. Appleton wanted permanence, so he worked for control.

Even if physical permanence were possible, shifting ideas could make it as undesirable in preservation as in other physical aspects of the city. Preservationists have become Ruskinians through the sobering experience of re-restoring earlier restorations; time has sometimes been more kind to their physical materials than to their scholarly basis. Whitmore's work on the Old State House was repudiated even in his lifetime, without detracting from his credit for defending the building. Restoration architects have come to embrace reversibility as a first principle governing their actions; even preservationists value control over permanence.

This version of control is expressed in James Marston Fitch's definition of preservation as "curatorial management" of the environment, an ongoing activity rather than a discrete act of salvation. When some restorers set out to freeze time at a particular moment, the resulting permanence smelled of embalming. People who appreciated the continuity of living historic neighborhoods tried managing rather than blindly resisting change; this philosophy together with the expansion of the movement's purview back to its original scope has once again removed the barriers between preservation and planning. One central idea of area preservation was that change could be good, could return things to a desirable prior state, not only at the scale of a restored building but at the larger urban scale. This idea was powerful, and it greatly expanded the fraction of the environment with which preservationists might concern themselves. It was more potent still in its effects on planning in general. Edward M. Bassett, reflecting in the mid-1920s about New York's experience with zoning, noted that *"No blighted districts have begun in this city since the zoning was established,* but on the contrary, some that had

begun have been redeemed."[1] Real estate theory, lagging behind practic
once again as it had with deed restrictions, debated during the 1930s anu
1940s whether it was really possible for neighborhoods to improve without
being physically reconstructed, whether all the ones that had been doing it
for forty years were somehow special cases.

Control of change does not necessarily lead to stability; those who wield a
tool, not those who made it, decide how it will be used. The mid-nineteenth-
century culture of change well accommodated that mainspring of city building, self-interest. Human nature had not changed since then, and the increased public power over the physical environment was explored by all
kinds of people, many looking to see what was in it for them.[2] Speculation
depends on anticipating change, and any expansion of controls on change
offered expanded speculative possibilities.

The simplest speculative subversion of zoning was "overzoning," the clas-
sification of far more land in intense use categories than the market was
likely to allocate for them, so that a zoning ordinance served not as a limitation on development but as mere boosterism. Marc Weiss, in *The Rise of
the Community Builders,* chronicles Los Angeles' adoption of land-use regulations and the real estate industry's adaptive response in which "the 'rabid
speculator' who at first balked at zoning soon found it to be a very conge-
nial ally [and] . . . zoning became the ultimate promotional device, a form
of government-subsidized free advertising." William B. Munroe, a contemporary expert on municipal administration, observed that "the signs went
up on vacant lots: 'Zoned for business,' or 'Zoned for apartments,' with the
definite implication that such action on the part of the public authorities
had resulted in giving the property a higher and more assured value than it
would otherwise have."[3]

Other manipulations of zoning could also enrich speculators at the expense of environmental stability. Zone changes, variances, and exceptions,
intended as refinements of public control, could also become methods
of achieving publicly enforced land-use monopolies. "Unlike deed restrictions," notes Weiss, zoning offered opportunities for speculation because
"zoning classifications and regulations could easily be changed by a majority
vote of the City Council. Real estate values could therefore be manipulated
by acquiring property with one zoning designation and having it changed to
another, or by selling property with the implied promise that its current zoning designation could be changed." These practices pointed to one advantage
of deed restrictions over public controls: within the limits of their specific
provisions and durations, deed restrictions provided reliable if cumbersome
protection, with enforcement in the hands of the aggrieved neighbors. Zoning provided more flexible control, but the flexibility was in the hands of

municipal officials, who might or might not respond to neighborhood concerns. Subdividers continued imposing restrictions, both to control matters that were beyond the reach of the police power, such as architectural style, minimum cost, and the race of occupants, and to provide long-term buttresses to neighborhood character independent of municipal caprice.[4]

Planners campaigned against these perversions of zoning. Overzoning, they argued, kept supply out of balance with demand in the land market, thus contributing to rather than relieving uncertainty in urban development. Many of zoning's original advocates were unpleasantly surprised by the frequency and deviousness with which the variance, exception, and zone-change mechanisms were used. They had conceived these as escape valves to be used for making infrequent adjustments in keeping with the original spirit of districts, or for recognizing substantially changed conditions. Instead they swiftly became the most frequently invoked portions of zoning ordinances, used not to carry out but to undermine their original intentions.[5]

But plannerly dismay at these shenanigans missed the essential difference from old ways: the context for speculation now was a public policy of control over environmental change. Since zoning supplemented rather than supplanted deed restrictions, if it offered any protection at all it was protection in addition to the private methods which remained available. By its very existence, zoning indicated a presumption in favor of stability, continuity, and preservation.

One conclusion we can easily reach about Americans' turn-of-the-century search for permanence in the urban environment is that it worked. Metropolitan Boston has changed as much in the sixty-five years since 1930 as it did in the sixty-five years preceding. Yet almost all of the icons that those Bostonians set out to save remain saved.

The center of the city has been remade almost completely, but it has been remade around its landmarks—all of the ones identified by nineteenth-century preservationists, and many more that have been added to the list. The Old South Church, the Old State House, Faneuil Hall, the Paul Revere House—all remain and now make up parts of the Boston National Historical Park. The Bulfinch statehouse, Park Street and St. Paul's Churches, and the Athenaeum all stand in their familiar places, still put to their original uses. The street numbers on the Granary and King's Chapel burial grounds remain unused.

The structures and places newly built for permanence have mostly achieved it so far. At Copley Square, Richardson's Trinity Church faces McKim's Public Library; each seems headed for its intended immortality.

Neighborhoods built for permanence, and neighborhoods resolutely defended, mostly retain their intended qualities after a century. In the 1870s

FIGURE 11.1 *The Old South meetinghouse, c. 1937–41. Courtesy Bostonian Society, Old State House*

there was no urban residential district in the country of which that could be said. But today Beacon Hill west of the statehouse remains much as it was, and the buildings that first provoked height restrictions there remain the tallest structures on its Beacon Street skyline. The Back Bay too is now an <u>historic district</u>, and most of the buildings that survived the 1920s have lasted to the present. Olmsted's deed-restricted Brookline subdivisions, and many others of their type, remain among the most attractive and prized residential locations in the Boston area, and the same story can be found in cities around the United States, at Llewellyn Park outside New York, Roland Park in Baltimore, and Shaker Heights outside Cleveland, where the century-long restrictions remain in force. These neighborhoods, designed for permanence, have in fact been the places where American city dwellers stood their ground and most closely achieved it.

The Common remains, as do fights about it. In the 1960s, Bostonians again argued over the sanctity of the space beneath it as they decided to put a parking garage there; in the 1980s they even replayed the subway imbroglios as they expanded Park Street station and fretted over its effect on the trees. Boston's Common, like New York's Central Park, will remain fertile ground for controversy because each in its respective city is the litmus test for commitment to environmental permanence; they are the screens on which people project their images of stability.

The triumph over the culture of change has not been limited to conspicuous symbolic locations but has permeated the way we make and remake cities. Even at the growing edges of metropolitan areas, we seldom find anything quite like the wide-open frontier of nineteenth-century suburbs, with their miles of paper streets outlining neighborhoods that might become mansions, or tenements, or factories, or all three. Instead, even where change is admitted to be inevitable, it is usually tightly confined by as-of-right zoning, and where developers wish to depart from these marked channels their neighbors look to government with every expectation that it will protect them from unwanted surprises. For every exception to the pattern—Urban Renewal and its modern-day Poletown equivalents, organized sellouts in which neighborhoods use their zoning to profit from land-use conversion—there are many more examples of no-growth opposition to all change, a contemporary quest for permanence. These modern antidevelopment constituencies want to keep it the way it was, the same rallying cry as a hundred years ago, but applied now to a far more encompassing environment than any nineteenth-century preservationist would ever have dared.

We face the same issues of change, permanence, and control, and we debate them in terms Americans first sketched out then. We fight many of the same battles, often with weapons forged then. We have created some new ones of our own: police-power regulations applied to individual historic landmarks; growth controls that directly regulate not only the substance but the rate of change. But most of what we do in regulating ordinary development today would have been understandable to anyone familiar with the development world of the 1920s, while that world would have been largely incomprehensible to a developer from fifty years earlier. Everything that we have added since then has refined a basic premise first agreed upon by that generation: change in the urban environment is not an unalloyed good but rather a necessary evil, and it is the public's right and responsibility to control it.

Notes

Abbreviations

AA&BN — *American Architect and Building News.*

BET — *Boston Evening Transcript.*

BG — *Boston Globe.*

BH — *Boston Herald.*

BPL — Boston Public Library.

FLO Papers — Charles Capen McLaughlin, ed., and Charles E. Beveridge, assoc. ed. *The Papers of Frederick Law Olmsted.* 6 vols. Baltimore, 1977–92.

MA&R — *Massachusetts Acts and Resolves.*

OTNE — *Old-Time New England.*

SPNEA — Society for the Preservation of New England Antiquities.

Introduction

Epigraph: Samuel Kirkland Lothrop, *A Discourse Preached in the Church in Brattle Square, on the Last Sunday of Its Use for Public Worship, July 30, 1871 . . . and an Account of Laying the Corner-stone of the New Church* (Boston, 1871), 27.

1. Homer Hoyt, *One Hundred Years of Land Values in Chicago: The Relationship of the Growth of Chicago to the Rise of Its Land Values, 1830–1933* (Chicago, 1933), 189–92; Walter Firey, *Land Use in Central Boston* (Cambridge, Mass., 1947), 61–68.

2. Charles H. Cheney, "Building for Permanency: The Esthetic Considerations in a Master or City Plan," in *Planning Problems of Town, City, and Region: Papers and Discussions at the Twentieth National Conference on City Planning* (Philadelphia, 1928), 32. See also discussion in Marc A. Weiss, *The Rise of the Community Builders: The American Real Estate Industry and Urban Land Planning* (New York, 1987), 61.

3. Quoted in David Schuyler, *The New Urban Landscape: The Redefinition of City Form in Nineteenth-Century America* (Baltimore, 1986), 26–27.

4. Kevin Lynch, *A Theory of Good City Form* (Cambridge, Mass., 1981), 112;

Josef W. Konvitz, *The Urban Millennium: The City-Building Process from the Early Middle Ages to the Present* (Carbondale, Ill., 1985); Christine Meisner Rosen, *The Limits of Power: Great Fires and the Process of City Growth in America* (New York, 1986); Anne Vernez Moudon, *Built for Change: Neighborhood Architecture in San Francisco* (Cambridge, Mass., 1986); Stewart Brand, *How Buildings Learn: What Happens after They're Built* (New York, 1994). "I asked Moudon," writes Brand (193), "if she thought the San Francisco Victorians were designed for change. 'No,' she said, 'they were just designed to appeal to a variety of tenants.'"

5. John J. Costonis, *Icons and Aliens: Law, Aesthetics, and Environmental Change* (Urbana, 1989), xv, 46.

6. Deuteronomy 27:17; *Oxford English Dictionary* (Oxford, 1989), 8:627, 9:1045.

7. Henry James, *The American Scene* (1907; Bloomington, Ind., 1968), 229.

8. James M. Lindgren, *Preserving the Old Dominion: Historic Preservation and Virginia Traditionalism* (Charlottesville, 1993); James M. Lindgren, *Preserving Historic New England: Preservation, Progressivism, and the Remaking of Memory* (New York, 1995).

9. Susan Mulcahey Chase, "Working-Class Suburbs and Restrictive Covenants, Wilmington, Delaware, 1900–1941," paper delivered at Sixth National Conference on American Planning History, Knoxville, Tenn., Oct. 14, 1995.

10. Charles B. Hosmer Jr., *Presence of the Past: A History of the Preservation Movement in the United States before Williamsburg* (New York, 1965), 124–26.

11. Garrett Power, "High Society: The Building Height Limitation on Baltimore's Mt. Vernon Place," *Maryland Historical Magazine* 79 (1984): 197–219; Seymour I. Toll, *Zoned American* (New York, 1969).

CHAPTER 1: *The Culture of Change*

Epigraph: Nathaniel Hawthorne, *Our Old Home: A Series of English Sketches* (1863; Columbus, 1970), 5:60.

1. *BG,* Aug. 9, 1873, 8.

2. Christine Meisner Rosen, *The Limits of Power: Great Fires and the Process of City Growth in America* (New York, 1986), 177–79.

3. Editorial, "Historical Aspect of the Fire," *BG,* Nov. 15, 1872, 4; *BG,* Nov. 21, 1872, 4.

4. Editorial, "The Bright Side," *BG,* Nov. 15, 1872, 4; Ross Miller, *American Apocalypse: The Great Fire and the Myth of Chicago* (Chicago, 1990).

5. Homer Hoyt, *One Hundred Years of Land Values in Chicago: The Relationship of the Growth of Chicago to the Rise of Its Land Values, 1830–1933* (Chicago, 1933), 279.

6. Lowell was also the third largest city in New England. *Seventh Census of the United States: 1850* (1853), table 34.

7. Charles S. Damrell, *A Half Century of Boston's Building* (Boston, 1895), 356, 358. For the years 1871–74—the first for which building statistics are available—the increase came about two-thirds through appreciation and one-third through new

construction. See John F. Fitzgerald, *Annual Address of . . . Mayor of Boston, to the City Council* (City doc. 1, 1907), app. 9.

8. Henry C. Binford, *The First Suburbs: Residential Communities on the Boston Periphery, 1815–1860* (Chicago, 1985); Kenneth T. Jackson, *Crabgrass Frontier: The Suburbanization of the United States* (New York, 1985), 34–38.

9. Edward Stanwood, "Topography and Landmarks of the Last Hundred Years," in *The Memorial History of Boston, Including Suffolk County, Massachusetts, 1630–1880*, ed. Justin Winsor (Boston, 1881), 3:25.

10. Alexander H. Rice, *Inaugural Address of . . . Mayor of the City of Boston, to the City Council* (City doc. 1, 1856), 12.

11. Rosen, *Limits of Power*, 185.

12. Rice, *Inaugural Address*, 13.

13. Sam Bass Warner, *The Private City: Philadelphia in Three Periods of Its Growth* (Philadelphia, 1968), 53, 3; Hendrik Hartog, *Public Property and Private Power: The Corporation of the City of New York in American Law, 1730–1870* (Chapel Hill, 1983), 175, 77; see also 203.

14. Peter R. Knights, *The Plain People of Boston, 1830–1860: A Study in City Growth* (New York, 1971), 59.

15. Figure derived from ibid., 57, 56, tables IV-6, IV-5: 11.4 percent of 1860 sample members "present in Boston at start of" 1830, multiplied by 33,633 households in 1860.

16. Walter Muir Whitehill, *Boston: A Topographical History* (Cambridge, Mass., 1959), 106–11.

17. Bulfinch to his son, June 12, 1843, in *The Life and Letters of Charles Bulfinch, Architect*, ed. Ellen Susan Bulfinch (Boston: Houghton Mifflin, 1896), 301.

18. Walter Firey, *Land Use in Central Boston* (Cambridge, Mass., 1947), 59.

19. Ibid., 61; William Dean Howells, *The Rise of Silas Lapham* (1885; New York, 1982), 21.

20. Frederick D. Allen, discussing the area bounded by Washington, State, and Essex Streets, and the harbor, in Massachusetts Supreme Judicial Court, *Old South Society, Petitioners, vs. Uriel Crocker et als. Report of Evidence Taken at the Hearing . . . before Mr. Justice Colt* (Boston, 1876), 56. See also "Old Landmarks Removed," *Christian Register*, Aug. 5, 1871, quoted in Samuel Kirkland Lothrop, *A Discourse Preached in the Church in Brattle Square, on the Last Sunday of Its Use for Public Worship, July 30, 1871 . . . and an Account of Laying the Corner-stone of the New Church* (Boston, 1871), 42.

21. Chandler Robbins, *Two Sermons, Delivered before the Second Church and Society, Sunday, March 10, 1844, on the Occasion of Taking down Their Ancient Place of Worship* (Boston, 1844), 3.

22. Chandler Robbins, *History of the Second Church, or Old North, in Boston, to Which Is Added, a History of the New Brick Church* (Boston, 1852), 146–48, 159.

23. Robbins, *Two Sermons . . . March 10, 1844*, 40–41.

24. George H. Eager, comp., *Historical Sketch of the Second Church in Boston* (Boston, 1894), 35–36; Robbins, *History of the Second Church*, 155–57. Even this church,

though dedicated in 1874 to stand for "years, even through centuries, to come" (Chandler Robbins, *A Sermon Preached at the Dedication of the Second Church, Boylston Street, November 4th, 1874* [Boston, 1875], 4), lasted only until 1912, when the Second Church, again finding its fashionable residential location overtaken by business, once again moved, this time to a more or less suburban location at the Brookline border, where it remains. The building was once again dismantled, this time to be reused elsewhere in the city by a different congregation (John Nicholls Booth, *The Story of the Second Church in Boston* [Boston, 1959], 44–47).

25. Trinity first considered one site at the foot of Beacon Hill. See Trinity Church, *Report of Committee, January 12, 1871* (Boston, 1871), 3. See also [Bishop] William Lawrence, *Address . . . Delivered in Trinity Church, Boston . . . [upon] the Fiftieth Anniversary of Its Consecration* (Boston, 1927), 8.

26. Old South Society, *Report of Committee to Consider Building on Boylston Street* (Boston, June 24, 1870), 6.

27. Whitehill, *Topographical History,* 42; Douglass Shand Tucci, *Built in Boston: City and Suburb, 1800–1950* (Boston, 1978), 4.

28. *BG,* Oct. 8, 1872, 4.

29. David Lowenthal, *The Past Is a Foreign Country* (Cambridge, England, 1985), 75–148.

30. Hawthorne, *Our Old Home,* 5:59–60.

31. Jefferson to Samuel Kerscheval, July 12, 1816, in *The Writings of Thomas Jefferson,* ed. Albert Ellery Bergh (Washington, D.C., 1903), 15:42–43; Daniel Boorstin, *The Lost World of Thomas Jefferson* (Boston, 1960), 208–10; Lowenthal, *Past Is a Foreign Country,* 108.

32. Nathaniel Hawthorne, *The House of the Seven Gables* (1851), quoted in Lowenthal, *Past Is a Foreign Country,* 111.

33. James Kent, *Commentaries on American Law,* 2d ed. (1832), quoted in Lawrence M. Friedman, *A History of American Law,* 2d ed. (New York, 1985), 413.

34. Friedman, *History of American Law,* 413–14.

35. John Bouvier, *A Law Dictionary, Adapted to the Constitution and Laws of the United States of America* (Philadelphia, 1858), 2:332.

36. Samuel Kirkland Lothrop, *A History of the Church in Brattle Street, Boston* (Boston, 1851), 112; *Proprietors of the Church in Brattle Square v. Moses Grant & Others,* 69 Mass. 142 (1855). The case was decided not on the facts of change in the neighborhood but on the "rule against perpetuities," the general principle of allowing no permanent legal instruments beyond the reach of modification by the living.

37. Robbins, *Two Sermons . . . March 10, 1844,* 48.

38. Henry James, *Washington Square* (1881; London, 1949), 37.

39. Hamilton Andrews Hill, *History of the Old South Church, 1669–1884* (Boston, 1890), 548.

40. *New York Tribune,* May 3, 1855, quoted in Edward K. Spann, *The New Metropolis: New York City, 1840–1857* (New York, 1981), 101.

41. *BG,* Aug. 26, 1872, 4; Sam Bass Warner, *Streetcar Suburbs: The Process of Growth in Boston, 1870–1900* (Cambridge, Mass., 1962); Jackson, *Crabgrass Frontier.*

42. Ralph Waldo Emerson, "Works and Days" (1870), quoted in Lowenthal, *Past Is a Foreign Country,* 105; James, *Washington Square,* 37; Warner, *Streetcar Suburbs,* 156.

43. Records of the Board of Trustees of the Washington Monument Association, July 19, 1826, MS, Bostonian Society Library.

44. Boston City Council, Joint Standing Committee on Public Buildings, *The Old State House: Report of a Hearing . . . on the Petitions for and against the Removal of the Old State House* (City doc. 71B, 1881), 4; editorial, *BG,* May 31, 1872, 4.

45. Massachusetts General Court, Committee on Federal Relations, *Arguments in Behalf of . . . Preservation of the Old South Meetinghouse . . . March 4, 1878* (Boston, 1878), 36.

46. Nathaniel Hawthorne, *The Marble Faun* (1859; Columbus, 1968), 4:301–2.

47. Spann, *New Metropolis,* 102; Warner, *Streetcar Suburbs,* 119–20.

48. Fanny Kemble, *Journal of a Residence in America* (1835), quoted in Lowenthal, *Past Is a Foreign Country,* 126; Spann, *New Metropolis,* 116.

49. Spann, *New Metropolis,* 106–8.

50. Boston City Council, Special Committee on the South Burying-Ground, *Report* (City doc. 153, 1884), 36.

51. *Report of the Joint Special Committee on Intramural Interments* (City doc. 96, 1879), 16. See also *MA&R,* 1885, Acts ch. 278, § 1.

52. George Adams, pub., *Directory of the City of Boston, 1850–51* (Boston, 1850), 68.

53. Trinity Church, *Report . . . January 12, 1871,* 2; David Charles Sloane, *The Last Great Necessity: Cemeteries in American History* (Baltimore, 1991), 13–43; Blanche Linden-Ward, *Silent City on a Hill: Landscapes of Memory and Boston's Mount Auburn Cemetery* (Columbus, 1989), 15–33.

54. James J. Farrell, *Inventing the American Way of Death, 1830–1920* (Philadelphia, 1980), 125.

55. Chandler Robbins, *Sermon, Delivered before the Proprietors of the Second Church, Wednesday, September 17, 1845, at the Dedication of Their New House of Worship* (Boston, 1845), 15.

56. Robbins, *Sermon . . . November 4th, 1874,* 22–23.

57. Samuel Kirkland Lothrop, cornerstone service, in *Memorial of the Church in Brattle Square* (Boston, 1871), 52 ("turned their backs"); Samuel Kirkland Lothrop, *A Sermon Preached at the Dedication of the Church of Brattle Square Society, on the Corner of Clarendon Street and Commonwealth Avenue, Dec. 22, 1873* (Boston, 1874), 3 ("cannot annul").

58. "H.H.A." letter, *BG,* Jan. 31, 1874, 3; *BET,* May 14, 1878, 4.

59. At a hearing on the Old South Church, Avery Plumer "spoke of the rapid growth of the city and the retirement of dwellings before the march of business. Within twenty years he prophesied that all Beacon Hill east of Charles street would be used for mercantile purposes, and that the entire peninsula would in time be swept of dwelling-houses and devoted to business purposes." *BG,* Jan. 28, 1874, 2.

60. *BG,* Mar. 28, 1872, 2.

61. Michael J. Doucet, "Urban Land Development in Nineteenth-Century North

America: Themes in the Literature," *Journal of Urban History* 8 (1982): 299–342; Warner, *Streetcar Suburbs,* 117–32; Hoyt, *One Hundred Years of Land Values,* 388–91.

62. James E. Vance, *This Scene of Man: The Role and Structure of the City in the Geography of Western Civilization* (New York, 1977), 34; Richard Sennett, *The Fall of Public Man: On the Social Psychology of Capitalism* (New York, 1974), 139–40; Paul Goodman, "Ethics and Enterprise: The Values of the Boston Elite, 1800–1860," *American Quarterly* 18 (Fall 1966): 437–51.

63. Spann, *New Metropolis,* 200. See also *BG,* Feb. 3, 1878, 2.

64. Richard M. Hurd, *Principles of City Land Values* (1903; New York, 1924), 52; Frederick Law Olmsted and J. James R. Croes, "Preliminary Report of the Landscape Architect and the Civil and Topographical Engineer, upon the Laying out of the Twenty-third and Twenty-fourth Wards . . . " (1876), in *Landscape into Cityscape: Frederick Law Olmsted's Plans for a Greater New York City,* ed. Albert Fein (Ithaca, N.Y., 1967), 352.

65. Spann, *New Metropolis,* 106. For a contemporary expression, see 456, n. 33: "Samuel Halliday, something of an expert on housing, said in 1859 that 'the class of houses in a neighborhood has much more to do in fixing the price of building lots than the geographical position of the lots.'" See also *Real Estate Register and Rental Guide* (Providence), Mar. 30, 1892, 6.

66. Advertisement, *BG,* Mar. 10, 1874, 5: "Seashore residence at Cohasset. . . . The land will cut up to good advantage for building lots." This was presented as one option to pay for an estate that was otherwise marketed not for speculation but for occupation by the purchaser.

67. *Real Estate Register and Rental Guide* (Providence), May 18, 1892, 2.

68. Spann quotes an advertisement for Fordham, N.Y., in 1852: "The object of the above restrictions . . . is to endeavor to secure a good neighborhood, and prevent nuisances and little village lots from being laid out." Spann, *New Metropolis,* 199.

CHAPTER 2: *Problems with Change*

Epigraph: William James quoted in Edward K. Spann, *The New Metropolis: New York City, 1840–1857* (New York, 1981), 158.

1. Oscar Handlin, *Boston's Immigrants: A Study in Acculturation* (1941; New York, 1975), 187–89.

2. Francis Parkman, "The Failure of Universal Suffrage," *North American Review,* July–Aug. 1878, 4, quoted in Robert M. Fogelson, *America's Armories: Architecture, Society, and Public Order* (Cambridge, Mass., 1989), 24.

3. Paul S. Boyer, *Urban Masses and Moral Order in America, 1820–1920* (Cambridge, Mass., 1978), 69; Fogelson, *America's Armories,* 168–69.

4. James Ford Rhodes, *History of the United States from Hayes to McKinley, 1877–1896* (New York, 1919), 46; the quoted passage was written in 1909. See also Fogelson, *America's Armories,* 27–28.

5. Quoted in Fogelson, *America's Armories,* 56.

6. Ibid., 24–25.

7. *BG,* Oct. 8, 1873. Boston voters, by contrast, approved annexing Brookline by a higher margin than they gave to any other town.

8. Thomas Parsons, *BG,* Oct. 1, 1873, 5.

9. Boston remained with the smallest area of any major American city. Kenneth T. Jackson, *Crabgrass Frontier: The Suburbanization of the United States* (New York, 1985), 139–40, tables 8-1 and 8-2.

10. David Schuyler, *The New Urban Landscape: The Redefinition of City Form in Nineteenth-Century America* (Baltimore, 1986), 150; Spann, *New Metropolis,* 109; John P. Marquand, *The Late George Apley* (1936; New York, 1964), 19.

11. David Lowenthal, *The Past Is a Foreign Country* (Cambridge, England, 1985), 122.

12. Chandler Robbins, *Address Delivered at the Laying of the Corner-stone of the Second Church . . . May 30, 1844* (Boston, 1844), 3. "I believe," he continued, "that few buildings have ever been taken down in this city, whose demolition has excited such general interest, whose loss has been so universally felt."

13. "After the demolition of the old brick," complained one of these preservationists, "there is scarcely a vestige of antiquity left in the town." Quoted in Charles B. Hosmer Jr., *Presence of the Past: A History of the Preservation Movement in the United States before Williamsburg* (New York, 1965), 29. See also William Hayden appendix in Rufus Ellis, *The Last Sermon Preached in First Church, Chauncy Street, May 10, 1868* (Boston, 1868), 22–24.

14. Ellis, *Last Sermon . . . May 10, 1868,* 13–15, 6. Similarly, Phillips Brooks had worked to get rid of old Trinity Church on Summer Street so that his friend H. H. Richardson could build a magnificent new one on the Back Bay, but two days after the old one burned in the Great Fire, he wrote to a friend, "I did not know how much I liked the gloomy old thing, till I saw her windows bursting, and the flames running along the old high pews. I feel it was better for the Church to go so than to be torn down stone by stone." [Bishop] William Lawrence, *Address . . . Delivered in Trinity Church, Boston . . . [upon] the Fiftieth Anniversary of Its Consecration* (Boston, 1927), 9.

15. Samuel Kirkland Lothrop, *A Discourse Preached in the Church in Brattle Square, on the Last Sunday of Its Use for Public Worship, July 30, 1871. . . . and an Account of Laying the Corner-stone of the New Church* (Boston, 1871), 49; Frederic C. Detwiller, "Thomas Dawes's Church in Brattle Square," *OTNE* 69 (1979): 1–17; Samuel Kirkland Lothrop, *A History of the Church in Brattle Street, Boston* (Boston, 1851), 107–8.

16. Lothrop, *Discourse . . . July 30, 1871.* See also account in *BG,* July 18, 1877, 2; *Proprietors of the Church in Brattle Square v. Moses Grant et al.,* 69 Mass. 142 (1855). The parsonage, on Court Street, was given by Lydia Hancock, John Hancock's aunt.

17. Lothrop, *Discourse . . . July 30, 1871,* 30. Similarly, Samuel Kirkland Lothrop, *A Sermon Preached at the Dedication of the Church of Brattle Square Society, on the Corner of Clarendon Street and Commonwealth Avenue, Dec. 22, 1873* (Boston, 1874), 5: "Bricks and mortar are not alive. It is the living organization that gives power to the memories and associations that gather around them, and these memories and associations go where the living organization goes."

18. Lothrop, *Discourse . . . July 30, 1871,* 28; Lothrop, *Sermon at the Dedication . . . Dec. 22, 1873,* 3, 25.

19. Lothrop, *Discourse . . . July 30, 1871,* 29–30.

20. Samuel K. Lothrop, *Letters of Rev. S. K. Lothrop to the Proprietors of Brattle Street Church . . .* (Boston, 1876), 7–9.

21. Lothrop, *Sermon at the Dedication . . . Dec. 22, 1873,* 4.

22. T. Cole to Luman Reed, Mar. 26, 1835, quoted in David Schuyler, "The Sanctified Landscape: Scenic Values and Historic Preservation in the Mid-Hudson Valley, 1820–1850" (American Studies Program, Franklin and Marshall College, Lancaster, Pa., 1989, photocopy), 14; Henry Philip Tappan, *The Growth of Cities: A Discourse Delivered before the New York Geographical Society, on the Evening of March 15th, 1855,* quoted in Spann, *New Metropolis,* 115.

23. [Robert Morris Copeland], editorial, *Boston Daily Advertiser,* Oct. 16, 1873, quoted in Cynthia Zaitzevsky, *Frederick Law Olmsted and the Boston Park System* (Cambridge, Mass., 1982), 18.

24. Quoted in Spann, *New Metropolis,* 158.

25. Norton to James Russell Lowell, Aug. 30, 1868, in *Letters of Charles Eliot Norton,* ed. Sara Norton and M. A. DeWolfe Howe (Boston, 1913), 1:306; Charles Eliot Norton, "The Lack of Old Homes in America," *Scribner's Magazine* 5 (1889): 638, 639.

26. H. Hudson Holly, an architectural pattern-book publisher, quoted in Jean A. Follett, "Colonial Revival Origins," in Providence Preservation Society, *The Colonial Revival in Rhode Island, 1890–1940* (Providence, 1989), 2.

27. Gwendolyn Wright, *Building the Dream: A Social History of Housing in America* (Cambridge, Mass., 1981), 96. The emergence of this set of ideas of home has been traced in a number of recent histories of housing and suburban development: Wright, *Building the Dream,* and also her *Moralism and the Model Home: Domestic Architecture and Cultural Conflict in Chicago, 1873–1913* (Chicago, 1980); David Handlin, *The American Home: Architecture and Society, 1815–1915* (Boston, 1979); Jackson, *Crabgrass Frontier;* John Stilgoe, *Borderland: Origins of the American Suburb, 1820–1939* (New Haven, 1988); Robert Fishman, *Bourgeois Utopias: The Rise and Fall of Suburbia* (New York, 1987).

28. Jackson, *Crabgrass Frontier,* 48, 49; Wright, *Building the Dream,* 96. "The American Home" was the "Safeguard of American Liberties," according to the title of a painting commissioned in 1893 by the founder of the United States League of Building and Loan Societies. Wright, *Building the Dream,* 101.

29. Wright, *Building the Dream,* 107. See also Jackson, *Crabgrass Frontier,* 52.

30. Wright, *Building the Dream,* 99.

31. Jackson, *Crabgrass Frontier,* 58. Frederick Law Olmsted in 1869 referred to fenced yards as "private outside apartments." Quoted in Schuyler, *New Urban Landscape,* 162.

32. Stilgoe, *Borderland,* 178.

33. Jackson, *Crabgrass Frontier,* 51.

34. Alan Gowans, *The Comfortable House: North American Suburban Architecture, 1890–1930* (Cambridge, England, 1986), 102–65.

35. Andrew J. King, *Law and Land Use in Chicago: A Prehistory of Modern Zoning* (New York, 1986), chap. 6; *BG,* Oct. 21, 1875, 2; James Means, "Shall We Save Marlborough Street? or Shall It Be Sacrificed for the Benefit of Land Speculators?" circular letter, May 6, 1890, Codman family MS collection, 30.668, SPNEA; Eleanora W. Schoenebaum, "Emerging Neighborhoods: The Development of Brooklyn's Fringe Areas, 1850–1930" (Ph.D. diss., Columbia University, 1976), 192–97; Richard M. Hurd, *Principles of City Land Values* (1903; New York, 1924), 118.

36. Wright, *Building the Dream,* 108; Hurd, *City Land Values,* 117; Frank J. Scott, *The Art of Beautifying Suburban Home Grounds* (1870; Watkins Glen, N.Y., 1982), 60–69.

37. Jackson, *Crabgrass Frontier,* 198.

38. Spann, *New Metropolis,* 106; Michael J. Doucet, "Urban Land Development in Nineteenth-Century North America: Themes in the Literature," *Journal of Urban History* 8 (1982): 329; Sam Bass Warner, *Streetcar Suburbs: The Process of Growth in Boston, 1870–1900* (Cambridge, Mass., 1962), 68.

39. E.g., Chevy Chase, Md. (1893) (Jackson, *Crabgrass Frontier,* 124), and Roland Park, Md. (1894), where these houses were sold at a loss (Harry G. Schalck, "Planning Roland Park, 1891–1910," *Maryland Historical Magazine* 67 [1972]: 423). See also *First Annual Conference of Developers of High Class Residential Property, 1917* (microfilm of transcript, Manuscripts and Archives, Olin Library, Cornell), b55–57, b72–73; *Second Annual Conference of Developers of High Class Residential Property, 1918,* 528–29.

40. Joseph Laronge, "The Subdivider of Today and Tomorrow," *Journal of Land and Public Utility Economics* 18 (1942): 427; Marc A. Weiss, *The Rise of the Community Builders: The American Real Estate Industry and Urban Land Planning* (New York, 1987), 30–31, 40–48; William S. Worley, *J. C. Nichols and the Shaping of Kansas City: Innovation in Planned Residential Communities* (Columbia, Mo., 1990), 202–4.

41. Laronge, "Subdivider of Today and Tomorrow," 427; Weiss, *Community Builders,* 61–62.

42. J. C. Nichols, "Financial Effect of Good Planning in Land Subdivision," in *Proceedings of the Eighth National Conference on City Planning, Cleveland, June 5–7, 1916* (New York, 1916), 93; Weiss, *Community Builders,* 64–67. See also quantification of the economic effects of neighborhood change in Lawson Purdy, "Remarks at the Closing Dinner," in *Proceedings of the Ninth National Conference on City Planning, Kansas City, Mo., May 7–9, 1917* (New York, 1917), 293–94.

43. He made the remarks in 1877, as alderman. Boston City Council, *Public Parks in the City of Boston: A Compilation of Papers, Reports, and Arguments Relating to the Subject* (City doc. 125, 1880), 93.

44. Nichols, "Financial Effect of Good Planning," 95.

45. Hugh O'Brien, *Inaugural Address of . . . Mayor of Boston* (City doc. 1, 1885), 33. Richard M. Hurd in 1903 cited Boston as the main American example of this form of "sheer waste." Hurd, *City Land Values,* 41.

46. Boston Common Council, Committee on Streets, *Report . . . on the Widening of North Street* (City doc. 72, 1860), 4. See also *BET,* Jan. 27, 1915, 3. Boston and

other American cities long sought "excess condemnation" powers that would allow them to take these remnants (see editorial, *BH,* Jan. 29, 1903, 6; Boston Society of Architects' campaign for excess condemnation amendment), in order, they thought, to realize a profit on private improvements planned in a rational whole with the newly widened streets. When Massachusetts cities finally received this power by constitutional amendment in 1911, they discovered that this profit was a chimera (*BET,* Jan. 27, 1915, 3). Even when consciously planned to maximize public and private gain together, these infrastructure changes were a net drag on the common wealth.

47. Josef W. Konvitz, *The Urban Millennium: The City-Building Process from the Early Middle Ages to the Present* (Carbondale, Ill., 1985), 131–66; Stanley K. Schultz, *Constructing Urban Culture: American Cities and City Planning, 1800–1920* (Philadelphia, 1989), 184–94.

48. Quoted in Spann, *New Metropolis,* 115–16.

49. Boston City Council, Committee on Laying out and Widening Streets, *Final Report* (City doc. 116, 1870), 24–25.

50. Frederick Law Olmsted, "Public Parks and the Enlargement of Towns" (1870), in *Civilizing American Cities: A Selection of Frederick Law Olmsted's Writings on City Landscapes,* ed. S. B. Sutton (Cambridge, Mass., 1971), 68.

51. Frederick Law Olmsted et al., "Report to the Staten Island Improvement Commission of a Preliminary Scheme of Improvements" (1871), in *Landscape into Cityscape: Frederick Law Olmsted's Plans for a Greater New York City,* ed. Albert Fein (Ithaca, N.Y., 1967), 173–205.

52. Schuyler, *New Urban Landscape,* 167–79.

53. Frederick Law Olmsted and J. James R. Croes, "Preliminary Report of the Landscape Architect and the Civil and Topographical Engineer, upon the Laying out of the Twenty-third and Twenty-fourth Wards . . ." (1876), in *Landscape into Cityscape,* ed. Fein, 352–54.

54. Ibid., 356, 352. Landscape architect H. W. S. Cleveland earlier invoked the same metaphor when he termed the provision of uniform blocks for differing uses "as absurd as would be the assertion that the convenience and comfort of every family would be best served by living in a square house, with square rooms, of a uniform size." Quoted in Jackson, *Crabgrass Frontier,* 75.

55. Olmsted and Croes, "Preliminary Report," 361.

56. Ibid., 357; David Schuyler and Jane Turner Censer, introd., *FLO Papers,* 6:34–37.

57. Olmsted and Croes, "Preliminary Report," 362, 364.

58. Ibid., 362–63; Seymour J. Mandelbaum, *Boss Tweed's New York* (New York, 1965), 116–17; Schuyler, *New Urban Landscape,* 177–78.

59. Olmsted, Vaux & Co., "Preliminary Report upon the Proposed Suburban Village at Riverside, Near Chicago" (1868), in *Civilizing American Cities,* ed. Sutton, 292.

60. Frederick Law Olmsted, "Report upon a Projected Improvement of the Estate of the College of California, at Berkeley, near Oakland" (1866) in *Civilizing American Cities,* ed. Sutton, 288. Olmsted first discussed these ideas in an 1860 letter to H. H. Elliott, one of the commissioners laying out northern Manhattan's streets. *FLO*

Papers, 3:265. For Fisher Hill, see Zaitzevsky, *Olmsted and the Boston Park System,* 115–17.

61. Jackson, *Crabgrass Frontier,* 124; Weiss, *Community Builders,* 48–52; Nichols, "Financial Effect of Good Planning," 92. On the heavy costs of improvement at Riverside, see Olmsted, "Report to the Staten Island Improvement Commission," 196. On the difficulty of carrying the land assembled for Roland Park, see Schalck, "Planning Roland Park," 422. The developers of Riverside defaulted during the Panic of 1873, and the Roland Park Company and J. C. Nichols struggled through the depression of the 1890s.

62. William Seton Gordon, "Building Restrictions—Right to Enforce," *Albany Law Journal* 43 (1891): 349; Hurd, *City Land Values,* pref., summ., and chap. 8.

CHAPTER 3: *Selling Permanence*

Epigraph: Alexander S. Taylor, "Districting through Private Effort," in *Proceedings of the Eighth National Conference on City Planning, Cleveland, June 5–7, 1916* (New York, 1916), 178.

1. *Parker v. Nightingale,* 88 Mass. 341 (1863), at 342; "Warrant and Partition of Hayward Estate," Suffolk County Land Records, Deed Book 277:269–81.

2. Testimony in *Equity Records, S. J. C., April–October 1863,* 412, Supreme Judicial Court Archives, Boston. One of the heirs took the mansion house itself, and two—still minors when the doctor died—were living a few years later on what had been his garden.

3. Peter R. Knights, *The Plain People of Boston, 1830–1860: A Study in City Growth* (New York, 1971), 59.

4. *Equity Records, S. J. C., April–October 1863,* 411–12. Loeber had first opened his restaurant three years earlier at 401 Washington Street, directly opposite Hayward Place. *Boston City Directory,* 1859.

5. *Equity Records, S. J. C., April–October 1863,* 415.

6. Allen Chamberlain, *Beacon Hill: Its Ancient Pastures and Early Mansions* (Boston, 1925), 181, 89; *Jeffries v. Jeffries,* 117 Mass. 184 (1874).

7. *Keppel v. Bailey,* Myl. & K. 517, 534 (1834), quoted in Anthony J. King, *Law and Land Use in Chicago: A Prehistory of Zoning* (New York, 1986), 10.

8. John Bouvier, *A Law Dictionary, Adapted to the Constitution and Laws of the United States of America* (Philadelphia, 1858), 1:345.

9. "Uniform": *Codman v. Bradley,* 201 Mass. 361 (1909), an 1811 Boston deed; "religious or literary": *Hubbell v. Warren,* 90 Mass. 173 (1864), at 173–74, a Charlestown covenant from some time before 1846; "roof of slate": *Lowell Institute for Savings v. City of Lowell,* 153 Mass. 530 (1891), at 530–31, a Lowell deed from 1839.

10. Church: *Canal Bridge v. Methodist Religious Society,* 54 Mass. 335 (1847), an 1823 Cambridge deed; houses: *Estabrook v. Smith,* 72 Mass. 572 (1856), an 1852 Worcester deed; *Hopkins v. Smith,* 162 Mass. 444 (1894), the 1867 Oak Bluffs subdivision.

11. Bouvier, *Law Dictionary,* 1:346.

12. See, e.g., *Badger v. Boardman,* 82 Mass. 559 (1860); also *Skinner v. Shepard,*

130 Mass. 180 (1881), in which the court holds that the restrictions cannot be enforced even by the grantor's heirs.

13. E.g., deeds at Monument Square, Charlestown, in 1846 include conditions "to the end that there may be an uniformity in the buildings to be erected fronting the said Monument Square, and for determining the character and style thereof," specifying that they were to be "not less than three nor more than four stories high, . . . built of brick or stone." *Hubbell v. Warren,* 90 Mass. 173, at 173, 174.

14. Chamberlain, *Beacon Hill,* 89, 188; Stephen Garmey, *Gramercy Park: An Illustrated History of a New York Neighborhood* (New York, 1984), 31.

15. *American Unitarian Association v. Minot,* 185 Mass. 589 (1904), was decided on this point. Some restrictions were indeed meant to be permanent, such as the Mount Vernon Street indenture (1820), which formalized an 1801 setback agreement as a permanent restriction (Chamberlain, *Beacon Hill,* 89). Some of the Pemberton Square restrictions (1835) applied to a single generation of building (Suffolk County Land Records, Deed Book 397:257), some for thirty years, and some perpetually ("Conditions of Sale of Building Lots on Phillips Place . . . ," SPNEA). These were unusual; more often those drafting deeds simply did not address the question of duration, leading at least to the conclusion that they did not think it important. This leads also to the paradox that a deed restriction without duration—nominally permanent— was, as time passed, less likely to be enforced than one with a stated expiration. A long finite term made clear that the restriction meant to regulate more than a single act of building, and it offered little room for reinterpretation at the hands of unpredictable courts. See, e.g., *Gray v. Blanchard,* 25 Mass. 283 (1829).

16. "Catalogue of Forty-two Lots of Land on Worcester Square . . . ," SPNEA. Some deeds specified that their restrictions applied to any future rebuilding, suggesting that this was not the ordinary interpretation. Margaret Supplee Smith, "Between City and Suburb: Architecture and Planning in Boston's South End" (Ph.D. diss., Brown University, 1976), 107, n. 80.

17. *Codman v. Bradley,* 201 Mass. 361, at 365. Chief Justice Knowlton suggested that when the parties recorded a release of this condition in 1857, they did not consider it as applying only to the initial buildings, but he goes on to say (at 367) that the applicability of the condition at that time was "doubtful" and its release more in the nature of removing a cloud on the title.

18. E.g., 1867 Cottage City conditions requiring that a house be erected "within one year." *Hopkins v. Smith,* 162 Mass. 444.

19. Smith, "Between City and Suburb," 72–73; Hermione Hobhouse, *Thomas Cubitt, Master Builder* (New York, 1971), 103–8. Bostonians' "mimicry" of English institutions in general, writes social historian Ronald Story, was "omnipresent" in the mid-nineteenth century. Story, *Harvard and the Boston Upper Class: The Forging of an Aristocracy, 1800–1870* (Middletown, Conn., 1980), 166.

20. *Linzee v. Mixer,* 101 Mass. 512 (1869): the Back Bay; *Sharp v. Ropes,* 110 Mass. 381 (1872): a small-time subdivider exercising personal control. See release of condition on Mount Vernon Place by heirs of grantor, May 29, 1850, Suffolk County Land Records, Deed Book 610:262. See also petition of residents of Concord Sq.

[n.d.] asking that Boston Water Power Co. not release restrictions on adjacent land, New Lands folder, Boston Water Power Co. collection, Baker Library, Harvard.

21. *Hano v. Bigelow,* 155 Mass. 341 (1892), in which the last lot in a subdivision was sold unrestricted in 1869. Subdividers sold lots for triple-deckers as restrictions' expiration approached: in 1894, *Roak v. Davis,* 194 Mass. 481 (1907); in 1899, *Ivarson v. Mulvey,* 179 Mass. 141 (1901).

22. "Condition of Sale of Building Lots on Phillips Place . . . ," SPNEA. This subdivision's remarkable restrictions allowed action against violators by "the owner of any lot interested in such breach," though reserving special powers for the developer. See *Codman v. Bradley,* 201 Mass. 361: the heirs of the beneficiaries of an 1811 condition were able to be located in 1857 only because they still owned nearby property.

23. Smith, "Between City and Suburb," 59, 71–74.

24. *Allen v. Mass. Bonding and Insurance Co.,* 248 Mass. 378 (1924); *Sanborn v. Rice,* 129 Mass. 387 (1880); form of deed in Massachusetts, Commission on the Back Bay, *Catalogue of Fifty Lots of Land on the Back Bay . . . to Be Sold by Public Auction, on Wednesday, October 24, 1860* (Boston, 1860), 6; Smith, "Between City and Suburb."

25. *Equity Records, S. J. C., April–October 1863,* 414.

26. *Parker v. Nightingale,* defendants' brief, 4, Social Law Library, Boston.

27. *Whitney v. Union Railway,* 77 Mass. 359 (1860), at 362.

28. *Parker v. Nightingale,* 88 Mass. 341, at 346, 348. He continues: "Circumstances may exist which might warrant a refusal to grant equitable relief. . . . If, for instance, it was shown that one or two owners of estates were insisting on the observance of restrictions and limitations contrary to the interests and wishes of a large number of proprietors . . . by which great pecuniary loss would be inflicted on them, or a great public improvement be prevented, a court of equity might well hesitate to use its powers to enforce a specific performance or restrain a breach of the restriction" (at 349). See also Lawrence M. Friedman, *A History of American Law* (New York, 1985), 421.

29. *Parker v. Nightingale,* 88 Mass. 341, at 347.

30. *Gray v. Blanchard,* 25 Mass. 283, at 289–90; 145 Ill. 336 (1893), quoted in King, *Law and Land Use in Chicago,* 44.

31. *Whitney v. Union Railway,* 77 Mass. 359, at 366.

32. A building line in Cambridge brought the question of permanence squarely before the court in 1881. "Though unlimited in point of time," wrote Chief Justice Horace Gray in what was afterward cited as the definitive national precedent on the question, "it is a valid restriction." *Tobey v. Moore,* 130 Mass. 448 (1881), at 450; *Corpus Juris* 18:386.

33. *Ladd v. Boston,* 151 Mass. 585 (1890), at 587, quoting 1835 deeds on Pemberton Square. The Pemberton Square restrictions are remarkable for having fully anticipated equitable-easement doctrine. See also *Tobey v. Moore,* 130 Mass. 448, which quotes 1850 deeds in Cambridge that include "restrictions and conditions" violation of which "shall not subject the said grantees or their heirs or assigns to a forfeiture of their estate in said land" (at 449).

34. The leading case on the subject before *Parker v. Nightingale* had been *Gray*

v. *Blanchard,* 25 Mass. 283, in which the Supreme Judicial Court enforced a thirty-year condition by forfeiture of an estate after twenty-five years had elapsed, saying, "We cannot help the folly of parties who consent to take estates upon onerous conditions, by converting conditions into covenants" (at 287). In 1847 the court voided a twenty-four-year-old condition rather than enforce it by forfeiture. *Canal Bridge v. Methodist Religious Society,* 54 Mass. 335.

After *Parker,* the court in 1874 explicitly reinterpreted an 1807 "condition" as a restriction in order to enforce it in *Jeffries v. Jeffries,* 117 Mass. 184. The following year in *Episcopal City Mission v. Appleton,* 117 Mass. 326, it declared an 1847 condition to be a restriction but refused to enforce it. By 1879, in *Keening v. Ayling,* 126 Mass. 404, it had blurred this boundary enough to refer to conditions as "conditions or restrictions." See also *Skinner v. Shepard,* 130 Mass. 180 (1881), an 1859 deed; *Cassidy v. Mason,* 171 Mass. 507 (1898), an 1847 subdivision. The question received a final airing in 1900 in *Clapp v. Wilder,* 176 Mass. 332, in which a 4-to-3 majority declared that a condition imposed in 1867 really was a condition, in order to decide that it was too late to enforce it. In the dissenting opinion, Associate Justice Marcus Morton III explained what had become the settled practice: "Conditions are construed as restrictions . . . not because the courts have any special fondness for or leaning towards building schemes or plans of general improvement, but because it would be inequitable and unjust as against the owners of adjoining and neighboring estates to construe them otherwise" (at 344).

35. Suffolk County Land Records, Deed Book 1034:181.

36. *MA&R,* 1866, Acts ch. 264; *Linzee v. Mixer,* 101 Mass. 512.

37. *Parker v. Nightingale,* 88 Mass. 341, at 347. Fifty years later another case challenged the legal fiction that such restrictions had always existed. Lawyers for the Massachusetts Institute of Technology claimed that provisions in its 1861 deed from the commonwealth could not have been meant as equitable easements because they did not exist until the *Parker* decision created them two years later. The court was "not impressed" by this argument. *M.I.T. v. Boston Society of Natural History,* 218 Mass. 189 (1914), at 196.

38. Arbitrary control: *Sharp v. Ropes,* 110 Mass. 381 (1872); Back Bay: *Linzee v. Mixer,* 101 Mass. 512 (1869); Beacon Hill: *Jeffries v. Jeffries,* 117 Mass. 184 (1874).

39. *Sanborn v. Rice,* 129 Mass. 387 (1880): South End; *Tobey v. Moore,* 130 Mass. 448 (1881): Dana Estate, Cambridge; *Hano v. Bigelow,* 155 Mass. 341 (1892): Roseland Street, Cambridge, held to have a general plan despite several lots left unrestricted.

40. For deeds following case law, see, e.g., an 1886 deed by a private developer in the Back Bay, which recited that its restrictions were imposed in "furtherance of a general scheme for the improvement of the granted property and that the same were imposed to benefit the parcels conveyed," not merely to benefit the subdivider. *Evans v. Foss,* 194 Mass. 513 (1907), at 514–15. "'Natural' assumption": *Locke v. Hale,* 165 Mass. 20 (1895), at 23, referring to an 1871 deed.

41. *Ladd v. Boston,* 151 Mass. 585, at 588; *Parker v. Nightingale,* 88 Mass. 341, at 348.

42. King, *Law and Land Use in Chicago,* 50; *Attorney General v. Algonquin Club,* 153 Mass. 447 (1891), at 454. Where restrictions had only a short time to run—that is, where permanence did not enter into the question—Massachusetts judges were more likely to award damages than to order violations corrected. E.g., an 1894 subdivision in Jamaica Plain included restrictions of only eight years' duration, one of which limited construction to one- or two-family dwellings. The court found it "very clear" that a "triple-decker" three-family tenement built five years later violated the restrictions, but it awarded monetary damages rather than ordering compliance, "considering the short time the restrictions were to run." *Ivarson v. Mulvey,* 179 Mass. 141, at 142–43. See also *Scollard v. Normile,* 181 Mass. 412 (1902), in which the restrictions' short time to run (six years left of fifteen) contributed to a decision not to enforce them.

43. *Riverbank Improvement Co. v. Bancroft,* 209 Mass. 217 (1911), at 223.

44. Gordon, "Building Restrictions," 349; Susan Mulcahey Chase, "Working-Class Suburbs and Restrictive Covenants, Wilmington, Delaware, 1900–1941," paper delivered at Sixth National Conference on American Planning History, Knoxville, Tenn., Oct. 14, 1995. By the turn of the century, restrictions were prevalent enough in Boston that advertisements stated when they were offering "unrestricted land." *BH,* Nov. 1, 1902, 13.

45. "The whole subject of restrictions is still in its infancy. Outside England, Massachusetts, and New York, the cases are few." Charles I. Giddings, "Restrictions upon the Use of Land," *Harvard Law Review* 5 (1892): 284. See also King, *Law and Land Use in Chicago,* 52.

46. *Tobey v. Moore,* 130 Mass. 448, at 449.

47. Clement E. Vose, *Caucasians Only: The Supreme Court, the NAACP, and the Restrictive Covenant Cases* (Berkeley, 1959), 8–11. Racially restrictive covenants were most common in midwestern and border states, and in California where they were directed against Asians (Helen Monchow, *The Use of Deed Restrictions in Subdivision Development* [Chicago, 1928], 47–50, table 3). Patricia Burgess, in a study of deed restrictions in Columbus, Ohio, found two subdivisions that "prohibited ownership or occupancy by "foreign undesirables," and a third singled out foreigners of the "Dago class" (Burgess, "Real Estate Development and Urban Form: Roadblocks in the Path to Residential Exclusivity," *Business History Review* 63 [Summer 1989]: 375). Sam Bass Warner, in his study of Boston between 1870 and 1900, found "no evidence, however, of the use of covenants against any racial, religious, or national group" (Warner, *Streetcar Suburbs: The Process of Growth in Boston, 1870–1900* [Cambridge, Mass., 1962], 122). I found only one, from West Roxbury in 1858, a house lot where "no part of said premises shall ever be conveyed to any Irish man or woman" (Norfolk County Deed Book 264:36, quoted in Suffolk County Land Registrations 1A:2). Racial covenants had appeared in California by the 1890s, but they came into most widespread use between 1917, when the U.S. Supreme Court declared racial zoning unconstitutional in *Buchanan v. Warley* (245 U.S. 60), and 1948, when the court did likewise with racial covenants in *Shelley v. Kraemer* (334 U.S. 1). The use of deed covenants to enforce racial segregation was a relatively late use of a legal tool that

had already been developed to deal with issues of uniformity and permanence of environmental design.

48. J. C. Nichols, "Financial Effect of Good Planning in Land Subdivision," in *Proceedings of the Eighth National Conference on City Planning,* 94; "Westover: A New England Village of the Twentieth Century," n.d., 5, Loeb Library, Harvard (italics original); "Oak Hill Village, Newton Centre, Mass.," rpt. from *National Real Estate Journal,* Nov. 15, 1926, SPNEA.

49. Alexander S. Taylor discussed the substance of typical restrictions in "Districting through Private Effort," 180–82. See advertisements in *BET,* Apr. 18, 1896, 11 (Babcock Hill, Brookline); Oct. 2, 1897, 23 (Wellington Hill); May 3, 1924, VI/3 (Winchester, "in one of the finest restricted residential streets"). My favorite is an ad for lots in Chestnut Hill: "Fine location. Restrictions." *BET,* May 3, 1924, VI/2.

50. *BET,* Sept. 18, 1897, 23. See also auction advertisement for Hunnewell Hill Land Co., in Newton: "Single houses to cost not less than $4000 to build, and two-family houses to cost not less than $6000 to build—all to have a twenty foot setback from line of street." *Boston Sunday Herald,* June 28, 1903, 23.

51. *BET,* Apr. 18, 1896, 5 (Battery Heights, Cushing Hill, Hull). See also Apr. 3, 1915, IV/13: "fully restricted" (Brookline); Apr. 3, 1915, IV/12: "properly restricted" (Allindale Homesteads, Dedham).

52. *BET,* Jan. 16, 1896, 5; Antoinette F. Downing, Elisabeth MacDougall, and Eleanor Pearson, *Survey of Architectural History in Cambridge, Report Two: Mid-Cambridge* (Cambridge, Mass., 1967), 30. See also Charles W. Eliot, ed., *Charles Eliot, Landscape Architect* (Boston, 1902), 214–15. Charles Eliot Norton had commissioned an earlier, aborted subdivision plan from Frederick Law Olmsted. *FLO Papers,* 6:257–61.

53. Monchow, *Use of Deed Restrictions,* 71; *Second Annual Conference of Developers of High Class Residential Property, 1918* (microfilm of transcript, Manuscripts and Archives, Olin Library, Cornell), 546–47.

54. *Second Annual Conference of Developers,* 546, 548.

55. Taylor, "Districting through Private Effort," 178; Monchow, *Use of Deed Restrictions,* 57.

56. "Jamaica Plain," *BET,* Apr. 28, 1896, 11; "Parkway Land," *BET,* May 3, 1924, VI/4; *Second Annual Conference of Developers,* 540; William C. Worley, *J. C. Nichols and the Shaping of Kansas City* (Columbia, Mo., 1990), 282; Van Sweringen advertisement quoted in Eugene Rachlis and John E. Marqusee, *The Land Lords* (New York, 1963), 72.

CHAPTER 4: *Preservation*

Epigraphs: William H. H. Murray quoted in Everett Watson Burdett, *History of the Old South Meetinghouse in Boston* (Boston, 1877), 96; James Freeman Clark in *BG,* Dec. 9, 1872, 1.

1. David Lowenthal, *The Past Is a Foreign Country* (Cambridge, England, 1985), 322; Jane Holtz Kay, *Lost Boston* (Boston, 1980), 129–33.

2. Adams quoted in Alfred Seelye Roe, *The Old Representatives' Hall, 1798–1895: An Address Delivered before the Massachusetts House of Representatives, January 2, 1895* . . . (Boston, 1895), 42; Thomas Baldwin, *A Discourse Delivered Jan. 1, 1811, at the Opening of the New Meeting-house Belonging to the Second Baptist Church* . . . (Boston, 1811), 33; Massachusetts General Court, House of Representatives, *Objections in Behalf of Several Proprietors of Pews and Tombs to a Bill to Authorize Trinity Church, in Boston, to Sell Land* . . . (Boston, 1871), 6. Similarly, the New York City Council in 1803 said that its new city hall "is intended to endure for ages." Quoted in Hendrik Hartog, *Public Property and Private Power: The Corporation of the City of New York in American Law, 1730–1870* (Chapel Hill, 1983), 95.

3. Quoted in Walter Firey, *Land Use in Central Boston* (Cambridge, Mass., 1947), 167–68.

4. Charter art. 25: "The city council also shall have the care and superintendence of the public buildings, and the care, custody, and management of all the property of the city, with power to lease or sell the same, except the common and Faneuil Hall." *Municipal Register* (City doc. 2, 1851). See also George Adams, pub., *The Directory of the City of Boston, 1850–51* (Boston, 1850), 67–68.

5. Sara B. Chase, "A Brief Survey of the Architectural History of the Old State House, Boston, Massachusetts," *OTNE* 58 (1978): 43.

6. Brooks quoted in [Bishop] William Lawrence, *Address . . . Delivered in Trinity Church, Boston . . . [upon] the Fiftieth Anniversary of Its Consecration* (Boston, 1927), 25; Alan Gowans, *Images of American Living* (Philadelphia, 1964), 352.

7. Ronald F. Lee, *The Antiquities Act of 1906* (Washington, D.C., 1970), 4.

8. Quoted in Charles B. Hosmer Jr., *Presence of the Past: A History of the Preservation Movement in the United States before Williamsburg* (New York, 1965), 23.

9. John Ruskin, *The Seven Lamps of Architecture* (1849; New York, 1971), 183, 185.

10. A building should be "more lasting . . . than . . . the natural objects of the world around it." Ibid., 177; see also 172.

11. Ibid., 186.

12. Quoted in Martin S. Briggs, *Goths and Vandals: A Study of the Destruction, Neglect, and Preservation of Historical Buildings in England* (London, 1952), 210, 208.

13. Quoted in ibid., 210; Robert Kerr, "English Architecture Thirty Years Hence" (1884), quoted in Lowenthal, *Past Is a Foreign Country,* 396.

14. Gwendolyn Wright, *Moralism and the Model Home: Domestic Architecture and Cultural Conflict in Chicago, 1873–1913* (Chicago, 1980), 12; Hosmer, *Presence of the Past,* 25.

15. Donald J. Olsen, *The City as a Work of Art: London, Paris, Vienna* (New Haven, 1986), 306.

16. "Quaint": *Ballou's Pictorial* 8 (May 26, 1855): 332, quoted in Abbott Lowell Cummings, "The Old Feather Store in Boston," *OTNE* 48 (1958): 86. See 99–102 for his "Check-list of known contemporary views of the Old Feather Store." Cummings quotes the *Daily Evening Traveller* of July 10, 1860, as saying that "the front wall of the building will be carefully taken down, in as good condition as possible, and will

be removed to East Cambridge, where it will probably be set up in some place where it can be preserved"; he reports that "nothing further is said about any such project, however" (87).

17. James Marston Fitch, *Historic Preservation: Curatorial Management of the Built World* (New York, 1982).

18. J. M. Arms Sheldon, "The 'Old Indian House' at Deerfield, Mass., and the Effort Made in 1847 to Save It from Destruction," *OTNE* 12 (1922): 98–108.

19. Hosmer, *Presence of the Past,* 36, 37–38.

20. Quoted in ibid., 44, 49.

21. Ibid., 41–62; *BG,* June 17, 1875, 1.

22. Hosmer, *Presence of the Past,* 30.

23. "The minutes for his will to this effect were under his pillow when he died." Boston City Council, *Report of Committee on the Preservation of the Hancock House* (City doc. 56, 1863), 9.

24. Charles L. Hancock petition, Mar. 18, 1863, Massachusetts State Archives, legislative documents, 1863, Resolves ch. 45.

25. Boston City Council, *Preservation of the Hancock House,* 8; *MA&R,* 1859, Acts ch. 175.

26. Charles L. Hancock to Thomas C. Amory, May 23, 1863, in Boston City Council, *Preservation of the Hancock House,* 6.

27. Boston City Council, *Preservation of the Hancock House,* 5.

28. Ibid., 11–12; Hosmer, *Presence of the Past,* 39.

29. O. H. Burnham, pub., "Bostonians! Save the Old John Hancock Mansion," June 6, 1863, SPNEA.

30. Boston City Council, *Preservation of the Hancock House,* 11.

31. *Christian Register,* Aug. 5, 1871, quoted in Samuel Kirkland Lothrop, *A Discourse Preached in the Church in Brattle Square, on the Last Sunday of Its Use for Public Worship, July 30, 1871 . . . and an Account of Laying the Corner-stone of the New Church* (Boston, 1871), 42.

32. *BG,* Dec. 4, 1872, 4; G. G. Wolkins, *Freedom and the Old South Meeting-house,* Old South leaflets no. 202 (Boston, 1945), 17. See also Frederic C. Detwiller, "Thomas Dawes's Church in Brattle Square," *OTNE* 69 (1979), 8–9, fig. 7.

33. Old South Society, *List of Pastors, Officers, and Members of Old South Church* (Boston, 1870); Richard Henry Dana Jr., *The Old South: Argument . . . before the Committee on Parishes and Religious Societies, November 27, 1872* (Boston, 1872), 3. Dana quotes an earlier pastor of the society as saying "he wished the funds were in the sea, for they kept people in the church whose chief object was to administer them" (2).

34. Hamilton Andrews Hill, *History of the Old South Church, 1669–1884* (Boston, 1890), 521.

35. Report by Charles Stoddard, Loring Lothrop, Avery Plumer, and the church's two pastors, Apr. 30, 1866, quoted in ibid., 524. They were speaking of the congregation's Spring Lane chapel, on another side of the same block; the congregation voted to give up the chapel and rent one on Beacon Hill instead.

36. "Extracts from the Records of the Old South Church," 2 (Oct. 19, 1869, meeting), in Massachusetts Supreme Judicial Court, *Old South Society v. Crocker*, and *Attorney General v. Old South Society* (Boston, 1874–96), various papers bound as one vol., BPL.

37. Jacob Dresser quoted in *BG*, Nov. 27, 1872, 4; Old South Society, *Report of Committee to Consider Building on Boylston Street* (Boston, June 24, 1870), 2.

38. Hill, *History*, 507–8. See "Brief for the Attorney General," 11, in Supreme Judicial Court, *Old South Society v. Crocker*, BPL.

39. Joseph Ballard, *Reasons for the Appointment of a Committee, to Investigate the Prudential Affairs of the Old South Church in Boston* (Boston, 1859), 22; *Attorney General v. Old South Society in Boston*, 95 Mass. 474 (1866); *Crocker v. Old South Society in Boston*, 106 Mass. 489 (1871).

40. Hill, *History*, 527–29.

41. [Charles Francis Adams], "The Fate of an Historic Edifice," *Nation* 15 (Nov. 28, 1872): 346; Hill, *History*, 528; Dana, *Argument*, 3.

42. *BG*, Dec. 3, 1872, 4. These remonstrants were represented by Richard Henry Dana Jr., former U.S. attorney for Boston. Dana, *Argument*, 2–3.

43. [Adams], "Fate of an Historic Edifice," 347.

44. Stoddard in *BG*, Nov. 23, 1872, 4; Manning sermon, May 2, 1869, quoted in Hill, *History*, 525.

45. *BG*, June 24, 1876, 1; Phillips quoted in Massachusetts General Court, Committee on Federal Relations, *Arguments in Behalf of . . . Preservation of the Old South Meetinghouse . . . March 4, 1878* (Boston, 1878), 31.

46. "Extracts from the Records," 6, in Supreme Judicial Court, *Old South Society v. Crocker*, BPL; Hill, *History*, 530–31.

47. Hill, *History*, 531; *MA&R*, 1872, special session, Acts ch. 368.

48. *Old South v. Crocker*, 119 Mass. 1 (1875), at 7; *MA&R*, 1874, Acts ch. 120.

49. *Old South v. Crocker*, 119 Mass. 1; Hill, *History*, 547.

50. *Old South Society v. Crocker*. This decision was not published in the *Massachusetts Reports* but appears in *Transactions of the Colonial Society of Massachusetts* 3 (1896): 264–67; quotation on 267.

51. Wolkins, *Freedom and the Old South*, 24–25.

52. *BG*, June 9, 1876, 2; June 10, 1876, 4.

53. Burdett, *History*, 89.

54. Ibid., 90. Directors of the Old South Work, *The Old South Meeting House*, Old South leaflets no. 183, 15, quotes Burdett as "one who was present."

55. *Old South Meeting House*, Old South leaflets no. 183, 7.

56. Quoted in *BG*, July 14, 1876, 4.

57. Quoted in *BG*, July 8, 1876, 4.

58. According to Burdett (*History*, 97), at the first mass meeting on June 14, journalist Curtis Guild spoke "highly commending the part women took in such movements," in apparent reference to the preservation of Mount Vernon.

59. *BG*, July 20, 1876, 5. If they bought the Copley Square lot, "rumor states that

an injunction restraining the erection of the ancient edifice will be applied for by the Old South Society." *BG,* July 19, 1876, 2. This, said the chairman of the standing committee, was "a lie." *BG,* July 27, 1876, 5.

60. *BG,* July 15, 1876, 8.

61. *Dictionary of American Biography,* 518–19; *BG,* June 19, 1876, 2; July 13, 1876, 4; Oct. 14, 1876, 2. Did G. W. Simmons's "last $100,000" offer indicate an arrangement with Hemenway from the beginning?

62. Quoted in Hill, *History,* 544.

63. Old South Society, *To the Legislature of Massachusetts: Answer to the Reply of Petitioners to the Remonstrance of the Old South Society* (Boston, 1877), 3.

64. *BG,* Apr. 26, 1877, 2; Apr. 27, 1877, 2; *MA&R,* 1877, Acts ch. 222. After winning this battle, the Old South Association did not actually use the building on Sundays. "Should anything be attempted at any time in the future under the sanctions of this law," warned Hamilton Andrews Hill in the congregation's official history in 1890, "it will, of course, be competent to the Old South Society to take measures to test the question of its constitutionality." Hill, *History,* 546.

65. One of the business firms was New England Mutual Life Insurance Company, which held the mortgage on the property. Another signatory was Avery Plumer, a member of the Old South Church standing committee. Mrs. Henry Warren Paine and Mrs. Arthur T. Lyman, whose husbands signed the petition, were on the preservation committee; Mrs. Lyman's father was John Amory Lowell, another petitioner against the appropriation. Massachusetts State Archives, legislative documents, 1877, Acts ch. 222.

66. Massachusetts General Court, Committee on Federal Relations, *Hearing,* 9 (Shattuck), 5, 7, 43; *MA&R,* 1878, Resolves ch. 26.

67. Burdett, *History,* 95–96; *BG,* Aug. 22, 1876, 5.

68. Quoted in *BET,* Jan. 28, 1880, 4.

69. *BG,* June 21, 1878, 4; Edwin D. Mead, *The Old South Historical Work* (Boston, 1887); Old South Association, *The Old South Association in Boston: List of Officers, Members, Committees* (Boston, 1912), 17–24.

70. *BG,* June 13, 1876, 4; *BET,* June 1, 1881, 4.

71. Chase, "Old State House," 31–49; Elizabeth Reed Amadon, *Old State House: Historical Report* (Boston, 1970).

72. *BG,* May 28, 1872, 4.

73. *BG,* June 27, 1876, 8; Feb. 22, 1876, 2; Curtis Guild Sr., president's address, in *Proceedings of the Bostonian Society at Its Twenty-third Annual Meeting, January 12, 1904* (Boston, 1904), 7. Clark's arguments in favor of preserving the Old South were clearly meant to distinguish the two cases: "It has never been prostituted to the use of traffic or gain [but] only once in its history, and then in an emergency such as was never before known in the history of the city, and which we trust we shall never again know, nor has it been used except for the purpose of sacred worship. Its retention will not interfere with public improvements, as there is room enough to move it back when the time comes for the widening of the street." *BG,* June 15, 1876, 2.

74. *BG,* June 16, 1876, 2.

75. *BET,* Jan. 14, 1880, 1; Feb. 11, 1880, 1. The earlier "Historical Commission" lapsed into inactivity; most of the same people, including Whitmore, were involved three years later in organizing the Antiquarian Club. *BG,* Aug. 22, 1876, 5; *BET,* June 19, 1879, 1.

76. *BET,* Jan. 16, 1880, 2; Jan. 20, 1880, 3.

77. *BET,* June 10, 1881, 2.

78. *BG,* June 19, 1881, quoted in *BET,* June 21, 1881, 2.

79. *BET,* June 24, 1881, 3; June 18, 1881, 4.

80. *BET,* June 24, 1881, 3. Before beginning work, Clough in a letter to Whitmore referred to "the restoring of the outside walls to conform with its original outline and appearance as shown by your sketches." *BET,* June 24, 1881, 2.

81. *BET,* May 27, 1881, 2.

82. Boston City Council, *Re-dedication of the Old State House, Boston, July 11, 1882,* 5th ed. (Boston, 1889), 158.

83. Amadon, *Old State House,* 10; George Henry Moore, *Prytaneum Bostoniense: Examination of Mr. William H. Whitmore's Old State House Memorial and Reply to His Appendix N,* 2d ed. (Boston, 1887); William Henry Whitmore, *The Old State House Defended from Unfounded Attacks upon Its Integrity: Being a Reply to Dr. G. H. Moore's Second Paper* . . . (Boston, 1886).

CHAPTER 5: *Parks and the Permanent Landscape*

Epigraph: H. W. S. Cleveland, "Landscape Gardening," *Christian Examiner,* 4th ser., 23 (May 1855): 398, quoted in David Schuyler, *The New Urban Landscape: The Redefinition of City Form in Nineteenth-Century America* (Baltimore, 1986), 67.

1. Cynthia Zaitzevsky, *Frederick Law Olmsted and the Boston Park System* (Cambridge, Mass., 1982), 15, 33; *Report of Committee on the Improvement of the Public Garden* (City doc. 63, 1859), 3, 6.

2. Norman T. Newton, *Design on the Land: The Development of Landscape Architecture* (Cambridge, Mass., 1971), 309.

3. Schuyler, *New Urban Landscape;* Zaitzevsky, *Olmsted and the Boston Park System;* Newton, *Design on the Land;* Irving D. Fisher, *Frederick Law Olmsted and the City Planning Movement in the United States* (Ann Arbor, 1986); Albert Fein, *Frederick Law Olmsted and the American Environmental Tradition* (New York, 1972); Charles E. Beveridge, introd., *FLO Papers,* vol. 3; David Schuyler and Jane Turner Censer, introd., *FLO Papers,* vol. 6.

4. In City Council debate, Apr. 1, 1875, quoted in Boston City Council, *Public Parks in the City of Boston: A Compilation of Papers, Reports, and Arguments Relating to the Subject* (City doc. 125, 1880), 34. Olmsted's 1870 Boston talk, in which he outlined the metaphor of the city as a house of many rooms, was arranged in aid of legislation for such a park plan. Zaitzevsky, *Olmsted and the Boston Park System,* 37.

5. Daniel Bluestone describes a similar experience in Chicago. Bluestone, *Constructing Chicago* (New Haven, 1991), 30.

6. Zaitzevsky, *Olmsted and the Boston Park System,* 37–43.

7. *Second Report of the Board of Commissioners of the Department of Parks for the City of Boston* (City doc. 42, 1876), 31, 29; Alexander von Hoffman, *Local Attachments: The Making of an American Urban Neighborhood, 1850 to 1920* (Baltimore, 1994), 87–88.

8. Former council president William H. Whitmore, who worked to spend city money restoring the Old State House, argued that the city should wait until it could afford parks. Boston City Council, *Public Parks,* 184; Zaitzevsky, *Olmsted and the Boston Park System,* 41–47.

9. Frederick Law Olmsted, *The Justifying Value of a Public Park* (Boston, 1881), 4, 20; "Notes on the Plan of Franklin Park and Related Matters" (1886), in *Civilizing American Cities: A Selection of Frederick Law Olmsted's Writings on City Landscapes,* ed. S. B. Sutton (Cambridge, Mass., 1971), 256–57.

10. Boston City Council, Committee on Common and Public Grounds, *Evidence Taken at the Hearing . . . on the Petition of the Mass. Charitable Mechanics Association, for Leave to Erect a Building on Boston Common* (City doc. 26, 1877) (hereafter cited as *Hearing on the Charitable Mechanics Building*), 38; J. Mason and Franklin Dexter, *Legal Opinion . . . on the Title of Boston Common* (Boston, 1843).

11. Joseph Bennett (1740) quoted in M. A. DeWolfe Howe, *Boston Common: Scenes from Four Centuries* (Boston, 1921), 26, 34, 38.

12. John G. Hales, *Survey of Boston and Its Vicinity* (1821), quoted in ibid., 57; 39–42.

13. *BG,* May 13, 1873, 8.

14. Howe, *Boston Common,* 57.

15. *BG,* Feb. 13, 1877, 4; Boston City Council, *Hearing on the Charitable Mechanics Building,* 72; Howe, *Boston Common,* 62–63.

16. Boston City Council, *Report of Committee on the Preservation of the Hancock House* (City doc. 56, 1863), 11; Howe, *Boston Common,* 67; *BG,* Nov. 12, 1872, 4; Nov. 14, 1872, 4; Nov. 15, 1872, 8.

17. Boston City Council, *Hearing on the Charitable Mechanics Building,* 15, 65, 17.

18. Ibid., 40; see also 41, 42, 57.

19. *BG,* Mar. 9, 1877, 4; *MA&R,* 1877, Acts ch. 223.

20. *BG,* Apr. 10, 1872, 8.

21. "R.L.S." letter, *BG,* May 28, 1874, 2.

22. *BG,* May 23, 1874, 4; Nov. 17, 1874, 2; "Nauticus" letter, *BG,* Jan. 16, 1874, 5.

23. Editorial, *BG,* May 27, 1874, 4; italics original.

24. *MA&R,* 1875, Acts ch. 163.

25. Walter Firey, *Land Use in Central Boston* (Cambridge, Mass., 1947), 145.

26. *BG,* May 26, 1875, 8.

27. Petition quoted in *BET,* Mar. 25, 1887, 5.

28. *BET,* Feb. 1, 1893, 1, quoted in Charles W. Cheape, *Moving the Masses: Urban Public Transit in New York, Boston, and Philadelphia, 1880–1912* (Cambridge, Mass., 1980), 134; see also 120, 124.

29. Cheape, *Moving the Masses,* 135–136; Nathan Matthews to Horace G. Allen,

Mar. 14, 1893, Nathan Matthews papers, 4:237, Littauer Library, Harvard; *MA&R, 1893, Acts* ch. 481.

30. Since the existing streetcar system would continue in operation alongside any elevated railroads, the problem of surface congestion was to some extent independent of the question of rapid transit, and the same legislature that approved the alley elevated also authorized a subway. *MA&R, 1893, Acts* ch. 478.

31. "Father of the subway": Sylvester Baxter letter, *BET*, Sept. 24, 1898, 17; "prove a safeguard": *BET*, Dec. 18, 1893, 8. Upham later served as the first president of the Boston Common Society. *BG*, Apr. 17, 1900, 6.

32. Both letters in *Boston Daily Advertiser*, Apr. 1, 1895, 8. "M.P.L." was perhaps Mary P. Lanza, who signed the May 11, 1895, petition in *BET*.

33. They did not ask for construction by tunneling, which leaves the ground's surface undisturbed, rather than by the more economical cut-and-cover, even though the distinction was well understood and true tunneling was clearly what they wanted. They were evidently willing to settle for the long-term prospect of mature trees replacing those lost, and willing to trust the commissioners to do the right thing. *BET*, May 11, 1895, 7.

34. *BET*, May 13, 1895, 4.

35. Boston Transit Commission, *First Annual Report* (Boston, 1895), 17, 30. See also app. C, D, E, and *Second Annual Report* (Boston, 1896), 7 and pl. C, D, E.

36. Boston Transit Commission, *First Annual Report*, 19; *BET*, Aug. 11, 1896, 4; *BG*, Apr. 17, 1900, 6.

37. Arthur Pickering, in Boston City Council, *Hearing on the Charitable Mechanics Building*, 40; Howe, *Boston Common*, 39–40. The visible traces evidently were obliterated in the 1830s.

38. *BG*, June 24, 1875, 4.

39. Thaddeus William Harris quoted in Blanche Linden-Ward, *Silent City on a Hill: Landscapes of Memory and Boston's Mount Auburn Cemetery* (Columbus, 1989), 172–73.

40. Ibid., 208–11, 295–320; David Charles Sloane, *The Last Great Necessity: Cemeteries in American History* (Baltimore, 1991), 55–56; Schuyler, *New Urban Landscape*, 50–55.

41. *Annual Report of the Trustees of Mount Hope Cemetery* (City doc. 16, 1860), 5, 6; Linden-Ward, *Silent City*, 334–35.

42. *An Ordinance in Relation to Mount Hope Cemetery* (City doc. 72, 1857), 8; *Annual Report . . . Mount Hope Cemetery* (1860), map. See also Sloane, *Last Great Necessity*, 84.

43. *Address Delivered by Hon. J. V. C. Smith, Mayor . . . January 1, 1855* (City doc. 1, 1855), 19; *Annual Report of the City Registrar* (City doc. 7, 1852), 24–25; *Annual Report of the City Registrar* (City doc. 10, 1855), 32–33; Linden-Ward, *Silent City*, 329.

44. *Annual Report of the City Registrar* (1855), 32–33; *Report of the Joint Special Committee on Intramural Interments* (City doc. 96, 1879), 29.

45. *Fifth Annual Report of the Board of Health* (City doc. 67, 1877), 19.

46. See, for example, *Report . . . on Intramural Interments,* 55, 56, 60; *BET,* Sept. 5, 1879, 1, 4; *Proceedings of the Common Council,* Oct. 9, 1879, 586. Other owners expressed willingness to trade their tombs for plots in Mount Auburn or other rural cemeteries, but the Board of Health could not enter such negotiations because the police-power basis of its actions did not permit treating burial rights as property.

47. *Report . . . on Intramural Interments,* 55; *BET,* Sept. 5, 1879, 1.

48. *Proceedings of the Common Council,* Oct. 9, 1879, 586; *Report . . . on Intramural Interments,* 30.

49. *Proceedings of the Massachusetts Historical Society,* Sept. 1879, 127, 131–32.

50. *Report . . . on Intramural Interments,* 56, 58.

51. Massachusetts Historical Society petition, Jan. 7, 1880, Massachusetts State Archives, legislative documents, 1880, Acts ch. 153; *BET,* Jan. 20, 1880, 3.

52. *BET,* July 11, 1879, 2; *Annual Report of the City Registrar* (1852), 25.

53. *BG,* Feb. 17, 1875, 8.

54. Newton, *Design on the Land,* 557; Laura Wood Roper, *FLO: A Biography of Frederick Law Olmsted* (Baltimore, 1973), 282–83.

55. Roper, *FLO,* 287.

56. Lamar (1886) quoted in Roderick Nash, *Wilderness and the American Mind* (New Haven, 1982), 115; Newton, *Design on the Land,* 518–20.

57. *FLO Papers,* 6:65; Roper, *FLO,* 379–82, 395–96. The commission was set up in 1883, its acquisitions funded in 1885.

58. Art. 7, § 7, quoted in American Scenic and Historic Preservation Society, *Eighteenth Annual Report* (Albany, 1913), 242–43; Newton, *Design on the Land,* 557–58; Roper, *FLO,* 415; Nash, *Wilderness,* 120.

59. Charles W. Eliot, ed., *Charles Eliot, Landscape Architect* (Boston, 1902), 204.

60. Letter to editor, *Garden and Forest,* Mar. 5, 1890, in ibid., 317–18.

61. Trustees of Public Reservations, *First Annual Report . . . 1891* (Boston, 1892), 5, 7–8.

62. *MA&R,* 1891, Acts ch. 352; Trustees of Public Reservations, *Third Annual Report . . . 1893* (Boston, 1894), 13.

63. Eliot, ed., *Charles Eliot,* 352.

64. Zaitzevsky, *Olmsted and the Boston Park System,* 121–23.

65. Trustees of Public Reservations, *First Annual Report,* in Eliot, ed., *Charles Eliot,* 344.

66. The Waverley Oaks were part of the Beaver Brook Reservation. Trustees of Public Reservations, *Third Annual Report,* 13; Eliot, ed., *Charles Eliot,* 740.

67. Eliot, ed., *Charles Eliot,* 741.

68. Charles B. Hosmer Jr., *Presence of the Past: A History of the Preservation Movement in the United States before Williamsburg* (New York, 1965), 94–100; Edward Hagaman Hall, "The Palisades of the Hudson River: The Story of Their Origin, Attempted Destruction and Rescue," in American Scenic and Historic Preservation Society, *Eleventh Annual Report* (Albany, 1906), 198–212.

69. Eliot, ed., *Charles Eliot,* 15, 154, 161–62.

70. Trustees of Public Reservations, *Third Annual Report,* 16.

71. Trustees of Public Reservations, *Eighth Annual Report . . . 1898* (Boston, 1899), 14; *1938 Annual Report,* 8–9.

CHAPTER 6: *From Monuments to Landmarks*

Epigraph: Prescott F. Hall, "Circular of the Preservation Committee," Feb. 7, 1903, in Committee for the Preservation of Park Street Church, *The Preservation of Park Street Church, Boston* (Boston, 1903), 35.

1. Massachusetts Executive Department, *Report of Commissioners on the Subject of Remodelling or Rebuilding the State House* (Senate doc. 60, 1867), 3 ("most pressing"), 28–29 ("additional importance"); House doc. 449, 1867, quoted in James M. Stone, *The Improvements of the State House: The Investigation Thereof Investigated and Misrepresentations Exposed* (Boston, 1868), 8 ("the necessities"). See also MA&R, 1878, Resolves ch. 43.

2. *Governor's Address* (Senate doc. 1, 1888), 24; *Salem Public,* rpt. in Malcolm Sillars, *The State House, a Comprehensive Project of Enlargement* (Boston, 1888), 32.

3. E.g., BET, Nov. 27, 1886: "The State House is not entirely safe in the hands of a people who could let the old Hancock House go."

4. Governor Oliver Ames, Senate doc. 6, 1887, 2; BET, Nov. 27, 1886.

5. *Commercial Bulletin,* Apr. 30, 1887 (rpt. in Sillars, *State House,* 27), writing of Rep. Justin Perry of Natick. The bill Mr. Perry actually submitted a month later made no mention of "colonial" style but called for "a plain, three-story building." House bill 520, 1887, 2.

6. Governor Oliver Ames, Senate doc. 6, 1887, 2.

7. Boston City Council, *Majority and Minority Reports of Joint Special Committee on Sale of Reservoir Lot* (City doc. 96, 1887), 7.

8. "Procure a new State House": *House Journal,* 1885, 176; "other locations": BET, Mar. 10, 1888, rpt. in Sillars, *State House,* 26; "removed or remodelled": AA&BN, June 26, 1886, 301.

9. MA&R, 1886, Resolves ch. 87; *House Journal,* 1886, 739. See also account of the act's passage by Dr. William A. Rust, then member of the House, in Massachusetts General Court, Committee on the State House, *Hearings Mar. 16, 17, 18, 1896, Concerning the Bulfinch Front,* typescript, Massachusetts State Library Special Collections, 1:2–4.

10. Massachusetts, Governor and Council, *State House Annex* (Boston, 1888), [1]. The competition was advertised November 28, 1888, with a deadline of January 20, 1889. It provoked a nationwide protest among architects, because of its short duration, inadequate prizes, failure to provide for expert evaluation of the entries, and failure to promise the commission to the winner. AA&BN, Dec. 15, 1888, 273; Dec. 22, 1888, 285; Jan. 19, 1889, 31. Most major architects refused to participate — nor could they effectively, given the time frame. The winner, Charles Brigham, was already intimately familiar with the building from making measured drawings for the state. AA&BN, Feb. 9, 1889, 61.

11. Brigham explained the modified plan in House doc. 334, 1889 (Apr. 10, 1889),

3, and recalled the modification process in Massachusetts General Court, *Hearings . . . Concerning the Bulfinch Front,* 2:39–40. Albert W. Cobb attributes the modified bridge to Carl Fehmer. See letter, *BET,* Feb. 14, 1895, 6.

12. Former governor John D. Long, chairman; William Endicott Jr.; and Benjamin D. Whitcomb. Subsequent members were Charles Everett Clark and George W. Johnson.

13. Massachusetts State House Construction Commissioners, *Seventh Annual Report, 1895* (Senate doc. 3, 1896), 7.

14. Massachusetts State House Construction Commissioners, *Fourth Annual Report, 1892* (House doc. 6, 1893), 8. The commissioners' proposal not surprisingly brought charges of disingenuousness. "The move for the destruction of the State House has been a covert one," said Arthur Rotch. "Following the diplomatic tactics of those in charge, the great 'Annex' has crept up in the rear under cover of the old building, and now suddenly asserts itself, and from behind it stabs to death" (*Save the State House: The Memorial of a Century of Freedom* [Boston, 1894], 28). Alden Sampson speculated that this "plot" was conceived as a way of building a whole new capitol piecemeal to avoid confronting demands that it be moved elsewhere in the state (Sampson letter in Boston Evening Transcript, *State House Reconstruction* [Boston, 1894]). The *American Architect* thought that "if it had been known that the public was not to be cajoled into giving up the old building," Massachusetts would have picked a different design (*AA&BN,* Mar. 10, 1894, 109). Arthur T. Lyman suggested a different sort of ulterior motive. With restoration estimated at $375,000, and new construction at $1.25 million, he quoted "a friend from the corrupt city of Philadelphia" who thought that the way to save the building was to raise the restoration price to $2 million (letter, *BET,* Apr. 22, 1896, 6).

15. Massachusetts State House Construction Commissioners, *Sixth Annual Report, 1894* (Senate doc. 3, 1895), 15. *AA&BN,* Dec. 4, 1886, 261, referred to the annex as "the permanent part" of the statehouse.

16. *AA&BN,* Jan. 14, 1893, 17. The experts, appointed March 14, 1895, were Charles A. Cummings (president of the Boston Society of Architects), David H. Andrews, and E. Noyes Whitcomb. Their report, presented April 13, is reprinted in *AA&BN,* Apr. 27, 1895, 39–40.

17. Massachusetts General Court, *Hearings . . . Concerning the Bulfinch Front,* 1:21 (see also Walter H. Wentworth, a Boston mason and builder: "I never saw a better-built wall," 1:32); 2:36.

18. Ibid., 2:25.

19. Construction commission chairman John D. Long, letter in *BET,* Feb. 2, 1894, 5. It "might, with such opportunities for effect as the lot afforded, have been made one of the most splendid buildings in the world." *AA&BN,* Feb. 10, 1894, 61.

20. Speech re Chicago Columbian Exposition, at Nov. 1893 Massachusetts Historical Society meeting, rpt. in *Save the State House,* 30. Three years later a crowd in Faneuil Hall applauded Mayor Josiah Quincy when he said, "I do not feel like trusting the architects of today to improve upon the work of Bulfinch." *BET,* Apr. 21, 1896, 1.

21. *Save the State House,* 15; *Worcester Spy,* rpt. in Sillars, *State House,* 32. An

1895 appeal by nonarchitects asked, "At this time of reawakening interest in a noble and severe civic architecture, symbolized by the new Public Library, what more fitting celebration of the centenary of Bulfinch's State House . . . than to hand down to another century unmoved, this landmark of a century preceding our own?" *BET,* Feb. 9, 1895, 9.

22. Edward Robinson, secretary of the Boston Art Commission, in Massachusetts General Court, *Hearings . . . Concerning the Bulfinch Front,* 1:45.

23. Albert W. Cobb, in ibid., 2:12. Cobb himself proposed in 1895 a "design for preserving and extending the front of the Massachusetts State House," but the legislature, rather than hiring him to carry out his plan, created the expert commission on which Cummings sat as the sole architect, which may explain Cobb's vehemence. When Cummings later served as consulting architect for the actual restoration, he refused to accept any compensation. *AA&BN,* July 11, 1896, 10.

24. Clement K. Fay, in Massachusetts General Court, *Hearings . . . Concerning the Bulfinch Front,* 3:17. The committee consisted of Fay, H. Langford Warren, and William R. Ware (1:14–15).

25. State House Construction Commissioners, *Fourth Annual Report,* 8.

26. Letter, *BET,* Feb. 2, 1894, 5.

27. *BET,* Feb. 26, 1894, 1. An opponent quoted the commissioners: " 'We would raze the building,' they said, 'in order to preserve it, in order to preserve the idea of which it is the material embodiment.' " Sampson letter in Boston Evening Transcript, *State House Reconstruction.*

28. Endicott letter: *BET,* Feb. 17, 1894, 12; Tuttle: Massachusetts General Court, *Hearings . . . Concerning the Bulfinch Front,* 3:33; Walker: *Save the State House,* 24. Even this to some people understated the value of the building: "Bulfinch was great because he built the State House, and not the State House great because Bulfinch built it." Sampson letter in Boston Evening Transcript, *State House Reconstruction.*

29. *AA&BN,* Mar. 10, 1894, 109; *MA&R,* 1892, Acts ch. 404; 1893, ch. 450; 1894, ch. 532; House bill 427, 1895.

30. Fay, in Massachusetts General Court, *Hearings . . . Concerning the Bulfinch Front,* 1:9; *AA&BN,* Mar. 10, 1894, 109.

31. State House Construction Commissioners, *Fourth Annual Report,* 8; Senate bill 182, 1894. Compare with Senate bill 318, 1893—essentially the same language, without the clause allowing dimensions to be increased.

32. Letter, *BET,* Feb. 2, 1894, 5. See also Arthur T. Lyman letter, *BET,* Apr. 22, 1896, 6: "Even if we had Bulfinch's original plans, it would be absurd to reproduce them when the building that we have is the building that he erected."

33. Massachusetts General Court, Committee on the State House, *Views of a Minority . . . on the Preservation of the State House* (Senate doc. 189, 1894), 2–3. The minority included Joseph F. Bartlett and E. G. Frothingham, of the Senate; Royal Robbins, the committee's chair; and F. H. Bradford and Henry A. Whitney, of the House.

34. Ibid., 4. The committee was adopting a position earlier taken by the Boston Society of Architects. See William G. Preston letter, *BET,* Feb. 7, 1894, 8.

35. "Faults": Sampson letter in Boston Evening Transcript, *State House Reconstruc-*

tion; Preston letter, *BET,* Feb. 7, 1894, 8; Eugène Emmanuel Violet-le-Duc (1875) quoted in Charles B. Hosmer Jr., *Presence of the Past: A History of the Preservation Movement in the United States before Williamsburg* (New York, 1965), 23; Wheelwright: Massachusetts General Court, *Hearings . . . Concerning the Bulfinch Front,* 1:42.

36. *BH,* Apr. 8, 1896, 6. Winslow Warren, in a letter to John D. Long, referred to the building's preservation as "destroying the effect of the new for the sake of the not very old." The building had "more an imaginary than a real antiquity," he said. "I confess that with an anxious antiquarian spirit I have endeavored to understand what are the associations connected with the present state house front. It was built by Mr. Bulfinch about 100 years ago. Well, what of it!" *BG,* Feb. 11, 1894, 10.

37. Charles A. Cummings wanted to "put it as nearly as possible in the condition it was in when Governor Andrews was here." Massachusetts General Court, *Hearings . . . Concerning the Bulfinch Front,* 1:10. See also Alfred Seelye Roe, *The Old Representatives' Hall, 1798–1895: An Address Delivered before the Massachusetts House of Representatives, January 2, 1895 . . .* (Boston, 1895), 42; Sampson letter in Boston Evening Transcript, *State House Reconstruction.*

38. Massachusetts General Court, *Hearings . . . Concerning the Bulfinch Front,* 1:44; Henry Lee, *The Value of Sentiment,* pamphlet rpt. from *AA&BN,* Mar. 9, 1895, 5.

39. *BG,* Apr. 26, 1877, 2; Old South Association, *The Old South Association in Boston: List of Officers, Members, Committees* (Boston, 1912).

40. Massachusetts General Court, *Hearings . . . Concerning the Bulfinch Front,* 1:11 (Fay); 2:26–27 (Long).

41. *Boston Morning Journal,* Mar. 27, 1896, 10; *AA&BN,* Apr. 25, 1896, 33; *BET,* May 13, 1896, 7; Massachusetts State Archives, legislative documents, 1896, Acts ch. 531; *Boston Morning Journal,* Apr. 16, 1896, 1; Massachusetts General Court, *Centennial of the Bulfinch State House: Exercises before the Massachusetts Legislature, January 11, 1898* (Boston, 1898), 30.

42. *AA&BN,* Apr. 18, 1896, 32; Apr. 27, 1896, 33; May 5, 1896, 45–47; Roe in Massachusetts General Court, *Centennial,* 19–20. See also James M. Lindgren, *Preserving the Old Dominion: Historic Preservation and Virginia Traditionalism* (Charlottesville, 1993), 206.

43. Massachusetts General Court, *Centennial,* 27; Senate bill 253, 1896 (as amended Senate bill 259, 1896). The president of the Senate was George P. Lawrence of North Adams, and the speaker of the House was George V. L. Meyer of Boston; Meyer was an investment banker whose sister Helen Meyer was later an important supporter of the Society for the Preservation of New England Antiquities. See also James Michael Lindgren, "The Gospel of Preservation in Virginia and New England: Historic Preservation and the Regeneration of Traditionalism" (Ph.D. diss., College of William and Mary, 1984), 260.

44. Massachusetts General Court, *Centennial,* 28 (architects); 25 ("old yet new"); 17 ("*Esto perpetua*").

45. For an appreciation of the Park Street spire, see *AA&BN,* Oct. 31, 1896, 33.

46. *BET,* June 16, 1881, 4 ("most conspicuous"); May 11, 1881, 4 ("vague idea"); May 7, 1881, 2; May 10, 1881, 1.

47. *BET*, Oct. 11, 1881, 4; June 16, 1881, 4; advertisement cited in letter to the editor, *BET*, Oct. 11, 1881, 5; [George B. Chase], "Brattle St. Church Tower," MS subscription book, T. Chase papers, Massachusetts Historical Society. Chase calculated that selling off the rest of the lot would leave at most $30,000 to be raised, and he obtained pledges for more than $20,000. The pledges ranged from $250 to $5,000. As the *Springfield Republican* wrote, "The appeal is rather to the wealthy than the sentimental citizen." Quoted in George B. Chase letter to the editor, *Boston Daily Advertiser*, July 29, 1881, clipping in subscription book. One pledge of $500 came from bank president Franklin Haven, who had led the effort to demolish the Old State House just a few weeks earlier but evidently felt less comfortable with change in the Back Bay, where he also enforced deed restrictions as a commissioner of public lands.

48. *BET*, Apr. 1, 1902, 12; Douglass Shand Tucci, *Built in Boston: City and Suburb, 1800–1950* (Boston, 1978), 13; *Boston Sunday Journal*, Feb. 17, 1901, 1, 2; *AA&BN*, Mar. 2, 1901, 66.

49. Quoted in H. Crosby Englizian, *Brimstone Corner: Park Street Church, Boston* (Chicago, 1968), 202.

50. *Springfield Republican*, Dec. 17, 1902, quoted in Committee for the Preservation of Park Street Church, *Preservation*, 52. The mortgage was due July 15, 1903 (23).

51. Quoted in Englizian, *Brimstone Corner*, 205.

52. *BH*, Dec. 8, 1902, 12; Dec. 14, 1902, 7; Dec. 18, 1902, 8; Englizian, *Brimstone Corner*, 204; Committee for the Preservation of Park Street Church, *Preservation*, 22–23.

53. Committee for the Preservation of Park Street Church, *Preservation*, 31, 51 (quoting Prescott F. Hall letter, *BET*, Dec. 31, 1902). Pledges: *BET*, Jan. 15, 1903; *BG*, Apr. 2, 1903, quoted in Committee for the Preservation of Park Street Church, *Preservation*, 32, 64.

54. Englizian, *Brimstone Corner*, 205. The three pew owners who later led the internal opposition, Dr. Fred T. Lewis, William K. Porter, and B. Frank Silsby, did not join this committee. *BG*, July 1, 1903, quoted in Committee for the Preservation of Park Street Church, *Preservation*, 72. The eighteen members of the committee included only two who had been active in saving the Bulfinch front. Pledges: *BET*, Feb. 27, 1903, 1; *BH*, Mar. 7, 1903, 9. The increase from $200,000 to $300,000 in a week, and the casualness with which these round figures were offered, suggests that they be treated with a certain skepticism.

55. Committee for the Preservation of Park Street Church, *Preservation*, 10 ("Wren"), 5 ("seen by more"); *BET*, Feb. 27, 1903, 1.

56. "Most conspicuous": Henry Whitmore in *BET*, Dec. 15, 1902; Committee for the Preservation of Park Street Church, *Preservation*, 4 ("essential"), 6 ("retain it"); Walter Firey, *Land Use in Central Boston* (Cambridge, Mass., 1947), 163.

57. Committee for the Preservation of Park Street Church, *Preservation*, 60 (quoting "M.N.O." letter to the editor, *BET*, Jan. 31, 1903), 56 ("Vistas," *BH*, n.d.).

58. "Ruined": *BET*, Feb. 27, 1903, 1; Committee for the Preservation of Park Street Church, *Preservation*, 60 ("noble approach": "M.N.O." letter to the editor, *BET*,

Jan. 31, 1903); 50 ("a well": *BET,* Dec. 31, 1902), 5–6 ("monumental building," "head of the Common").

59. Letter, *BET,* Jan. 5, 1903, 8; for biographical detail on Joseph Lee, see Elisabeth M. Herlihy, ed., *Fifty Years of Boston* (Boston, 1932), 771.

60. *BET,* Feb. 27, 1903, 1.

61. Hosmer, *Presence of the Past,* 146; House bill 712, 1903; *BET,* Feb. 27, 1903, 1.

62. Edwin D. Mead and Prescott Hall testimony at legislative hearing, *BET,* Feb. 27, 1903, 1.

63. Hosmer, *Presence of the Past,* 111; *BH,* Mar. 7, 1903; Apr. 2, 1903; *Springfield Republican,* Feb. 10, 1903, quoted in Committee for the Preservation of Park Street Church, *Preservation,* 32. On March 9, three days after the Parker House meeting, the legislature received a negative report on the Park Street Church bill from the Committee on the State House, which had held the hearing. *House Journal,* 1903, 542.

64. *BET,* Feb. 27, 1903, 1; Firey, *Land Use in Central Boston,* quoting *Boston Sunday Journal,* Mar. 15, 1903.

65. *BG,* Apr. 2, 1903, quoted in Committee for the Preservation of Park Street Church, *Preservation,* 66; Eugenie Ladner Birch and Deborah S. Gardner, "The Seven-Percent Solution: A Review of Philanthropic Housing, 1870–1910," *Journal of Urban History* 7 (1981): 403–38.

66. *BH,* Apr. 2, 1903; also *BG,* July 1, 1903, and *Boston Morning Journal,* July 1, 1903, both quoted in Committee for the Preservation of Park Street Church, *Preservation,* 71–74. See also *Preservation,* 22–23.

67. *BH,* June 15, 1904; Englizian, *Brimstone Corner,* 205–6.

68. Quoted in Englizian, *Brimstone Corner,* 207.

69. Ibid.

70. Committee for the Preservation of Park Street Church, *Preservation,* 74, quoting *Boston Morning Journal,* July 1, 1903. Englizian (*Brimstone Corner,* 209) says it is not in that issue of the *Journal.*

71. Rev. A[rcturus] Z. Conrad, ed., *Commemorative Exercises at the One Hundredth Anniversary of the Organization of Park Street Church, February 26–March 3, 1909* (Boston, 1909), 27 ("on the condition"), 161–62 ("it preaches"); Englizian, *Brimstone Corner,* 211, 219. Other than painting, all of the $10,000 was spent on the building's interior.

72. Ronald Story, *Harvard and the Boston Upper Class: The Forging of an Aristocracy, 1800–1870* (Middletown, Conn., 1980), 13–19; *BG,* Jan. 14, 1873; trustees' circular letter to proprietors, Dec. 1, 1903, William Sumner Appleton scrapbook [10], SPNEA.

73. *BET,* Mar. 7, 1903 ("an heirloom"); May 23, 1901 ("reliance"); *BH,* Feb. 17, 1912 ("breach of trust"); *Boston Sunday Post,* Dec. 3, 1911; petition, Appleton scrapbook [10], SPNEA; Jane S. Knowles, *Change and Continuity: A Pictorial History of the Boston Athenaeum* (Boston, 1985).

74. Charles Zueblin, "'The White City' and After," *Chautauquan,* Dec. 1903, 373–78.

75. Charles Zueblin, "Metropolitan Boston," *Chautauquan,* Jan. 1904, 486; Zueblin, "White City'; William H. Wilson, *The City Beautiful Movement* (Baltimore, 1989), 48, 53–74; William H. Jordy, "The Beaux-Arts Renaissance: Charles McKim's Boston Public Library," in *American Buildings and Their Architects* (New York, 1976), 3:314–75.

76. Charles Mulford Robinson, *The Improvement of Towns and Cities* (New York, 1901), 200, 201.

77. "Fragment": Baxter quoted in Tucci, *Built in Boston,* 147; "*dégagement*": Donald J. Olsen, *The City as a Work of Art: London, Paris, Vienna* (New Haven, 1986), 306; Robinson, *Improvement,* 206–8; *Boston Real Estate Record and Building News,* Nov. 18, 1893, 4; Nov. 4, 1893, 4.

78. Jon A. Peterson, "The City Beautiful Movement: Lost Origins and Forgotten Meanings," *Journal of Urban History* 2 (1976): 415–34; Charles Brigham testimony in *BET,* Feb. 10, 1896, 8; Senate doc. 385, 1899.

79. C. R. Ashbee, *A Report . . . to the Council of the National Trust for Places of Historic Interest and Natural Beauty, on His Visit to the United States in the Council's Behalf* (London, 1901), 13, 5.

80. Ibid., 7, 11.

CHAPTER 7: *The Sacred Sky Line*

Epigraph: Oliver Wendell Holmes Sr., *The Autocrat of the Breakfast Table* (1858; Boston, 1886), 125.

1. C. R. Ashbee, *A Report . . . to the Council of the National Trust for Places of Historic Interest and Natural Beauty, on His Visit to the United States in the Council's Behalf* (London, 1901), 7.

2. The Athenaeum trustees, shortly before their aborted attempt to relocate, advocated further height restrictions on buildings around them. *Boston Morning Journal,* Apr. 4, 1899.

3. *MA&R,* 1891, Acts ch. 355. The restriction exempted "steeples, domes, towers, or cupolas erected for strictly ornamental purposes." For this citywide height restriction, see Michael Holleran, "Boston's 'Sacred Sky Line': From Prohibiting to Sculpting Skyscrapers, 1891–1928," *Journal of Urban History* 22 (1996): 552–85.

4. *AA&BN,* Mar. 26, 1887, 145.

5. Altona, outside Hamburg. Heights of Buildings Commission, *Report . . . to the Committee on the Height, Size, and Arrangement of Buildings of the Board of Estimate and Apportionment of the City of New York* (New York, 1913), 94–95.

6. *AA&BN,* Mar. 26, 1887, 145.

7. Anthony J. King, *Law and Land Use in Chicago: A Prehistory of Zoning* (New York, 1986), 124–27.

8. Christopher Tiedemann, *A Treatise on the Limitations of the Police Power in the United States* (St. Louis, 1886), 426, n. 1; *MA&R,* 1868, Acts ch. 281; Christine Cousineau, "Tenement Reform in Boston, 1870–1920: Philanthropy, Regulation, and

Government Assisted Housing," in *Proceedings, Third National Conference on American Planning History, Cincinnati, 1989* (Hilliard, Ohio, 1990), 600; Ernst Freund, *The Police Power: Public Policy and Constitutional Rights* (Chicago, 1904), v.

9. *BET*, Feb. 21, 1896, 12. See also Holleran, "Boston's 'Sacred Sky Line.'"

10. *Boston Real Estate Record and Building News,* July 28, 1894.

11. *BET*, Mar. 31, 1896, 7.

12. Douglass Shand Tucci, *Built in Boston: City and Suburb, 1800-1950* (Boston, 1978), 106.

13. See "Boston's Tallest Skyscrapers," *Boston Sunday Globe,* Jan. 14, 1894, 27, which lists and illustrates Boston's twenty-nine tallest structures (down to 103 feet); there are no apartment houses on the list.

14. "Vox Populi" letter to the editor, *BET,* Jan. 22, 1896, 6; Tucci, *Built in Boston,* 106.

15. *BET*, Feb. 7, 1896, 4. Ironically, J. Pickering Putnam, the architect of Haddon Hall, had been one of the club's founders and remained a member. Officially, the club was neutral on this as on all issues and merely "extended the facilities of its rooms and of its machinery of publicity to any of its members who were fighting any sort of campaign." Twentieth Century Club, *A Survey of Twenty Years* (Boston, 1914), 9.

16. House bill 522, 1896.

17. *AA&BN,* Feb. 1, 1896, 49.

18. *BH,* Apr. 17, 1896, 5.

19. *MA&R,* 1896, Acts ch. 313.

20. Quoted in Upham letter, *BET,* June 20, 1896, 15; *Senate Journal,* 1896, 788 (May 7); *House Journal,* 1896, 1040 (May 14).

21. *BET,* June 20, 1896, 15; *Senate Journal,* 1896, 875 (May 19). The next year Upham returned with a police-power bill modified to meet many of the exchange's objections (House bill 287, 1897); it included a larger area within the high-building district and included a variance procedure modeled on a proposed New York City height law, by which tall buildings could be erected outside the high-building district if approved by the mayor, the parks commissioners, and the Board of Health. The legislature's Committee on Metropolitan Affairs reported a version that applied only to Beacon Hill and the Back Bay (House bill 970, 1897). The Senate amended it to reduce heights in the whole city—even downtown—to eighty feet but then failed to pass the bill (*Senate Journal,* 1897, 596). The following year Upham made one more try (House bill 763, 1898). The Senate again eliminated the district provision so that the bill would lower heights throughout the city—this time to one hundred feet (Senate bill 205, 1898)—and once again failed to pass it (*Senate Journal,* 1898, 538).

22. The limit was imposed August 3, 1896. Commission on Height of Buildings in the City of Boston, *Final Report* (City doc. 133, 1905), 14–15; Heights of Buildings Commission (New York), *Report,* 141. No one appeared, either in favor or opposed, at the parks commissioners' hearing on the restrictions. *BET,* July 20, 1896, 1. A claim of damages at this hearing would normally be the first step in seeking compensation under eminent domain.

23. *Robert Treat Paine v. Commonwealth,* transcript of hearings, 1902–3, MS, Massachusetts State Library Special Collections.

24. *AA&BN,* Mar. 4, 1893, 129; William H. Wilson, *The City Beautiful Movement* (Baltimore, 1989), 58; William H. Jordy, "The Beaux-Arts Renaissance: Charles McKim's Boston Public Library," in *American Buildings and Their Architects* (New York, 1976), 3:314–75.

25. J. H. Benton Jr., *Argument . . . for Legislation to Limit the Height of Buildings on and near Copley Square* (Boston, 1898), 32.

26. *BET,* Apr. 3, 1901, 6.

27. Quoted in David Alan Levy, "The Sacred Skyline: The Conflict over Height Restrictions for Copley Square" (M.C.P. thesis, Massachusetts Institute of Technology, 1985), 30, 35.

28. *BET,* Jan. 24, 1898, 4; Edmund A. Whitman, *Change of Limitation in Height of Buildings in Copley Square: Address . . . Opening the Case for the Remonstrants against the Bills for the Change in the Limitation* (Boston, 1903), 9.

29. Letter to "a prominent member of Trinity Church," Sept. 23, 1897, cited in Samuel J. Elder, *Limitation of Height of Buildings Near Copley Square: Argument . . . on Behalf of the Museum of Fine Arts and Massachusetts Institute of Technology* (Boston, 1898), 10–11. In the same letter the syndicate offered to construct the building with only seven stories and sell it for $1,085,000, and claimed that it would yield an 8–10 percent return at that price. Since the price named represented an $85,000 construction profit for the syndicate on its already inflated $1 million capitalization, and apartments were then expected to yield around 6 percent (*BET,* Sept. 20, 1898, 5), the project's opponents used this offer to argue that a height restriction would in fact entail no damages (Benton, *Argument,* 35–36.)

30. Elder, *Limitation of Height,* 11. As Justice David J. Brewer later put it for the U.S. Supreme Court, "There may be novel questions in respect to the measure of damage, the value of the property that is taken." *Williams v. Parker,* 188 U.S. 491 (1903), at 504.

31. J. M. Crafts (president of MIT), letter to the editor, *BET,* in Massachusetts General Court, Committee on Cities, *Schedules to Accompany Petition for Legislation to Protect Copley Square in the City of Boston* (Boston, 1898), schedule H; Levy, "Sacred Skyline," 46; *Attorney General v. Williams,* 140 Mass. 329 (1885).

32. Elder, *Limitation of Height,* 11, 3; Benton, *Argument,* 10. Boston's total real estate valuation in 1898 was $870 million. *Municipal Register* (City doc. 37, 1916), 260.

33. Benton, *Argument,* 11; House bill 114, 1898. Another petition defined its area with an exact boundary, within which it sought a seventy-foot limit (House bill 291, 1898). George Upham for one last time submitted his citywide height-district bill (House bill 763, 1898), with Copley Square and all the rest of the Back Bay in the eighty-foot district.

34. King letter, *BET,* Jan. 27, 1898, 6; Levy, "Sacred Skyline," 47; Benton, *Argument,* 8.

35. Benton, *Argument,* 30. Benton insisted that the Parks and Parkways Act itself was a police-power measure (28). See also Elder, *Limitation of Height,* 12.

36. *MA&R,* 1898, Acts ch. 452, § 3; Whitman, *Change of Limitation,* 10.

37. *MA&R,* 1898, Acts ch. 452, § 1. Similar exceptions had been inserted into the Parks and Parkways Act by an amendment the previous year. *MA&R,* 1897, Acts ch. 379.

38. *MA&R,* 1898, Acts ch. 452, § 3; 1894, Acts ch. 257; Whitman, *Change of Limitation,* 10.

39. Henry L. Higginson, *BH,* Feb. 1, 1898, cited in Levy, "Sacred Skyline," 34.

40. See entries in Conrad Reno, *Memoirs of the Judiciary and the Bar of New England for the Nineteenth Century* (Boston, 1901), 2:114, 124.

41. *Attorney General v. Williams,* 174 Mass. 476 (1899), at 478.

42. Woodbury & Leighton letter to the editor, *BET,* Mar. 22, 1900, 10.

43. Albert E. Pillsbury, *The Truth about Westminster Chambers* (Boston, 1901), 11.

44. Senate doc. 234, 1900: "I am unable to give my sanction to a measure inclined to relieve citizens of the Commonwealth from the consequences of deliberate disregard of the provisions of a statute of the General Court." See Massachusetts General Court, House of Representatives, *Statements Made by Members Speaking to Questions of Personal Privilege in the House of Representatives on Tuesday, May 29, 1900, Concerning Newspaper Criticisms of Their Votes . . .* (House doc. 1385, 1900).

45. Future U.S. Supreme Court justice Louis Brandeis argued for the committee that "this is a case where the majesty of the law must be maintained for the sake of its influence upon the community." *BET,* Apr. 3, 1901, 1.

46. *BET,* Apr. 4, 1901, 5.

47. *BET,* Mar. 14, 1901, 5; *Williams v. Parker,* 188 U.S. 491.

48. *Cole v. Boston,* 181 Mass. 374 (1902). The case was filed September 6, 1898, three and a half months after the restrictions went into effect. Whitman, *Change of Limitation,* 15–16.

49. Trustees of the Museum of Fine Arts, *Twenty-fourth Annual Report, for the Year Ending December 31, 1899* (Boston, 1900), 7–8. The museum's president was William Endicott Jr., who as a statehouse commissioner had advocated rebuilding the Bulfinch front in "enduring materials" (Whitman, *Change of Limitation,* 13). The possibility of moving had already been publicly discussed during 1898 (*AA&BN,* Nov. 5, 1898, 41; Nov. 19, 1898, 57; Nov. 26, 1898, 69); the trustees were nervous about not only Westminster Chambers but also the impending removal of a nearby fire station in order to construct a new Back Bay railroad station.

50. Museum of Fine Arts, *Twenty-fourth Annual Report,* 9; Woodbury & Leighton letter, *BET,* Mar. 22, 1900, 10.

51. *BH,* Mar. 1, 1903, 10. See also, even before Copley Square restrictions, "Boston's Fifth Avenue," advertisement, *BET,* Dec. 8, 1897, 6; "Boylston Street as It Was and Is," *BET,* Dec. 9, 1897, 10.

52. Charles Zueblin, "Metropolitan Boston," *Chautauquan,* Jan. 1904, 486. On the City Beautiful movement as urban self-discipline, see Paul Boyer, *Urban Masses and*

Moral Order in America, 1820–1920 (Cambridge, Mass., 1978), 261–76. The total damages under Acts 1898, ch. 452, including those paid to other owners, were $396,079.72 (Elisabeth M. Herlihy letter, n.d., Loeb Library VF, Harvard).

53. *Boston Morning Journal,* Jan. 5, 1899.

54. Massachusetts Executive Department, *Report of Commissioners on the Subject of Remodelling or Rebuilding the State House* (Senate doc. 60, 1867), 7.

55. Ibid.

56. Ibid., 7, 3, 30; *Parker v. Commonwealth,* 178 Mass. 199 (1901), at 202.

57. Tucci, *Built in Boston,* 147. The legislature pursued this approach further in 1898 when it had the dome outlined in lights at night. *MA&R,* 1898, Acts ch. 395.

58. *BET,* Nov. 27, 1886, n.p., clipping, Massachusetts State Library Special Collections.

59. Ibid.; *Report of Committee on Finance* (House doc. 457, 1886), 2; Senate doc. 6, 1887, 1. Governor Ames's plan assumed "the buildings to be removed at such time as shall seem to be for the best interests of the Commonwealth." Senate doc. 6, 1887, 2.

60. *Boston Journal,* Mar. 28, 1887, in Malcolm Sillars, *The State House, a Comprehensive Project of Enlargement* (Boston, 1888), 34.

61. *AA&BN,* Feb. 11, 1899, 41; Massachusetts State Archives, legislative documents, 1899, Acts ch. 457.

62. *Boston Morning Journal,* Mar. 18, 1899, 5.

63. House bill 681, § 1, 1899.

64. *Boston Morning Journal,* Apr. 4, 1899, 5; *Boston Evening Globe,* Mar. 17, 1899, 4.

65. *Boston Evening Globe,* Mar. 30, 1899, 6.

66. Ibid.

67. Ibid.

68. *Boston Evening Globe,* May 18, 1899, 2.

69. Including the Hotel Bellevue, which was under construction to thirty-nine feet above the Bulfinch cornice. *AA&BN,* Mar. 25, 1899, 89.

70. *Boston Evening Globe,* Mar. 30, 1899, 6; *Boston Morning Journal,* Apr. 13, 1899, 4.

71. *MA&R,* 1899, Acts ch. 457; 1901, Acts ch. 525; 1902, Acts ch. 543. The provision may also have been a cynical attempt to minimize compensation, since owners could claim damages on only half of their property but were unlikely to build above the limit on the other half.

CHAPTER 8: *The Limits of Permanence*

Epigraph: C. Eliot, "The Necessity of Planning," *Garden and Forest* Aug. 26, 1896, in *Charles Eliot, Landscape Architect,* ed. Charles W. Eliot (Boston, 1902), 663.

1. Stewart Brand, "The Romance of Maintenance," in *How Buildings Learn: What Happens after They're Built* (New York, 1994), 110–31.

2. Blanche Linden-Ward, *Silent City on a Hill: Landscapes of Memory and Boston's Mount Auburn Cemetery* (Columbus, 1989), 280–82, 327; James J. Farrell, *Inventing the American Way of Death, 1830–1920* (Philadelphia, 1980), 136–38; David Charles

Sloane, *The Last Great Necessity: Cemeteries in American History* (Baltimore, 1991), 71, 109–10; Alexander von Hoffman, *Local Attachments: The Making of an American Urban Neighborhood, 1850 to 1920* (Baltimore, 1994), 75.

3. Frederick Law Olmsted Jr. and Theodora Kimball, eds., *Forty Years of Landscape Architecture* (New York, 1928), 2:99, 58–60, 78; Eliot, ed., *Charles Eliot*, 620.

4. Eliot, ed., *Charles Eliot*, 475; Eliot, "Necessity of Planning," 664.

5. Olmsted and Kimball, eds., *Forty Years*, 2:362; Eliot, ed., *Charles Eliot*, 665.

6. Charles B. Hosmer Jr., *Presence of the Past: A History of the Preservation Movement in the United States before Williamsburg* (New York, 1965), 292; Trustees of Public Reservations, *Twenty-fifth Annual Report . . . 1915* (Boston, 1916), 17–18; also *Sixth Annual Report . . . 1896* (Boston, 1897), 16; *Eighth Annual Report . . . 1898* (Boston, 1899), 16.

7. Trustees, *Ninth Annual Report . . . 1899* (Boston, 1900), 19–20.

8. American Scenic and Historic Preservation Society, *Fifteenth Annual Report* (Albany, 1910), 94.

9. William Sumner Appleton scrapbook [23], SPNEA; *MA&R*, 1907, Acts ch. 385; James M. Lindgren, *Preserving Historic New England: Preservation, Progressivism, and the Remaking of Memory* (New York, 1995), 160–61.

10. Roderick Nash, *Wilderness and the American Mind*, 3d ed. (New Haven, 1982), 113–15, 161–81; Norman T. Newton, *Design on the Land: The Development of Landscape Architecture* (Cambridge, Mass., 1971), 530.

11. Edward Hagaman Hall, "History of Central Park in the City of New York," in American Scenic and Historic Preservation Society, *Sixteenth Annual Report* (Albany, 1911), 484–88; *Twenty-first Annual Report* (Albany, 1916) 21, 154–55; Laura Wood Roper, *FLO: A Biography of Frederick Law Olmsted* (Baltimore, 1973), 366; Galen Cranz, *The Politics of Park Design: A History of Urban Parks in America* (Cambridge, Mass., 1982), 8–24.

12. Alexander von Hoffmann, "'Of Greater Lasting Consequence': Frederick Law Olmsted and the Fate of Franklin Park, Boston," *Society of Architectural Historians Journal* 47 (1988): 348; Cynthia Zaitzevsky, *Frederick Law Olmsted and the Boston Park System* (Cambridge, Mass., 1982), 77–79; Newton, *Design on the Land*, 296–99.

13. John C. Olmsted to W. M. Elliott, president, Licton Mineral Springs Co., Seattle, Aug. 2, 1907, 8, box B232, Olmsted Associates papers, Library of Congress, Manuscript Division. Roland Park's first restrictions were modeled on those of Llewellyn Park, N.J., and Tuxedo Park, N.Y. Harry G. Schalck, "Planning Roland Park, 1891–1910," *Maryland Historical Magazine* 67, 427–28; *First Annual Conference of Developers of High Class Residential Property, 1917* (microfilm of transcript, Manuscripts and Archives, Olin Library, Cornell), b90.

14. *Linzee v. Mixer*, 101 Mass. 512 (1869), at 514, 522–23. The new deeds provided that

steps, windows, porticos and other usual projections appurtenant to said front wall are to be allowed in this reserved space of twenty feet, subject to the following limitations, namely, first, that no projection of any kind (other than door-steps and balustrades connected therewith, and also cornices at the roof of the building) will be allowed to extend more than five feet from said front wall into said space; and second, that no projection in the nature of a bay-window, circular front or octagon front, with the foundation wall sustaining the same, (such foundation wall being a projection of front wall,) will be allowed, unless any horizontal section of such projection would fall within the external lines of a trapezoid, whose base upon the rear line of the aforesaid space does not exceed seven-tenths of the whole front of the building, nor exceed eighteen feet in any case, and whose side lines make an angle of forty-five degrees with the base.

"The commissioners always considered that this was a fair construction of the restrictions and limitations of the former deed," said one of them, Franklin Haven (at 523).

15. Helen Monchow, *The Use of Deed Restrictions in Subdivision Development* (Chicago, 1928), 32–33. The reason for this was cases like *Stone v. Pillsbury,* 167 Mass. 332 (1897), in which the Supreme Judicial Court allowed an alcoholism hospital in an 1887 Roxbury subdivision restricted to single-family construction. *Single dwelling-house,* said the court, was a technical real estate term that did not bind the owners because they were not real estate professionals.

16. J. C. Nichols, "A Developer's View of Deed Restrictions," *Journal of Land and Public Utility Economics* 5 (1929): 133.

17. Monchow, *Use of Deed Restrictions,* 65–71; Elvon Musick, "Legal Authority for Architectural Control," in *Planning Problems of Town, City and Region: Papers and Discussions at the Nineteenth National Conference on City Planning* (Philadelphia, 1927), 269–83. E.g., Roland Park Co., *Deed and Agreement . . . Guilford* (Baltimore, 1913), 13–14, covers care of common areas and provision of services, and also "expenses incident to the examination and approval of plans as herein provided, and to the enforcement of the restrictions, conditions, covenants, easements, charges and agreements herein contained" (14). Nichols, "Developer's View of Deed Restrictions," 139; Charles S. Ascher, "Reflections on the Art of Administering Deed Restrictions," *Journal of Land and Public Utility Economics* 8 (1932): 376–77. For a critical study of the more recent growth of homeowners' associations, see Evan McKenzie, *Privatopia: Homeowner Associations and the Rise of Residential Private Government* (New Haven, 1994).

18. Monchow attempted such an arrangement and concluded that there was no discernible trend. Monchow, *Use of Deed Restrictions,* 56–60. See H. V. Hubbell, "Land Subdivision Restrictions," *Landscape Architecture,* Oct. 1925, 53–54, showing all restrictions drawn up by the Olmsted firms to 1925. I am indebted to Patricia Burgess for access to her raw data on restrictions in Columbus, Ohio, which further reinforce these conclusions. I have not attempted any systematic sampling of Boston restrictions for this study, and this discussion is based instead on an examination of restrictions described in Supreme Judicial Court decisions and a variety of other sources.

19. *Parker v. Nightingale,* 88 Mass. 341 (1863); *Jeffries v. Jeffries,* 117 Mass. 184 (1874), at 184–85.

20. See Monchow, *Use of Deed Restrictions,* 24, for a version of this list organized somewhat differently.

21. Eighteen signatures appear on the petition; of the seventeen legible names,

nine are listed in the 1886 *Boston City Directory* as lawyers, two as conveyancers, and one as both. Petition, presented by Mr. Bailey of Everett, Feb. 3, 1886, Massachusetts State Archives, legislative documents, 1887, Acts ch. 418.

22. House bill 406, 1886.

23. *MA&R*, 1887, Acts ch. 418.

24. *Stewart v. Finkelstone,* 206 Mass. 28 (1910), at 32. Justice Loring favored environmental permanence in other forms as well. He had worked to save the Bulfinch statehouse, and shortly after this decision he would join the new Society for the Preservation of New England Antiquities as a life member (see chap. 9). See also the South End deed in *Hamlen v. Werner,* 144 Mass. 396, a decision handed down by the Supreme Judicial Court on March 7, 1887, during the month the Committee on Judiciary was considering the bill to limit restriction terms.

25. *Brown v. O'Brien,* 168 Mass. 484 (1897). The decision does not mention Acts 1887, ch. 418, and was based on other grounds.

26. *Baptist Social Union v. Boston University,* 183 Mass. 202 (1903), at 205.

27. *Jenney v. Hynes,* 282 Mass. 182 (1933), which enforced a thirty-seven-year-old use restriction imposed in the new Back Bay in 1896, terminating in 1950.

28. E.g., the 1900 "Montvale" subdivision in Worcester. *Allen v. Barrett,* 213 Mass. 36 (1912).

29. *MA&R*, 1889, Acts ch. 442, § 1.

30. *Jackson v. Stevenson,* 156 Mass. 496 (1892), at 502.

31. Lawrence Veiller, "Districting by Municipal Regulation," in *Proceedings of the Eighth National Conference on City Planning, Cleveland, June 5–7, 1916* (New York, 1916), 149.

32. Monchow, *Use of Deed Restrictions,* 61.

33. Nichols, "Developer's View of Deed Restrictions," 135. Nichols had earlier discussed his self-renewing restrictions at the Eighth National Conference on City Planning in 1916. J. C. Nichols, "Financial Effect of Good Planning in Land Subdivision," in *Proceedings of the Eighth National Conference on City Planning,* discussion, 109.

34. Nichols, "Financial Effect of Good Planning," discussion, 109; *Riverbank Improvement Company v. Bancroft,* 209 Mass. 217 (1911).

35. Musick, "Legal Authority for Architectural Control," 278; Robert A. M. Stern, ed., *The Anglo-American Suburb* (London, 1981), 80.

36. *Third Annual Conference of Developers of High Class Residential Property, 1919* (microfilm of transcript, Manuscripts and Archives, Olin Library, Cornell), 704, 698; Joseph Laronge, "The Subdivider of Today and Tomorrow," *Journal of Land and Public Utility Economics* 18 (1942): 428.

37. Nichols, "Developer's View of Deed Restrictions," 138. See also *First Annual Conference of Developers,* b100–101; *Third Annual Conference of Developers,* 706–8.

38. Monchow, *Use of Deed Restrictions,* 35. See also Nichols, "Developer's View of Deed Restrictions," 137. For an example in Springfield and Longmeadow, Mass., see *Parsons v. Duryea,* 261 Mass. 314 (1927). As of 1868, by contrast, Frederick Law Olmsted thought, "We cannot judiciously attempt to control the form of the houses

which men shall build" in Riverside; "we can only, at most, take care that if they build very ugly and inappropriate houses, they shall not be allowed to force them disagreeably upon our attention," through setback and landscaping requirements. Olmsted, Vaux & Co., "Preliminary Report upon the Proposed Suburban Village at Riverside, Near Chicago" (1868), in *Civilizing American Cities: A Selection of Frederick Law Olmsted's Writings on City Landscapes,* ed. S. B. Sutton (Cambridge, Mass., 1971), 301–2.

39. Ascher, "Art of Administering Deed Restrictions," 375, 376.

40. Olmsted to Bouton, Dec. 1, 1900, quoted in Schalck, "Planning Roland Park," 425; Roland Park Co., *Deed and Agreement . . . Guilford,* 9–10. Similarly, 1920 Merrymount Co. deeds cited in *Abbott v. Stegman,* 263 Mass. 585 (1928).

41. Monchow, *Use of Deed Restrictions,* 54. See also Nichols, "Developer's View of Deed Restrictions," 136.

42. *Beekman v. Schirmer,* 239 Mass. 265 (1921), at 266, 270; *Riverbank Improvement Co. v. Bancroft,* 209 Mass. 217; *Third Annual Conference of Developers,* 696–705.

43. Marc A. Weiss, "Urban Land Developers and the Origins of Zoning Laws: The Case of Berkeley," *Berkeley Planning Journal* 3 (1986): 16. There are scattered examples of voluntary imposition of restrictions after land passed into many hands: Rancho Santa Fe, near San Diego, where owners of more than thirty-five hundred acres converted ten-year restrictions to permanent ones (Charles H. Cheney, "Building for Permanency: The Esthetic Considerations in a Master or City Plan," in *Planning Problems of Town, City, and Region,* 43); Cohasset, Mass., 1937, a voluntary fifty-year restriction to residential use around the Common (Lewis Barrington, *Historic Restorations of the Daughters of the American Revolution* [New York, 1941], no. 17); another in Cleveland (Thomas W. Larwood Jr. discussion of Nichols, "Financial Effect of Good Planning," 107). The only widespread use of restrictions after subdivision was not a land-use issue but an appropriation of this land-use tool for other ends: the twentieth-century imposition of racially restrictive covenants through "protective associations" in already developed areas; see chap. 3, n. 47.

44. Weiss, "Urban Land Developers," 8. J. C. Nichols in 1929 claimed that "the effectiveness of the use of deed restrictions by the subdividers of the country really gave birth to the idea of zoning." Nichols, "Developer's View of Deed Restrictions," 142.

45. Anthony J. King, *Law and Land Use in Chicago: A Prehistory of Zoning* (New York, 1986), 231, 253–58; *MA&R,* 1881, Acts ch. 255, § 2. Later the legislature extended the veto to all owners within twenty-five feet of the premises. *MA&R,* 1887, Acts ch. 323.

46. *MA&R,* 1893, Acts ch. 462; House bill 506, 1893 (Feb. 7); House bill 230, 1893 (Jan. 31). The minimum could be as much as twenty-five feet.

47. George W. Pope and Horace G. Allen in *Board of Street Commissioners* 23 (Dec. 7, 1893): 223.

48. *Proceedings of the City Council of Boston,* 1893, 594.

49. John K. Berry in *Board of Street Commissioners* 24 (Dec. 20, 1894): 274; John Carleton in *Board of Street Commissioners* 23 (Dec. 7, 1893): 224. Similarly, in Chi-

cago in 1912 the city council considered ways of preventing business encroachment onto residential streets and concluded that the best available mechanism was municipally established building lines. King, *Law and Land Use in Chicago*, 334.

50. *Board of Street Commissioners* 24 (1894): 253, 272, 278–79, 287, 301–4. The building line in Beacon Street's deed restrictions had been upheld and enforced in 1886 in *Payson v. Burnham*, 141 Mass. 547; residents may have wished to avoid the trouble of private lawsuits to enforce it in the future.

51. *BET*, May 26, 1915, 14; May 31, 1915, 3.

52. Board of Street Commissioners, *Annual Report* (Boston, 1895). In the next twenty years Boston imposed municipal building lines in only three more places, all of them streets in the new Back Bay. Brookline: *BET*, May 26, 1915, 14.

53. See Christine Cousineau, "Tenement Reform in Boston, 1870–1920: Philanthropy, Regulation, and Government Assisted Housing," in *Proceedings, Third National Conference on American Planning History, Cincinnati, 1989* (Hilliard, Ohio, 1990), 600, re the Tenement House Act (*MA&R*, 1868, Acts ch. 281). See also *MA&R*, 1869, Acts ch. 369, "An act concerning the erection of stables in the city of Boston."

54. *MA&R*, 1913, Acts ch. 577. The following year the legislature raised the threshold for change by deleting consideration of public convenience. *MA&R*, 1914, Acts ch. 119.

55. For 1889 parkway restrictions, see *Flynn v. Caplan*, 234 Mass. 516 (1920), at 517.

56. House doc. 1305, 1902, 3, 5. Parker was articulating an argument that the American City Beautiful movement had recently imported from English antibillboard activists. See William H. Wilson, "The Billboard: Bane of the City Beautiful," *Journal of Urban History* 12 (1987): 397.

57. *MA&R*, 1903, Acts ch. 331; *Commonwealth v. Boston Advertising Co.*, 74 N.E. 601, cited in Wilson, "Billboard," 414.

CHAPTER 9: *Institutionalized Preservation*

Epigraph: William Sumner Appleton to Murray Corse, May 16, 1919, quoted in Charles B. Hosmer Jr., *Presence of the Past: A History of the Preservation Movement in the United States before Williamsburg* (New York, 1965), 285.

1. *AA&BN*, June 26, 1886, 301.

2. See Hosmer, *Presence of the Past*, 114–15.

3. *Proceedings of the Bostonian Society*, 1903, [74]. John Ritchie, a neighbor of the Bulfinch statehouse who would later join the preservation committee to save it, said at the 1887 hearings that he was "astounded that the Bostonian Society . . . did not appear to enter their plea." *BET*, Mar. 24, 1887, 1.

4. *Proceedings of the Bostonian Society*, 1914, 23; 1903, 6. Of the Park Street committee's eighteen members, the only officer or former officer of the Bostonian Society was William H. Lincoln, president of the Chamber of Commerce.

5. Lewis Barrington, *Historic Restorations of the Daughters of the American Revolution* (New York, 1941), pref.; Hosmer, *Presence of the Past*, 131–32.

6. Rev. Thomas Franklin Waters quoted in Hosmer, *Presence of the Past,* 113; see also 109–11.

7. Samuel Adams Drake, *Our Colonial Homes* (1893), quoted in James M. Lindgren, *Preserving Historic New England: Preservation, Progressivism, and the Remaking of Memory* (New York, 1995), 37; *BG,* Apr. 11, 1905, North Square/Paul Revere scrapbook, SPNEA.

8. Printed circular letter, 1905, and "Paul Revere's House Saved," unidentified clipping, 1907, both in North Square/Paul Revere scrapbook, SPNEA.

9. "Original condition": WSA letter, *Boston Post,* June 16, 1905, North Square/ Paul Revere scrapbook, SPNEA; "would not recognize": Walter Muir Whitehill, foreword, in Hosmer, *Presence of the Past,* 13; Joseph Everett Chandler, "Notes on the Paul Revere House," *Handbook of the Paul Revere Memorial Association* (Boston, 1950), 17–25; Chandler to Walter Gilman Page, Mar. 2, 1907, North Square/Paul Revere scrapbook, SPNEA; William Sumner Appleton, "Destruction and Preservation of Old Buildings in New England," *Art and Archaeology* 8 (1919): 144.

10. William Sumner Appleton Jr.'s background is best described in Lindgren, *Preserving Historic New England,* and Katherine H. Rich, "Beacon," *OTNE* 66 (1976): 42–60. Other information below comes from Hosmer, *Presence of the Past,* 237–39, and "William Sumner Appleton, 1874–1947," *OTNE* 38 (1948): 71–72.

11. *Proceedings of the Bostonian Society,* 1907, 47; James Michael Lindgren, "The Gospel of Preservation in Virginia and New England: Historic Preservation and the Regeneration of Traditionalism" (Ph.D. diss., College of William and Mary, 1984), 51, 238, n. 37; Lindgren, *Preserving Historic New England,* 17.

12. Lindgren, *Preserving Historic New England,* 19–23; Charles Eliot Norton, "The Lack of Old Homes in America," *Scribner's Magazine* 5 (1889): 636–40.

13. Unidentified clipping, North Square/Paul Revere scrapbook, SPNEA.

14. Harvard College, *Twenty-fifth Anniversary Report of the Class of 1896* (1921), quoted in Rich, "Beacon," 56; *SPNEA Bulletin* 1 (1910): 4.

15. Rich, "Beacon," 57–58.

16. "Fixed it up": Appleton quoted in Lindgren, "Gospel of Preservation," 242; "connections": Charles B. Hosmer Jr., *Preservation Comes of Age: From Williamsburg to the National Trust, 1926–1949* (Charlottesville, 1981), 1:151, quoting letter to Hosmer from Philip Dana Orcutt. See also Lindgren, *Preserving Historic New England,* 60–67.

17. *SPNEA Bulletin* 1 (1910): 4.

18. The project was initiated and carried out by the Colonial Dames (James M. Lindgren, *Preserving the Old Dominion: Historic Preservation and Virginia Traditionalism* [Charlottesville, 1993], 126–29). In 1922–23, again at the Dames' instigation, the APVA cannibalized the 1622 ruins of the Jamestown mill to construct a memorial shrine (Lindgren, "Gospel of Preservation," 181–82, n. 81). For Appleton on the APVA, see Lindgren, "Gospel of Preservation," 130–31.

19. See American Scenic and Historic Preservation Society, *Sixteenth Annual Report* (Albany, 1911), 123–31; *Eighteenth Annual Report* (Albany, 1913), 147–60.

20. *SPNEA Bulletin* 1 (1910): 5.

21. Ibid., 6.

22. *SPNEA Bulletin* 3 (July 1912): 14. The second property was the 1808 Fowler House in Danversport, bought subject to life occupancy by its owners.

23. *SPNEA Bulletin* 3 (July 1912): 18, 20.

24. *SPNEA Bulletin* 6 (Apr. 1915): 22; 4 (Aug. 1913): 2–8; 6 (Apr. 1915): 13.

25. *OTNE* 11 (1920): 6; 38 (1948): 77.

26. Massachusetts General Court, Committee on the State House, *Hearings Mar. 16, 17, 18, 1896, Concerning the Bulfinch Front,* typescript, Massachusetts State Library Special Collections, 1:39.

27. See, e.g., *SPNEA Bulletin* 2 (1911): 4.

28. *SPNEA Bulletin* 3 (July 1912): 20 ("supreme interest"), 13 ("make a beginning"); 7 (Dec. 1916): 14 ("the minimum").

29. *SPNEA Bulletin* 7 (May 1916): 14 ("be our policy"); 5 (Apr. 1914): 7 ("warrant local effort").

30. *SPNEA Bulletin* 1 (1910): 4. For a specific case, in Greenfield, Mass., see *SPNEA Bulletin* 9 (Nov. 1918): 27–28.

31. Hosmer, *Presence of the Past,* 205–8; *SPNEA Bulletin* 5 (Apr. 1914): 23; Lindgren, "Gospel of Preservation," 284–86; Lindgren, *Preserving Historic New England,* 137; Hosmer, *Preservation Comes of Age,* 1:173–74; *AA&BN,* Mar. 31, 1915, 213.

32. *SPNEA Bulletin* 9 (Nov. 1918): 22; Lindgren, *Preserving Historic New England,* 81–84.

33. *SPNEA Bulletin* 6 (Apr. 1915): 8.

34. *OTNE* 11 (1920): 178; 13 (1923): 191; see also 62, no. 4 (1972), special Province House issue.

35. In contrast to the period of interest—1607 to 1861—set out explicitly in APVA's 1889 charter. Lindgren, *Preserving the Old Dominion,* 10.

36. *SPNEA Bulletin* 5 (Apr. 1914): 5 ("not very"); *OTNE* 12 (1921): 178 ("absolutely nothing"), 182 ("gratifying"); 11 (1920): 173–75 ("mid-Victorian"). SPNEA accepted a 1904 house in 1921, but it was the building's furniture rather than the structure itself that was deemed historic. The acceptance had little to do with any system of preservationist value: the house came with a $20,000 endowment. *OTNE* 12 (1921): 163.

37. *OTNE* 11 (1920): 166.

38. Ibid., 176 (Buckman Tavern), 167–68 ("thoroughly conservative"); *SPNEA Bulletin* 5 (Dec. 1914): 19 (SPAB); 9 (Nov. 1918): 34 ("documentary value"); Lindgren, *Preserving Historic New England,* 134–44.

39. Robert Campbell and Peter Vanderwarker, *Cityscapes of Boston: An American City through Time* (Boston, 1992), 13. The quotation refers to the removal of storefronts from in front of the Otis House. *SPNEA Bulletin* 3 (Feb. 1913): 18 (campaign for Cooper-Austin corner lot); 5 (Apr. 1914): 4 (Fowler House lots "forever safeguard the setting" of the house); 7 (May 1916): 11 (a list of properties where "each should have a little more land"); 9 (Feb. 1919): 4–5 (Cambridge Street shops purchased in front of Otis House).

40. Joseph Chandler to Appleton, Oct. 8, 1917, quoted in Lindgren, "Gospel of Preservation," 326; *SPNEA Bulletin* 7 (Dec. 1916): 13.

41. Lindgren, *Preserving Historic New England*, 101.

42. *SPNEA Bulletin* 4 (Aug. 1913): 2–3 ("best portion"); 6 (Apr. 1915): 16–17 (Bulfinch).

43. Proceedings of the forty-ninth convention, AIA (1915), quoted in Hosmer, *Presence of the Past*, 252.

44. Lindgren, "Gospel of Preservation," 313.

45. William Sumner Appleton, "The Province House, 1922," *OTNE* 62 (1972): 91.

46. T. J. Jackson Lears, *No Place of Grace: Antimodernism and the Transformation of American Culture, 1880–1920* (New York, 1981). The Arts and Crafts Movement was represented in Boston by the Boston Society of Arts and Crafts, founded in 1897 with Appleton's teacher C. E. Norton as its first president. Lindgren, *Preserving Historic New England*, 19–22, 68–95.

47. Lindgren, *Preserving Historic New England*, 85 ("little houses"), 79 ("disappointed"), 70 ("Anglo-Saxon"); *SPNEA Bulletin* 2 (1911): 14–15 ("almost brutal").

48. Lindgren, "Gospel of Preservation," 331 ("foreigners"); *SPNEA Bulletin* 6 (Apr. 1915): 17 ("family names"). See also *BH*, Jan. 11, 1915, SPNEA clipping file.

49. *OTNE* 12 (1921): 177; Appleton to Millar, May 6, 1916, quoted in Lindgren, "Gospel of Preservation," 298; see also 286.

50. Lindgren, "Gospel of Preservation," 299; *OTNE* 12 (1921): 180.

51. Quoted in Hosmer, *Presence of the Past*, 133. Prescott F. Hall, chairman of the Committee to Preserve the Park Street Church, helped found the Immigration Restriction League. Mrs. Prescott F. Hall, *Immigration and Other Interests of Prescott Farnsworth Hall* (New York, 1922).

52. Curtis Guild to PRMA, Nov. 29, 1907, North Square/Paul Revere scrapbook, SPNEA; *OTNE* 13 (1922): 94; 11 (1920): 170–71.

53. Hosmer, *Preservation Comes of Age*, 1:141; Lindgren, *Preserving Historic New England*, 71–78, 88–89.

54. *SPNEA Bulletin* 1 (1910): 6 ("wise restrictions"); 3 (Feb. 1913): 11; Lindgren, "Gospel of Preservation," 293.

55. *OTNE* 12 (1921): 176 ("be continued"); 11 (1920): 30 ("financial weakness"); *SPNEA Bulletin* 4 (Aug. 1913): 28 ("security of the Society"); 3 (July 1912): 19; 6 (Apr. 1915): 13; *AA&BN*, Dec. 10, 1913, 234. See also Lindgren, *Preserving Historic New England*, 127.

56. Appleton, "Destruction and Preservation," 155, 168–69.

57. Hosmer, *Preservation Comes of Age*, 1:178.

58. Hosmer, *Presence of the Past*, 36, 111. Even in this case, like the Park Street Church proposal to the legislature, the catalyst was a private campaign that raised a substantial fraction of the purchase price.

59. Bolton, "Note-book," Feb. 23, 1914, quoted in Lindgren, *Preserving Historic New England*, 34; Jack Beatty, *The Rascal King: The Life and Times of James Michael Curley, 1874–1958* (Reading, Mass., 1992), 167–68; Alexander von Hoffmann, *Local Attachments: The Making of an Urban Neighborhood, 1850 to 1920* (Baltimore, 1994), 201–39.

60. *Massachusetts Special Acts and Resolves*, 1915, Acts ch. 306; Lindgren, "Gospel

of Preservation," 273. O'Hearn was not being arbitrary; on the contrary, he systematically enforced building and fire codes for the first time in the city's history, causing the demolition of 654 substandard structures in his first fifteen months in office. *BET,* May 12, 1915, III/3.

61. *BH,* Mar. 9, 1923; May 6, 1924; Dec. 26, 1930.

62. Appleton, "Destruction and Preservation," 179. When Appleton in 1936, under the financial pressures of the depression, relinquished one house to the National Park Service to become a part of the National Historic Site in Salem, Mass., he complained that "the government, if it runs true to its usual form, will want to receive the property without any conditions of any kind, which will permit it at some time in the future to pull the house down and take it out for re-erection at a World's Fair in Salem, Oregon, if the vote of Oregon senators should be needed to putting something of the kind over, and it is exactly this sort of thing that our Society exists to prevent." Quoted in Hosmer, *Preservation Comes of Age,* 1:143.

63. Ronald F. Lee, *The Antiquities Act of 1906* (Washington, D.C., 1970), 1 ("first . . . policy"), 117 (text of 34 Stat. L. 225, § 2), 94–96, tables 1–3; Appleton to Charles D. Walcott, Dec. 2, 1912, microfiche correspondence archive, "Preservation legislation," SPNEA.

64. C. D. Walcott to Appleton, Dec. 5, 1912, and Appleton to Secretary of the Interior, Dec. 9, 1912, both in microfiche correspondence archive, "Preservation legislation," SPNEA; *SPNEA Bulletin* 6 (Apr. 1915): 7; Lee, *Antiquities Act,* 94. The other four designated on October 15, 1924, were Fort Pulaski, Ga.; Castle Pinckney, S.C.; and Fort Matanzas and Castillo de San Marcos, Fla. No national monument was created in New England until 1949 (Saint Croix, Me.).

65. Stephen W. Jacobs, "Architectural Preservation in the United States: The Government's Role," *Curator* 9 (1966): 313.

66. Hosmer, *Preservation Comes of Age,* 1:75.

67. Case 2, Frederic H. Viaux papers, Baker Library, Harvard; *BH,* Apr. 28, 1894, 1; *BG,* Nov. 25, 1894; *Boston Sunday Journal,* Feb. 17, 1901, 1; *SPNEA Bulletin* 7 (May 1916): 46; for a similar example, see Franklin Haven, in chap. 6, n. 47.

68. E.g., Moses Williams offered the Sun Tavern to SPNEA in 1912; when Appleton declined it for lack of a site to move it to, Williams cooperated in allowing Norman Isham to make measured drawings as the building was taken down. Sun Tavern file, SPNEA.

69. *Providence Magazine,* Dec. 1914, 807; May 1914, 374–77; *Current Affairs,* Mar. 3, 1924, SPNEA clipping file.

70. William Sumner Appleton, Chairman, The Com. Soc. Sons of the Revolution, printed letter to Boston Transit Commission, Dec. 12, 1905, and [WSA] to Geo. G. Crocker, May 4, 1906, both in William Sumner Appleton scrapbook [23], SPNEA; *Proceedings of the Bostonian Society* (1903): 6.

71. Appleton privately called the Custom House Tower "one of the fiercest architectural aberrations in America" but publicly did little to oppose it. Lindgren, *Preserving Historic New England,* 109.

72. Lindgren, *Preserving the Old Dominion,* 93; Georgie Boge and Margie Holder

Boge, *Paving over the Past: A History and Guide to Civil War Battlefield Preservation* (Washington, D.C., 1993), 15–23; *U.S. v. Gettysburg Electric Railway Co.,* 160 U.S. 668.

73. Quoted in Hosmer, *Presence of the Past,* 167.

74. Lindgren, "Gospel of Preservation," 339; Ancient Monuments Consolidation and Amendment Act (1913), 3 & 4 Geo. 5, ch. 32. Nicholas Boulting, "The Law's Delays: Conservationist Legislation in the British Isles," in *The Future of the Past: Attitudes to Conservation, 1174-1974,* ed. Jane Fawcett (London, 1976), 19; David Lowenthal, *The Past Is a Foreign Country* (Cambridge, England, 1985), 394. See also Stephen W. Jacobs, "Architectural Preservation in Europe: French and English Contributions," *Curator* 9 (1966): 196–215, 201.

75. Constitution of the Commonwealth of Massachusetts, amendments art. 51, in *Massachusetts General Acts,* 1919, act 63.

76. Appleton to Mr. R. Peabody Bellows, Dec. 6, 1935, microfiche correspondence archive, "Preservation legislation," SPNEA.

77. Henry M. Hutchings to Appleton, Oct. 22, 1918, microfiche correspondence archive, "Preservation legislation," SPNEA. The vote is not easy to interpret, as all thirteen amendments on the ballot passed, most by similar margins, and the high number of blank ballots indicates apathy toward all the referenda. The preservation amendment won without an actual majority of all ballots cast in either the city or the state. Unidentified clipping, microfiche correspondence archive, "Preservation legislation," SPNEA.

78. Appleton to Senator Cavanagh, May 2, 1919, 2, and Appleton to President, Boston Society of Architects, Dec. 2, 1935, both in microfiche correspondence archive, "Preservation legislation," SPNEA; House bill 767, 1919; *SPNEA Bulletin* 10 (Oct. 1919): 18–19.

CHAPTER 10: *Public Control*

Epigraph: *Parker v. Commonwealth,* 178 Mass. 199 (1901), at 203–4.

1. House bill 668, § 2, 1899. Mayor Quincy instead requested, and the Committee on Cities once again reported, a bill lowering the citywide limit to one hundred feet (House bill 1137, 1899); once again it failed to pass.

2. The U.S. Congress passed a similar act that year regulating building heights in the District of Columbia, specifying different limits for "business streets," which were those designated by the commissioners of the District of Columbia as being in predominantly business use, and for "residence streets," which were all others. The act made no provision for compensation and was thus in effect the first imposition of height districts in any American city under the police power. Congress was under the impression that it was following Boston precedent (House rept. 1704, 55th Cong., 3d sess., 1899, 2), and Bostonians do not appear to have known of the D.C. regulations. The act was not tested in court. Heights of Buildings Commission, *Report . . . to the Committee on the Height, Size and Arrangement of Buildings of the Board of Estimate and Apportionment of the City of New York* (New York, 1913), 150–51.

3. *MA&R*, 1899, Acts ch. 457, § 2. The restricted area was extended in 1901 (Acts ch. 525), and a 1902 amendment (Acts ch. 543) to the 1901 extension of these restrictions made a final refinement in drafting height limits under eminent domain, providing that any damages were to be offset against benefits to property owners arising from the whole statehouse and park project. Justice Marcus Knowlton, who had to sort all this out in 1906 in *American Unitarian Association v. Commonwealth*, 193 Mass. 470, suggested (at 477) that the 1901 act might have been the first American height zoning under the police power. It provided compensation for owners on Beacon and Park Streets (§ 4), but not those on Bowdoin Street (§ 3); the provision offsetting benefits against damages, covering all these areas including Bowdoin Street, was not enacted until the following year. Knowlton used the idea of a police-power district to avoid the otherwise inescapable conclusion that the 1901 act was an error in legislative draftsmanship.

4. *Parker v. Commonwealth*, 178 Mass. 199, at 204–5.

5. Minneapolis traveled a similar detour, using eminent domain to keep apartment buildings out of residential areas between 1917 and 1925. Matthew B. Seltzer, "Zoning by Eminent Domain in Minneapolis, 1912–1925," in *Proceedings, Fifth National Conference on American Planning History, Chicago, 1993* (Hilliard, Ohio, 1993), 76.

6. *Robert Treat Paine v. Commonwealth*, transcript of hearings, 1902–3, MS, Massachusetts State Library Special Collections, 5; *Parker v. Commonwealth*, 178 Mass. 199, at 201; *BET*, Jan. 5, 1903, 6; *Boston Evening Globe*, Mar. 17, 1899, 4.

7. The legislature passed a new kind of height-restriction legislation, authorizing the governor to issue bonds to cover the damages, "to such an amount as may be necessary." *MA&R*, 1903, Acts ch. 234. I have been unable to determine the actual total of damages awarded. Two statutes (1901, ch. 417, and 1905, ch. 224) extended the deadlines for claiming damages, indicating that at least some owners were lax in pursuing compensation. In *Raymond v. Commonwealth*, 192 Mass. 486, the court awarded $32,500 damages at the corner of Park and Beacon Streets, probably one of the more valuable lots affected. Taken together, this evidence suggests that total compensation must have been much less than $5–6 million but still a substantial sum.

8. "Hard to say": *Attorney General v. Williams*, 174 Mass. 476 (1899), at 478; "grave difficulties": *Parker v. Commonwealth*, 178 Mass. 199, at 205; *Williams v. Parker*, 188 U.S. 491 (1903), at 504; *BH*, Dec. 11, 1902, 7.

9. *MA&R*, 1904, Acts ch. 333, § 1; Commission on Height of Buildings in the City of Boston, *Final Report* (City doc. 133, 1905), 18; House bill 507, 1904, submitted by petition of G. H. Richards and others; *Boston City Council Minutes*, 1904, 113 (Mar. 24).

10. House doc. 507, 1904; House doc. 1250, 1904.

11. The other two members of the "Commission on Height of Buildings in the City of Boston," all appointed June 7, 1904, were Henry Parkman and Joseph A. Conry.

12. Commission on Height of Buildings (Boston), *Final Report*, 17 ("considerable part"), 20 ("gridiron"), 19 ("distinctly residential"). See also editorial, *BET*, Dec. 6, 1904, 12.

13. Richard M. Hurd, *Principles of City Land Values* (1903; New York, 1924), 81; advertisement, *BET*, Dec. 8, 1897, 6; Dec. 9, 1897, 10; *BH*, Mar. 1, 1903, 10.

14. Commission on Height of Buildings (Boston), *Final Report*, 22, 9, 21. See also map, *BH*, Dec. 6, 1904, 12.

15. Commission on Height of Buildings (Boston), *Final Report*, 21. "If it were not for . . . the great number of high buildings already erected in the downtown districts," they said, "we should recommend a maximum limit for the entire city of 100 feet" (22).

16. *BET*, Dec. 6, 1904, 12; Commission on Height of Buildings (Boston), *Final Report*, 23.

17. *Petitioners for the Repeal of Chapter 333 of the Acts of 1904*; *MA&R*, 1905, Acts ch. 383. The act again delegated to a commission the details of where and under what conditions such buildings would be permitted; the mayor appointed the same three commissioners. Rather than drawing more boundaries, this time they formulated a rule: on any B-district street more than sixty-four feet wide, buildings could rise to one and one-quarter times the width of the street, to a maximum of one hundred feet on streets of eighty feet or wider. Order of July 21, 1905; Commission on Height of Buildings (Boston), *Final Report*, 26.

18. *Boston City Council Minutes*, 1904, 113 (Mar. 24). Four of the petitioners for repeal had protested any state appropriation for saving the Old South. *Petitioners for the Repeal of Chapter 333 of the Acts of 1904*.

19. *Welch v. Swasey*, 193 Mass. 364 (decision Jan. 1, 1907).

20. *Welch v. Swasey*, 214 U.S. 91 (1909), at 107–8. Jacob H. Morrison, quoting this passage, says, "There is no doubt that *Welch v. Swasey* established a judicial pattern of circumvention and evasion where regulations based on aesthetic considerations were concerned." Morrison, *Historic Preservation Law* (Washington, D.C., 1965), 23.

21. *Welch v. Swasey*, 214 U.S. 91, at 106–8.

22. Boston Transit Commission, *Twelfth Annual Report* (Boston, 1906), 46 ("in which direction"), 49; *Thirteenth Annual Report* (Boston, 1907), 8–10; *Seventeenth Annual Report* (Boston, 1911), 5–6, 11, 36 ("difficult to see"), app. B, C; *MA&R*, 1907, Acts ch. 573.

23. *BET*, Feb. 10, 1915, 1. The transit commission had already announced, with respect to an issue elsewhere, that its "aim should be to facilitate the extension of the business district rather than its contraction." Report to the Legislature on Boylston Street Subway Terminal, May 9, 1913, app. A in Boston Transit Commission, *Nineteenth Annual Report* (Boston, 1913), 52.

24. Editorial, *BET*, Feb. 8, 1915, 10.

25. Boylston Street Owners' Association letter to Mayor Curley, *BET*, Mar. 24, 1915, 3. See also earlier rumblings in testimony before legislative committee, *BET*, Feb. 10, 1915, 3; Senate doc. 177, 1915.

26. *Massachusetts Special Acts and Resolves*, 1915, Acts ch. 297 (Arlington Street station); 1915, Acts ch. 333 (building heights). The members of the commission, ex officio, were the chairman of the City Planning Board (Ralph Adams Cram), the city building commissioner (Patrick O'Hearn), and the fire commissioner (John Grady).

27. *Massachusetts Special Acts and Resolves,* 1915, Acts ch. 333. Once again, no mechanism for revision was specified.

28. See Commission on Height of Buildings in the City of Boston, *Hearings* (Boston, 1916), 98, 127.

29. Ibid., 107.

30. Ibid., 104 ("permanent as possible"), 48 ("My idea"), 31 ("present uncertainty").

31. Ibid., 171 ("Back Bay"), 143 ("Commonwealth avenue"). See also 36, 51–52, 140, 171–72. Commission on Height of Buildings in the City of Boston, *Report* (City doc. 114, 1916), 4 ("probable trend").

32. Commission on Height of Buildings (Boston), *Hearings,* 155; see also 141, app., 155.

33. Ibid., 15, 17.

34. Ibid., 160.

35. Commission on Height of Buildings (Boston), *Report,* 114; Nov. 29, 1916, and Jan. 13, 1917, clippings, Beebe Communications Center, Boston University; Commission on Height of Buildings in the City of Boston, *Order . . . Amending Boundaries* (City doc. 45, 1917).

36. Massachusetts made an early attempt to generalize from Boston's innovation, a 1907 proposal (House doc. 416) that would have given all the state's cities and towns the same right as Boston to establish business and residential districts with different height limits. It failed in the legislature.

37. Marc A. Weiss, *The Rise of the Community Builders: The American Real Estate Industry and Urban Land Planning* (New York, 1987), 81; W. L. Pollard, "Outline of the Law of Zoning in the United States," *Annals of the American Academy of Political and Social Science* 155, pt. 2 (1931): 19.

38. Frederick Law Olmsted Jr., "The Scope and Results of City Planning in Europe," in *City Planning* (Senate doc. 422, 61st Cong., 2d sess., 1909), 63–70; Seymour I. Toll, *Zoned American* (New York, 1969), 123–25; Frank Backus Williams, "The German Zone Building Regulations," in Heights of Buildings Commission (New York), *Report,* 94–119; John R. Mullin, "American Perceptions of German City Planning at the Turn of the Century," *Urbanism Past and Present* 3 (1977): 5–15.

39. Senate doc. 422, 61st Cong., 2d sess., 1909, 60, 69, 72. The U.S. Supreme Court in fact had not yet ruled on such broad use categories. Frank Backus Williams, *The Law of City Planning and Zoning* (New York, 1922), 288.

40. *Proceedings of the Third National Conference on City Planning, Philadelphia, Pennsylvania, May 15–17, 1911* (Boston, 1911), 240.

41. Ibid., 245, 258.

42. Heights of Buildings Commission (New York), *Report,* 39; MA&R, 1912, Acts ch. 334; *Kilgour v. Gratto,* 224 Mass. 78 (1916). For example, Lawrence Veiller, "Protecting Residential Districts," in *Proceedings of the Sixth National Conference on City Planning, Toronto, May 25–27, 1914* (Boston, 1914), 92–111, makes no mention of Massachusetts in an otherwise exhaustive survey.

43. Heights of Buildings Commission (New York), *Report,* 38–42.

44. Ibid., 269; Toll, *Zoned American,* 93–116, 146, 158–59.

45. Heights of Buildings Commission (New York), *Report,* 1 ("zones"), 71–75; Lawson Purdy quoted in S. J. Makielski Jr., *The Politics of Zoning: The New York Experience* (New York, 1966), 20; Toll, *Zoned American,* 167.

46. Heights of Buildings Commission (New York), *Report,* 72, 51–53; Toll, *Zoned American,* 159–60.

47. Paul Goldberger, *The Skyscraper* (New York, 1981), 13; Heights of Buildings Commission (New York), *Report,* 64; Stephen Zoll, "King Kong in New York," *Space and Society* 18 (1982): 16; Toll, *Zoned American,* 180.

48. Marc A. Weiss, "Urban Land Developers and the Origins of Zoning Laws: The Case of Berkeley," *Berkeley Planning Journal* 3 (1986): 13 ("restricted sections"), 16; Toll, *Zoned American,* 196–97.

49. Discussion of Lawrence Veiller, "Districting by Municipal Regulation," in *Proceedings of the Eighth National Conference on City Planning, Cleveland, June 5–7, 1916* (New York, 1916), 165 ("strictly residential"), 162.

50. Robert M. Fogelson, *The Fragmented Metropolis: Los Angeles, 1850–1930* (Cambridge, Mass., 1967), 261–62. Duncan McDuffie argued for zoning in Berkeley to "protect the business districts of the city against the competition created by scattering stores through residence districts." Quoted in Weiss, "Urban Land Developers," 13.

51. Toll, *Zoned American,* 173; Veiller, "Districting by Municipal Regulation," 153. The same constitutional convention put forward, and the voters approved at the same election, a similar amendment defining conservation of natural resources as a public use (amendments art. 49) and another permitting the regulation of advertising "on private property within public view" (amendments art. 50). Unidentified clipping, microfiche correspondence archive, "Preservation legislation," SPNEA; Morrison, *Historic Preservation Law,* 6.

52. Frederic H. Fay, "The Planning of a City," in *Fifty Years of Boston,* ed. Elisabeth M. Herlihy (Boston, 1932), 50; Massachusetts constitution, amendments art. 60: "The general court [the legislature] shall have power to limit buildings according to their use or construction to specified districts of cities or towns." The amendment's brevity caused problems, as it made no provision for the legislature to delegate this power to cities and towns. Action in the 1919 session was stymied by the attorney general's insistence that such delegation would be unconstitutional (*Opinions of the Attorney General* 5 [1917–20]: 362–65), but the Supreme Judicial Court contradicted him in an advisory opinion (*Opinion of the Justices,* 234 Mass. 597 [1920]), so the measure was enacted the following year: *MA&R,* 1920, Acts ch. 601.

53. Boston City Planning Board, "Growth of the Zoning Movement," Jan. 15, 1924, typescript, Loeb Library, Harvard, 4.

54. The project was directed by Arthur C. Comey. Boston City Planning Board, *Zoning for Boston: A Survey and a Comprehensive Plan* (Boston, 1924), 9–10. The planning board decided to submit Boston's zoning to the legislature because it was not clear, even with the zoning-enabling act, that a city ordinance could supersede the legislature's many special enactments on building construction and heights for Boston. *MA&R,* 1924, Acts ch. 488.

55. Oliver Ames, *Governor's Address* (Senate doc. 1, 1888), 24; editorial, *BET,* Mar. 10, 1888, rpt. in Malcolm Sillars, *The State House, a Comprehensive Project of Enlargement* (Boston, 1888), 26.

56. Walter Firey, *Land Use in Central Boston* (Cambridge, Mass., 1947), 120.

57. [Margaret Deland], "The Regeneration of Beacon Hill: How Boston Goes about Civic Improvement," *Craftsman* 16 (1909): 92.

58. Ibid., 95; *BET,* Dec. 6, 1922, quoted in Firey, *Land Use in Central Boston,* 111; *OTNE* 11 (1920): 171.

59. *BET,* May 15, 1915, III/2.

60. "Old Favorite Residential Quarters, Now Somewhat Down-at-the-Heel, Will Some Day Regain Their Former Dignity. A Phenomenon of Modern City Growth," *Providence Magazine,* Jan. 1915, 17.

61. See, e.g., the street commissioners' hearing on a garage proposed for Charles Street, *BET,* Feb. 23, 1915, 1.

62. Boston City Planning Board, *Zoning for Boston,* 34 ("direct benefit"), 29; Kenneth T. Jackson, *Crabgrass Frontier: The Suburbanization of the United States* (New York, 1985), 242; Weiss, *Community Builders,* 11–12.

63. Firey, *Land Use in Central Boston,* 129–32; *BH,* Oct. 2, 1926; Beacon Hill Association, Zoning Defence Committee, *The Menace to Beacon Hill* (Boston, 1927); *BH,* June 22, 1929; June 29, 1929; *BET,* Mar. 8, 1933; *BH,* Apr. 7, 1933.

64. "Zoning, Autos, and Subways," W. C. Codman letter to the editor, *BET,* n.d., clipping, W. C. Codman papers, SPNEA; *BH,* Oct. 30, 1926.

65. There is some confusion in the published record about what New Orleans actually did in the mid-1920s. Jacob H. Morrison, an authority on preservation law and a New Orleans resident, wrote that the city passed an historic district ordinance in 1924, "but it was never put into effect" (Morrison, *Historic Preservation Law,* 17, n. 11). Charles Hosmer in his first history of preservation wrote that New Orleans architects in 1926 and 1927 worked on "the first effort to create a municipal historic preservation law in the United States" (Charles B. Hosmer Jr., *Presence of the Past: A History of the Preservation Movement in the United States before Williamsburg* [New York, 1965], 205), but in the sequel to that work he said they "evidently failed. There is no evidence that any ordinance actually came up for consideration at this time" (*Preservation Comes of Age: From Williamsburg to the National Trust, 1926–1949* [Charlottesville, 1981], 1:294). However, he cites "a weak law in New Orleans," extant in 1929, as the sole precedent for Charleston's historic district zoning (239).

66. Hosmer, *Preservation Comes of Age,* 1:240.

67. Ibid., 239 ("incompetent to judge"), 241; Morrison, *Historic Preservation Law,* 21. The main branch of aesthetic control, around which most litigation centered, was billboard regulation.

68. Morrison, *Historic Preservation Law,* 39, 41–42.

69. Stoney to Appleton, Mar. 21, 1929, microfiche correspondence archive, SPNEA; Hosmer, *Preservation Comes of Age,* 1:237.

70. Appleton to Stoney, Mar. 26, 1929, 2 ("any particular house"), and Apr. 4, 1929, microfiche correspondence archive, SPNEA.

71. Morrison, *Historic Preservation Law,* 47.

72. Ibid., 12–14. The historic district campaign on Beacon Hill was led by John Codman (Jacobs, "Architectural Preservation in the United States," 328), son and business successor of William Coombs Codman (Oct. 1, 1932, clipping, W. C. Codman papers, SPNEA).

Conclusion

1. Edward M. Bassett quoted in Seymour I. Toll, *Zoned American* (New York, 1969), 193; italics original. See also Eugenie Birch and Douglas Roby, "The Planner and the Preservationist: An Uneasy Alliance," *Journal of the American Planning Association* 50 (1984): 194.

2. Toll, *Zoned American,* 207–10.

3. Marc A. Weiss, *The Rise of the Community Builders: The American Real Estate Industry and Urban Land Planning* (New York, 1987), 96–105 (Weiss refers [98–99] to a quotation by Huber Smutz, Los Angeles zoning administrator, regarding a 1921 zoning revision: "It was either a proposition of zoning the rabid speculator's property for the purpose for which he was holding it or having no zoning at all and hence no protection for residential districts"); William B. Munroe, "A Danger Spot in the Zoning Movement," *Annals of the American Academy of Political and Social Science* 155, pt. 2 (1931): 203; Toll, *Zoned American,* 206–7.

4. Weiss, *Community Builders,* 99; Marc A. Weiss, "The Real Estate Industry and the Politics of Zoning in San Francisco, 1914–1928," *Planning Perspectives* 3 (1988): 311–24; Toll, *Zoned American,* 207–10. See also Lawrence Veiller, "Districting by Municipal Regulation," in *Proceedings of the Eighth National Conference on City Planning, Cleveland, June 5–7, 1916* (New York, 1916), 156.

5. Weiss, *Community Builders,* 102; Robert M. Fogelson, *The Fragmented Metropolis: Los Angeles, 1850–1930* (Cambridge, Mass., 1967), 255–57, 261–62. Boston's experience was less disturbing. From the organization of the Board of Zoning Adjustment in 1924 through the end of 1930, 64 petitions for zone changes were granted out of 219 applications. Frederic H. Fay, "The Planning of a City," in *Fifty Years of Boston,* ed. Elisabeth M. Herlihy (Boston, 1932), 52–53.

Index

Related Books in the Series

The Library of Congress has cataloged the hardcover edition
of this book as follows:

Holleran, Michael.
Boston's "Changeful times" : origins of preservation and planning in America / Michael
Holleran.
p.   cm. — (Creating the North American landscape)
Includes bibliographical references and index.
ISBN 0-8018-5729-5 (acid-free paper)
1. Historic preservation—Massachusetts—Boston.   2. Historic buildings—
Massachusetts—Boston—Conservation and restoration.   3. Boston (Mass.)—History.
4. City planning—Massachusetts—Boston—History.   I. Title.   II. Series.
F73.37.H5   1998
974.4′61—DC21   97-25750

ISBN 0-8018-6644-8 (pbk.)